GUIDE TO
LITERARY MANUSCRIPTS
IN THE HUNTINGTON LIBRARY

GUIDE TO LITERARY MANUSCRIPTS IN THE HUNTINGTON LIBRARY

HUNTINGTON LIBRARY

1979

Library of Congress Card Number 79–84369
ISBN 0–87328–102–0
Printed in the United States of America by Kingsport Press
Designed by Ward Ritchie

The preparation of this work was made possible through a grant from the Research Collections Program of the National Endowment for the Humanities

FOREWORD

The two foundations of the Huntington Library are its rare books, prints, maps, music scores, ephemera, and reference books (all together, about one million items); and its manuscripts (consisting of about five million pieces). To provide fuller access to its manuscripts, the Huntington began in 1975 a six-year project to survey its holdings, summarize groups of related manuscripts and single pieces of major significance, and then publish the results in a four-part *Guide to Manuscripts in the Huntington Library.*

The first two parts of the *Guide,* on American historical manuscripts and on literary manuscripts, are being published in 1979. The final two parts, on British historical manuscripts and on medieval and renaissance manuscripts, will be published in 1981. When the entire project is completed, scholars around the world will have comprehensive information about one of the great repositories of research materials on British and American history and literature. We hope that these *Guides* will assist them in their scholarly investigation, whether they decide to request photocopies by mail and then work at home, or whether they choose to travel to San Marino and explore at first hand the riches of the Huntington.

DANIEL H. WOODWARD
LIBRARIAN

PREFACE

The purpose of this guide is to list as completely as possible the literary manuscripts in the Huntington Library, which number at least 125,000 pieces by more than 1,000 authors. The guide includes the items listed by Herbert C. Schulz in "American Literary Manuscripts in the Huntington Library" (*Huntington Library Quarterly*, vol. 22: no. 3, May 1959) and in "English Literary Manuscripts in the Huntington Library" (*Huntington Library Quarterly*, vol. 31: no. 3, May 1968), as well as the materials that have been acquired since the publication of these articles. While it reflects the Huntington's strong emphasis on British and American literature, it also includes a few European and Canadian authors. Manuscripts written by authors who died before 1600 are excluded since they are described in the *Guide to Medieval and Renaissance Manuscripts in the Huntington Library* that forms a part of this series.

The two primary criteria for including an author in the guide are common identification as a literary figure and the appearance of his name in at least one standard biographical dictionary. Historians and scientists are generally excluded unless they were writing for the general public or were dealing critically with literature. A few persons have been included who are not known primarily as writers but who have attained significance because of their importance in literary circles; they include publishers, and artists, such as painters, sculptors, actors, musicians, and entertainers.

Manuscripts are listed according to author and arranged alphabetically. Under the author entries the manuscripts are divided into five possible categories: 1) Verse, 2) Prose, 3) Letters, 4) Documents, and 5) Other. The Verse and Prose (1 and 2) are listed alphabetically by title (with square brackets used to indicate supplied titles or portions of titles), and untitled poems designated by the first line, enclosed within quotation marks. Each entry is followed by the number of pages or leaves. When available, the Huntington Manuscript call number or collection prefix (or name) is also given. Manuscripts are in the author's own handwriting unless otherwise indicated. In the category of Letters (3) the total number of letters written by the author is given, followed by inclusive dates. The abbreviation "ca." designates "circa," indicating an approximate date, while "n.d." in place of a date stands for "no date." If a significant number of letters were addressed to an author, these too are noted. Documents (4) include items such as checks, receipts, bills, financial statements, wills, notes of authorization, etc., which are not individually described but for which the number of pieces and inclusive dates are given. The last group, Other (5), includes annotations, corrections or marginal notes in printed books or other manuscripts, drawings, sketches, lists, and miscellaneous items. In general, facsimile copies are not listed, nor are inscriptions in books unless they are of uncommon length, significance, or rarity.

A few of the larger literary collections have full descriptions in the regular alphabetical sequence. The following collections are fully described: Conrad Potter Aiken, Mary (Hunter) Austin, James Thomas Fields, Jack London, and Wallace Stevens. Prominent correspondents in these collections are listed within the collection description as well as in the alphabetical sequence of the guide. In addition, three collections are described but cannot be represented adequately by a listing of authors: the California Poetry File, the Commonplace Books Collection, and the Larpent Plays. For this last collection, single authors are not entered because most of the plays are official copies and not in the author's hand, and because a comprehensive listing of these plays has already been published

(Dougald MacMillan, *Catalogue of the Larpent Plays in the Huntington Library*, San Marino, 1939). All of the authors in the Larpent Collection are listed (as well as the plays of unidentified authorship) in an Appendix at the end of the guide.

The *Guide to Literary Manuscripts at the Huntington Library* was compiled and edited by Sue Hodson under the supervision of Mary L. Robertson, Curator of Manuscripts, with special help from Jean F. Preston, former Curator of Manuscripts. Some of the descriptions of larger collections were written by David Mike Hamilton, and preliminary cataloging was done by many members of the Department of Manuscripts staff. Special guidance was provided by Virginia Rust, Associate Curator of Manuscripts. The project was supported by a grant from the National Endowment for the Humanities. Further editorial assistance was provided by Edwin H. Carpenter, Jane Evans, and Betty Leigh Merrell.

GUIDE TO
LITERARY MANUSCRIPTS
IN THE HUNTINGTON LIBRARY

ABBEY, Henry, *American poet,* 1842–1911

Letters: 2 (1886–94)

ABBOTT, Lyman, *American clergyman, editor,* 1835–1922

Letters: 13 (1865–1916)

ABDULLAH, Achmed, *American novelist, playwright,* 1881–1945

Letters: 1 (1919)

A BECKETT, Gilbert Arthur, *English comic writer,* 1837–91

Letters: 2 (1873–79)

ABINGTON, Frances (Barton), *English actress,* 1737–1815

Letters: 2 (1775–90)

ADAMIC, Louis, *Austrian-born American author,* 1899–1951

Letters: 26 (1927–30), including 21 to Mary (Hunter) Austin

ADAMS, Andy, *American cowboy, miner, author,* 1859–1935

Letters: 26 (1904–33), including 22 to Mary (Hunter) Austin

ADAMS, Charles, *American diplomat, editor,* 1807–86

Letters: 21 (1858–77), including 17 to Thomas Haines Dudley

ADAMS, Charles Follen, *American poet,* 1842–1918

Letters: 1 (1878)

ADAMS, Franklin Pierce, *American journalist, columnist, poet,* 1881–1960

Letters: 3 (1915 and n.d.)

ADAMS, George Matthew, *American columnist,* 1878–1962

Letters: 4 (1942)

ADAMS, Henry Brooks, *American historian, essayist,* 1838–1918

Letters: 24 (1864–1912)

ADAMS, James Truslow, *American historian,* 1878–1949

Letters: 2 (1934–40)

ADAMS, Ramon Frederick, *American author,* 1889–

Letters: 2 (1936–49)

ADAMS, Samuel Hopkins, *American novelist,* 1871–1958

Letters: 5 (ca. 1920–36)

ADDAMS, Jane, *American settlement worker, sociologist, author,* 1860–1935

Letters: 11 (1899–1928)

ADDISON, Joseph, *English statesman, poet, essayist,* 1672–1719

Letters: 1 (1706)

Documents: 1 (1712)

ADE, George, *American humorist, playwright,* 1866–1944

Letters: 19 (1903–42)

ADY, Julia Mary (Cartwright), *English author,* d. 1924

Prose:

Isabella d'Este (544 pp.: HM 17248)

AGASSIZ, Jean Louis Rodolphe, *American naturalist, author,* 1807–73

Letters: 48 (1847–73)

Documents: 2 (1863 and ca. 1870)

Other:

Annotations in *Mitchell's School Atlas,* 1853 (HM 32434)

AGEE, James, *American author,* 1909–55

Letters: 1 (1931)

AGUILAR, Grace, *English novelist,* 1816–47

Letters: 1 (1842)

AIKEN, Conrad Potter, *American poet, novelist,* 1889–1973

Conrad Potter Aiken was born in Savannah, Georgia, where he spent his first eleven years until witnessing the murder-suicide of his father and mother in 1901. After his parents' deaths, he went to live with his great aunt, uncle, and aunt in New England. His writing career began at Middlesex

School in Concord, Massachusetts, where he contributed to the school magazine, *The Anvil.* He continued to write while at Harvard, publishing articles in *The Harvard Monthly* and *The Harvard Advocate,* and upon graduation chose to continue writing as a profession. Aiken was married three times, first, shortly after graduation from Harvard, to Jessie McDonald, by whom he had three children: Jane, Joan, and John. In 1929 Aiken's marriage to Jessie terminated, and the following year he married Clarice Lorenz. This marriage also ended in divorce, in 1937. Shortly afterwards, Conrad Aiken married Mary Augusta Hoover, with whom he lived for the rest of his life.

Subject matter: the collection (most of which falls between 1851 and 1976) is rich in original autograph and typescript versions of Aiken's works. The heart of the collection, however, is the voluminous correspondence written to Aiken from his contemporaries, neighbors, and friends, mostly dealing with business and literary matters related to Aiken's work or to the work of his contemporaries.

Significant persons: persons having the largest representation include Aiken's third wife, Mary Augusta (Hoover) AIKEN, Edward John BURRA, John DAVENPORT, Thomas Stearns ELIOT, Clarence Malcolm LOWRY, and John Lincoln SWEENEY. Material by these and others appears within each author's individual entry in this Guide.

Physical description: chiefly letters and manuscripts; the 4378-piece collection also contains a number of photographs, a few documents, and some business ephemera.

Source: acquired from Mary Augusta Hoover Aiken in 1975. Some of Aiken's original letters have been acquired from booksellers or other persons.

Bibliography: most of Aiken's manuscripts have been published; the heaviest concentration of manuscripts of poems contained in the collection was published in *Skylight One*

(1949), *The Divine Pilgrim* (1949), *A Letter from Li Po* (1955), *Sheepfold Hill* (1955), and *The Morning Song of Lord Zero* (1962).

AIKIN, Charles Rochemont, *English doctor, medical writer,* 1775–1847

Letters: 1 (1800)

AIKIN, Lucy, *English writer,* 1781–1864

Letters: 3 (1819 and n.d.)

AINSWORTH, William Harrison, *English novelist,* 1805–82

Verse:

Henley—A Poem (HM 14962)
Jeny Jumper's Chaunt (HM 14961)
To a Young Italian Lady (HM 14981)
[Untitled fragment of verse] (RB 320006, vol. 2, p. 134)

Prose:

Crichton (111 leaves: HM 14960)
Crichton (10 leaves: HM 14959)
Crichton: [Epoch the First: Book II] (13 leaves: HM 14953)
[Fragment from unidentified ms.] (2 leaves: HM 14988)
Hilary St. Ives: [Books I, II, and III] (492 leaves: HM 14952)
Jack Sheppard: [chaps. IV and IX] (12 leaves: HM 14954)
Journal of a Tour through Italy (142 leaves: HM 14955)
Journal of a Tour through Italy [Naples only] (21 leaves: HM 14956)
Journal of a Tour through Italy (8 leaves: HM 14957)
The Tower of London: [chaps. 30–33] (20 leaves: HM 14958)

Guy Fawkes: [Book the First, chap. 16] (1 p.: RB 137399, vol. 2, p. 266)

Letters: 305 (1827–81)

Documents: 1 (1873)

AKENSIDE, Mark, *English poet, physician,* 1721–70

Verse:

Ode, beginning: "From pompous life's dull Masquerade . . ." (not autograph: JE 6)

AKERS, Elizabeth (Chase), see ALLEN, Elizabeth Ann (Chase) Taylor Akers

AKINS, Zoë, *American playwright, poet,* 1886–1958

Verse:

8 poems (also: miscellaneous addenda, 75 pieces: Akins Collection)

Prose:

83 articles, book reviews, lectures, etc.

3 novels: (Life of a Young Man [unpublished], *Wastelands,* and *The White Doe:* Akins Collection)

73 plays

78 outlines and synopses

30 short stories

Letters: 982 (1919–58), and approximately 4,000 addressed to her

ALABASTER, William, *English Latin poet, divine,* 1567–1640

Verse:

Ninium ne crede colori: [poems, Latin and English] (HM 39464)

[Poems ascribed to Alabaster in commonplace books] (HM 172, HM 41536)

Letters: 1 (ca. 1616)

ALCOTT, Louisa May, *American novelist,* 1832–88

Verse:

With a Rose That Bloomed on the Day of John Brown's Martyrdom (not autograph: HM 957)

Prose:

How I Went Out to Service (33 leaves: HM 13133)

Jimmy's Cruise in the Pinafore (31 leaves: HM 13132)

Letters: 2 (1863–64) to James Thomas Fields and Annie (Adams) Fields

ALDEN, Henry Mills, *American editor, author,* 1836–1919

Letters: 84 (1861–1912)

ALDINGTON, Richard, *English novelist, poet,* 1892–1962

Letters: 42 (1918–61)

ALDRICH, Thomas Bailey, *American author,* 1836–1907

Verse:

A. D. 2893 (HM 7815)

Cradle Song (HM 7818)

Frost Work (HM 7878)

Garnaut Hall (FI 230)

Identity (HM 32437)

Imogen (HM 1229)

Kismet (HM 13130)

Lost at Sea (HM 38486)

Miantowohan (FI 180)

Rococo (RB 7061)

To A. F. (Fields Addenda, Box 12 [1])

"We live on tombs, and live our day, and die" (John Anson Ford Album)

"What time the moon her silv'ry fingers laid . . ." (HM 13125)

When I am Dead (HM 13128)

With Three Flowers (HM 13129)

Prose:

Among the Studios, No. I (11 leaves: HM 7816)

Among the Studios, No. III (17 leaves: HM 7817)

The Chevalier de Resseguier (43 leaves: HM 17239)

Leaves from a Notebook (22 leaves: HM 13119)

Memoranda (15 leaves: HM 13120)

Mother Michel and her Cat (80 leaves: HM 17238)

A Note on L'Aiglon (8 leaves: HM 13121)

Père Antoine's Date Palm (14 leaves: HM 13122)

Robert Herrick, the Man and the Poet (partly typed, 26 leaves: HM 13131)

Robert Herrick, the Man and the Poet (corrected typescript, 28 leaves: HM 7786)

Letters: 110 (1855–1906)

Other:

[Marginal notes on Bliss Carman's *A Trail,* 1890] (HM 12770)

ALEXANDER, Hartley Burr, *American educator, editor, author,* 1873–1939

Letters: 6 (1931–36) to Neeta Marquis

ALEXANDER, Samuel John, *American author,* fl. 1912

Verse:

The Quenching of the Star—To the Great Memory of Ambrose Bierce (G. W. James Collection)

The Recall of the Ghost (G. W. James Collection)

A Wayside Ghost (G. W. James Collection)

ALGER, Horatio, Jr., *American author,* 1834–99

Verse:

Strive and Succeed! The world's temptations flee [poem of 4 lines from Alger's book titles] (HM 32600)

Letters: 88 (1870–99)

ALLEN, Charles Dexter, *American author,* 1865–1926

Letters: 20 (1892–1907)

ALLEN, Elizabeth Ann (Chase) Taylor Akers, *American poet, novelist,* 1832–1911

Verse:

Bed-Time (HM 532)

Letters: 2 (1863–1900)

ALLEN, Francis Henry, *American editor, ornithologist,* 1866–1953

Letters: 15 (1918–42)

ALLEN, George, *American educator, clergyman, author,* 1808–76

Letters: 3 (1863–72)

ALLEN, James, *American author,* 1739–1808

Documents: 1 (1808)

ALLEN, James Lane, *American novelist*, 1849–1925

Prose:

Father Palemon [published as *The White Cowl*] (71 pp.: HM 1499)

A Kentucky Episode [published as *King Solomon of Kentucky*] (82 pp.: HM 14989)

ALLEN, Willis Boyd, *American author*, 1855–1938

Letters: 1 (1916)

ALLIBONE, Samuel Austin, *American lexicographer, librarian, compiler*, 1816–89

Prose:

Commonplace book containing, among other matters, A Visit to Washington Irving, June 12, 1855 (39 pp.: AL 401)

Letters: 45 (1855–70), and several hundred addressed to him

ALLINGHAM, William, *English poet*, 1824–89

Letters: 8 (1844–88)

ALLISON, Young Ewing, *American editor, author*, 1853–1932

Letters: 1 (1896) to Simon Bolivar Buckner.

ALMA-TADEMA, Sir Lawrence, *English artist*, 1836–1912

Letters: 6 (1876–1908)

ALTROCCHI, Julia (Cooley), *American poet*, 1893–

Verse:

Astronaut to Vega (typewritten, carbon copy. Also, tape recording of the poem: California Poetry File)

Prose:

California Biography in Poetry (typewritten, carbon copy, 20 pp.: California Poetry File)

Letters: 136 (1939–68), and 28 addressed to Mrs. Altrocchi

AMES, Charles Gordon, *American clergyman, editor,* 1828–1912

Verse:

Collection of 17 poems for Mrs. Ann L. North (52 pp.: HM 35315)

Hidden Life (Burdette Collection)

To Lady A. F. (FI 122)

Letters: 8 (1866–1906)

AMES, Fisher, *American statesman, publicist, author,* 1758–1808

Documents: 1 (1788)

AMIS, Kingsley William, *English author,* 1922–

Verse:

Memory [8 drafts of poem] (HM 41012)

ANDERSON, Alexander, *American wood engraver,* 1775–1870

Verse:

Selkirk and the Yarrow (HM 44522)

ANDERSON, Frederick Irving, *American author,* 1877–1947

Letters: 1 (1914)

ANDERSON, Judith, *English-born American actress,* 1898–

Letters: 1 (1948)

ANDERSON, Melville Best, *American educator, author,* 1851–1933

Letters: 76 (1894–1933)

ANDERSON, Sherwood, *American essayist, novelist,* 1876–1941

Letters: 4 (1923) to Mary (Hunter) Austin.

ANDREWS, Elisha Benjamin, *American educator, historian,* 1844–1917

Letters: 1 (1896)

ANDREWS, Mary Raymond (Shipman), *American novelist,* 1865?–1936

Letters: 1 (n.d.)

ANGELO, Valenti, *American author, illustrator,* 1897–

Letters: 2 (1936)

ANSPACH, Elizabeth, Margravine of, *English dramatist,* 1750–1828

Letters: 7 (1780–1810)

ANSTEY, Christopher, *English poet,* 1724–1805

Letters: 2 (1776–95)

ANTHONY, Susan (Brownell), *American reformer,* 1820–1906

Prose:

An address on women's rights (58 leaves: AF 79)

Letters: 432 (1848–1905)

Documents: 1 (1899)

ANTIN, Mary, *American essayist,* 1881–1949

Letters: 2 (1925–27) to Mary (Hunter) Austin

APPERLEY, Charles James, *English sporting writer,* 1779–1843

Letters: 1 (1840)

APPLETON, Thomas Gold, *American essayist, poet, artist,* 1812–84

Letters: 2 (n.d.) to Annie (Adams) Fields

ARBLAY, Frances (Burney) d', *English author,* 1752–1840

Prose:

Consolatory Extracts Daily Collected or Read in My Extremity of Grief at the Sudden and Tragical Loss of My Beloved Susan (49 pp.: HM 293)

Letters: 2 (1794–1816)

ARBUTHNOT, John, *English physician, wit, poet,* 1667–1735
Documents: 1 (1724/5)

ARCHER, Kate Rennie (Aitken), *American poet,* 1863–1960?

Verse:

Angus (typewritten: Archer Collection)

Big Shot (Yeatman Collection)

Bird on the Farallones (typewritten: Archer Collection)

Blue-Printing (typewritten: Archer Collection)

Cliff-Home (typewritten: Archer Collection)

Daybreak in a Mountain District (typewritten: California Poetry File)

The Dead Must Laugh (typewritten: California Poetry File)

Emeritus (Archer Collection)

Freeway—Hollywood (Archer Collection)

"From east to west" (Archer Collection)

The Green Lady (typewritten: Keene Collection)

Intermission (typewritten: Archer Collection)

The Mountain (typewritten: Archer Collection)

New Colt (Archer Collection)

"No seats on the rocks" (Archer Collection)

November Vineyard (typewritten: Keene Collection)

"Now, if I had a hungerness" (Archer Collection)

"Only the racing of the night stream, waken" (Archer Collection)

The Order of Mary (typewritten: California Poetry File)

Passing Camp Roberts (Archer Collection)

Prayer on the Cotswolds—England (typewritten: Keene Collection)

Question to God (typewritten, enclosed in letter: Archer Collection)

Ranch Grove (typewritten: Keene Collection)

Return to Barra [two copies—variants] (Archer Collection)

Rhythm of Suspense (typewritten: California Poetry File)

Silver (typewritten: Archer Collection)

Single Breakfast (Yeatman Collection)

Target (Yeatman Collection)

Texas in Africa (typewritten: Archer Collection)

Universal Harvest (typewritten: Archer Collection)

Up at Sunrise (typewritten: California Poetry File)

Valley Evening (California Poetry File)

Valley Evening. San Diego (Archer Collection)

Prose:

Of Quiet Things: [two prose sketches] (typewritten, 4 pp.: Archer Collection)

Transit of Culture (5 pp.: Archer Collection)

Letters: 251 (1934–59), including 197 to Jennette Yeatman, and 301 letters addressed to Mrs. Archer

Other:

Biographical notations (9 pieces: Archer Collection)

Miscellaneous manuscripts and notes (20 pieces: Archer Collection)

Memoranda and receipts (10 pieces: Archer Collection)

ARENSBERG, Walter Conrad, *American author,* 1878–1954

Verse:

To a Poet: [dedicatory poem to Wallace Stevens] (WAS 4091)

Letters: 14 (1916–51)

ARMITAGE, Merle, *American impresario, author,* 1893–1975

Letters: 1 (1944)

ARMOUR, Richard Willard, *American educator, humorist,* 1906–

Letters: 2 (1948–60)

ARNOLD, Sir Edwin, *English poet,* 1832–1904

Verse:

The Gateway of the "Garden" of Sa'di (HM 13179)

The Light of the World (HM 14992)

Pearls of the Faith (HM 13180)

Potiphar's Wife (HM 17192)

The Shadow of the Cross (HM 14991)

Prose:

The Flower Pageants of Japan (32 pp.: HM 7445)

Gesta Venatica, Being a Record of Game . . . Bagged in India (with drawings, 69 pp.: HM 32436)

Letters: 13 (1861–1900)

ARNOLD, Matthew, *English poet, critic,* 1822–88

Letters: 23 (1858–ca. 1884)

ARNOLD, Samuel James, *English dramatist,* 1774–1852

Letters: 6 (1814–22)

ARREOLA, Juan Jose de, *Mexican author,* 1918–

Prose:

Vida y Virtudes de la Esclarecida Virgen Santa Rosalia . . . (216 pp.: HM 735)

ARTHUR, John S., *English bookseller,* fl. 1879–1910

A collection of 109 autograph and 5 typed letters from booksellers and publishers, between ca. 1804 and ca. 1910, with the majority falling between 1880 and 1910. Most of the letters are addressed to John S. Arthur, Liverpool bookseller. (HM 31196)

ARTHUR, Timothy Shay, *American editor, author,* 1809–85

Prose:

Hiring a Servant (2 pp.: HM 17196)

Letters: 2 (1855–58)

ASHLEY, Robert, *English miscellaneous writer,* 1565–1641

Prose:

Of Honour: [prose treatise] (EL 1117)

ASHTON, Winifred (Clemence Dane, pseud.), *English novelist, dramatist,* d. 1965

Letters: 4 (1932–59)

ATHERTON, Gertrude Franklin (Horn), *American novelist,* 1857–1948

Prose:

The Conqueror (346 pp.: HM 29306)

Letters: 59 (1902–42)

ATKINSON, Joseph, *English dramatist,* 1743–1818

Letters: 32 (1802–10). Also, 9 letters (1806–07) from Joseph and John Atkinson (firm)

AUSLANDER, Joseph, *American author,* 1897–

Verse:

"Against brutality and wrong" (HM 39490)

AUSTIN, Alfred, *English poet,* 1835–1913

Verse:

Two Autumn Sonnets (HM 7790)

Letters: 1 (1892)

AUSTIN, Jane (Goodwin), *American novelist,* 1831–94

Letters: 1 (ca. 1893) to James Ripley Osgood

AUSTIN, Mary (Hunter), *American essayist, novelist, playwright,* 1868–1934

Mary (Hunter) Austin, born in Carlinville, Illinois, moved in her early twenties to Bakersfield, California, for reasons of health. Following her marriage there, she and her husband settled in the Owens Valley, where the first of her published books, *The Land of Little Rain,* was written. She divorced her husband, and moved in 1900 to Carmel, George Sterling's literary bohemia on the California seacoast. *The Atlantic Monthly* bought her first book for serial publication the same year. With the royalties from *The Land of Little Rain,* Mary Austin traveled to Europe in 1903, and remained on the continent, traveling infrequently to New York, for the next fifteen years. In 1918 Mary Austin returned to the desert she loved, settling in Taos, New Mexico, where she lived for the rest of her life.

Subject matter: primarily letters addressed to Mary Austin, most of which fall between 1861 and 1952, dealing not only with literary matters but also with botany, the Colorado River Project, the Owens Valley and Death Valley, penitentiary reform, and women's suffrage. Because of Mary Austin's deep interest in the Southwest, there are many letters which are concerned with this region and its inhabitants, including Indians and Indian lore, and New Mexican art and literature.

Significant persons: authors represented include Gertrude Franklin (Horn) ATHERTON, Willa CATHER, Ina COOLBRITH, Sinclair LEWIS, Vachel LINDSAY, Jack LONDON, Amy LOWELL, Henry L. MENCKEN, and George STERLING. Material by these and others appears within each author's individual entry in this Guide.

Physical description: mostly letters and manuscripts, by a large number of authors. Included in the 11,000 pieces are the manuscripts of all her books except *The Land of Little Rain,* several notebooks and outlines for her novels, short stories and plays, and over 400 photographs.

Source: acquired from Indian Arts Fund, New Mexico, 1951. Several acquisitions from booksellers have been added to the collection since the original purchase.

Bibliography: versions of all the book-length manuscripts have been published.

Prose:

Hymns of the Penitentes (13 pp.: HM 41060)

Rimas Infantiles of New Mexico (6 pp.: HM 41601)

Letters: 219 (1903–34)

AUSTIN, Sarah (Taylor), *English author,* 1793–1868

Letters: 5 (1834–36), 4 to Francis Lieber

AVERY, Benjamin Parke, *American journalist, author,* 1828–75

Verse:

"Out where the misty Golden Gate" (HM 35075)

AYSCOUGH, George Edward, *English dramatist,* d. 1779

Letters: 1 (1769)

B

BABBAGE, Charles, *English mathematician,* 1792–1871

Letters: 7 (1835–63)

BACHELLER, Irving, *American novelist,* 1859–1950

Verse:

Whisperin' Bill (AP 23)

Letters: 33 (1895–1931)

BACHMAN, John, *American naturalist, clergyman,* 1790–1874

Prose:

Address delivered before the Horticultural Society of Charleston (6 pp.: HM 12791)

An Introductory Lecture on the habits of Insects (32 pp.: HM 12793)

[Lecture on the organization, classification, and habits of insects] (34 leaves; also, a corrected copy: HM 12794 A & B)

Notes for an Introductory Lecture to the Phil. Society (9 pp.: HM 12792)

BACON, Francis, 1st Viscount St. Albans, *English essayist, philosopher,* 1561–1626

Prose:

An Advisement Touching an Holy Warre [with dedicatory letter to Bp. Lancelot Andrewes] (incomplete, 4 pp.: EL 1594a)

Certain Considerations Touching the Plantations in Ireland (90 pp.: EL 1721)

[Modern copy of same] (EL 1747)

Certaine Observacons vpon a Libell . . . intituled a Declaracon of the True Causes of the Greate Troubles Presupposed to be Intended Against the Realme of England (71 pp.: EL 1604)

Consideracons Touching a Warre with Spaine (33 pp.: EL 1594)

[Speech delivered at the opening of Parliament, Jan. 30, 1620/1] (EL 1214)

[Speech delivered in the Court of Exchequer Chamber on Calvin's case] (10 pp., incomplete: EL 1890)

Letters: 5 (1597–1620)

Documents: 6 (1594–1616/7)

BACON, Leonard, *American clergyman, editor, author,* 1802–81

Letters: 4 (1873–80)

BAILEY, Irene Temple, *American novelist,* d. 1953

Letters: 14 (1891–1927)

BAILLIE, Joanna, *Scottish dramatist, poet,* 1762–1851

Verse:

A Sailor's Song (HM 41083)

Letters: 20 (1810–45)

BAINBRIDGE, Oliver, *English author,* fl. 1900–20

Letters: 2 (1910), and approximately 300 addressed to him

BAKER, George Pierce, *American educator, author,* 1866–1935

Letters: 14 (1927–30)

BAKER, Ray Stannard, *American editor, biographer, essayist,* 1870–1946

Letters: 7 (1902–39)

BALDERSTON, John Lloyd, *American playwright,* 1889–1954

Verse:

Goddess and God: a play in verse (HM 30311)

Also: by Marion (Rubincam) Balderston—

Aneurin Bevan [author's reminiscences of Aneurin Bevan] (typewritten, 5 pp.: HM 44093)

George Moore (typescript of the author's reminiscences of George Moore: 5 pp.: HM 40397)

BALESTIER, Charles Wolcott, *American publisher, novelist,* 1861–91

Letters: 4 (1890–91)

BALMER, Edwin, *American editor, novelist,* b. 1883

Letters: 1 (1928)

BALZAC, Honoré de, *French novelist,* 1799–1850

Prose:

[Scènes de la vie privée et publiques des animaux: the end of chap. VI, vol. II, and the beginning of chap. VII, the latter entitled:] A la grande serre du Jardin des Plantes (1 p.; also, printed proof with corrections: HM 7791, A & B)

Letters: 1 (1843)

BAMFORD, Frederick Irons, *American author, poet, librarian,* fl. 1906–17

Letters: 8 (1906–17)

BAMFORD, Samuel, *English poet, weaver,* 1788–1872

Letters: 2 (1845–50)

BANCROFT, Aaron, *American clergyman, author,* 1755–1839

Letters: 1 (1816)

BANCROFT, George, *American diplomat, historian,* 1800–91

Prose:

History of the United States. The American Revolution, vol. VIII, chap. LI (2 leaves: HM 2163)

Letters: 65 (1839–89)

BANCROFT, Hubert Howe, *American editor, publisher, historian, essayist,* 1832–1918

Letters: 22 (1871–90)

BANCROFT, Lady Marie Effie (Wilton), *English actress, theatrical manager,* 1839–1921

Letters: 4 (1909–11) to Walford Graham Robertson

Other:

"Stage masks may cover honest faces" [quotation] (1 p.: HM 16063)

BANCROFT, Sir Squire Bancroft, *English actor, theatrical manager,* 1841–1926

Letters: 7 (1868–1911)

Other:

"I don't see what harm it can do me . . ." [quotation] (1 p.: HM 16065)

BANGS, John Kendrick, *American editor, lecturer, humorist,* 1862–1922

Verse:

The Author's Boomerang (HM 20511)

A Literary Order (CM 24)

Letters: 40 (1891–1913)

BANIM, John, *Irish novelist, dramatist, poet,* 1798–1842

Letters: 1 (n.d.)

BARBAULD, Anna Letitia (Aikin), *English author,* 1743–1825

Letters: 8 (ca. 1776–1825)

BARHAM, Richard Harris, *English author,* 1788–1845

Verse:

The Lay of St. Medard. Golden Legends No. VII (HM 14392)

Letters: 1 (1844)

BARING, Maurice, *English novelist, essayist, poet,* 1874–1945

Letters: 5 (1896–1931)

BARING-GOULD, Sabine, *English author,* 1834–1924

Verse:

Onward, Christian Soldiers (HM 17358)

Letters: 1 (1921)

BARKER, Squire Omar, *American poet,* 1894–

Letters: 2 (1957) to Eugene Lafayette Cunningham

BARLOW, Joel, *American poet,* 1754–1812

Verse:

Advice to a Raven in Russia (BN 46)

Letters: 5 (1787–1811), and 3 postscripts (1810); and 70 addressed to him

Documents: 3 (1797–1809)

BARNARD, Lady Anne (Lindsay), *English author,* 1750–1825

Verse:

Auld Robin Gray (MO 153)

Letters: 3 (1802–ca. 1808)

BARNARD, Edward William, *English divine, poet,* 1791–1828

Verse:

Jemima (RB 109990, vol. 3, pt. 2, p. 210)

BARNARD, Frederick Augustus Porter, *American clergyman, educator, editor,* 1809–89

Letters: 16 (1860–83)

BARNARD, Henry, *American educator,* 1811–1900

Letters: 7 (1838–69)

BARNES, Albert, *American clergyman, author,* 1798–1870

Prose:

Home Missions: [a sermon on a text from] Josh. 13:1 (44 pp.: HM 301)

Letters: 1 (1861)

BARNES, William, *English poet,* 1801–86

Letters: 9 (1863–76)

BARR, Amelia Edith (Huddleston), *American author,* 1831–1919

Letters: 5 (1896–1902)

BARRETT, Wilson, *English actor, manager, dramatist,* 1846–1904

Letters: 5 (1886–98)

BARRIE, Sir James Matthew, *English playwright, novelist,* 1860–1937

Prose:

A Scotch Student's Dream (7 pp.: HM 44519)

Letters: 101 (1907–27), including 98 to R. Golding Bright, his agent

BARRY, John Daniel, *American journalist, novelist,* 1866–1942

Letters: 2 (1901–07)

BARRYMORE, John, *American actor,* 1882–1942

Letters: 1 (1920)

BARTLETT, John, *American editor, publisher,* 1820–1905

Letters: 5 (1858–97)

BARTLEY, George, *English comedian, actor,* 1782?–1858

Letters: 3 (1836–53)

BARTOL, Cyrus Augustus, *American clergyman, author,* 1813–1900

Verse:

The Dew of Death (FI 260)

Prose:

The Duty of Encouraging One Another (17 pp.: HM 298)

Letters: 29 (1854–83), including 28 to James Thomas Fields and Annie (Adams) Fields

BARTON, Bernard, *English poet,* 1784–1849

Verse:

A visit to Grandmamma (HM 14498)

Letters: 4 (1814–47)

BATEMAN, Sidney Frances (Cowell), *English actress,* 1823–81

Letters: 1 (n.d.)

BATES, Arlo, *American author, educator,* 1850–1918

Verse:

To My Infant Son (Kane Literary Collection)

Letters: 2 (1882–1900)

BATES, Charlotte Fiske, *American poet,* 1838–1916

Letters: 1 (1888)

BATES, Herbert Ernest, *English author,* 1905–74

Prose:

The Baker's Wife (17 pp.: HM 17246)

Letters: 15 (1926–68)

BATES, Katharine Lee, *American educator, poet,* 1850–1929

Letters: 1 (1920)

BAYLEY, Frederick William Naylor, *English editor, publisher,* 1808–53

Letters: 1 (n.d.)

BAYLOR, Frances Courtenay, *American novelist, short-story writer, poet,* 1848–1920

Letters: 2 (1894 and n.d.)

BAYLY, Ada Ellen, *English novelist,* 1857–1903

Prose:

Donovan (546 pp.: HM 17240)

Letters: 3 (1888–92)

BEACH, Rex Ellingwood, *American novelist,* 1887–1949

Letters: 1 (1906)

BEARD, Charles Austin, *American educator, historian,* 1874–1948

Letters: 15 (1908–46)

BEARDSLEY, Aubrey Vincent, *English artist,* 1872–98

Prose:

[Autobiographical note] (2 pp.: HM 14998)

Letters: 157 (1894–98)

BEATTIE, James, *English poet, professor of moral philosophy,* 1735–1803

Letters: 12 (1774–92)

BEATTIE, William, *English physician, poet,* 1793–1875

Letters: 1 (1839)

BEAUMONT, Francis, *English dramatist,* 1584–1616

Verse:

[Song] from the Nice Valour, or the Passionate Mad-man (MO 163)

[Poem ascribed to him in commonplace book] (HM 198)

BEAUMONT, Sir George Howland, 7th Bart., *English art patron, landscape painter,* 1753–1827

Letters: 11 (1796–1823)

BEAUMONT, Sir John, *English poet,* 1583–1627

Letters: 1 (1617/18)

Documents: 1 (1626)

BEAZLEY, Sir Charles Raymond, *English author,* 1868–1955

Prose:

John Cabot and his Son (416 pp.: HM 45713)

BECHDOLT, Frederick Ritchie, *American author,* 1874–1950

Letters: 8 (1907–32)

BECKFORD, William, *English author,* 1759–1844

Letters: 1 (1831)

BEDE, Cuthbert, see BRADLEY, Edward

BEDINGFELD, Edward, *English poet,* b. 1730

Verse:

Elegy Written in a Church-yard in South Wales (HM 1210)

Occasioned by Seeing a Copy of Verses to the Memory of Miss Blandy (HM 1209)

Ode . . . (HM 1205)

On the Victory off the Mouth of the Nile (HM 1207)

To Lady Viscountess Montague (HM 1208)

To Sickness (HM 1215)

To the Memory of Miss Blandy (HM 1212)

To William Jerningham, Esquire (HM 1206)

Under a Mezzotinto of Mr. Mason (HM 1213)

Written in 1801 (HM 1214)

Letters: 2 (1753–58)

BEECHER, Henry Ward, *American clergyman, author,* 1813–87

Letters: 19 (1856–85)

Other:

[Inscription:] "May the republic live! itself free and giving freedom to all" (1 p.: HM 2146)

BEERBOHM, Sir Max, *English critic, essayist, caricaturist,* 1872–1956

Prose:

The Guerdon (3 pp.: HM 32697)

Letters: 9 (1946–51)

BEETHOVEN, Ludwig van, *German composer,* 1770–1827

[One leaf of music from a notebook] (HM 15631)

BEHRMAN, Samuel Nathaniel, *American playwright,* 1893–

Letters: 52 letters (1939–41) addressed to him.

BELASCO, David, *American playwright, producer, actor,* 1859–1931

Prose:

The Wife (written jointly with Henry Churchill De Mille, 137 pp.: HM 2950)

Letters: 11 (1915–30)

BELKNAP, Jeremy, *American clergyman, historian,* 1744–98

Letters: 1 (1784)

BELL, Charles Frederic Moberly, *English journalist,* 1847–1911

Letters: 13 (1897–98)

BELL, Clive, *English art critic,* 1881–1964

Letters: 1 (1914)

BELL, Digby Valentine, *American comedian, operatic baritone,* 1849–1917

Letters: 4 (1841–98)

BELL, Horace, *American author,* 1830–1918

Prose:

Atlantis (Money's Zwirro-Zwirro, corrected typescript, 33 pp.: HM 39789)

Dona Vicente Murrieta [chap. II] (corrected typescript, 4 pp.: HM 39790)

Gold Bricks (corrected typescript, 35 pp.: HM 39791)

Jack Power, El Campeador. A California Romance (corrected typescript, 241 pp.: HM 39797)

The Jews and the Courts (corrected typescript, 16 pp.: HM 39792)

Junipero Serra's Conquest of California from the Manuscript of Don Guillermo Embustero y Mentiroso (corrected typescript, 158 pp.: HM 39798)

Leonis (corrected typescript, 22 pp.: HM 39799)

Los Angeles 1882 [chap. XVII] (corrected typescript, 22 pp.: HM 39793)

Manifest Destiny as it appeared in Nicaragua in 1855–'56–'57 (corrected typescript, 179 pp.: HM 39800)

On the Old West Coast [20 chapters] (corrected typescript, 301 pp.: HM 39788)

Pioneer Characters and Elections [chap. 23] (corrected typescript, 22 pp.: HM 39794)

Pioneer Relic (typewritten, 1 p.: HM 39795)

Saddle and Sword (corrected typescript, 602 pp.: HM 39787)

Scouting Adventures during 1861–1865 (corrected typescript, 179 pp.: HM 39786)

The Vasquez Vendetta (typewritten, 62 pp.: HM 39796)

Letters: 25 (1863–1901)

BELL, Robert, *English author,* 1800–67

Letters: 4 (1845–61)

BELL, Thomas Hastie, *American author,* 1867?–1942

Prose:

Catherine Breshkovsky (typewritten, xerox copy, 11 pp.: HM 42295)

Frank Harris (typewritten, 1 p.: HM 42296)

[Plagiarism by Frank Harris and others] (typewritten, 2 pp.: HM 42297)

Letters: 42 (1923–42), including 19 to Upton Sinclair

BELLAMY, Edward, *American author,* 1850–98

Prose:

Notebooks (typewritten, carbon copy, 592 pp.: HM 45714)

BELLAMY, Thomas, *English miscellaneous writer,* 1745–1800

Letters: 1 (1796)

BELLAW, Americus Wellington, *American author,* fl. 1873–1915

Prose:

Chevalier Bayard (14 pp.: HM 33695)
My Last Naval Engagement (12 pp.: HM 33696)
Preface to Almanac (7 pp.: HM 33697)
Whitehorn's Dictionary (34 pp.: HM 33698)

Letters: 1 (1915)

BELLEW, Harold Kyrle, *English actor,* 1855–1911

Letters: 1 (n.d.)

BELLOC, Hilaire, *English poet, writer,* 1870–1953

Letters: 1 (1918)

BELOE, William, *English divine, literary writer,* 1756–1817

Letters: 3 (1795–1815)

BEMAN, Nathaniel Sydney Smith, *American clergyman,* 1785–1871

Prose:

Address to the Church and Congregation on resigning my Pastoral Charge (16 pp.: HM 3589)

BENEFIELD, John Barry, *American author,* 1877–1956?

Letters: 1 (1924)

BENÉT, Laura, *American poet, biographer,* fl. 1921–59

Verse:

Christmas Crown (OC 1)

BENÉT, William Rose, *American poet, essayist,* 1886–1950

Letters: 105 (1920–50)

BENJAMIN, Park, *American lawyer, editor, author,* 1849–1922

Letters: 4 (1842–ca. 1863)

BENJAMIN, Samuel Greene Wheeler, *American artist, author,* 1837–1914

Verse:

Ode on the death of Abraham Lincoln [opening lines only] (HM 3144)

Letters: 3 (ca. 1890–1907)

BENNETT, Charles Henry, *English artist,* 1829–67

Letters: 1 (1855–66)

BENNETT, Enoch Arnold, *English novelist,* 1867–1931

Prose:

Giralda: A Melodrama in One Act (21 pp.: HM 36693)

Rivals for Rosamund: [play in one act] (52 pp.: HM 20690)

Whom God Hath Joined. A novel (164 pp.: HM 6903)

Letters: 6 (1911–23)

BENNETT, James Gordon, *American editor,* 1841–1918

Letters: 11 (1876–1908)

BENNETT, John, *American illustrator, author,* 1865–1956

Letters: 11 (1900–02) to Albert Bigelow Paine

BENNETT, Sanford Fillmore, *American physician, hymn writer, novelist,* 1836–98

Verse:

Sweet By-and-By (HM 45673)

Letters: 1 (1881)

BENNETT, William Cox, *English miscellaneous writer,* 1820–95

Verse:

An Invocation (RB 109990, vol. 3, pt. 1, p. 102)

BENNOCH, Francis, *English silk merchant,* 1812–90

Prose:

Fine Art Exhibition: [Impressions of a Benjamin Robert Haydon Painting Exhibition] (3 pp.: BE 1)

Letters: 5 (1845–85), and 290 addressed to him; also 56 letters from Benjamin Robert Haydon addressed to Bennoch and Richard Samuel Twentyman

BENSON, Arthur Christopher, *English essayist, poet, scholar,* 1862–1925

Letters: 5 (1905–24)

BENSON, Edward Frederic, *English novelist, essayist, biographer,* 1867–1940

Letters: 1 (1917)

BENSON, Stella, *English novelist,* 1892–1933

Letters: 2 (1922–32)

BENTHAM, Jeremy, *English writer on jurisprudence,* 1748–1832

Prose:

Constitutional Code (1 p.: RB 131334, vol. 2, p. 98)

Letters: 1 (1830)

Other:

[Endorsement and notes on letter from Sir Evan Nepean, 1st Bart.] (HM 6596)

BENTLEY, Richard, *English publisher,* 1794–1871

Letters: 12 (1835–63)

BENTON, Joel, *American journalist, author,* 1832–1911

Letters: 3 (1894–1910)

BERENSON, Bernard, *American art critic, author,* 1865–1959

Letters: 1 (n.d.)

BERESFORD, John Davys, *English novelist,* 1873–1947

Letters: 10 (1921–27)

BERKELEY, George Charles Grantley Fitzhardinge, *English writer,* 1800–81

Letters: 1 (1838)

BERKMAN, Alexander, *American anarchist author,* 1870–1936

Letters: 3 (1911–12)

BERNHARDT, Sarah, *French actress,* 1844–1923

Letters: 4 (1889–1902)

BERRY, Mary, *English author,* 1763–1852

Letters: 5 (1792–1831)

BERRYMAN, John, *American author,* 1914–

Letters: 4 (1948–64)

BESANT, Sir Walter, *English writer,* 1836–1901

Prose:

Andromeda (402 pp.: HM 7116)
[Autobiographical sketch] (4 pp.: HM 10785)
David and Jonathan (25 pp.: HM 7111)
The Demoniac (230 pp.: HM 7190)
Dorothy Forster (2 vols.: HM 7194)
The Fourth Generation (376 pp.: HM 7811)
Monmouth (published as *For Faith and Freedom,* 471 pp.: HM 7208)
No Other Way (title originally typewritten: The Way Out; partly typewritten, with corrections, 371 pp.: HM 8294)
Old Portsmouth (13 leaves: HM 7456)
Over the Sea with a Sailor (written with James Rice, 181 leaves: HM 33694)
Westminster (chap. 1 lacking, 204 pp.: HM 8283)

Letters: 49 (1874–1901)

BETHUNE, George Washington, *American clergyman, poet,* 1805–62

Letters: 7 (1832–58)

BEWICK, Thomas, *English wood engraver,* 1753–1828

Letters: 28 (1796–1824); and 28 letters (1796–1836) and 2 documents (1806–15) by Jane Bewick

BIDDLE, George, *American painter, illustrator, author,* 1885–

Letters: 7 (1956–69)

BIERCE, Ambrose Gwinnett, *American author,* 1842–1914?

Prose:

Collected Works—

Ashes of the Beacon (proof sheets with ms. corrections, 310 pp.: HM 10455)

Black Beetles in Amber (proof sheets with ms. corrections, 322 pp.: HM 10452)

The Devil's Dictionary (proof sheets with ms. and typewritten corrections, 349 pp.: HM 10450)

In the Midst of Life (proof sheets with ms. corrections, 438 pp.: HM 10453)

The Monk and the Hangman's Daughter; and Fantastic Tales (largely proof sheets with ms. corrections, 393 pp.: HM 10454)

Negligible Tales, and Kings of Beasts (proof sheets with ms. corrections, 135 pp.: HM 10458)

The Opinionator (partly ms. and partly typewritten, 49 pp.: HM 10456)

Shapes of Clay (proof sheets with ms. corrections, 428 pp.: HM 10451)

in the Huntington Library

Essays from Tangential Views, Opinionator, and Antepenultimata (typewritten, 87 pp.: HM 10457)

Miscellaneous stories (mss. and proof sheets, 266 pp.: HM 10459)

Contents:

Write It Right
The Stranger
Death of Halpin Frayser
The Moonlight Road
Secret of Macarger's Gulch
One Summer Night
The Diagnosis of Death
Moxon's Master
One of Twins
The Haunted Valley
A Jug of Sirup
Stanley Fleming's Hallucinations
A Baby Tramp
The Night-doings at Deadman's
Beyond the Wall
The Middle Toe of the Right Foot
John Mortenson's Funeral
The Realm of the Unreal
A Psychological Shipwreck
John Bartine's Watch
Haita the Shepherd
An Inhabitant of Carcosa
The Way of Ghosts
A Cold Greeting
A Wireless Message

An Arrest
Soldier-folk
Three and Three Are One
A Baffled Ambuscade
Two Military Executions
Some Haunted Houses
A Fruitless Assignment
A Vine on a House
At Old Man Eckert's
The Thing at Nolan
The Spook House
The Other Lodgers
Bodies of the Dead
Mysterious Disappearances

Letters: 373 (1871–1913)

Other:

[Annotations on George Sterling's works, "Duandon" (HM 2082) and "Testimony of the Suns" (HM 2064)]

[Note in *The Shadow on the Dial*] (RB 112471)

[Signed quote in *Fantastic Fables*] (RB 112469)

BIERSTADT, Albert, *American landscape painter,* 1830–1902

Letters: 3 (1862–89)

BIGELOW, John, *American editor, biographer,* 1817–1911

Letters: 26 (1846–1910)

BINDLOSS, Harold, *English novelist,* 1866–1945

Letters: 3 (1912–22)

BINYON, Laurence, *English poet,* 1869–1943

Letters: 13 (ca. 1898–1923)

BISHOP, Elizabeth, *American poet,* 1911–

Letters: 3 (1949–50)

BISHOP, Sir Henry Rowley, *English composer,* 1786–1855

Prose:

A Journal from London to Paris . . . (HM 20334)

A Journal &c, through France, and The Netherlands . . . (HM 20408)

BJORKMAN, Edwin August, *Swedish-American journalist, author, translator,* 1866–1961

Letters: 4 (1912–14) to Mary (Hunter) Austin

BLACK, William, *English novelist,* 1841–98

Prose:

A Hallowe'en Wraith (16 pp.: HM 14396)

The Monarch of Mincing Lane (153 pp.: HM 14397)

A Snow Idyll (36 pp.: HM 11351)

Letters: 13 (ca. 1870–89)

BLACKFORD, Martha, see STODDART, Lady Isabella (Moncrieff-Wellwood)

BLACKIE, John Stuart, *Scottish professor, man of letters,* 1809–95

Verse:

Burns (HM 44074)

May-Song (HM 44065)

To a Fair Lady Who Wished She had Been Born a Man (HM 44066)

Prose:

Carlyle [a critical paragraph] (1 p.: HM 44067)

BLACKMORE, Richard Doddridge, *English barrister, novelist,* 1825–1900

Verse:

Fringilla (corrected proofs: RB 43720)

John Howard's Rub-adub (HM 36090)

Kadisha (corrected typescript, incomplete: HM 14475)

Lita of the Nile (corrected typescript, incomplete: HM 14474)

To My Pen (HM 39313)

Prose:

Lorna Doone (416 pp.: HM 14399)

Letters: 107 (1860–99)

Other:

[Annotations on a bill from The Savoy Type-writing Office] (HM 14415)

BLACKMUR, Richard Palmer, *American educator, literary critic, poet,* 1904–

Letters: 6 (1931–61)

BLACKSTONE, Sir William, *English judge, legal writer,* 1723–80

Letters: 1 (1765)

BLACKWELL, Alice Stone, *American editor, author,* 1857–1950

Letters: 38 (1879–1940)

BLACKWOOD, Algernon, *English novelist,* 1869–1951

Letters: 3 (1911–22)

BLACKWOOD, William, *English publisher,* 1776–1834

Letters: 3 (1819–30)

BLAIR, Hugh, *Scottish divine, professor of rhetoric,* 1718–1800

Letters: 8 (1769–99)

BLAKE, William, *English poet, painter,* 1757–1827

Letters: 16 (1800–27)

Other:

[Marginal notes in]:

J. C. Lavater, *Aphorisms on Man,* 1788 (RB 57431)

Robert J. Thornton, *The Lord's Prayer,* 1827 (RB 113086)

Richard Watson, *An Apology for the Bible,* 1797 (RB 110260)

[38 drawings, as listed in *Catalogue of William Blake's Drawings in the Huntington Library*]

BLAND, Henry Meade, *American poet,* 1863–1931

Prose:

The Poetry of Robert Browning: [draft of lecture] (George W. James Collection)

Letters: 21 (1905–16)

BLANDING, Don, *American artist, traveler, poet,* 1894–1957

Letters: 24 (1933–46)

BLESSINGTON, Countess of, see GARDINER, Marguerite (Power) Farmer, Countess of Blessington

BLIND, Mathilde, *English poet,* 1841–96

Verse:

Love's Completeness (Russell Collection)

Letters: 2 (1888 and n.d.)

BLIVEN, Bruce Ormsby, *American editor, author,* 1889–

Letters: 11 (1925–43)

BLOMFIELD, Charles James, Bishop of London, *English writer,* 1786–1857

Letters: 9 (1814–ca. 1845)

BODENHEIM, Maxwell, *American poet, novelist,* 1893–1954

Letters: 7 (1918–19)

BOK, Edward William, *American editor, author,* 1863–1930

Letters: 27 (1883–1923)

BOKER, George Henry, *American poet, playwright,* 1823–1900

Verse:

"O, heart of mine" (FI 300)

"Wheel on thy axle" (FI 324)

Letters: 38 (1851–67), including 36 to James Thomas Fields

BOLTON, Sarah (Knowles), *American biographer, poet,* 1841–1916

Letters: 9 (1870–1907)

BOND, Carrie (Jacobs), *American songwriter, poet,* 1862–1946

Letters: 30 (1904–43)

BONER, John Henry, *American lexicographer, poet,* 1845–1903

Verse:

Elizabeth (BR Box 171)

In a Ball-Room (BR Box 171)

BONNER, Charles, *American author,* 1896–

Letters: 1 (1865)

BOOKER, Moore, *English clergyman, author,* fl. 1751–52

Verse:

An Elegiac Poem on ye Death of ye Rt Honble Mary Ponsonby late Countess of Drogheda (HM 14352)

A Tale: [poem in 90 lines] (HM 14353)

BOOTH, Edwin Thomas, *American actor,* 1833–93

Letters: 5 (1881–92)

BOOTH, Junius Brutus, *English actor,* 1796–1852

Letters: 1 (1833)

BOOTH, Samuel, *American poet,* fl. 1853–86

Verse:

Scrapbook: [poems] (HM 26352)

BOOTHBY, Guy Newell, *English novelist,* 1867–1905

Letters: 2 (n.d.)

BORROW, George Henry, *English author,* 1803–81

Verse:

Balder's Dreams, from the Ancient Norse (HM 14491)

The Death of Balder, a Heroic Play with Songs, in three acts. Translated from the Danish of Ewald (HM 14398)

The Giant's Head (HM 400)

The National Song of Denmark, from the Danish of Ewald (HM 14499)

"O merciful God creator of man and Djinn" (translated from the Arabic: HM 402)

Ribolt's Combat with the Dragon and Aller (HM 17245)

Romantic Ballads: [14 poems] (HM 15485)

Prose:

Celtic Bards, Chiefs and Kings (185 leaves: HM 17381)

Wild Wales: Its People, Language and Scenery (497 leaves: HM 12076)

Other:

Note, alterations and corrections in:

Borrow, George (trans.) *Bible. New Testament. Luke. Gitano* (RB 55275)

BOSWELL, James, *English writer, biographer of Johnson,* 1740–95

Letters: 6 (1771–91)

BOSWORTH, Hobart Van Zandt, *American scenario writer, actor,* 1867–1940?

Letters: 137 (1913–15)

BOTTA, Anne Charlotte (Lynch), *American author,* 1815–91

Verse:

Ab Astris (HM 14495)

Accordance (HM 14492)

Endurance (HM 14493)

A Modern Hero (HM 14494)

Prometheus (HM 14496)

Prose:

American Civilization (45 pp.: HM 14497)

Letters: 1 (1849)

BOTTOMLEY, Gordon, *English poet,* 1874–1948

Letters: 99 (1919–48)

Documents: 1 (1948)

BOUCHER, Jonathan, *American divine, author,* 1738–1804

Verse:

The American Times—see ODELL, Jonathan

Letters: 4 (1790–98)

BOUCICAULT, Aubrey, *English-American actor,* 1869–1913

Letters: 1 (1892)

BOUCICAULT, Dion, *Irish-born actor, playwright,* 1820–90

Prose:

Used Up (71 leaves, with corrections in hand of Charles Dickens: HM 17513)

Letters: 9 (1862–ca. 1880)

BOUGHTON, George Henry, *English painter, illustrator,* 1833–1905

Letters: 9 (1861–71)

BOWDLER, Thomas, *English editor,* 1754–1825

Letters: 4 (1777–98)

BOWLES, William Lisle, *English divine, poet, antiquary,* 1762–1850

Letters: 13 (1800–36)

BOWRING, Sir John, *English linguist, writer, traveler,* 1792–1872

Letters: 7 (1828–42), and 150 addressed to Bowring

BOYD, Andrew Kennedy Hutchinson, *Scottish divine,* 1825–99

Prose:

Recreations of a Country Parson: [table of contents only] (2 pp.: FI 395)

Letters: 22 (1861–62), including 8 to James Thomas Fields and 13 to Ticknor and Fields (firm)

BOYD, Ernest Augustus, *Irish-American critic, author,* 1887–1946

Letters: 1 (1917)

BOYD, Hugh Stuart, *English Greek scholar,* 1781–1848

Prose:

St. Basil's Homily on Paradise, translated from the Greek by Hugh Stuart Boyd (in the handwriting of Elizabeth [Barrett] Browning, 18 pp.: HM 4880)

Other:

[List of H. S. Boyd's works] (16 pp.: HM 4881)

BOYESEN, Hjalmar Hjorth, *Norwegian-American author,* 1848–95

Letters: 3 (1902)

BOYLE, John, 5th Earl of Orrery and Cork, *English author,* 1707–62

Verse:

To Mr. Pope (HM 14354)

Prose:

Letters from Italy in the years 1754 and 1755 (3 vols.: HM 6257)

Letters: 3 (1740/41–50)

BOYLE, Roger, 1st Earl of Orrery, *English statesman, soldier, dramatist,* 1621–79

Verse:

Henry the Fifth (EL 11642)
Henry the Fifth (HM 20)
Henry the Fifth (HM 11619)

Letters: 27 (1660/1–67)

BOYS, Thomas Shotter, *English painter, lithographer,* 1803–74

Letters: 5 (1829–54)

BRACKENRIDGE, Henry Marie, *American lawyer, author,* 1786–1871

Letters: 1 (ca. 1840)

BRADBROOK, Muriel Clara, *English author,* 1909–

Prose:

Yeats and Elizabethan Love Poetry (typewritten, with author's autograph corrections, 19 pp.: Dublin Magazine Collection)

BRADFORD, Gamaliel, *American biographer, essayist,* 1863–1932

Letters: 3 (1914–16)

BRADFORD, Roark, *American novelist,* 1896–1948

Letters: 4 (1934–36) to Eugene Lafayette Cunningham

BRADLEY, Edward, *English humorist,* 1827–89

Letters: 1 (1877)

BRADLEY, Mary Emily (Neely), *American novelist, poet,* 1835–98

Letters: 3 (1885–89)

BRADLEY, Will H., *American book designer, type designer, art director, author,* 1868–1962

Letters: 1 (n.d.), and 1 letter to him (1952)

BRADLEY, William Aspenwall, *American editor, author,* 1878–1939

Letters: 3 (1902–06), including 2 to Annie (Adams) Fields and 1 to Albert Bigelow Paine

BRADY, Cyrus Townsend, *American clergyman, novelist,* 1861–1920

Prose:

The Doctor of Philosophy (first draft; typewritten with corrections in author's hand, 162 leaves: HM 34547)

The Doctor of Philosophy (corrected draft; typewritten with author's and printers' corrections; galley proofs enclosed, 193 leaves: HM 34548)

Letters: 4 (1898–1910)

BRAHAM, John, *English singer,* 1774–1856

Letters: 5 (1835–52)

Other:

Leaves of music in ms. in: Braham, John. *Dulce Domum* (RB 150300)

BRAITHWAITE, William Stanley Beaumont, *American poet, anthologist,* 1878–1962

Letters: 7 (1912–29)

BRANCH, Anna (Hempstead), *American poet,* 1875–1937

Letters: 7 (1908–17), including 6 to Annie (Adams) Fields

BRAND, Barberina, Lady Dacre, *English poet, dramatist,* 1768–1854

Letters: 2 (1815–30)

BRANDT, Harry Alonzo, *American educator,* 1885–

Collection of approximately 500 pieces, including correspondence to and from Brandt, and typescripts of some of his articles, books, and collections of poetry.

BRAYBROOKE, Neville Patrick Bellairs, *English author,* 1925–

Prose:

Ford Madox Ford: A Reappraisal (carbon copy, 13 pp.: Dublin Magazine Collection)

Letters: 1 (1967)

BRETON, Jules Adolphe Aimé Louis, *French painter, writer,* 1827–1906

Letters: 1 (1884)

BRETT, Richard, *English divine,* 1560?–1637

Verse:

[Verses in Latin, Greek, Hebrew, Chaldaic, Syriac, and Arabic on the deliverance of James I from the Gunpowder Plot] (EL 1140)

BREWER, George, *English miscellaneous writer,* b. 1766

Letters: 1 (1809)

BREWSTER, Sir David, *English natural philosopher,* 1781–1868

Prose:

Colours of Natural Bodies (3 pp.: RH 648)

Letters: 14 (1826–67)

BRIDGES, Robert, *American editor, poet,* 1858–1941

Verse:

To a Young Convalescent (RB 21637)

Letters: 1 (1921)

BRIDGES, Robert Seymour, *English poet,* 1844–1930

Verse:

A Peace Ode (HM 36062)

To the United States of America (HM 27235)

Letters: 7 (1881–1919)

BRIDGMAN, William, *English author,* d. 1847

Prose:

The Commentary of Hierocles on the Golden Verses of the Pythagoreans (171 pp.: HM 13904)

The Commentary of Simplicius on the Enchiridion of Epictetus, translated from the Greek (596 pp.: HM 13903)

The Golden Verses of the Pythagoreans, translated from the Greek with a parallel translation by Nicholas Rowe, 1804; A Commentary on the Lord's Prayer . . . Nov. 1805; [and] The Enchiridion of Epictetus, translated from the Greek . . . 1806 (HM 13902)

BRIGGS, Charles Frederick, *American author,* 1804–77

Verse:

A Caution to Sea Travellers (HM 15484)

BRININSTOOL, Earl Alonzo, *American author,* 1870–1957

Letters: 4 (1934) to Eugene Lafayette Cunningham

Other:

Statement of wife of General Jesse M. Lee re the killing of Ogalala Sioux Chief Crazy Horse at Fort Robinson, Nebraska, in 1877 (HM 31260)

BRISBANE, Arthur, *American journalist,* 1864–1936
Letters: 10 (1899–1922)

BROCK, Charles Edmund, *English illustrator, portrait painter,* 1870–1938

Letters: 1 (1922)

BRONTË, Anne, *English author,* 1820–49

Verse:

Poems (HM 2576)

Contents:

Song [dated] Sep. 3, 1845

Song [signed] A. B. [dated] Sep. 4, 1845

Parting address from L. L. to A. B. [signed] Zerona A. Brontë, Oct. 1, 1845

"Why should such gloomy silence reign" [dated] Monday night, May 11, 1846

Mirth and Mourning, July 15, 1846, [signed] Zerona

"Weep not too much my darling" [signed] A. B. [dated] July 28, 1848

BRONTË, Charlotte, *English author,* 1816–55

Verse:

"My darling, thou wilt never know" (HM 2574)

"There's little joy in life for me" (HM 2575)

"We wove a web in childhood" (HM 2578)

Prose:

Anne Askew, Imitation (in French, 7 pp.: HM 2560)

Corner Dishes, Being a Small Collection of Mixed and Unsubstantial Trifles in Prose and Verse, by Lord Charles, Albert Florian Wellesley (contains: A Peep into a Picture Book; A Day Abroad in Four Chapters; and Stanzas on the Fate of Henry Percy: HM 2577)

The Lord's Prayer [written on the size of a three-penny piece] (1 p.: HM 33702)

Letters: 122 (1832–54), including 107 to Ellen Nussey

BRONTË, Emily, *English author,* 1818–48

Verse:

Poems: [34 untitled poems, in the handwriting of A. B. Nicholls] 91 pp.: HM 2581)

For a detailed list of contents of this and other Brontë manuscripts, see *The Trollopian,* 2 (1947–48): 177–99, 241–59; and 3 (1948–49): 55–72.

BROOKE, Henry, *English author,* 1703?–83

Verse:

Prologue to Gustavus Vasa (LO 10484)

BROOKE, Rupert Chawner, *English poet,* 1887–1915

Prose:

[Review of The Plays of August Strindberg] (9 pp.: HM 13905)

BROOKE, Samuel, *English master of Trinity College, Cambridge; writer of Latin plays and religious treatises,* d. 1631

Prose:

De Auxilio Divinae Coratiae et Libero Arbitrio (EL 1158)

BROOKS, Charles Timothy, *American poet, clergyman, translator,* 1813–83

Letters: 5 (1845–47)

BROOKS, Charles William Shirley, *English writer,* 1816–74

Letters: 24 (1842–73)

BROOKS, Cleanth, *American educator, author,* 1906–

Letters: 7 (1951–56)

BROOKS, Eldridge Streeter, *American editor, author,* 1846–1902

[Quotation from *The Song of the Knifemen*] (Kane Literary Collection)

BROOKS, John Graham, *American sociologist, reformer, writer,* 1846–1938

Letters: 5 (1888–91) to Annie (Adams) Fields

BROOKS, Maria (Gowen), *American poet,* 1794?–1845

Letters: 1 (1830)

BROOKS, Noah, *American editor, author,* 1830–1903

Letters: 3 (1860–92)

Other:

Notes in Carl Schurz's *Abraham Lincoln* (RB 16361)

BROOKS, Phillips, *American Episcopal bishop, author,* 1835–93

Prose:

"Let us give thanks to God upon Thanksgiving Day" (not autograph, 1 p.: FI 367)

Letters: 17 (1867–91)

Other:

[Inscription in his *Tolerance: Two Lectures . . .*] (RB 323522)

BROOKS, Van Wyck, *American critic, biographer,* 1886–1963

Letters: 48 (1907–58), including 20 to Mary (Hunter) Austin

BROUGH, Lionel, *English actor,* 1836–1909

Letters: 1 (1876)

BROUGHAM, Henry Peter, 1st Baron Brougham and Vaux, *English Lord Chancellor,* 1778–1868

Letters: 56 (1811–63)

BROUGHAM, John, *American actor, playwright,* 1810–80

Prose:

Anything for a Change (48 pp.: HM 13906)

Letters: 11 (ca. 1850–75)

BROUGHTON, Rhoda, *English novelist,* 1840–1920

Letters: 5 (1884–1900)

BROUN, Heywood Campbell, *American journalist, critic,* 1888–1939

Letters: 1 (1923) to Mary (Hunter) Austin

BROWN, Abbie Farwell, *American author,* d. 1927

Verse:

Windows (Kane Literary Collection)

Letters: 1 (n.d.)

BROWN, Alice, *American novelist,* 1857–1948

Prose:

The Cave of Adullam (41 pp.: HM 17249)

Letters: 9 (1906–35)

BROWN, Ford Madox, *English painter,* 1821–93

Letters: 48 (1853–93), and 106 letters addressed to Brown

BROWN, John, *English essayist,* 1810–82

Letters: 37 (1861–82), including 22 to James Thomas Fields and Annie (Adams) Fields

Other:

[Extracts from letters written to Annie (Adams) Fields and James Thomas Fields] (in the hand of Annie Fields; extracted for her book *A Shelf of Old Books,* 8 pp.: FI 418)

BROWNE, Hablot Knight, *English painter, book illustrator* (known as "Phiz"), 1815–82

Letters: 9 (1841–65), including 3 to Charles Dickens

Other:

[Pencil note in Dickens's Instructions to "Phiz" for Illustrating *Martin Chuzzlewit*] (HM 17501)

Drawings:

Illustrations to *Nicholas Nickleby:* 49 pen and ink drawings (HM 39999)

Illustrations to *Barnaby Rudge:* 60 pencil and watercolor drawings (HM 39997)

Illustrations to *The Old Curiosity Shop:* 60 pencil and watercolor drawings (HM 39998)

Pencil drawings of Puck, by "Phiz" in: Jerrold, Blanchard, *Life of George Cruikshank* (RB 137399, vol. 2, p. 238)

BROWNE, John Ross, *California pioneer, journalist, traveler, author,* 1821–75

Letters: 4 (1859–68)

Documents: 1 (1855)

BROWNE, Lewis, *American author,* 1897–1949

Letters: 1 (1932)

BROWNE, Lewis Allen, *American editor, author,* 1876–1937

Letters: 5 (1935–36) to Theodore Perceval Gerson

BROWNE, Maurice, *English-born American theatrical director, playwright,* 1881–1954

Letters: 17 (1922–52)

BROWNELL, Henry Howard, *American poet,* 1820–72

Letters: 30 (1865–67), including 29 to James Thomas Fields

Documents: 1 (n.d.)

BROWNELL, William Crary, *American critic,* 1851–1928

Prose:

Poe: [essay published in *American Prose Masters* in 1923] (45 pp.: HM 4285)

Letters: 6 (1890–1903)

BROWNING, Elizabeth (Barrett), *English poet,* 1806–61

Verse:

[Copy-book, containing poems, short essays, and notes, composed before the age of ten years and afterwards transcribed] (HM 4883)

[A Drama of Exile: incomplete draft] (HM 4877)

The Enchantress (HM 12765)

[The Enchantress: incomplete] (HM 12764)

Hector in the Garden (HM 4887)

Hiram Powers's Greek Slave (HM 4930)

Kings (HM 12766)

Manuscript Poems by Elizabeth B. Barrett: [notebook containing copies of eleven poems in the handwriting of Arabella Barrett] (HM 4932)

[Poem addressed to Hugh Stuart Boyd with a translation of "Prometheus Bound" of Aeschylus] (HM 4886)

[Prometheus Bound, translated from the Greek of Aeschylus, with a preface] (HM 4931)

[A Reed: first two stanzas only] (HM 4999)

Song of the Rose (HM 4888)

Sonnet on a Nun (RB 22866)

Stanzas [on her love for poetry] (HM 4889)

Stanzas on the Present State of Greece (HM 12759)

Suggested by Miss Landon's Lines on the Death of Mrs. Hemans (HM 42510)

The Sword of Castruccio Castracani (HM 4890)

[Thumbnail portraits, in verse, of Mary Maddox and of various members of Elizabeth Barrett's family] (HM 4885) Followed by: "Impromptu on a Candlestick"

To Mary Hunter on her Birthday (HM 4933)

To my Sweet George on his Birthday (HM 4892)

To the Mother of a Dead Blind Boy (HM 26070)

Two Poems (HM 39939)

[A Translation of Dante's Inferno: fragment] (HM 12762)

[Translation of "Sonetto di Vittorelli"] (RB 22866, vol. 3)

A True Dream, Dreamed at Sidmouth 1833 (HM 4884)

"A while ago and we were not" (HM 12767)

Wisdom Unapplied (HM 4893)

Prose:

[Commonplace book, containing passages copied from various authors] (43 pp.: HM 4934)

[Essay on Mind]: Analysis of the Second Book (2 pp.: HM 12760)

A glimpse into my own life and literary character (80 pp.: HM 4879)

Le Souvenir, or Pocket Tablet for 1844: [printed almanac, containing addresses and miscellaneous memoranda in the handwriting of Elizabeth (Barrett) Browning] (31 pp.: HM 4878)

[Notebook containing Greek exercises, translations, a draft of portions of the "Essay on Mind," and religious memoranda] (39 pp.: HM 4882)

[Remarks on a work by Sir Uvedale Price] (7 pp.: HM 12761)

St. Basil's homily on Paradise, translated from the Greek by Hugh Stuart Boyd [with corrections by Elizabeth (Barrett) Browning] (18 pp.: HM 4880)

[Thoughts on a Sickroom] (4 pp.: HM 4891)

[A translation of] The Epitaph of Moschus on Bion (4 pp.: HM 12763)

[A translation of] The Medea of Euripides (incomplete, 5 pp.: HM 12758)

Letters: 49 (1827–60)

BROWNING, Robert, *English poet,* 1812–89

Verse:

Christmas Eve and Easter Day (HM 4955)

[Epitaph for the Tomb of Levi Lincoln Thaxter] (HM 4954)

Helen's Tower (in the handwriting of F. J. Furnivall: FU 77)

How We Brought the Good News from Ghent to Aix (HM 4957)

[My Star] (HM 4999)

[Quotation of 4 lines only, from an unknown author, beginning: "Yellow and pale as ripened corn"] (HM 4956)

Spring Song (HM 44064)

Prose:

[Red Cotton Night-cap Country: biographical notes on Antonio Mellerio] (4 pp.: HM 12833)

Letters: 203 (1833–89)

Documents: 1 (1861)

Other:

[Endorsement on the cover of Elizabeth (Barrett) Browning's "A Glimpse into My own Life and Literary Character"] (HM 4879)

BRUNO, Guido, *American editor, author,* 1884–

Letters: 2 (1921)

BRYAN, William Jennings, *American political leader, orator,* 1860–1925

Letters: 9 (1903–22)

BRYANT, William Cullen, *American editor, poet,* 1794–1878

Verse:

After the Tempest (HM 2555)

The Ascension (HM 2569)

Autumn Woods (HM 2553)

The Conjunction of Jupiter and Venus (HM 2563)

The Damsel of Peru (HM 2564)

The Disinterred Warrior (HM 2566)

[A fragment of translation: Homer's] *Odyssey,* Book V, the Cave of Calypso (HM 1223)

The Grecian Partizan (HM 24380)

Hymn of the Waldenses (HM 2558)

Hymn to the North Star (HM 24377)

An Indian at the Burying Place of His Fathers (HM 2558)

An Indian Story (HM 2559)

An Invitation to the Country (SL 231)

The Lapse of Time (HM 2561)

The Life of the Blessed, [translated] from the Spanish of Ponce de León (HM 2565)

March (HM 2556)

Monument Mountain (HM 2557)

The Murdered Traveller (HM 24378)

Niagara [translated] from the Spanish of José María Hérédia (HM 2570)

The Old Man's Funeral (HM 2556)

On the Last Judgement (HM 2548)
The Prodigal's Return (HM 24379)
A Rain Dream (HM 2568)
The Return of Youth (HM 24387)
The Rivulet (HM 2556)
Rizpah (HM 24379)
Song—"Love's Seasons" (HM 2558)
Song of the Grecian Amazon (HM 2554)
Song of the Stars (HM 2561)
Sonnet: Mutation (HM 2554)
Sonnet: November (HM 2554)
Spring in Town (HM 2567)
[Springtime, translated] from the Spanish of Villegas (HM 2571)
The Spring's Walk (HM 2549)
Summer Wind (HM 2559)
Thanatopsis: [early version, in 49 lines] (HM 2551)
To —, beginning, "Aye, thou art for the grave" (HM 2559)
To a Cloud (HM 24378)
To a Waterfowl (HM 2550)
[Translated] from the French of Clement Marot: On a Person Called Friar Lubin (RB 79749, vol. 4, pt. 1)
Translation of a fragment of Simonides (HM 2550)
"Truth, Crushed to earth, shall rise again" (SW 65)
The Two Graves (HM 2562)

Prose:

[Legal casebook and notebook] (84 leaves: HM 2294)

Letters: 49 (1824–77)

Documents: 2 (1823–59)

Other:

[Corrections on Willis Gaylord Clark's *A Changeful Picture*] (HM 2573)

[Fragment of manuscript (6 lines)] (RB 114359, vol. d)

BRYCE, James, 1st Viscount Bryce, *English writer*, 1838–1922

Prose:

England and Ireland (37 pp.: HM 12834)

Letters: 6 (ca. 1880–1921)

BRYCE, Lloyd Stephens, *American diplomat, editor, novelist*, 1851–1917

Letters: 4 (1879–91)

BRYDGES, Sir Samuel Egerton, 1st Bart., *English bibliographer, genealogist*, 1762–1837

Verse:

Sonnets [eight] (HM 3169)

Letters: 11 (1800–36)

BUCHANAN, Robert Williams, *English poet, novelist*, 1841–1901

Verse:

Idyls and Legends of Inverburne [12 poems] (HM 12837)

Prose:

The Charlatan (corrected typescript, 262 pp.: HM 12835)

Foxglove Manor (400 pp.: HM 12836)

Letters: 8 (1864–97)

BUCK, Pearl (Sydenstricker), *American novelist*, 1892–1973

Letters: 2 (1945 and n.d.)

BUCKLAND, Francis Trevelyan, *English naturalist, writer,* 1826–80

Letters: 1 (1880)

BUCKLE, Henry Thomas, *English historian of civilization,* 1821–62

Letters: 6 (1858–60)

BUCKSTONE, John Baldwin, *English comedian, solicitor's clerk,* 1802–79

Prose:

Widow Wiggins: a monopolylogue (1 vol.: HM 43328)

Letters: 21 (1840–78)

Documents: 1 (1874)

BULLEN, Arthur Henry, *English author,* 1857–1920

Letters: 20 (1890–1907)

BULLEN, Thomas, *English poet,* fl. 1700

Verse:

Poems Written on Several Occasions (RB 352764)

BULWER, William Henry Lytton Earle, Baron Dalling and Bulwer, *English diplomatist,* 1801–72

Letters: 15 (1824–51)

Documents: 2 (1831)

BULWER-LYTTON, Edward George Earle Lytton, 1st Baron Lytton, *English novelist,* 1803–73

Verse:

Chant d'hommage pour Pausanias de Sparte (HM 7880)

One of the Crowd (corrected proof sheets: RB 131482)

Prose:

Godolphin (incomplete, 317 pp.: HM 7975)

I Think on Italy (7 leaves: HM 17145)

Letters from Sir Edward Bulwer-Lytton to Lady Blessington (corrected proof: RB 131482)

Walpole, or Every Man Has His Price (corrected proof: RB 131481)

Letters: 153 (1827–72)

Other:

[Corrections on: Report on a speech on Odd Fellows delivered by Edward . . . Bulwer-Lytton] (HM 17185)

BULWER-LYTTON, Edward Robert, 1st Earl of Lytton, *English statesman, poet,* 1831–91

Letters: 51 (ca. 1855–87)

Documents: 1 (1856)

BULWER-LYTTON, Rosina Doyle (Wheeler), Baroness Lytton, *English novelist,* 1802–82

Verse:

"I sits with my feet in a brook" (HM 10068)

Monody on the Year 1847 (JP 32)

To My Children (JP 31)

Letters: 66 (1838–61)

Documents: 1 (1852)

BUNCE, Oliver Bell, *American publisher, editor, playwright, anthologist,* 1828–90

Letters: 6 (1885–87)

BUNN, Alfred, *English theatrical manager*, 1796?–1860

Letters: 7 (1829–40)

BUNNER, Henry Cuyler, *American poet, editor, short-story writer*, 1855–96

Verse:

Deaf (HM 12755)

Edmund Clarence Stedman (HM 10057)

For the First Page of the Album (RB 113686)

Forty (HM 12753)

Grandfather Watts (RB 113686)

Grant (HM 12849)

Home Sweet Home, with Variations (HM 12848)

In a Paris Restaurant (HM 12843)

Leopold Damrosch (proof sheet, signed: HM 12845)

Les Morts Vont Vite (HM 12844)

March in Janiveer, Janiveer in March I fear (HM 12846)

The New Girls (HM 12756)

Puck's Exchanges: Garden and Forest (HM 12757)

She Was a Beauty (HM 12847)

Prose:

Classic Journalism (1 p.: HM 12754)

General Benjamin F. Butler (9 leaves: HM 32689)

In 1888 the vote for mayor in New York City was . . . (9 leaves: HM 32691)

Once Upon a Time . . . (6 leaves: HM 32692)

The Red Silk Handkerchief (65 pp.: HM 12850)

Summer is the true vacation time . . . (10 leaves: HM 32690)

Letters: 6 (1880–96)

BURDETTE, Robert Jones, *American humorist, author,* 1844–1914

Prose:

[Journal of a tour through Europe, Egypt, and Palestine, beginning in London and ending in Pasadena, California] (2 vols.: HM 12851)

[Manuscript notes for lectures, sermons, speeches, etc.] (Burdette Collection)

Diaries and memo books (ca. 45 vols.: Burdette Collection)

Letters: 951 (1883–1914), also, 1,255 (1871–1953) letters by Clara (Bradley) Burdette

BURGES, Sir James Bland, *English politician, author,* 1752–1824

Letters: 1 (1800)

BURGESS, Frank Gelett, *American humorist, author,* 1866–1951

Verse:

Arnold His Book [collection of 7 short rhyming verses, including "The Purple Cow," each with a pen and watercolor illustration] (1 vol.: HM 30900)

The Goops (HM 34814)

Letters: 15 (1897–1932)

BURGESS, Richard, *English divine, writer,* 1796–1881

Letters: 14 (1841–59), including 13 to John Arnold Rockwell

BURGOYNE, John, *English dramatist, general,* 1722–92

Letters: 6 (1773–78)

Documents: 1 (1773)

BURKE, Edmund, *English statesman, critic,* 1729–97

Letters: 19 (1759–96)

BURKE, Kenneth Duva, *American music critic, author,* 1897–

Letters: 4 (1964–72)

BURNABY, Frederick Gustavus, *English cavalry officer, author,* 1842–85

Letters: 1 (1882)

BURNE-JONES, Sir Edward Coley, *English painter,* 1833–98

Letters: 76 (1857–97)

Documents: 1 (1886)

BURNET, Dana, *American playwright, novelist, poet,* 1888–

Verse:

Lincoln (HM 3142)

Letters: 1 (n.d.)

BURNET, Gilbert, *English bishop, writer,* 1643–1715

Letters: 2 (1710–30)

BURNETT, Frances Eliza (Hodgson), *American novelist,* 1849–1924

Prose:

Editha's Burglar (36 pp.: HM 33693)

Letters: 10 (ca. 1885–1902)

BURNEY, Charles, *English organist, musical historian,* 1726–1814

Letters: 2 (1787)

BURNEY, Frances, see ARBLAY, Frances (Burney) d'

BURNHAM, Clara Louise (Root), *American novelist, poet,* 1854–1927

Letters: 2 (1894–1917)

Other:

[Signed quotation] (Kane Literary Collection)

BURNS, Robert, *Scottish poet,* 1759–96

Verse:

"And I'll kiss thee yet, yet . . ." (Tune—Brae's o' Balquidder: HM 13046)

"Behold, my love, how green the groves . . ." (HM 2584)

"A down winding 'Nith I did wander . . ." (Song-Tune, Geordie's byre: HM 13044)

Elegy on Captain Matthew Henderson (HM 13054)

Epigrams (HM 13042)

Epithalamium: [a poem] and Epitaph . . . (Forgery?: HM 13042)

"The friend who wild from Wisdom's way . . ." (HM 13026)

"Fy, let us a' to Kirk-t, . . ." A Ballad-Tune, Fy let us a' to the bridal (HM 13048)

Glenriddel Hermitage, June 28th, 1788 (HM 13061)

"Green sleeves and tartan ties . . ." (HM 13046)

"Here, where the Scottish muse immortal lives . . ." (RB 124145, vol. 1)

The Humble Petition of Bruar Water to the Noble Duke of Athole (HM 13027)

Johnie B's Lament (Tune—The babes o' the wood: HM 13045)

The Kirk's Alarm—A Ballad (Tune—Push about the brisk bowl: HM 13058)

Lament for James, Earl of Glencairn (missing the first two verses: HM 13050)

"The last time I came o'er the moore . . ." (HM 13049)

"Lassie wi' the lint-white locks, . . ." (HM 13057)

"My Chloris, mark how green the groves, . . ." (HM 13042)

"No Churchman am I for to rail and to write . . ." A Song (Tune—Prepare, my dear brethren, to the tavern let's fly: HM 13036)

On a Scotch Bard, gone to the West Indies (HM 13056)

On Captn. Grose's present peregrination through Scotland collecting the Antiquities of that Kingdom (HM 13055)

On Mr. Pit's Hair-Powder Tax (HM 13025)

On Scaring Some Water-Fowl in Loch Turit (HM 13040)

[Poems on leaves in the beginning and end of "Geddes Burns"] (RB 124145, vol. 1)

Queen Mary's Lament (HM 13051)

"Their groves o' sweet myrtles let Foreign Lands reckon . . ." Tune, Humors of Glen (HM 13045)

"There was an auld man and he has a bad wife . . ." (HM 13047)

"Thou lingering star with lessening ray . . ." (HM 13035)

To Miss Jeany Cruikshank (HM 13022)

To Miss Susan Logan, Park[house]—With Beattie's Poems (HM 13021)

To Mr. McMurdo, with a Pound of Lundiefoot Snuff (HM 13024)

To Mrs. Mc—alias Clarinda (HM 13040)

" 'Twas where the birch and sounding thong are ply'd . . ." (HM 13059)

The Wedding Day, A Song . . . (HM 13034)

The Whistle—A Ballad—[and] The Prose Story of the Whistle (HM 13053)

Why should na poor people mow (HM 34699)

Poems in RB 151851, in order:

On reading in a Newspaper the death of John McLeod Esqre . . .

On the death of Sir J. Hunter Blair

Written on the blank leaf of a copy of my first Edition

Epitaph on a friend

The humble Petition of Bruar Water to the noble Duke of Athole

Epistle wrote in the commencement of my poetical career . . .

On the death of Robr. Dundas . . . with note by Burns

On scaring some waterfowl in Loch Turit . . .

Written in the Hermitage at Taymouth

Written at the Fall of Fyers

Written in Friar's Carse Hermitage on the banks of Nith—June—1788

Altered from the Foregoing—Dec. 1788

To Robert Graham of Fintry

Letters: 18 (1786–95). Also photostats of letters regarding "Geddes Burns" (RB 151851) in Robert Burns box

Documents: 1 (1793)

Other:

[Annotation in pencil in hand of Robert Burns and addressed to Jean Lorimer] (RB 120027)

[Annotation and corrections in Burns's *Poems,* 1792] (RB 110909)

[Annotations of 39 localities and names filled in and an extra stanza at end of "Tam Samson's Elegy," in Burns's *Poems*, 1787] (RB 110190, p. 152)

BURR, Amelia Josephine, *American poet, novelist,* b. 1878

Letters: 1 (1922)

BURRA, Edward John, *English surrealist painter,* 1905–76

Letters: 200 (1930–73) to Conrad Aiken

Other:

Pencil drawing (AIK 2196)

BURRITT, Elihu, *American linguist, reformer, author,* 1810–79

Prose:

The Reality and Mission of Ideal Characters (46 pp.: HM 13292)

Walk from London to Land's End and Back (693 leaves: HM 33692)

Letters: 11 (1854–78)

Documents: 1 (1860)

BURROUGHS, John, *American naturalist, author,* 1837–1921

Verse:

Early April (HM 33764)

To the Golden Crowned Sparrow in Alaska (HM 33770)

"What matter if I stand alone?" (HM 33740)

Prose:

About spiders and other things (18 leaves: HM 33761)

The art of seeing things (61 leaves: HM 33762)

Carlyle and Emerson (incomplete, pp. 23–78: HM 33763)

The Early Writings of John Burroughs (28 pp.: HM 12798)

Essay written for the Whitman Centenary (26 pp.: HM 12797)

The Ether (5 leaves: HM 15483)

Flies in Amber (typescript with corrections in the hands of Burroughs and Clara Barrus: HM 15479)

Glimpses of Wild Life about My Cabin (69 leaves: HM 15480)

Glimpses of Wild Life about my Cabin (corrected typescript, 27 leaves: HM 15481)

"Look Nature Through Tis Revolution All" (essay and pencil drawings: RB 54819)

Men and Animals (27 leaves: HM 33766)

Notebook containing printed notices of "Wake Robin," notes made on the South Downs of England (October 13, 1871), accounts of expenses, and miscellaneous memoranda (7 leaves: HM 15477)

Notebooks written during the Harriman Alaskan Expedition in 1899 (2 vols.: HM 33770)

Reading the Book of Nature (18 leaves: HM 33767)

The Real and the Ideal—A Hint from Nature (12 leaves: HM 33739)

The Still Small Voice [draft of an essay] (incomplete, 10 pp.: HM 15482)

Thoreau (17 leaves: HM 33768)

Two Birds' Nests (including two photographs and one pen and ink drawing of Burroughs; printed text of MS. as it appeared in chap. 6 of *Far and Near,* 1904; 17 leaves: HM 33769)

Work and Wait (6 pp.: HM 15478)

Letters: 72 (1866–1913)

BURT, Katharine (Newlin), *American novelist,* b. 1882

Letters: 1 (1920)

BURTON, Sir Frederic William, *English painter,* 1816–1900

Letters: 1 (1875)

BURTON, Richard Eugene, *American poet, critic,* 1861–1940

Verse:

If We Had Time (HM 15486)

Letters: 4 (1903–04)

BURTON, Sir Richard Francis, *English explorer, scholar,* 1821–90

Prose:

Four Lectures: The Visitation to El Medinah; The Pilgrimage to Meccah; What Led to the Discovery of the Sources of the Nile; A Mission to Dahome (121 leaves: HM 27955)

The Uruguay: [translation of the Portuguese Epic by the Brazilian poet José Basilio da Gama] (This is *not* the manuscript described in Penzer's *Bibliography,* 1923, and sold at Parke-Bernet in 1953, April 14, Lot 157; 98 leaves: HM 27954)

Letters: 85 (1885–90), and 34 (1888–92) by Isabel Burton

BURTON, Robert, *English author,* 1577–1640

Autograph and marginal annotations in: Giovio, Paolo. *Novocomensis episcopi Nvcerini Historiarum sui temporis* (n.p., 1556: RB 151881)

BURY, Catherine Maria (Dawson) Tisdall, Countess of Charleville, *English poet,* 1762–1851

Verse:

To Mr. [William] Sotheby, on reading his Italy (SY 16)

Letters: 1 (1834)

BURY, Lady Charlotte Susan Maria (Campbell), *English novelist,* 1775–1861

Verse:

[Poetical and prosaic commonplace book] (Includes poems ascribed to: Sir Walter Scott, Richard Brinsley Sheridan, John Wolcot; 354 pp.: HM 33691)

Poetical commonplace book (210 pp.: HM 29165)

Prose:

Diary (239 pp.: HM 19481)

Letters: 5 (1821–37)

BUTLER, Ellis Parker, *American humorist, author,* 1869–1937

Letters: 1 (1916) to Mary (Hunter) Austin

BUTLER, Frances Anne (Kemble), see KEMBLE, Frances Anne

BUTLER, Henry Montagu, *English headmaster, writer,* 1833–1918

Letters: 2 (1890–1912)

BUTLER, William Allen, *American lawyer, biographer, novelist, poet,* 1825–1902

Letters: 19 (1859–99)

BUTLER-BURKE, Vivian, *American writer,* fl. ca. 1920

Prose:

Mythological Traditions Connected with Berchtesgaden and District, Bavaria and Austria (typewritten with corrections; 10 pp.: Butler-Burke Collection).

Memoranda, etc. (Butler-Burke Collection)

Notes for mythology research (Butler-Burke Collection)

Notebooks (4 vols.: Butler-Burke Collection)

Dictionary of Terms (16 vols.: Butler-Burke Collection)

Notes on Gaelic Mythology (arranged alphabetically; ca. 1000 pieces: Butler-Burke Collection)

BUTTERWORTH, Hezekiah, *American author*, 1839–1905

Letters: 2 (1899 and n.d.)

BUXTON, Sir Thomas Fowell, 1st Bart., *English philanthropist, author*, 1786–1845

Letters: 6 (1824–40)

BYNNER, Witter, *American poet, playwright*, 1881–1968

Verse:

"The agitation and the use of war . . ." (RB 297228)

Drouth (typewritten: California Poetry File)

Ghost (typewritten: California Poetry File)

Spring (HM 14993)

Three Songs to Celia (California Poetry File)

Letters: 58 (1905–55)

BYRD, William, *American planter, colonial official, author*, 1674–1744

Prose:

Journal, in shorthand; also, in longhand, with volume in reverse: A Credo, and Abstracts of law cases from *Cases de Leases* in the Reports of Sir Edward Coke (161 leaves: BR 61)

Letter and Representation concerning the office of Auditor of Public accounts in Virginia (2 pieces: BL 96, BL 98)

Notebook containing drafts of addresses, petitions, etc. prepared while acting as counsel for Sir Edmund Andros, and as Agent for the Colony of Virginia (46 leaves: BR 744)

Letters: 1 (1722)

Documents: 5 (1728–43/44)

BYRON, George Gordon Noel, 6th Baron Byron, *English poet,* 1788–1824

Verse:

"And thou art dead, as young and fair" (HM 12540)

Answer: [epistle to a friend, Francis Hodgson, in answer to some lines exhorting the author to be cheerful, and to "banish care"] (HM 6515)

"Could I remount the river of my years" (HM 12539)

Epistle to Augusta (HM 12546)

[Lines addressed by Lord Byron to his Lady, when the latter was labouring under illness] (in handwriting of James Clarence Morgan: HM 2851)

Monody on the Death of the Right Honorable R. B. Sheridan (HM 12859)

On the Death of Thyrza: "Without a stone to mark the spot" (HM 12536)

On the eyes of Miss A. H. (a copy in an unidentified hand: HM 12376)

Oscar of Alva (stanzas 29–34 only: HM 12379)

Stanzas, beginning, "Away, away, ye Notes of Woe" (HM 12537)

Stanzas to Augusta (HM 12538)

Stanzas to Thyrza (HM 12545)

Corrections on proof sheets of:

Siege of Corinth and Parisina (RB 90590)

The Corsair (RB 89524)

Manfred (RB 90270)

Childe Harold (RB 92328)

Lament of Tasso (RB 90272)

Prose:

[Lord Byron's draft of a footnote to accompany a reference to Southey's *Curse of Kelama,* in his Hints from Horace] (HM 12380)

Letters: 29 (1805–24)

Documents: 2 (1814–16)

BYRON, Henry James, *English dramatist,* 1834–84

Letters: 6 (1860–81)

C

CABELL, James Branch, *American novelist, essayist, poet,* 1879–1958

Letters: 1 (1920)

CABLE, George Washington, *American novelist,* 1844–1925

Letters: 14 (1884–1907)

CADELL & DAVIES (English firm)

Collection of 496 pieces (1769–1832), consisting primarily of letters to the publishing firm from literary clients.

CAHAN, Abraham, *Russian-American novelist, editor,* 1860–1951

Letters: 1 (1921)

CAINE, Sir Thomas Henry Hall, *English novelist,* 1853–1931

Verse:

With the Night (HM 33771)

Prose:

[An Imaginary Interview with Himself] (7 leaves: HM 33785)

Letters: 26 (1880–1914)

CAIRNS, Huntington, *American lawyer, author,* 1904–

Letters: 8 (1949–73)

CALDECOTT, Randolph, *English artist,* 1846–86

Letters: 2 (1871–83)

CALDER, John, *English author,* 1733–1815

[Annotations relative to Jonathan Swift's *Character of the Earl of Wharton:* extract from the new edition of the *Tatler*] (3 pp.: HM 14358)

[Notation on a title page] (Kane Literary Collection)

CALDERON, Philip Hermogenes, *English painter,* 1833–98

Letters: 1 (1865)

CALIFORNIA POETRY FILE

The California Poetry File, a collection of approximately 2,100 pieces, consists of poems, letters, and printed items written by and relating to Western writers and California poets in particular. The collection offers an interesting view of the California literary scene during the first half of the twentieth century, particularly in its concentration of many local and lesser-known writers. Among the more important authors represented are such writers as Kate Rennie (Aitken) Archer, Witter Bynner, Bliss Carman, Stanton Arthur Coblentz, Hamlin Garland, Langston Hughes, Charles Fletcher Lummis, and Don and Neeta Marquis. Specific items by these authors, as well as by others in the collection, are listed within each author's individual entry in this Guide.

CALVERT, George Henry, *American poet, essayist, novelist, playwright,* 1803–89

Letters: 2 (1867–69)

CAMBRIDGE, Richard Owen, *English author,* 1717–1802

Letters: 5 (1770–ca. 1790)

CAMPBELL, Thomas, *English poet,* 1777–1844

Verse:

Elegy Written in Mull (HM 31505)

"If strewn his ashes to the wind" (RB 131334, vol. 1)

Lochiel's Warning (HM 31476)

The Soldier's Dream, transcribed by Th. Campbell (HM 31477)

Systema (HM 31498)

Prose:

De Montfort [a revision of a Joanna Baillie play, "De Monfort"] (62 leaves: HM 32693)

Edmund Spenser: [a biographical sketch] (28 pp.: HM 33775)

Edmund Waller: [a biographical sketch] (8 pp.: HM 33777)

Life of Dryden: [a biographical sketch] (13 pp.: HM 33776)

Life of Robert Southwell born 1560: [a biographical sketch] (3 pp.: HM 33779)

Thomas Nash 1558–1600: [an extract from *Anecdotes of Literature and Scarce Books*] (7 pp.: HM 33778)

[Notebook for *Specimens of the British Poets*] (300 pp.: HM 33781)

Notes on The English Stage (239 pp.: HM 33780)

Preface to Mr. Moxon's Edition of Shakespeare: [a life of Shakespeare] (135 pp.: HM 33782)

[Note on intent to write a poem on Portugal] (RB 131334, vol. 1)

Letters: 56 (1794–1844)

CAMPBELL, Walter Stanley, *American educator, author,* 1887–1957

Letters: 20 (1930–51)

CAMPION, Thomas, *English poet, musician,* d. 1619

Verse:

"There is a gardine in her face" (copy: EL 8892)

CANBY, Henry Seidel, *American educator, editor, author,* 1878–1961

Letters: 31 (1920–37), including 29 to Mary (Hunter) Austin

CANNING, George, *English statesman,* 1770–1827

Letters: 8 (1806–18)

CANOVA, Antonio, *Italian sculptor,* 1757–1822

Letters: 4 (1811–18)

CANTOR, Eddie, *American comedian,* 1893–1964

Letters: 1 (1953)

CAREW, Rivers, *Editor, Dublin Magazine,* fl. 1961–68

Letters: 36 (1963–72), and 611 letters addressed to him

Other:

237 manuscripts submitted to him

CAREW, Thomas, *English poet,* 1595?–1639?

Verse:

[Poems ascribed to him in commonplace books]: (HM 116, HM 198, HM 1338)

CAREY, Henry Charles, *American publisher, economist, author,* 1793–1879

Letters: 120 (1829–78)

Documents: (1852)

CAREY, Mathew, *Irish-born American publisher, economist, author,* 1760–1839

Letters: 4 (1808–36)

CAREY, Rosa Nouchette, *English novelist,* 1840–1909

Letters: 3 (1890–1902)

CARHART, Arthur Hawthorne, *American conservationist, novelist,* 1892–

Letters: 18 (1929–32) to Mary (Hunter) Austin

CARLETON, William McKendree, *American poet,* 1845–1912

Prose:

A Classical Mud-Hole (25 pp.: HM 34554)

CARLILE, Richard, *English free-thinker, printer, author,* 1790–1843

Prose:

[Article on Religion] (incomplete, 8 pp.: RC 330)

Letter 3—Society (2 pp.: RC 334)

Note on the Letter of Edwinus (8 pp.: RC 347)

On Prison Discipline and on the Duties of Magistrates, Keepers and other Officers of Prisons (8 leaves: RC 335)

On the Science of God. Chapter 11. On the moral governance of mankind (18 pp.: RC 339)

To . . . Commons of Great Britain and Ireland in Parliament assembled. Petition (2 pp.: RC 342)

To the Editor of the Morning Advertiser. Political Mistakes in Jewish History. Letter 4 (13 pp.: RC 332)

To . . . the Lords . . . in Parliament assembled (4 pp.: RC 341)

To the Political Public (8 pp.: RC 340)

What is that most wanted in society? Free Discussion (1 p.: RC 338)

Letters: 248 (1822–43)

CARLYLE, Jane Baillie (Welsh), *English writer,* 1801–66

Letters: 17 (1844–64)

CARLYLE, Thomas, *English essayist, historian,* 1795–1881

Verse:

"The Future hides in it" (HM 34594)

Prose:

History of Frederick the Great (1 leaf only: HM 12769)

Last Words of Thomas Carlyle: On Trades-Unions; Promoterism; Signs of the Times (a fragment, 8 pp.: HM 11620)

On the erection of a statue in honor of Oliver Cromwell (8 pp.: HM 34579)

Picture of Husbandry in Annandale (2 pp.: HM 34595)

[Quotation:] "Paradise is under the shadow of our Swords," said the Emir: "Forward!" (1 slip: HM 12768)

Reminiscences of my Irish Journey (100 pp.: HM 31984)

Letters: 116 (1835–74)

Documents: 16 (1842–74)

CARMAN, Bliss, *American poet,* 1861–1929

Verse:

99 texts

Prose:

Address to the Graduating Class, 1911, of the Unitarian School of Personal Harmonizing (19 pp.: HM 35387)

[Essay on James Whitcomb Riley] (64 pp.: HM 35405)

[Essay on Personal Harmonizing] (20 pp.: HM 35406)

[James Whitcomb Riley: an essay] (50 pp.: HM 12780)

The Music of Life: First Draft (26 leaves: HM 35547)

[Notes on James Whitcomb Riley and his writings] (20 pp.: HM 35437)

Physical Training and the Art of Life (10 leaves: HM 35447)

The Poet in Modern Life (57 pp.: HM 12771)

Letters: 61 (1890–1928), including 45 to Susan (Hayes) Ward

CARNEY, James Patrick, *Irish author,* 1914–

Letters: 1 (n.d.)

CARPENTER, Edward, *English author,* 1844–1929

Letters: 1 (1914)

CARR, John, *English writer, translator of Lucian,* 1732–1807

Letters: 1 (1822)

CARROLL, Lewis, see DODGSON, Charles Lutwidge

CARRYL, Guy Wetmore, *American novelist, poet, humorist,* 1873–1904

Letters: 1 (1897)

CARTER, Elizabeth, *English miscellaneous writer,* 1717–1806

Letters: 5 (1782–1800)

CARTER, John, *English divine,* d. 1655

Prose:

Funerall Sermon for Frances Countess of Bridgewater (facsimile: EL 6887)

A Funerall Sermon vpon the Death of the Countess of Bridgewater my deare Lady and mother (facsimile: EL 6885)

Prayers and Two Sermons (EL 6884)

Sermon (EL 6880)

Sermon (EL 6882)

A Sermon Preached at Little Gaddesden at the Funeral of Lady Frances Stanley (facsimile: EL 6883)

CARUTHERS, William Alexander, *American novelist,* 1800–46

Letters: 5 (1822–33)

CARY, Alice, *American poet,* 1820–71

Verse:

"I have kept fancy travelling to and fro" (HM 1240)

Song of Sorrow (HM 22501)

"To search out all his mysteries . . ." (HM 429)

Letters: 20 (1856–68)

CARY, Lucius, 2nd Viscount Falkland, *English soldier, politician, writer,* 1610?–43

Letters: 1 (1642/3)

CARY, Phoebe, *American poet,* 1824–71

Verse:

A Ballad of Calden Water (HM 34553)

Prodigals (HM 428)

Letters: 1 (n.d.)

CASALS, Pablo, *Spanish cellist, conductor, pianist, composer,* 1876–1973

Letters: 1 (n.d.)

CASEY, Kevin, *Irish author,* 1940–

Letters: 2 (1962–63)

CASTLE, Egerton, *English novelist,* 1858–1920

Letters: 4 (1895–1919)

CATHER, Willa Sibert, *American novelist, poet,* 1873–1947

Letters: 103 (1909–ca. 1940)

CATLIN, George, *American artist, author,* 1796–1872

Prose:

The North Americans in the Middle of the Nineteenth Century (ms. of unpublished book, with 254 drawings by Catlin: HM 35183, vols. A and B)

Letters: 2 (1870 and n.d.)

CATTERMOLE, George, *English painter,* 1800–68

Letters: 10 (1841–64), including 6 addressed to Charles Dickens

CATTON, Charles Bruce, *American editor, author,* 1899–

Letters: 1 (1956) to Norreys J. O'Conor

CAWEIN, Madison Julius, *American poet,* 1865–1914

Verse:

Blooms of the Berry (HM 34546)

Kentucky Poems (extract from Prologue: HM 1204)

Letters: 4 (1896), and 29 to him from James Whitcomb Riley

Other:

[Description of photograph presented to him by James Whitcomb Riley] (1 p.: HM 44355)

CERF, Bennet Alfred, *American publisher, editor, author,* 1898–1971

Letters: 63 (1927–52), including 37 to the Merrymount Press and 25 to Sara Bard (Field) Wood

CHALMERS, Stephen, *American novelist, poet,* 1880–1935

Letters: 15 (1917–34)

CHALMERS, Thomas, *English theologian,* 1780–1847

Letters: 10 (ca. 1817–46)

CHALON, Alfred Edward, *English painter,* 1780–1860

Letters: 3 (1852–57)

CHAMBERLAIN, Arthur Henry, *American educator, author,* 1872–1942

Letters: 11 (1929–32) to Cyril Clemens

CHAMBERLAIN, Joseph, *English statesman, writer,* 1836–1914

Letters: 8 (1885–1900)

CHAMBERS, Robert, *English publisher, author,* 1802–71

Letters: 13 (1853–67)

CHAMBERS, Robert William, *American novelist,* 1865–1933

Verse:

Charles Warren Stoddard (Songs): [lyrics] (HM 35075)

Prose:

The Cambric Mask (484 leaves: HM 34543)

Lorraine! (863 leaves: HM 34544)

The Sinful City (published as *Ashes of Empire;* 847 leaves: HM 34545)

Yo Espero (a novelette published in *The Haunts of Men;* 68 leaves: HM 34551)

Letters: 1 (1903)

CHANNING, Edward Tyrrell, *American educator, editor, author,* 1790–1856

Letters: 1 (1839)

CHANNING, William Ellery, *American clergyman, poet,* 1780–1842

Letters: 3 (1838–42)

CHANNING, William Ellery, *American poet,* 1818–1901

Verse:

A Poet's Love (in hand of Thoreau: HM 13207)

Letters: 2 (1845–73)

CHANNING, William Henry, *American clergyman, abolitionist, author,* 1810–64

Letters: 11 (1860–83)

CHANTREY, Sir Francis Legatt, *English sculptor,* 1781–1841

Letters: 2 (1829–37)

CHAPMAN, John Jay, *American critic, poet,* 1862–1933

Letters: 55 (1891–1915), including 47 to the Merrymount Press

CHAPONE, Hester (Mulso), *English essayist,* 1727–1801

Letters: 4 (1762–74)

CHAPPLE, Joseph Mitchell, *American editor, anthologist, novelist, biographer,* 1867–1950

Letters: 13 (1900–12)

CHEEVER, George Barrell, *American clergyman, reformer, author,* 1807–90

Letters: 1 (1859) to Susan (Brownell) Anthony

CHENEY, David MacGregor, *American author,* fl. 1901–30

Verse:

A Cloud is Here (AP 350)

Elegy on the point of a Carpet Tack (AP 317)

The Ivy (AP 295)

Midnight (AP 326)

The Passing Day (AP 301)

A Sonnet of Autumn (AP 351)

Prose:

The Call of the Sea (4 leaves: AP 294)

Letters: 56 (1901–30)

CHENEY, John Vance, *American librarian, poet, essayist,* 1848–1922

Verse:

To Hope (HM 1238)

Letters: 9 (1887–1921), and ca. 200 letters addressed to Cheney

CHERRY, Andrew, *Irish actor, dramatist,* 1762–1812

Prose:

Thalia's Tears: A Tributory Sketch (4 leaves: HM 17431)

CHESEBROUGH, Caroline, *American author,* 1828?–73

Letters: 1 (1871)

CHESTERFIELD, Earl of, see STANHOPE, Philip Dormer, 4th Earl of Chesterfield.

CHESTERTON, Gilbert Keith, *English essayist, critic, novelist, poet,* 1874–1936

Verse:

The Three Conquistadors (illustrated: HM 26402)

CHILD, Francis James, *American educator, linguist,* 1825–96

Letters: 11 (1862–ca. 1879)

CHILD, Lydia Maria (Francis), *American editor, abolitionist, novelist,* 1802–80

Letters: 44 (1839–79)

CHILD, Richard Washburn, *American diplomat, novelist,* 1881–1935

Letters: 1 (1923)

CHIVERS, Thomas Holley, *American poet, playwright,* 1809–58

Verse:

Apples of Eros No. 1—Cupid in Search of Venus Doves (HM 2518)

De Ole Gray Hoss (HM 2522)

Elen Æyre (HM 2532)

Hymn of Faith (HM 2517)

Lament for Shelley Lost at Sea (HM 2523)

Lyra Coeli: a song of sorrow (HM 2521)

Milton (HM 2528)

Noises of the Night (HM 2520)

The Roll of Fame (HM 2525)

The Rosebud of Beauty (in hand of J. Hunt, Jr.: HM 2536)

The Vigil in Aiden (HM 2538)

Prose:

A Brief Summary of Poe's Birth, Life and Death (32 pp.: HM 2530)

Letters from the North. New Series. No. 10 (4 pp.: HM 2527)

A New Life of Edgar Allan Poe (43 leaves: HM 2529)

Notes and Criticisms on a New Edition of Shakespeare's Works (2 pp.: HM 2533)

Notes Concerning the Criticism by Willis of Tennyson in the *Home Journal* (4 pp.: HM 2534)

Notes on the Widower, Ulalume, Dream Land, Israfel, To One in Paradise, etc. (6 pieces: HM 2535)

Notes on N. P. Willis, R. W. Griswold, and J. R. Lowell; and on Poe's criticism of "Plato Contra Athenos" and on "Charles O'Malley" (3 pp.: HM 2516)

Sketch of the Life of T. H. Chivers, M.D., with some remarks on a few of his earliest poems (6 pp.: HM 2537)

Statement concerning a letter from Ms. Elmira Shelton to Mrs. Maria Clem (2 pp.: HM 2531)

Thoughts on Capital Punishment (8 pp.: HM 2519)

Letters: 14 (1842–55)

CHRIST-JANER, Albert William, *American artist, educator,* 1910–

Letters: 5 (1944–45)

CHURCH, Richard, *English writer,* 1893–

Letters: 8 (1951–61)

CHURCHILL, Winston, *American novelist, author,* 1871–1947

Letters: 3 (1916)

CHUTE, Marchette Gaylord, *American author,* 1909–

Letters: 24 (1946–57) to Norreys J. O'Conor, and 100 to Chute

CIARDI, John, *American educator, poet,* 1916–

Letters: 3 (1956–67)

CIBBER, Colley, *English actor, dramatist,* 1671–1756

Letters: 1 (1753)

CLARE, Ada, see McELHENNEY, Jane

CLARK, Charles Heber, *American journalist, author,* 1847–1915

Letters: 2 (1882–1903)

CLARK, Kate (Upson), *American author,* 1851–1935

Letters: 2 (1889–1903), including one to Albert Bigelow Paine

CLARK, Lewis Gaylord, *American editor, poet,* 1808–73

Letters: 5 (1834–55)

CLARK, Willis Gaylord, *American editor, publisher, poet,* 1808–41

Verse:

A Changeful Picture (HM 2573)

Letters: 1 (1829)

CLARKE, Adam, *English theologian, author,* 1762–1832

Letters: 17 (1786–1830)

Documents: 1 (1810)

CLARKE, Austin, *Irish poet,* 1896–

Verse:

The Paper Curtain (with author's autograph corrections: Dublin Magazine Collection)

Letters: 26 (1932–67), including 22 to James Starkey

CLARKE, Charles Cowden, *English Shakespearean scholar,* 1787–1877

Letters: 17 (1823–77), of which 14 are in joint authorship with Mary Victoria (Novello) Cowden Clarke

CLARKE, James Freeman, *American Unitarian clergyman,* 1810–88

Verse:

July 9th, 1867: [poem on anniversary of birthday of William Lowell Putnam] (SL 235)

Prose:

Journal including record of journey to California via the Isthmus, notes on quartz mining in Nevada County, and account of trip east as far as Grey Town, Nicaragua (1 vol.: HM 18962)

Letters: 36 (1834–87)

Documents: 1 (1887)

CLARKE, John Sleeper, *American actor,* 1833–99

Letters: 1 (n.d.)

CLARKE, Mary Victoria (Novello) Cowden, *English wife of Charles Cowden Clarke,* 1809–98

Verse:

Sonnet: "Kind words! how good ye are, written or said!" (FI 812)

Letters: 49 (1851–96); other letters are written jointly with Charles Cowden Clarke

CLARKE, Rebecca Sophia, *American author,* 1833–1906

Letters: 2 (1883–96)

CLARKE, William Fayal, *American editor,* 1855–1935

Letters: 16 (1898–1933)

CLARKSON, Thomas, *English philanthropist, anti-slavery writer,* 1760–1846

Prose:

[Account of efforts, 1807–24, to abolish the foreign slave trade and slavery in the British colonies] (66 leaves: CN 33)

The African Prince (14 leaves: CN 70)

Paper . . . to interfere for better Treatment of Negroes in W. Indies (4 pp.: CN 56)

Letters: 86 (1789–1846)

Documents: 8 (1792–1843)

CLAYTON, John, *English actor,* 1843–88

Letters: 1 (1878)

CLEMENS, Samuel Langhorne (Mark Twain, pseud.), *American author,* 1835–1910

Verse:
Those Annual Bills (FI 5076)

Prose:

An American Pirate: letter to the editor of the Chronicle (2 pp.: HM 22253)

A Cure for the Blues: [a review of] *The Enemy Conquered; or, Love Triumphant,* by Samuel Watson Royston (HM 17378)

The Gilded Age (two fragments: 1 p. from chapter I and 2 pp. from chapter LXIII; partly in the hand of Charles Dudley Warner; 3 leaves: HM 453)

The Gilded Age: chapters XXIII and LX (partly in hand of Charles Dudley Warner; 34 pp.: HM 1315)

The Gilded Age: chapter XXXIII (64 pp.: HM 1312)

The Gilded Age: chapter XXXVII (15 pp.: HM 1309)

The Gilded Age: chapter XL (15 pp.: HM 1318)

The Gilded Age: chapter XLVIII (in the handwriting of Charles Dudley Warner; 20 pp.: HM 470)

The Gilded Age: chapter LV (in the handwriting of Charles Dudley Warner; 20 pp.: HM 1317)

The Gilded Age: chapter LVII (25 pp.: HM 1311)

The Gilded Age: Appendix (1 p.: HM 1310)

Meisterschaft (93 leaves: HM 11610)

Playing Courier (43 leaves: HM 1314)

The Prince and the Pauper (3 vols.: HM 1327)

[Suppressed chapter of *Life on the Mississippi*] (typewritten copy, 12 pp.: Hill Collection)

A Tramp Abroad: chapter VII (26 leaves: HM 1308)

Letters: 161 (1867–1910), including 105 to Mary J. (Mason) Fairbanks

CLEMENTS, Colin Campbell, *American playwright,* 1894–1948

Letters addressed to Clements and his wife, Florence (Willard) Ryerson Clements, are in the Willard Collection. Two letters by Mrs. Clements, written in 1927 and 1930, are included in the Marquis Collection.

CLEVELAND, John, *English poet,* 1613–58

Verse:

Epitaph upon the E[arl] of Strafford (copy: EL 8864)

CLIFTON, William, *American poet,* 1772–99

Prose:

Paddy's Plot, or the Old Fool Couzen'd at last (33 pp.: HM 34559)

CLIVE, Caroline (Meysey-Wigley), *English writer,* 1801–73

Verse:

"I sought you, friends of youth" (RB 109990, vol. 2, pt. 1)

CLOUGH, Arthur Hugh, *English poet,* 1819–61

Letters: 1 (n.d.)

CLOVER, Samuel Travers, *American journalist, author,* 1859–1934

Letters: 19 (1902–33)

COATES, Florence Earle, *American poet,* 1850–1927

Letters: 1 (1917)

COBB, Irvin Shrewsbury, *American humorist, novelist*, 1876–1944

Letters: 8 (1913–35)

COBB, James, *English dramatist*, 1756–1818

Verse:

Poor Old Drury! A Prelude (HM 17432)

COBB, Margaret Smith, *American author*, fl. 1910–26

Verse:

At Sea (typewritten: Jack London Collection)

The Brave (GS 21)

The Lame Lady (typewritten: Jack London Collection)

The Law (typewritten: Jack London Collection)

Redolence (typewritten: Jack London Collection)

The Suicide (typewritten: Jack London Collection)

Prose:

Love (4 leaves: GS 22)

Letters: 33 (1910–26)

COBBE, Frances Power, *English philanthropist, religious writer*, 1822–1904

Letters: 6 (1895–1904); also, several hundred letters addressed to her, including 238 from Anthony Ashley Cooper, 7th Earl of Shaftesbury

COBBET, William, *English political journalist, essayist*, 1762–1835

Prose:

To the Citizens of London [an address] (11 pp.: HM 17026)

Letters: 34 (1793–1832)

COBBOLD, Richard, *English novelist,* 1797–1877

Letters: 5 (1827–70)

COBDEN, Richard, *English statesman, writer,* 1804–65

Letters: 13 (1846–64)

COBLENTZ, Stanton Arthur, *American critic, poet,* 1896–

Verse:

Epitaph for a Poet (California Poetry File)

Intricate is the Weaving (California Poetry File)

Letters: 53 (1924–49)

COBURN, Walt, *American author,* b. 1889

Letters: 1 (1929) to Eugene Lafayette Cunningham

COCKERELL, Sir Sydney Carlyle, *English author,* 1867–1962

Letters: 21 (1896–1912), and 38 addressed to him

Documents: 1 (1893)

CODRINGTON, Robert, *English author,* d. 1665

Verse:

[Volume of verses in English and Latin on the death of the wife of Lord Bridgewater] (facsimile: EL 6850)

Letters: 1 (1661)

COFFIN, Charles Carleton, *American correspondent, author,* 1823–96

Letters: 1 (ca. 1870)

COGGESHALL, William Turner, *American editor, diplomat, author,* 1824–67

Letters: 1 (1862)

COGHLAN, Rose, *English-American actress,* 1853–1932

Letters: 1 (1880)

COHEN, Alfred J., *American drama critic, novelist,* 1861–1928

[Quotation from His Own Image] (Kane Literary Collection)

COLBURN, Frona Eunice Wait (Smith), *American author,* b. 1859

Letters: 1 (1914) to George Wharton James

COLCORD, Lincoln Ross, *American novelist, poet,* 1883–1947

Verse:

"I went out into the night of quiet stars" (Kane Literary Collection)

COLERIDGE, Derwent, *English author,* 1800–83

Letters: 6 (1860–68), including 5 to Frederick James Furnivall

COLERIDGE, Ernest Hartley, *English literary editor,* 1846–1920

Verse:

[Poems written in the 1860s] (HM 31991)

Letters: 10 (1877–94)

COLERIDGE, Hartley, *English poet, man of letters,* 1796–1849

Verse:

Contemplations on a Distant Prospect of a Church Yard at Night (HM 12296)

"Thou Baby Innocence—unseen of me . . ." (HM 12125)

To Wordsworth (HM 12309)

"A wanton Bard in heathen time . . ." (HM 12103)

Letters: 1 (1821)

COLERIDGE, Henry Nelson, *English editor, literary executor of S. T. Coleridge,* 1798–1843

Letters: 2 (1832–40)

COLERIDGE, Samuel Taylor, *English poet, critic,* 1772–1834

Verse:

Effusion 16 (published as "Pity": HM 260)

The Garden of Boccaccio (corrected draft: HM 360)

Know Thyself (RB 131334, vol. 2)

Lines suggested by the last words of Berengarius; Reflections on the above; also Epitaphium Testamentarium (HM 12122)

Lines to a Young Man of Fortune who Abandoned Himself to an Indolent and Causeless Melancholy (in letter to Benjamin Flower: HM 12290)

Osorio (contemporary copy with autograph corrections and additions: HM 361)

Osorio (contemporary copy: HM 362)

Song, or rather the Commencement of a Song (published as Glycine's Song in *Zapolya,* Act II, scene i: HM 12105)

Prose:

[Commonplace book, containing, among other pieces, "On the Divine Ideas" and a transcription of the German play "Adams und Evens Erschaffung und ihr Sundenfall"] (partly autograph; partly in German, 291 pp.: HM 8195)

The Grounds of Sir Robert Peel's bill vindicated (16 pp.: HM 12121)

[Hexameters: definition and remarks on structure, with examples] (1 leaf: HM 12123)

Notebook containing thoughts on the Trinity, imagination, studies of the Gospels, and philosophical matters (98 leaves: HM 17299)

The Reason and the Understanding (2 pp.: HM 34656)

My Advice and Scheme (RB 131334, vol. 2)

Letters: 53 (1794–1832)

Documents: 1 (1805)

Other:

[Marginal notes, annotations, and corrections in twelve printed books]

COLERIDGE, Sara (Coleridge), *English writer, editor,* 1802–52

Verse:

Vago angellato che contando vai [a sonnet translated into English from the Italian of Francesco Petrarca] (HM 12295)

Verses on Illness Written at Hampstead (HM 2171)

Letters: 6 (1838–49)

COLLIER, John Payne, *English Shakespearean critic,* 1789–1883

Verse:

Verses written of 20 good precepts, at the request of his Especiall good friend and kinsman M. Robert Cudden of Grayes Inne (RB 120526)

Letters: 52 (1830–81)

Other:

[Forged accounts of money and gifts, and forged letters in Ellesmere Collection] (EL 123–127, EL 138, and EL 11750–11755)

[Marginal notes and annotations in the Perkins Folio of Shakespeare's Works] (RB 56316)

COLLINS, Charles Allston, *English painter, author,* 1828–73

Prose:

Apology for his Art under a deep sense of High-minded Responsibility: [essay concerning "Electric Telegraph"] (23 pp.: HH 1)

Letters: 24 (1850–71), including 22 to William Holman Hunt

COLLINS: William Wilkie, *English novelist,* 1824–89

Prose:

Armadale, A Drama in Three Acts (66 pp.: HM 33790)

Armadale: a novel with title page, dedication, and introduction (577 pp.: HM 33786)

Armadale (1866 printed copy with corrections and additions by Collins: RB 83848)

The Frozen Deep (1866 printed copy, autographed by Collins: RB 122534)

The Haunted Hotel (printed copy with added pages of manuscript and ms. corrections: RB 120320)

How I Write My Books (contemporary copy with corrections by Collins, 5 pp.: HM 33791)

Lady Calista: A Drama in Four Acts and Five Tableaux (partly autograph, 169 pp.: HM 33792)

Miss Gwilt: A Drama in Five Acts (printed copy with corrections by Collins: RB 120054)

My Lady's Money (107 pp.: HM 12789)

No Name, A Drama in Four Acts (1870 printed copy with corrections by Collins: RB 120321)

[Unidentified Play] (fragment, 1 p. only: HM 12788)

The Woman in White: In a Prologue and Four Acts (partly autograph, 133 pp.: HM 33793)

Letters: 136 (1850–89)

Documents: (1868) concerning publication of *Moonstone*

COLLYER, Robert, *American Unitarian clergyman,* 1823–1912

Letters: 120 (1863–1912)

COLMAN, George, *English dramatist,* 1762–1836

Letters: 29 (1801–27)

COLTON, Arthur Willis, *American writer,* 1868–1943

Letters: 1 (1920)

COLTON, Charles Caleb, *English poet, essayist,* 1780–1832

Verse:

Society (HM 6521)

COLTON, Walter, *American naval chaplain, journalist, author,* 1797–1851

Letters: 1 (1850)

Documents: 5 (1846–48)

COLUM, Padraic, *Irish-American poet, miscellaneous author,* 1881–1972

Prose:

The Child of Sorrow [Thomas Dermody] (typewritten, with author's autograph corrections, 7 pp.: Dublin Magazine Collection)

John Davidson (typewritten, with author's autograph corrections, 9 pp.: Dublin Magazine Collection)

Stephen Phillips (typewritten, with author's autograph corrections, 5 pp.: Dublin Magazine Collection)

Thomas MacDonagh and His Poetry (typewritten, with author's autograph corrections, 8 pp.: Dublin Magazine Collection)

Letters: 8 (1965–68)

COMBE, William, *English adventurer,* 1741–1823

Letters: 5 (1790–1818)

COMFORT, Will Levington, *American editor, novelist,* 1878–1932

Letters: 7 (1902–31)

COMMONPLACE BOOK COLLECTION

The Commonplace Book Collection was artificially formed from 28 volumes of miscellaneous literary material which range from the sixteenth to the twentieth century. The volumes consist chiefly of verse and short prose pieces, with some letters, sermons, music, and (in the later volumes) numerous original pen-and-ink drawings. Included are several volumes of early seventeenth-century poetry, political satires from the time of the Rump Parliament and the Glorious Revolution, three volumes owned by Joseph Haselwood, the Samuel J. Sterrett Album, the Sibbald Album, the Lydia Woodworth Album, an album of French authors, and the Benjamin West and John and Charles Wesley albums. Among the more important later authors represented are George Gordon NOEL, 6th Baron BYRON, Reginald HEBER, Charles LAMB, Mary LAMB, John MILTON, and Alfred TENNYSON, 1st Baron TENNYSON. Specific manuscripts and letters, by the authors listed above as well as by others in the collection, are listed within each author's individual entry in this Guide.

Additional commonplace books in the Ellesmere Collection are noted in the description of that collection in the *Guide to British Historical Manuscripts in the Huntington Library.*

CONANT, Isabella Howe, *American poet,* b. 1874

Letters: 1 (n.d.)

CONE, Helen Gray, *American educator, poet,* 1859–1934

Letters: 2 (1892–94)

CONGREVE, William, *English dramatist,* 1670–1729

Letters: 1 (1723)

Documents: 1 (1715)

CONKLING, Grace Walcott (Hazard), *American poet,* 1878–1958

Letters: 2 (1917–20)

CONQUEST, George Augustus, *English actor, manager, writer of melodrama,* 1837–1901

Letters: 1 (1890)

CONRAD, Joseph, *Polish-born English novelist,* 1857–1924

Prose:

An Anarchist: [original draft of a novelette] (68 pp.: HM 33794)

Joseph Conrad, His Raison d'Être as a Writer: [annotations, corrections, and supplementary notes on a biographical sketch which was anonymously written ca. 1906] (16 pp.: HM 33795)

[Lord Jim: fragment, being a variant of a portion of chapters XXXIII and XXXIV] (8 leaves: HM 12997)

Nostromo. Part Third. The Lighthouse: [chapters i–vii] (mostly typescript with annotations and corrections by Conrad, 168 pp.: HM 33796)

Note [on *An Outcast of the Islands*] (4 pp.: HM 33797)

Note in Stephen Crane's *The Five White Mice* (HM 3995)

Letters: 2 (1915–20)

CONRAD, Robert Taylor, *American journalist, jurist, playwright, poet,* 1810–58

Letters: 1 (1856)

CONVERSE, Florence, *American editor, novelist, poet,* 1871–1964?

Letters: 1 (1916)

CONWAY, Katherine Eleanor, *American editor, poet,* 1853–1927

Verse:

"There's a woman at root of everyone's grief" (HM 35075)

Letters: 1 (1894)

CONWAY, Moncure Daniel, *American clergyman,* 1832–1907

Prose:

Avalon and the Holy Thorn (14 pp.: HM 17241)

Carlyle and His Circle (9 pp.: RB 441582)

Letters: 52 (1864–1906), and 63 letters to Conway

Other:

[Corrections on Frederick James Furnivall's report of inaugural meeting of the Browning Society] (FU 303)

CONWAY, Sir William Martin, Baron Conway of Allington, *English art critic, collector,* 1856–1937

Letters: 13 (1907–29)

COOK, Edward Dutton, *English drama critic,* 1829–83

Letters: 3 (1860–83)

COOK, Eliza, *English poet,* 1818–89

Verse:

On the Death of a Favourite Old Hound (HM 1794)

Vive La Follie (FR 43)

Letters: 1 (n.d.)

COOKE, John Esten, *American novelist,* 1830–86

Verse:

A Dream of the Cavaliers (BR Box 255)

Notebook containing poems written in 1848 and 1849, as follows (BR 759):

Ad Taylorem

Air-Far Away in Tennessee

"The bard whose life is written in this page"

Far Away in Tennessee, beginning, "I took her lily hand in mine"

Far Away in Tennessee, beginning, "Tom here's to your health my boy"

"Fill up, fill up the mighty cup"

"In my youth's summer all was bright and clear"

Libera Nos Domine

Life—a Poem

Lives—Stanzas

Look First upon This Picture [followed by another poem entitled] Then on This

Mr. Polk's Valedictory

Old Year, beginning, "A chill old man with a hoary beard"

The Old Year, beginning, "The new year gaily ambles up"

Song—Angelica, Do Come Home

Song, beginning, "Heard you aught of Lancelot"

Tom's Verdict

Translation of a Celtic Chant

Twelve O'clock

When Sorrow Comes

Who's Thar?

Prose:

Old Virginia: or, the fortunes of Henry St. John (212 pp.: BR 67; published in 1859 under the title *Henry St. John, Gentleman, of "Flower of Hundreds," in the County of Prince George, Virginia. A Tale of 1774–'75*)

Letters: 24 (1847–85)

COOKE, Rose (Terry), *American author,* 1827–92

Verse:

The New Sangreal (FI 624)

Out of the Body to God (FI 631)

Letters: 17 (1860–89)

COOKSLEY, S. Bert, *American poet,* fl. 1925

Verse:

Poems: (typewritten: GS 55)

With Change

Voyage

To a Poet

The Watchers

Old Friends

"So he believed, when all the world was still"

"We who have been confident of dawn"

COOLBRITH, Ina Donna, *American poet,* 1842–1928

Verse:

Blossom Time (HM 38419)

Bret Harte (2 ms. copies; 1 typewritten copy: Kozlay Collection)

Copa de Oro (Foy Collection)

James F. Bowman (HM 38420)

The Laurel: To Edmund Clarence Stedman (HM 34624)

A Leaf for Memory: Mrs. Martha E. Powell (HM 34623)

Longfellow (HM 34622)

Los Angeles (Foy Collection)

Mariposa Lily (Foy Collection)

A New Leaf (Foy Collection)

"A noise like of a hidden brook" (HM 38455)

"Oh balm and dew and fragrance of those nights" (HM 35075)

The Poet (HM 26321)

San Francisco (Keeler Collection)

To Charles Warren Stoddard, beginning, "For the old days' sake" (RB 44880)

Prose:

[A Meeting with John Greenleaf Whittier] (22 pp.: HM 38487)

[A Recollection of Francis Bret Harte and Charles Warren Stoddard] (51 pp.: HM 38488)

Letters: 253 (1876–1926)

COOLIDGE, Dane, *American novelist, naturalist,* 1873–1940

Letters: 6 (1912–39)

Other:

[Two signed quotations] (Kane Literary Collection)

COOLIDGE, Susan, see WOOLSEY, Sarah Chauncey

COOPER, James Fenimore, *American novelist,* 1789–1851

Prose:

The Autobiography of a Pocket Handkerchief: [the final draft] (154 pp.: HM 34535)

John Shaw (11 pp.: HM 34536)

Ned Myers; or A Life Before the Mast (final draft, with preface, 154 pp.: HM 34532)

Richard Dale (16 pp.: HM 34537)

The Water Witch (part of chap. IV, 4 pp.: HM 12796)

Letters: 11 (1824–50)

Documents: 4 (1834–46)

COOPER, Robert, *English engraver, publisher,* fl. 1800–56

Letters: 8 (1836–55)

COOPER, Susan Fenimore, *American author,* 1813–94

Letters: 3 (1876)

COPERARIO, Giovanni, or COPRARIO, or COOPER, John, *English musician,* d. 1626

Rules. How to Compose (EL 6863)

[Songs in 6-vol. Elizabethan part books] (EL 25/A/46–51)

COPLEY, John Singleton, Baron Lyndhurst, *English jurist, Lord Chancellor, son of J. S. Copley, painter,* 1772–1863

Letters: 10 (ca. 1830–62)

CORBET, Richard, *English bishop, poet,* 1582–1635

Verse:

An Elegie upon the Ladie Haddington (copy: EL 8798)
[Poems ascribed to him in commonplace books] (HM 116, HM 172, HM 198)

CORNELL, Sara (Hughes), *American author, physician,* 1862–1938

Prose:

A Valid Excuse (HM 34821)

Letters: 32 (1910–37), including 27 to Neeta Marquis

CORNWALL, Barry, see PROCTOR, Bryan Waller

CORSON, Hiram, *American educator, author,* 1828–1911

Letters: 2 (1886–91)

CORTISSOZ, Royal, *American journalist, lecturer, art critic,* 1869–1948

Letters: 42 (ca. 1905–24)

CORY, William Johnson, *English schoolmaster, lyric poet,* 1823–92

Letters: 42 (1848–85) to Frederick James Furnivall

COSTAIN, Thomas Bertram, *American editor, author,* 1895–

Letters: 2 (1930)

COTTLE, Joseph, *English bookseller, poet, publisher,* 1770–1853

Verse:

The Baronial Hall (HM 12130)

Letters: 1 (1827)

COTTON, Charles, *English poet,* 1630–87

[Ms. corrections in printed copy of his *The Confinement*] (RB 102322)

COUSINS, Samuel, *English mezzotint engraver,* 1801–87

Letters: 3 (1867–82)

COWLEY, Abraham, *English poet,* 1618–67

Verse:

On Drink: [paraphrase upon the Greek of Anacreon] (LO 10486)

A Satyre. The Puritan and the Papist (copy: EL 8780)

[Poems ascribed to him in commonplace book] (HM 16522)

COWLEY, Malcolm, *American editor, poet, translator,* 1898–

Letters: 60 (1935–73)

COWPER, William, *English poet,* 1731–1800

Verse:

The Iliad of Homer: a translation of Book XII, lines 108–241 (HM 12584)

The Odyssey of Homer: a fragment of translation (HM 10765)

Poems (3 volumes containing about 65 poems; vols. 1 and 2 in handwriting of John Johnson, and vol. 3 in handwriting of author: HM 12587)

[Poems, including "Table Talk," "The Progress of Error," "Truth," and "Anti-Thelyphthora"] (HM 12588)

Letters: 4 (1759–85)

Documents: 1 (1722)

COX, David, *English watercolor painter,* 1809–85

Letters: 1 (1874)

COZZENS, Frederic Swartwout, *American merchant, essayist, poet,* 1818–69

Letters: 3 (1861–65)

CRABBE, George, *English poet,* 1754–1832

Verse:
Tales of the Hall (early draft: HM 27621)

Prose:

Sermon on a text: "Abhor that which is Evil, cleave to that which is Good." Romans 12:9 (10 leaves: HM 33798)

Sermon on a text: ". . . Paul thou art beside thyself, Much Learning hath made thee Mad." Acts 26:24 (16 leaves: HM 4287)

Sermon on the text: "How can I do this great Wickedness and Sin against God." Genesis 39:9 (10 leaves: HM 4288)

Sermon on Matthew 24:3 (8 leaves: HM 17363)

Sermon (15 pp.: RB 131334, vol. 1)

Letters: 6 (1814–26)

CRADDOCK, Charles Egbert, see MURFREE, Mary Noailles

CRADOCK, Joseph, *English author,* 1742–1826

Letters: 1 (1823)

CRAIG, Hardin, *American educator, author,* 1875–1968

This collection, approximately 400 pieces, consists of Professor Craig's professional papers relating to his publications, including articles, random chapters of books, and notes and outlines. There is much correspondence with his publishers, as well as personal correspondence and autobiographical material.

CRAIGIE, Pearl Mary Teresa, *English novelist, dramatist,* 1867–1906

Letters: 4 (1896–1906)

CRAIK, Dinah Maria (Mulock), *English novelist,* 1826–87

Verse:

The African Slave (HM 1822)

Prose:

Girls in Their Teens: [preface and suggested title page only] (4 pp.: FI 863)

How She Told a Lie: [final draft] (21 pp.: HM 34556)

Letters: 9 (1866–69)

CRAIK, George Lillie, *Scottish author,* 1798–1866

Letters: 2 (1856–62)

CRANCH, Christopher Pearse, *American clergyman, artist, critic, poet,* 1813–92

Letters: 2 (1884–85)

CRANE, Ralph, *English poet,* fl. 1625

Prose:

The Faultie Favorite: [theological discourse] (EL 6870)

CRANE, Stephen, *American writer,* 1871–1900

Prose:

The Five White Mice (12 pp.: HM 3995)

Letters: 1 (1892)

CRASHAW, Richard, *English poet,* 1613?–49

Verse:

To the Reader, upon the Intent of Lessius his Booke concerning Temperance (RB 102361)

CRAVEN, Elizabeth, Countess of, see ANSPACH, Elizabeth, Margravine of

CRAWFORD, Francis Marion, *American novelist,* 1854–1909

Prose:

Bar Harbor: [article written by Mary (Cadwalader) Jones for Crawford and revised by him] (typewritten, with revisions in Crawford's hand, 26 pp.: HM 15550)

Francesca da Rimini (typewritten, 76 pp.: HM 4284)

[Synopsis of a story] (3 leaves: CM 57)

Washington as a Spectacle (6 pp.: HM 34558)

Letters: 33 (1893–1907)

CRESWICK, Thomas, *English landscape painter,* 1811–69

Letters: 2 (1852 and n.d.)

CRESWICK, William, *English actor,* 1813–88

Letters: 3 (1836–68)

CROKER, John Wilson, *English politician, essayist,* 1780–1857

Letters: 38 (1809–49)

Documents: 3 (1824)

Other:

[Note regarding a quotation about immortality from Boswell's life of Johnson] (1 leaf: LR 67)

CROKER, Thomas Crofton, *Irish antiquary,* 1798–1854

Letters: 7 (1827–54)

Documents: 1 (1847)

CROLY, George, *Irish author and Anglican clergyman,* 1780–1860

Letters: 5 (1825–31)

CROLY, Herbert David, *American editor, author,* 1869–1930

Letters: 13 (1912–25)

CROLY, Jane (Cunningham), *American editor, newspaperwoman, author,* 1829–1901

Letters: 1 (1890)

CRONIN, Archibald Joseph, *Scottish novelist, physician,* 1896–

Verse:

"Here comes the autograph of A. J. C.": [poem about signing his autograph] (Kane Literary Collection)

CROSS, Ada (Cambridge), *Australian novelist,* 1844–1926

Verse:

Poems: [with title page, introductory letter, index, and author's note] (HM 33774)

Letters: 2 (1911)

CROSS, Mary Ann (Evans) (George Eliot, pseud.), *English novelist,* 1819–80

Prose:

[Notes: brief essays and memoranda on various subjects, later published (in part) in two works: *Impressions of Theophrastus Such* (1879) and *Essays and Leaves from a Notebook* (1884)] (55 pp.: HM 12993)

Letters: 16 (1853–79)

Other:

[Memoranda and notes in two manuscripts of George Henry Lewes] (HM 12993–12994)

CROTHERS, Samuel McChord, *American clergyman, essayist,* 1857–1927

Letters: 2 (1909–11)

CROWE, Catherine (Stevens), *English novelist,* 1800?–76

Letters: 6 (1851–59), including 5 to Annie (Adams) Fields and 1 to James Thomas Fields

CROY, Homer, *American novelist,* b. 1883

Letters: 6 (1917–29), including 3 to Neeta Marquis

CRUIKSHANK, George, *English caricaturist, illustrator,* 1792–1878

Prose:

Hints on Good Manners (published as *More Hints on Etiquette, for the Use of Society at Large, and Young Men in Particular,* London, 1838, with nine woodcuts by Cruikshank), draft, in two versions. On the versos of two leaves are several trial sketches by Cruikshank for the plate "Oliver Plucks up a Spirit." One page in the hand of Charles Dickens on a similar subject is bound into the volume; on the verso are sketches and a pencil note by Cruikshank. (42 pp.: HM 30901)

Letters: 63 (1827–76)

Documents: 1 (1821)

Other:

[Notes and ink sketch on printed prospectus on the creation of weekly periodical entitled "The Prophet"] (HM 39284)

[Notes and illustrations for *Ainsworth's Magazine*] (1 p.: HM 42736)

[Notes for a report to his corps] (On verso: 4 sketches of heads: HM 42735)

Drawings: 57

CULLEN, Countee, *American poet,* 1903–46

Letters: 1 (1926) to George Sterling

CUMBERLAND, Richard, *English dramatist,* 1732–1811

Letters: 2 (1805)

CUNNINGHAM, Allan, *Scottish poet, man of letters,* 1784–1842

Verse:

The Mariner (RB 109990, vol. 3, pt. 1)

Letters: 5 (1827–41)

CUNNINGHAM, Eugene, *American author,* 1896–1957

Prose:

[Bound typescripts]: (Cunningham Collection)

Buckaroo

Bravo Trail, and Pistol Passport (bound together)

Deep Soundings
Outlaw Justice
Quick Triggers
The Ranger Way
Red Range
Riders of the Night
Trail of the Macaw
Triggernometry
Whistling Lead

[Unbound typescripts]: (Cunningham Collection)
Buscadero's Own Book
Buscadero Trail (and variant copy)
Nuestro Pueblo
Viva Buscadero

Letters: 1,588 (1921–57), and approximately 2,000 letters addressed to him

Other:
[Miscellaneous lists and notes] (Cunningham Collection)
[Five scrapbooks] (Cunningham Collection)

CUNNINGHAM, William, *American journalist, author,* 1901–

Letters: 1 (1943)

CURTIS, George Ticknor, *American constitutional lawyer, author,* 1812–94

Letters: 170 (1862–89)

CURTIS, George William, *American author, man of letters,* 1824–92

Prose:

Janet Walford's Portrait: [final draft] (18 pp.: HM 34695)
The Shrouded Portrait: [final draft] (31 pp.: HM 34694)

Letters: 94 (1852–90)

CURWOOD, James Oliver, *American novelist,* 1878–1927

Letters: 1 (1920)

CUSHMAN, Charlotte Saunders, *American actress,* 1816–76

Letters: 54 (1837–74), including 44 to James Thomas Fields and Annie (Adams) Fields

CUSTIS, George Washington Parke, *American playwright,* 1781–1857

Prose:

Montgomerie; or, The Orphan of a Wreck, a Dramatic Romance (93 pp.: HM 598)

Letters: 6 (1827–56)

D

DAHLGREN, Sarah Madeleine (Vinton) Goddard, *American novelist, essayist,* 1825–98

Verse:

To Charles Warren Stoddard (HM 35075)

Letters: 1 (1895)

DALL, Caroline Wells (Healey), *American suffragist, author,* 1822–1912

Letters: 18 (1859–93)

DALY, John Augustin, *American producer, playwright,* 1838–99

Letters: 4 (1865–96)

DAMON, Samuel Foster, *American poet, literary biographer,* 1893–1971

Letters: 1 (1966)

DANA, Charles Anderson, *American editor,* 1819–97

Letters: 66 (1851–93), including 45 to Samuel L. M. Barlow

DANA, Richard Henry, *American lawyer, miscellaneous writer,* 1787–1879

Verse:
"O listen, man": [nine lines from his poem, "The Husband and Wife's Grave"] (HM 8281)

Letters: 7 (1867–78), including 4 to Annie (Adams) Fields and 2 to James Thomas Fields

DANA, Richard Henry, *American sailor, author, lawyer,* 1815–82

Letters: 19 (1860–80), including 8 to James Thomas Fields

DANE, Clemence, see ASHTON, Winifred

DANIELL, Samuel, *English artist, travel writer,* 1775–1811

Letters: 1 (1792)

DARGAN, Olive (Tilford), *American playwright, poet,* 1869–1968

Letters: 3 (1913–54)

DARWIN, Charles Robert, *English naturalist,* 1809–82

Letters: 73 (ca. 1870–82)

DARWIN, Erasmus, *English physiologist, poet,* 1731–1802

Verse:
The Mechanism of the Body (MO 724)

Letters: 4 (1781–95)

DAUDET, Alphonse, *French novelist,* 1840–97

Prose:
Victor Hugo (23 leaves: HM 28163)

Letters: 1 (n.d.)

D'AVENANT, Sir William, *English poet, dramatist,* 1606–68

Letters: 1 (1652)

DAVENPORT, John, *English reviewer of modern literature,* 1908–66

Letters: 18 (1935–65) to Conrad Aiken

DAVIDSON, James Wood, *American journalist, author,* 1829–1905

Letters: 20 (1887–98)

DAVIES, Sir John, *English jurist, poet,* 1569–1626

Verse:
"You that in Judgment passion never show" (EL 76)

Letters: 10 (1607–26)

DAVIES, Mary Carolyn, *American poet,* fl. 1912–13

Letters: 4 (1912–13)

DAVIES, Thomas, *Scottish bookseller, writer,* 1712?–85

Letters: 1 (1769)

DAVIS, Harold Lenoir, *American author,* 1896–1960

Letters: 1 (1935)

DAVIS, Owen, *American playwright,* 1874–1956

Letters: 1 (n.d.) to Sonya Levien

DAVIS, Rebecca Blaine (Harding), *American novelist,* 1831–1910

Prose:
David Gaunt (55 pp.: FI 1169)
Life in the Iron Mills (24 pp.: FI 1170)

Letters: 15 (1861–96)

DAVIS, Richard Harding, *American journalist, war correspondent, novelist,* 1864–1916

Prose:

The Bar Sinister (85 pp.: HM 28164)

Letters: 11 (1887–1904)

DAVIS, Robert Hobart, *American editor, playwright,* 1869–1942

Letters: 49 (1909–32), including 47 to Neeta Marquis

DAVIS, William Heath, *American author,* 1822–1909

Prose:

Sixty Years in California (801 leaves: DA 1)

Sixty Years in California: [material assembled for a revised and enlarged edition] (typescript, 293 leaves: DA 2)

Seventy-five Years in California: [chapters comprising only the additional material included in the enlarged edition of his *Sixty Years in California,* published posthumously in 1929] (typescripts, 188 leaves: DA 3)

Letters: 19 (1847–1906)

Documents: 6 (1846–55)

Other:

[Typescript of biographical sketch of José Martínez in printed copy of *Seventy-five Years in California*] (RB 436357)

DAVY, Sir Humphrey, *English chemist,* 1778–1829

Verse:

The Glow Worm—Epping Forest (SY 40)

Letters: 4 (1814–26)

DAY, Henry Noble, *American Congregational clergyman, educator, author,* 1808–90

Prose:

The Nature of Beauty (53 pp.: HM 28166)

DAY, Holman Francis, *American poet, novelist, playwright,* 1865–1935

Letters: 2 (1920–21)

DAY, John, *English dramatist,* fl. 1606

Prose:

Peregrinatio Scholastica, or Learneings Pillgrimadge (copy, 56 pp.: EL 8728)

DAY, Julia, *English poet,* fl. 1849

Verse:

"Beneath the wave as in a tomb" (RB 109990, vol. 2, pt. 1, p. 127)

DAY-LEWIS, Cecil, *English poet,* 1904–

Verse:

Beechen Vigil and Other Poems (typewritten: HM 40994)

Beechen Vigil and Other Poems (corrected proofs for 1925 edition: HM 40996)

Beechen Vigil and Other Poems (corrected page proofs for 1925 edition: HM 40995)

Letters: 26 (1924–26)

DE CASSERES, Benjamin, *American author,* 1873–1945

Prose:

Auto-Irony (typewritten; 4 pp.: Jack London Collection)

The Mocker (typewritten; 3 pp.: Jack London Collection)

The Pal of the Lord (typewritten; 2 pp.: Jack London Collection)

Pierrot-Parabrahma (typewritten; 1 p.: Jack London Collection)

Preludes and Postludes (typewritten; 10 pp.: Jack London Collection)

[Play] (typewritten; 5 pp.: Jack London Collection)

Shelley (typewritten; 4 pp.: Jack London Collection)

Strindberg (typewritten; 4 pp.: Jack London Collection)

Victor Hugo (typewritten; 9 pp.: Jack London Collection)

Letters: 16 (1913–26)

DEFOE, Daniel, *English journalist, novelist,* 1661?–1731

Verse:

Meditations (seven poems written at the end of a notebook containing copies in his hand of six sermons preached by John Collins: HM 26613)

Parson Plaxton of Barwick in ye County of York Turned inside out (copy, in a letter of George Staniland, 1709, May 11, and followed by Plaxton's Retort, Tint for Tant, and A Fable: HM 20340)

DE FOREST, John William, *American novelist, poet,* 1826–1906

Letters: 1 (1874)

DEGGE, Sir Simon, *English author,* 1612–1704

Verse:

On the Famous Orinda and her Pompey (copy: EL 8868)

DE LA MARE, Walter John, *English poet, novelist,* 1873–1956

Letters: 299 (1919–56)

DELAND, Margaretta Wade (Campbell), *American novelist,* 1857–1945

Prose:

The Awakening of Helena Richie (incomplete; 13 pp.: HM 7272)

John Ward, Preacher (fragment; 3 pp.: HM 22563)

Letters: 120 (1890–1928)

DELANE, John Thaddeus, *English editor,* 1817–79

Letters: 2 (n.d.)

DELAPLAINE, Joseph, *American editor, publisher, author,* 1777–1824

Letters: 12 (1812–19)

DE LA RAMÉE, Marie Louise (Ouida, pseud.), *English novelist,* 1839–1908

Prose:

The Bullfinch, An Orchard, Ruffino, Trottolino (all bound together; printed copies with autograph notations and revisions: RB 114297)

An Orchard (77 pp.: HM 41265)

Ruffino (partly autograph typescript; corrections in author's hand; 3 vols.: HM 41266)

Trottolino (86 pp.: HM 41264)

Letters: 3 (n.d.)

DE LEON, Thomas Cooper, *American editor, historian, novelist, humorist,* 1839–1914

Letters: 2 (1866–68)

DELL, Floyd, *American novelist,* 1887–

Letters: 6 (1926–32)

DE MILLE, Henry Churchill, see BELASCO, David

DE MORGAN, William Frend, *English artist, novelist,* 1839–1917

Prose:

A Likely Story (170 pp.: HM 1734)

Letters: 1 (1915)

DENHAM, Sir John, *English poet,* 1615–69

Verse:

Cooper's Hill (copy: EL 8899)

An Elegie vpon Judge Crooke (copy: EL 8849)

Mr. Hampden's Speech against Peace (copy: EL 8876)

[Poems ascribed to him in commonplace book] (HM 16522)

DE QUINCEY, Thomas, *English author,* 1785–1859

Prose:

Leaders in Literature (corrected proof sheets; 345 pp.: HM 36039)

My Brother Pink: a short autobiographical sketch (incomplete; 3 pp.: HM 36040)

The Pagan Oracles (corrected proof sheet for 1853–60 Edinburgh edition of De Quincey's *Works,* vol. 8, entitled "Essay Sceptical . . ."; 1 p.: HM 36041)

The Spanish Military Nun (corrected proof sheets for 1853–60 Edinburgh Edition of De Quincey's *Works,* vol. 3, entitled "Miscellanies"; 85 pp.: HM 31019)

Whiggism in its Relations to Literature (corrected proof sheets; 18 pp.: HM 36042)

Letters: 3 (1823–59), and note (ca. 1805) in letter of Henry De Quincey, also, family letters including the following: Jane De Quincey, 13 (1806–19); Henry De Quincey, 9 (ca. 1805–14); Mary De Quincey, 18 (1807–13); Richard De Quincey, (1799–1812); and letters by his children, Emily Jane De Quincey, 12 (1856–63); Margaret (De Quincey) Craig, 10 (1852–55); and Florence (De Quincey) Baird-Smith, 7 (1853–69)

DERBY, George Horatio, (John Phoenix, pseud.) *American humorist,* 1823–61

Prose:

[Typewritten articles included in a scrapbook of William Gibbons Cohen] (AM 74)

Letters: 4 (1854–56)

Documents: 2 (1850–52)

Other:

Views of Sand Island: [pen and ink drawing] (HM 19340)

DERBY, James Cephas, *American publisher, author,* 1818–92

Letters: 5 (1862–84)

DE SELINCOURT, Hugh, *English author,* 1878–1951

Letters: 1 (1908)

DEUTSCH, Albert, *American author,* 1905–61

Letters: 3 (1947)

DEVERELL, Frances C., *English author,* fl. 1899–1920

Prose:

P. R. B. and Walter Howell Deverell (early draft; 167 pp.: HM 12981)

P. R. B. and Walter Howell Deverell (typewritten; 83 pp.: HM 12982)

Letters: 1 (1920)

DEVERELL, Walter Howell, *English pre-Raphaelite painter,* 1827–54

Prose:

Diary (fragment; 2 pp.: HM 12920)

Letters: 2 (1853 and n.d.)

DE VINNE, Theodore Low, *American master printer, author,* 1828–1914

Letters: 4 (1906–12)

D'EWES, Sir Simonds, *English antiquarian,* 1602–50

Letters: 1 (1649)

DIAZ, Abby (Morton), *American author,* 1821–1904

Letters: 49 (1863–1900), including 49 to James Thomas Fields and Annie (Adams) Fields

DIBDIN, Charles, *English dramatist, actor, composer,* 1745–1814

Verse:

Song (HM 3168)

DIBDIN, Charles, *English dramatist, composer,* 1768–1833

Letters: 20 (1826–33)

DIBDIN, John Bates, *English author,* fl. 1825–28

Prose:

Diary (1825–28; 180 pp.: HM 28176)

DIBDIN, Thomas Frognall, *English bibliographer,* 1776–1847

Prose:

[Corrected proof of 2 pp. relating to the University of St. Andrews, from his Bibliographical, Antiquarian and Picturesque Tour in the Northern Counties of England and in Scotland] (1 leaf: DI 162)

Letters: 65 (1813–45)

Documents: 1 (1838)

Other:

[Notes and corrections in *The Bibliographical Decameron*] (RB 32446)

DIBDIN, Thomas John, *English dramatist,* 1771–1841

Verse:

The Comet (HM 11459)

A Fragment (not autograph: FR 64)

Impromptu (FR 65)

The Scotch Greys (FR 66)

To Messrs. C. & A. Forrester (FR 67)

"When Folk commence the World anew!" (FR 68)

Letters: 3 (1807–35)

DICK, Sir Alexander, *English physician, correspondent of Dr. Johnson,* 1703–85

Letters: 4 (1762–65)

DICKENS, Charles, *English novelist,* 1812–70

Verse:

The Bill of Fare (not autograph: HM 17514)

The Response (HM 17520)

Two Verses written for Christiana Weller's (aft. Thompson) album, beginning, "I put in a book once, by hook or by crook" (HM 17518)

Prose:

A Child's History of England (chap. 12; 18 pp.: HM 17500)

The Demeanour of Murderers (7 pp.: HM 17502)

Dreadful Hardships, Endured by the Shipwrecked Crew of the "London" (1 p.: HM 17517)

Ecclesiastical Registries (8 pp.: HM 17504)

Essay on Manners (fragment; note in pencil with illustration on verso, probably by George Cruikshank; 1 p.: HM 42726)

[Five outlines for Christmas issues of *Household Words* and *The Year Round*] (8 pp.: HM 17508–17512)

Mr. Charles Dickens: a speech about sanitary reform delivered at Gore House, Kensington, May 10, 1851 (15 pp.: HM 17505)

New Uncommercial Samples: On an Amateur Beat (corrected proof: RB 114202)

Remaining List of Readings (in America; 1 p.: HM 17522)

Speech of Charles Dickens, Esquire, Delivered at the Meeting of the Administrative Reform Associations, at Drury Lane Theater, on Wednesday, June 27th, 1855 (corrected proof: RB 110335)

Supposing: [a short article on prison conditions] (2 pp.: HM 17506)

Letters: 993 (1833–70), and 136 letters addressed to Dickens

Letterbook of *All the Year Round* editorial office containing press copies of letters by Charles Dickens, W. H. Wills, and C. C. B. Dickens, 1859–80 (HM 17507)

Volume of typewritten copies of 118 letters by Dickens, 1836–70 (HM 27634)

Forgery of letter, dated Dec. 11, 1837 (HM 18751)

Also, 124 letters by Georgina Hogarth; and letters by other members of the Dickens family

Documents: 5 (1840–65)

Other:

[Corrections in pencil and ink of John Saunders's *Love's Martyrdom* for stage performance] (RB 121982)

[Corrections in manuscript copy of "Used up," by Dion Boucicault] (HM 17513)

[Directions to Browne for illustrations in *Martin Chuzzlewit*] (4 pp.: HM 17501)

[Sixteen titles suggested for *Household Words*] (HM 17521)

A Souvenir of Charles Dickens's Last Visit to America (162 items relating to the banquet given in 1867 before Dickens's departure for America, consisting mainly of letters addressed to Charles Kent: HM 18584–18746)

DICKINSON, Anna Elizabeth, *American writer, lecturer, author,* 1842–1932

Letters: 18 (1863–73)

DICKINSON, Emily Elizabeth, *American poet,* 1830–86

Letters: 1 (1885)

DIGBY, Sir Kenelm, *English author, naval commander, diplomat,* 1603–65

Verse:

[Poems ascribed to him in commonplace book] (HM 116)

Prose:

[Journal: 1627–1628/9] (EL 6858)

Copies of letters in commonplace book (HM 36836)

DILKE, Charles Wentworth, *English antiquary, critic,* 1789–1864

Letters: 1 (1837)

DILLON, Ellis, *Irish author,* 1920–

Letters: 1 (1967)

DISRAELI, Benjamin, 1st Earl of Beaconsfield, *English Prime Minister,* 1804–81

Prose:

[Speech on the death of the Duke of Wellington (contemporary copy)] (6 pp.: STG Box 95 [36])

The Tragedy of Count Alarcos (368 pp.: HM 36028)

Venetia (457 pp.: HM 36029)

Letters: 26 (1834–79)

D'ISRAELI, Isaac, *English man of letters,* 1766–1843

Letters: 7 (1796–1835)

D'ISRAELI, Israel, *English author,* fl. 1829–39

Letters: 3 (1829–39)

DIXIE, Lady Florence Caroline (Douglas), *English author, traveler,* 1857–1905

Prose:

Columbus Memorial (3 pp.: HM 1999)

Letters: 2 (1892–1904)

DIXON, Thomas, *American novelist, playwright,* 1864–1946

Letters: 3 (1914–32) to Albert Bigelow Paine

DIXON, William Hepworth, *English historian, traveler,* 1821–79

Letters: 15 (1860–68)

DOBELL, Bertram, *English bookseller, man of letters,* 1842–1914

Letters: 3 (1893–1912)

DOBELL, Sydney Thompson, *English poet, critic,* 1824–74

Letters: 3 (1868–72), also 8 letters (1859–82) by his wife, Emily (Fordham) Dobell

DOBIE, Charles Caldwell, *American novelist, playwright,* 1881–1943

Letters: 1 (1928)

DOBIE, James Frank, *American educator, editor, folklorist, author,* 1888–1964

Letters: 18 (1927–56), including 11 to Stuart Nathaniel Lake

DOBSON, Henry Austin, *English poet, man of letters,* 1840–1921

Verse:

[Doggerel verse announcing a temporary change of address] (HM 10764)

My First Prose Book (RB 122732)

Proverbs in Porcelain (HM 36025)

"Shades of Herrick, muse of Locker" (HM 403)

To E. G. on Pepys' Diary (HM 12078)

To George H. Broughton, beginning, "Spring stirs and wakes . . ." (RB 122705)

To G. H. B., beginning, "Spring has come . . ." (RB 122705)

The Water Cure (HM 36026)

Prose:

The Pupils of Bewick (31 pp.: HM 36027)

Letters: 10 (1881–1919)

Other:

[Two lines of Canto III of Sir Walter Scott's "Harold the Handy"] (HM 1937)

DODD, Lee Wilson, *American playwright, novelist, poet,* 1879–1933

Letters: 1 (1913)

DODDRIDGE, Philip, *English clergyman, religious writer,* 1702–51

Prose:

Lectures on the ministerial and pastoral offices . . . and A short system of Jewish antiquities (121 leaves: HM 34800)

Lectures 116 to 169 on Matthew (not autograph; 478 pp.: HM 109)

Sermon (in shorthand: HM 916)

Letters: 5 (1733–51)

DODGE, Mary Abigail (Gail Hamilton, pseud.), *American writer,* 1833–96

Letters: 3 (1862–73)

DODGE, Mary Elizabeth (Mapes), *American writer,* 1831–1905

Verse:

Lullaby from Rhymes and Jingles (HM 22459)

Letters: 76 (1866–1900)

DODGSON, Charles Lutwidge (Lewis Carroll, pseud.), *English mathematician, author,* 1832–98

Verse:

"Puck has fled the haunts of men" and "Puck has ventured back again" (two poems: HM 35954)

Letters: 94 (1849–97)

Other:

[Mathematical equations written in Dodgson's *Symbolic Logic*] (RB 28777)

DODINGTON, George Bubb, Baron Melcombe, *English politician, writer,* 1691–1762

Letters: 1 (1761)

DODSLEY, Robert, *English poet, playwright, bookseller,* 1703–64

Letters: 2 (1748)

DOLE, Nathan Haskell, *American editor,* 1852–1935

Verse:

The Building of the Organ (HM 36030)

Children's Voices: Outdoor Lyrics (HM 36031)

Flowers from Foreign Gardens (HM 36032)

The Pilgrims and Other Poems for Public Occasions (HM 36033)

Letters: 9 (1886–1921)

Other:

[Quotation from a poem by Bach] (RB 5457, vol. 1)

[Notation re music] (RB 5457, vol. 2)

DONNE, John, *English poet,* 1573–1631

Verse:

Poems and Paradoxes and Problems (192 leaves: EL 6893)

[Poems ascribed to Donne in commonplace books] (HM 116 and HM 198)

To God Æternall: "Wilt thou forgive that sinne where I begunne" in commonplace book of Sir Edward Dering, 2nd Bart. (HM 41536)

Letters: 1 (1626)

Other:

[Manuscript note in Paschal's *Legatus*] (RB 182692)

DOOLITTLE, Hilda, *American poet,* 1886–1961

Letters: 13 (1933–56)

DORR, Julia Caroline (Ripley), *American writer,* 1825–1913

Verse:

Two Paths (HM 22713)

Letters: 19 (1864–1910)

DOS PASSOS, John Roderigo, *American writer,* 1896–1970

Letters: 9 (1932–65)

DOUCE, Francis, *English antiquary,* 1757–1834

Letters: 10 (1808–26)

DOUGLAS, David, *English author,* 1823–1916

Letters: 17 (1888–1911), including 12 to Annie (Adams) Fields

DOUGLAS, James Dixon, *Scottish author,* 1922–

Letters: 2 (1965)

DOUGLAS, Lloyd Cassel, *American clergyman, novelist,* 1877–1951

Letters: 2 (1938 and n.d.)

DOUGLASS, Frederick, *American orator, statesman, author,* 1817?–95

Letters: 12 (1846–94)

Other:

[Signed autograph sentiment] (HM 39927)

DOWDEN, Edward, *Irish Shakespearean critic,* 1843–1913

Verse:

Poppies: a morsel of dramatic lyric (HM 39182)

Sequel to Certain Verses called "Poppies" (HM 39183)

A Sonnet concerning a Hazel Stick of a Price more than one-&-sixpence (HM 39184)

Letters: 74 (1868–1912)

DOWSON, Ernest Christopher, *English lyric poet,* 1867–1900

Prose:

Memoirs of Cardinal Dubois by Paul Lacroix, translated into English by Dowson (256 pp.: HM 36034)

The Mistresses of Louis XV (translated from the French of Edmond and Jules de Goncourt; 750 pp.: HM 36035)

DOYLE, Sir Arthur Conan, *English physician, novelist,* 1859–1930

Prose:

The Return of Sherlock Holmes: VIII, The Adventure of the Six Napoleons (26 pp.: HM 36022)

Letters: 2 (1890–1910)

DOYLE, Richard, *English artist, caricaturist,* 1824–83

Letters: 31 (1851–83)

DRAKE, Joseph Rodman, *American poet,* 1795–1820

Verse:

The Mocking Bird (in the hand of Charles Graham Tillou: HM 34247)

To Sarah (HM 15626)

Trifles in Rhyme—a notebook of poems—(Contents: The Culprit Fay, Song—air "What ye Wha," Song—air "The Legacy," To Miss McC—with a Withered Violet, To—, Miss R. H., Song—"Peggy na Levan," Meeting, Written on Leaving New Rochelle, To Miss McC—on Hearing Her Sing "Cuclamachree," The American Flag [last stanza in the hand of Fitz-Greene Halleck], Moimeme, Niagara). Pages 65–204 of notebook contain poems by Drake, Halleck, and Mrs. Tillou in the hand of Francis R. Tillou (HM 35316)

DRAPER, John William, *English scientist, author,* 1811–82

Letters: 4 (1860–75)

DREISER, Theodore, *American journalist, author,* 1871–1945

Verse:

Sweet Kathleen Mavourneen: a poem written to Elizabeth (Kearney) Coakley (HM 36256)

Prose:

Are Men Free and Morally Responsible for Their Actions? No (typescript of debate: Barrett Collection)

Concerning Love (typewritten; 2 pp.: HM 36250)

The Dawn is in the East (typed; 3 pp.: HM 36251)

Five Wishes (partly typewritten; 5 pp.: HM 36252)

Nikolai Lenin (typewritten; 1 p.: HM 36253)

An outline for a story (2 pp.: HM 36249)

Sherwood Anderson: a eulogy (typewritten; 1 p.: HM 36254)

Six ideas for magazine articles (2 pp.: HM 36255)

Letters: 73 (1909–45)

DRINKWATER, John, *English poet,* 1882–1937

Prose:

The Life of Poetry; The Poet's Words and Images; The History of English Poetry (three essays; 13 pp.: HM 28165)

Letters: 7 (1919–29)

DRISCOLL, Charles Benedict, *American editor, lecturer, author,* 1885–1951

Letters: 1 (1928)

DRISCOLL, Louise, *American poet,* 1875–1957

Letters: 2 (1918–20)

DRUMMOND, Henry, *English politician,* 1786–1860

Letters: 6 (1824–44)

DRYDEN, John, *English poet,* 1631–1700

Verse:

Epilogue at ye Opening the Theatre Royal (copy: EL 8925)

Epilogue to Amboyna (copy: EL 8918)

The Fall of Angells, or Man in Innocency (contemporary copy: EL 11640)

The Fall of Angells, or Man in Innocency (contemporary copy: RB 134219–29)

Prologue to Amboyna (EL 8917)

Prologue [to "An Evening's Love or, the Mock Astrologer"] (copy: EL 8922)

Prologue to the Prophetess (EL 8770)

Prologue to ye Opening ye Theatre Royall (copy: EL 8923)

DRYER, John, *American author,* fl. 1965

Prose:

Upton Sinclair is 87 (typescript of a speech; 7 pp.: HM 44531)

Other:

Upton Sinclair. Monrovia: your city: John Dryer interviews Upton Sinclair (4 eight-track tape recordings: HM 41094)

DU BOIS, William Edward Burghardt, *American author,* 1868–1963

Letters: 1 (1924)

DUCHE, Jacob, *American clergyman, Revolutionary patriot, author,* 1737–98

Letters: 1 (1776)

DUCIS, Jean François, *French playwright,* 1733–1816

Letters: 14 (1763–73)

DUCK, Stephen, *English poet,* 1705–56

Letters: 3 (1735–51)

DUFF, Edward Gordon, *English author,* 1863–1924

Letters: 5 (1908–24)

DUFFIELD, Samuel Augustus Willoughby, *American clergyman, hymnologist, poet, author,* 1843–87

Verse:

Benison (2 copies: Kane Literary Collection)

Memory (Kane Literary Collection)

A Song from a Sigh (Kane Literary Collection)

DUGANNE, Augustine Joseph Hickey, *American author,* 1823–84

Verse:

To My Friend, Thomas L. James (RB 41969)

Winthrop (FI 1188)

Letters: 2 (1867–75)

DUGDALE, Sir William, *English author, historian,* 1605–86

Prose:

Historical and geneologicall Collections, of the family of Hastings, Earls of Huntingdon (124 pp.: HA 16250)

Letters: 6 (1674–85)

DULAC, Edmund, *English illustrator,* b. 1882

Letters: 6 (1941–50)

DUMAS, Alexandre, *French dramatist, novelist,* 1802–70

Prose:

Une Aventure de Marie Michon (HM 30893)

Le Brevet de Zumere (HM 30895)

[Dramatic fragment] (HM 30898)

Epsom Races: Extract from Le Petit Journal (4 pp.: FR 73)

La France abandonnée par l'Angleterre et par l'Autriche dans la question de Bologne (5 pp.: HM 7636)

Le Mole et le Marche Neuf (HM 30897)

Monseigneur Valerga (HM 30899)

Reclamation à propos de Nelson (HM 34207)

La Reine Margot (HM 30894)

St. Antoine Usurpateur (HM 30896)

Letters: 2 (1837–52)

DUMAS, Alexandre, *French novelist, dramatist,* 1824–95

Prose:

[End of the Second Act of Loustel] (2 pp.: Notable French Authors, p. 21)

Letters: 1 (n.d.)

DU MAURIER, George Louis Palmella Busson, *English artist, novelist,* 1834–96

Prose:

Trilby (concluding part only; 67 pp.: HM 36037)

Letters: 15 (1867–92)

DUNIWAY, Abigail Jane (Scott), *American novelist, poet, editor,* 1834–1915

Letters: 4 (1904–11)

DUNKIN, William, *English poet,* 1709?–65

Verse:

A Full and true Vindication of Sir Thomas Prendergast from the many scandalous Libels lately written against him, with the Resolutions of the House (HM 14364)

. . . of the Furniture belonging to —s Room in Trinity College Dublin. In imitation of Dr. Swift's m—r written in ye year 1725 (HM 14363)

Letters: 1 (1742/3)

DUNLOP, Alison Hay, *Scottish author,* fl. 1890–96

Prose:

From Yarrow to Edinburgh College—Memories of Long Ago (33 pp.: HM 44523)

DUNN, Joseph Allan Elphinstone, *English-born American explorer, editor, novelist,* 1872–1941

Letters: 3 (1939) to Eugene Lafayette Cunningham

DUNSANY, Lord, see PLUNKETT, Edward John Morton Drax, Baron Dunsany

DUNTON, James Gerald, *American author,* 1899–

Letters: 14 (1927–34) to Eugene Lafayette Cunningham

DUPIN, Aurore Lucie, Baronne Dudevant (George Sand, pseud.), *French novelist,* 1804–76

Letters: 2 (1866–71)

DURANTY, Walter, *American correspondent, author,* 1884–1957

Letters: 1 (1937)

D'URFEY, Thomas, *English poet, dramatist,* 1653–1723

Verse:

"Why are mine eyes still flow—ing" (EL 8741)

DURRELL, Lawrence, *English author,* 1912–

Letters: 3 (1972–74)

DUYCKINCK, Evert Augustus, *American editor, biographer, compiler,* 1816–78

Prose:

Gilbert Mothier de Lafayette (92 pp.: HM 36024)

John Adams (80 pp.: HM 36023)

Letters: 7 (1854–72)

DUYCKINCK, George Long, *American editor, biographer,* 1823–63

Letters: 1 (1860)

DWIGHT, Theodore, *American lawyer, editor,* 1764–1846

Letters: 29 (1808–36)

DWIGHT, Theodore, *American educator, author,* 1796–1866

Letters: 5 (1858)

DWIGHT, Theodore William, *American author,* 1822–92

Letters: 2 (1864–67)

DWIGHT, Timothy, *American clergyman, educator, poet,* 1752–1817

Letters: 1 (1796)

DYCE, Alexander, *English scholar,* 1798–1869

Letters: 2 (n.d.)

DYCE, William, *English painter,* 1806–64

Letters: 4 (1836–52)

DYE, Eva (Emery), *American author,* 1855–1937

Letters: 6 (1889–1922)

DYER, George, *English author,* 1755–1841

Letters: 4 (1801–36)

E

EAMES, Wilberforce, *American bibliographer, librarian,* 1855–1937

Letters: 1 (1898) to Frederick Jackson Turner

EASTLAKE, Sir Charles Lock, *English artist,* 1793–1865

Letters: 5 (1843–61)

EASTMAN, Max Forrester, *American editor, essayist, poet,* 1883–1969

Letters: 19 (1913–44)

EATON, Charles Edward, *American author,* 1916–

Letters: 4 (1946–68)

EATON, Walter Prichard, *American educator, essayist,* 1878–1957

Letters: 3 (1915–23)

EBERHART, Richard, *American poet,* 1904–

Letters: 51 (1943–55)

EDDY, Mary Morse (Baker) Glover Patterson, *American author, founder of Church of Christ, Scientist,* 1821–1910

Letters: 153 (1889–1909)

EDGEWORTH, Maria, *English novelist,* 1767–1849

Prose:

Helen (incomplete; 1 p.: HM 7313)

Letters: 77 (1782–1849)

EDGEWORTH, Richard Lovell, *English author,* 1744–1817

Prose:

Notes on Sailing (1 p.: FB 1241)

Letters: 15 (1803–17)

EDMONDS, Walter Dumaux, *American author,* 1903–

Letters: 2 (1938–39)

EDWARDS, Amelia Ann Blanford, *English novelist,* 1831–92

Letters: 6 (1888–90)

EDWARDS, George Wharton, *American painter, author,* 1869–1950

Letters: 4 (1897–1921)

EDWARDS, Harry Stillwell, *American novelist, poet,* 1855–1938

Prose:

An Idyll of Sinkin' Mountin (typewritten with corrections; 30 pp.: HM 30324)

Letters: 2 (1895)

EDWARDS, Henry, *American author,* fl. 1868–91

Letters: 28 (1868–91) to Charles Warren Stoddard

EGAN, Pierce, *English author,* 1772–1849

Letters: 3 (1828–45)

EGERTON, Francis, 1st Earl of Ellesmere, *English statesman, poet,* 1800–57

Letters: 6 (1837–53)

EGGLESTON, Edward, *American Methodist preacher, author,* 1837–1902

Prose:

Some Western Schoolmasters (32 pp.: HM 12842)

Letters: 29 (1881–90)

Documents: 1 (1888)

EGGLESTON, George Cary, *American journalist, novelist,* 1839–1911

Letters: 8 (1873–95)

EHRMANN, Maximilian, *American author,* 1872–1945

Letters: 6 (1915–16)

ELIOT, George, see CROSS, Mary Ann (Evans)

ELIOT, Thomas Stearns, *American poet, essayist,* 1888–1965

Letters: 67 (1914–63), including 65 to Conrad Potter Aiken

ELLET, Elizabeth Fries (Lummis), *American author,* 1818–77

Letters: 4 (1838–61)

ELLIOTT, Ebenezer, *English poet,* 1781–1849

Letters: 2 (1844)

ELLIOTT, Maud (Howe), *American author,* 1854–1948

Letters: 2 (1932)

ELLIS, Sir Henry, *English librarian, editor,* 1777–1869

Letters: 10 (1808–53)

ELLIS, Henry Havelock, *English scientist and physician,* 1859–1939

Letters: 7 (1913–27)

ELLISTON, Robert William, *English actor,* 1774–1831

Letters: 6 (1807–20)

ELLSWORTH, William Webster, *American publisher, lecturer, author,* 1855–1936

Letters: 7 (1896–1904)

ELTON, Sir Charles Abraham, *English author,* 1778–1853

Prose:

Epistle to Elia (HM 12276)

Letters: 3 (1819–21)

ELWIN, Whitwell, *English prose writer,* 1816–1900

Letters: 29 (1856–96)

EMERSON, Edward Waldo, *American author,* 1844–1930

Letters: 8 (1897–1921)

EMERSON, Ralph Waldo, *American poet, essayist,* 1803–82

Verse:

Astraea (HM 7626)
Berrying (HM 7625)
Culture (HM 1216)
Étienne de la Boece (HM 7623)
Fate (HM 7627)

Merlin (HM 7624)

My Garden (HM 45715)

To Rhea (HM 7628)

Uriel (HM 7629)

The Visit (HM 7630)

Prose:

[Editor's Notice to *Letters to Various Persons* by Henry D. Thoreau] (2 pp.: FI 1363)

[Fragment of manuscript]: "The time to come will show us the influence of the American spirit on the Education . . ." (1 p.: HM 15610)

Quotation and Originality (84 pp.: HM 45716)

Thoreau (208 pp.: HM 187)

Letters: 67 (1828–75), and 46 by members of the Emerson family

Other:

List of Lecture Topics (1 p.: FI 1390)

ENGLISH, Thomas Dunn, *American editor, playwright, novelist, poet,* 1819–1902

Verse:

Ben Bolt (HM 7322)

Letters: 3 (1843–91)

ERVINE, St. John Greer, *Irish playwright, critic, novelist,* b. 1883

Letters: 1 (1912)

ETHEREGE, Sir George, *English dramatist,* 1635?–91

Verse:

Ephelia to Bajazet (attributed to him; copy: EL 8736A)

ETTY, William, *English painter,* 1787–1849

Letters: 2 (1842 and n.d.)

EUGÉNE, see SUE, Marie-Joseph

EUSDEN, Laurence, *English poet laureate,* 1688–1730

Letters: 1 (1727)

EVANS, Florence Wilkinson, *American novelist, poet, playwright,* fl. 1917

Letters: 1 (1917)

EVANS, Frederick William, *American Shaker leader, author,* 1808–93

Letters: 2 (1885–90)

EVELETH, George Washington, *American author,* fl. 1848

Prose:

The Nucleous of Our Planet in a State of Igneous Liquifaction (2 pp.: HM 1187)

EVELYN, John, *English author,* 1620–1706

Letters: 1 (1679) to Samuel Pepys

Documents: 1 (1706)

Other:

Loci Laudubilies: notes (1 p.: HM 42760)

[Manuscript corrections and three pages of manuscript additions and corrections in *Numismata*] (RB 65848)

[Marginal notes in Sir Richard Baker's *A Chronicle of the Kings of England*] (RB 53556)

EVERETT, Edward, *American clergyman, statesman, orator, author,* 1794–1865

Verse:

Unpublished lines addressed to Clevinger by Edw[d] Everett on receiving his bust (FI 570)

Prose:

A Defence of Powers' Statue of Webster (39 pp.: AL 398)

Recollections of Lord Byron (6 pp.: AL 394)

Recollections of Sir Walter Scott (6 pp.: AL 395)

Review of Henry Wheaton's "Elements of International Law" (43 pp.: HM 42762)

Letters: 159 (1824–64)

Documents: 2 (1837–53)

Other:

[Annotations in Monroe's *A View of the Conduct of the Executive*] (RB 7646)

[Annotation in his *Orations and Speeches,* 1836 (RB 323622)]

F

FAED, Thomas, *Scottish painter,* 1826–1900

Letters: 5 (1867)

FAIRBANKS, Douglas, *American actor,* 1883–1939

Letters: 1 (1925)

FALL, Eliza, *English poet,* 1821–81

Verse:

A Christmas Carol (HM 42764)
Invocation to the Gods (HM 42765)
The Island of the Dead (HM 42766)
"Kind Nature, how are all thy ways with me" (HM 42767)
Mary Magdalen (HM 42768)
"O gentle maidens that with snowy hands" (HM 42770)
To—with Autumnal Violets (HM 42771)

Prose:

Notes [on allusions in her own poetry] (6 pp.: HM 42769)

Letters: 45 (1851–56) to William Henry Harrison.

FANE, Julian Henry Charles, *English diplomat, poet,* 1827–70

Letters: 2 (1861–67)

FANSHAWE, Catherine Maria, *English poet,* 1765–1834

Verse:

Liberty (SY 52)

Letters: 2 (1805–31)

FARADAY, Michael, *English physicist, writer,* 1791–1867

Letters: 8 (1826–62)

FARJEON, Benjamin Leopold, *English novelist,* 1838–1903

Letters: 5 (1873–78)

FARLEY, Charles, *English actor, dramatist,* 1771–1859

Letters: 2 (1852 and n.d.)

FARRAR, Eliza Ware (Rotch), *American author,* 1791–1870

Letters: 12 (1864–66), including 11 to James Thomas Fields and 1 to Francis James Child

FARRAR, Frederic William, *English poet,* 1831–1903

Prose:

Minor Reminiscences of Dean Stanley (32 pp.: HM 42818)

Letters: 5 (1865–98)

FARREN, William, *English actor,* 1786–1861

Letters: 4 (1828–52)

FAWCETT, Edgar, *American poet, playwright, novelist,* 1847–1904

Verse:

Married Bohemians (HM 7876)

Letters: 15 (1893–98)

FAWCETT, John, *English actor, dramatist,* 1768–1837

Letters: 2 (1817)

FAY, Frank J., *Irish actor,* fl. 1905–1911

Letters: 35 (1906–11)

FAY, Theodore Sedgwick, *American diplomat, editor, poet, novelist,* 1807–98

Letters: 4 (1850–62)

FECHTER, Charles Albert, *English actor, dramatist,* 1824–79

Letters: 18 (1861–75), including 9 to Samuel L. M. Barlow

FENN, George Manville, *English novelist,* 1831–1909

Letters: 4 (1878–91)

FENOLLOSA, Mary (McNeill), *American novelist, poet,* 1866–1954

Letters: 1 (1920)

FENTON, Roger, *English divine,* 1565–1616

Prose:

De aequivocatione (EL 1134)

FERBER, Edna, *American novelist, playwright,* 1887–1968

Letters: 8 (1917–32)

FERGUSON, Sir Samuel, *English poet, antiquary,* 1810–86

Verse:

To Henrietta Guinness (RB 328392)

Letters: 1 (1878)

FERGUSSON, Erna, *American author,* 1888–1964

Letters: 2 (1933) to Mary (Hunter) Austin

FERNALD, Chester Bailey, *American storywriter, playwright,* 1869–1938

Letters: 5 (1895–96)

FERRIER, Susan Edmonstone, *English novelist,* 1782–1854

Letters: 1 (n.d.)

Other:

[Manuscript corrections in 1841 edition of *Destiny*] (RB 123523)

FICKE, Arthur Davison, *American essayist, poet,* 1883–1945

Letters: 16 (1927–37), including 14 to Mary (Hunter) Austin

FIELD, Eugene, *American poet,* 1850–95

Verse:

"And, Lo! tonight, the phantom light": [poem of inscription] (RB 13401)

Armenian Lullaby (not autograph, with music by D. B. Gillette, Jr.: HM 19440)

"As you, dear Lamon, soundly slept" (LN 2380; also, another copy, not autograph, in Burdette Collection)

Beard and Baby (HM 19409)

Bethlehem Town (HM 19876)

Bethlehem Town II (HM 19877)

A Birthday Wish (HM 19891)

Boccaccio (HM 19410)

Casey's Table d'Hote (HM 19878)

Clare Market (HM 30310)

Crumpets and Tea (HM 19442)

The Dead Babe (HM 19411)

Dear Old London (HM 19412)

Doctors (HM 19438)

The Dreams (HM 19413)

Echoes from the Sabine Farm: [table of contents only] (HM 19414)

"Go, missive mine, as valentine" (HM 19879)

The Hawthorne Children (HM 19415)

"His prey are of every size and age" (HM 42822)

Hymn, Xmas, 1888 (HM 19880)

"I asked to Occupy her": [verses written opposite four stanzas copied by Field from Percy's *Suppressed Poems of the Early English Poets*] (HM 19417)

Little Boy Blue: [last stanza only] (HM 19444)

Little Willie (HM 19443)

Love's Request (with music: HM 19441)

The Modern Cinderella (HM 19419)

The Morning Bird (HM 19420)

My Book: [37 poems copied into scrapbook inscribed to William C. Buskett] (HM 19435)

"My good friend Cox, the sly old fox": [poem of inscription] (RB 323707)

The Noontide (HM 19421)

The Onion Tart: an Idyllic Lyric Ballad Dedicated to the Hon. William Walter Phelps (HM 27371)

Picnic Time (HM 19422)

Plaint of the Missouri 'Coon in the Berlin Zoological Gardens (HM 19423)

Shuffle-Shoon and Amber Locks (HM 19424)

The Stork (HM 42827)
The Straw Parlor (HM 19426)
Teeny-Weeny (HM 19427)
"This is Posie's great big sister" (HM 19445)
To DeWitt Miller (HM 19428)
To Francis Wilson (HM 19429)
To W. I. Way (HM 19430)
The Truth about Horace (HM 19446)
The Twenty-third Psalm (HM 19881)
The Two Sleepers (HM 1230)
"What perfumed, posie-dizened sirrah" (RB 14439)
"Whenever I've this heartache" (HM 19431)
"The womenfolk are few up there" (HM 35075)

Prose:

The Buccaneers, a comic opera in three acts (49 pp.: HM 19434)
Human Sympathy on the "Jinin" Farms (8 pp.: HM 19416)
Memoirs of Mrs. Ruth Gray (10 p.: HM 19418)
Speech to introduce George W. Cable (1 p.: HM 19425)
Diary (1873; 17 leaves: HM 19436)
Diary (1890; 51 leaves: HM 19437)

Letters: 73 (1872–95)

FIELD, Kate, see FIELD, Mary Katherine Keemle

FIELD, Mary Katherine Keemle, *American journalist, lecturer, actress, author,* 1838–96

Letters: 13 (1881–95)

FIELD, Rachel Lyman, *American novelist, poet, playwright,* 1894–1942

Letters: 14 (1920–41)

FIELD, Roswell Martin, *American journalist, author,* 1851–1919

Verse:

"Impartially the feet of Death . . ." [poem in leaf of Eugene Fields's *Echoes from the Sabine Farm*] (RB 14439)

Three Gems from Theocritus:

The Statue of Anacreon

Epitaph on Hipponax

Orthon's Epitaph (HM 7225)

Letters: 2 (1905–10)

FIELD, Sara Bard, see WOOD, Sara Bard (Field)

FIELDING, Antony Vandyke Copley, *English painter,* 1787–1855

Letters: 1 (1834)

FIELDING, Henry, *English novelist,* 1707–54

Prose:

Extracts from Michael Dalton's The Countrey Justice (1 p.: HM 11618)

Letters: 3 (1741–54)

Documents: 2 (1753)

FIELDS, Annie (Adams), *American author,* 1834–1915

Verse:

Canticles of Married Love, 1865–68 (Fields Addenda, Box 2 [1])

Decoration Day (SL 243)

"Life is all youth to thee" (HM 35075)

Ten Years After (SL 244)

To France (SL 242)

Waiting (SL 240)

[Composition Books containing 98 poems] (Fields Addenda, Box 2 [2–8])

[Four poems in letters to Laura (Winthrop) Johnson] (Fields Addenda, Box 12 [5])

[Poems: 80 unbound poems, and 32 miscellaneous fragments of verse] (Fields Addenda, Box 2 [9])

[Three notebooks of poetry, containing a total of 266 poems] (Fields Addenda, Box 1 [1–3])

Prose:

[Biographical sketch of Marie Therese (de Solms) Blanc] (28 pp. [also typed transcript—18 pp.]: Fields Addenda, Box 3 [1])

[Biographical sketch of Oliver Wendell Holmes] (20 pp.: Fields Addenda, Box 3 [2])

[Biographical sketch of Shelley] (7 pp.: Fields Addenda, Box 3 [3])

Charles Reade and his Letters (69 pp.: Fields Addenda, Box 3 [4])

Days with Mrs. Stowe [a chapter of *Authors and Friends*] (73 pp.: Fields Addenda, Box 3 [5])

From "The Stones of Venice" (2 pp.: Fields Addenda, Box 3 [6])

A Gentleman of Fire (8 pp.: Fields Addenda, Box 3 [7])

George Eliot (18 pp.: Fields Addenda, Box 3 [8])

Illustrations from Life (31 pp.: Fields Addenda, Box 3 [9])

[Journal containing anecdotes about Oliver Wendell Holmes] (83 pp.: Fields Addenda, Box 3 [10])

Life of St. Catherine (37 pp.: Fields Addenda, Box 3 [11])

Longfellow (4 pp.: Fields Addenda, Box 3 [12])

[Memoir of General Armstrong] (10 pp.: Fields Addenda, Box 3 [13])

[Memoir of Robert Collyer] (1 p.: Fields Addenda, Box 3 [14])

Memoirs of a Physician: [book review] (25 pp.: Fields Addenda, Box 3 [15]; also corrected typescript; 11 pp.)

Saint Teresa (53 pp.: Fields Addenda, Box 4 [1]; also supplementary notes and papers—35 pp.: Box 4 [2])

A Second Shelf of Old Books: Edinburgh (103 pp.: Fields Addenda, Box 4 [3])

The Walk (5 pp.: Fields Addenda, Box 4 [4])

[Speech re life of Christ] (31 pp.: Fields Addenda, Box 4 [5])

[Speech in tribute to Julia (Ward) Howe] (6 pp.: Fields Addenda, Box 4 [6])

[Speech on patriotism to be delivered on Washington's birth] (24 pp.: Fields Addenda, Box 4 [7])

[Miscellaneous manuscripts] (15 pp.: Fields Addenda, Box 4 [8])

[Notation concerning number of Hawthorne letters on hand] 1 p.: Fields Addenda, Box 4 [9])

[18 speeches on charity, a notebook of drafts of speeches, and miscellaneous notes on charity] (Fields Addenda, Box 5 [1–16])

Letters: 166 (1857–1912), including 25 to Henry Wadsworth Longfellow

Other:

Miscellaneous notes and memoranda (16 pieces: FI 3037)

Announcement re memorial to Oliver Wendell Holmes (FI 3038)

Fragrant Memories: [scrapbook of some diary entries and many pressed flowers, with notes laid in] (Fields Addenda, Box 6 [1])

[Address book, with notes, cards, etc.] (Fields Addenda, Box 6 [2])

[Notebook of memoranda and addresses] (Fields Addenda, Box 6 [3])

FIELDS, James Thomas, *American editor, publisher, poet,* 1817–81

James Thomas Fields began his publishing career in 1831 when he became a clerk in "The Old Corner Bookstore," which later became William D. Ticknor and Company. Evolving into Ticknor and Fields in 1854, the firm achieved prominence as the publisher of *The Atlantic Monthly* (which Fields also edited from 1861 to 1870) and gained an increasing reputation as one of the foremost American book publishers. Fields was responsible for much of his firm's success, largely as a result of his equitable and generous treatment of authors and his talents as a recruiter of new writers and promoter of their books. With his wife, Annie (Adams) Fields, he formed the nucleus of a Boston literary circle which included prominent American and English authors. After his retirement from business in 1870, Fields continued his writing and lecturing, drawing upon his many literary friendships for source material.

Subject matter: primarily letters addressed to James and Annie (Adams) Fields, many dealing with business and literary matters related to *The Atlantic Monthly* or volumes to be published by Ticknor and Fields. Also included are manuscripts of works submitted to Fields for publication. Strongest for period 1850–1914.

The Fields Addenda contains the personal papers of the Fieldses, consisting largely of their literary efforts in verse and prose, as well as biographical sketches and anecdotes of their friends. There is also some correspondence, including letters from James to Annie Fields.

Significant persons: Authors having the largest representation include Oliver Wendell HOLMES, Henry Wadsworth LONGFELLOW, Harriet (Beecher) STOWE, and John Greenleaf WHITTIER. Material by these and others appears within each author's individual entry in this Guide.

Physical description: letters and manuscripts by a large number of authors (5095 pieces). The Fields Addenda, approximately 500 pieces, consists largely of notebooks and composition books of poetry, essays, and miscellaneous notes, with many loose leaves inserted between the pages.

Source: acquired from A. S. W. Rosenbach in 1922; the Fields Addenda from Boylston A. Beal through M. A. DeWolfe Howe in 1934.

Verse:

Anniversary Poem, delivered before the Mercantile Library Association, 1838: [printed copy, also containing 15 ms. poems, and clippings] (Fields Addenda, Box 7 [1])

[Dummy volume for his *Poems,* with ms. dedication, table of contents, and 2 ms. poems tipped in] (Fields Addenda, Box 7 [3])

A Handful of Merry Ballads: [ms. title page, table of contents, and list of possible mottoes for fly-leaf] (Fields Addenda, Box 8 [1])

A New and True Ghost Story: [rhymed narrative] (Fields Addenda, Box 8 [2])

[Poems—66 unbound poems, and 10 fragments of verse] (Fields Addenda, Box 8 [3])

[Volume of *Poems,* Cambridge, cut and corrected, with ms. notes, and clippings] (Fields Addenda, Box 7 [2])

Prose:

Cheerful Companions: [ms. title page and table of contents, with printed copies of several essays attached to ms. pages] (9 pp.: Fields Addenda, Box 8 [5])

Entry Photographs (corrected proofs, 10 pp.: Fields Addenda, Box 8 [6])

An Epistle to Leigh Hunt in Elysium (45 pp.: Fields Addenda, Box 8 [7])

Hints for Talks with Young Scholars (58 pp.: Fields Addenda, Box 8 [8])

[Memorandum concerning American men and women of letters] (8 pp.: Fields Addenda, Box 8 [9])

[Miscellaneous manuscripts and proofs re English literature] (39 pp.: Fields Addenda, Box 8 [10])

[Notes on American literature] (21 pp.: Fields Addenda, box 8 [11])

[Notes on Burns] (50 pp.: Fields Addenda, Box 8 [12])

[Notes on Byron] (54 pp.: Fields Addenda, Box 8 [13])

[Notes on Campbell] (10 pp.: Fields Addenda, Box 8 [14])

[Notes on cheerfulness] (115 pp.: Fields Addenda, Box 9 [1])

[Notes on DeQuincey] (88 pp.: Fields Addenda, Box 9 [2])

[Notes on Dickens] (21 pp.: Fields Addendum, Box 9 [3])

[Notes on Thomas Gray] (29 pp.: Fields Addenda, Box 9 [4])

[Notes on Adelaide Kemble] (10 pp.: Fields Addenda, Box 9 [5])

[Notes on literature] (40 pp.: Fields Addenda, Box 9 [6])

[Notes for lecture on Longfellow] (80 pp.: Fields Addenda, Box 9 [7])

[Notes on Milton] (17 pp.: Fields Addenda, Box 9 [8])

Notes on Shelley (68 pp.: Fields Addenda, Box 9 [9])

[Notes on John Wilson] (29 pp.: Fields Addenda, Box 9 [10])

[Misc. manuscripts] (58 pp.: Fields Addenda, Box 9 [11])

Letters: 422 (1845–80), including 58 to Annie (Adams) Fields, 20 to Nathaniel Hawthorne, 148 to Henry Wadsworth Longfellow, 52 to Mary Russell Mitford, and 105 to Bayard Taylor

Other:

[Manuscript notebook, with loose notes and clippings laid in, ca. 1860–75] (Fields Addenda, Box 10 [1])

[Marginal note on Henry Leigh Hunt's *Morgiana in England*] [HM 12243)

[Memoranda of poems] (2 pp.· FI 5094)

[Memorandum and account book with some loose sheets, ca. 1863–81] (Fields Addenda, Box 10 [2])

[Portfolio of miscellaneous notes, consisting largely of quotations] (Fields Addenda, Box 10 [3])

[Two scrapbooks of clippings, with notes and quotations copied in] (Fields Addenda, Box 11 [1–2])

FINGER, Charles Joseph, *American editor, author,* 1869–1941

Letters: 15 (1920–34)

FINLEY, John Huston, *American editor, educator, author,* 1863–1940

Letters: 3 (1900)

FIRTH, Sir Charles Harding, *English historian,* 1857–1936

Prose:

Memorandum on the proposals made by the conference of northern universities . . . at Manchester (typewritten, 7 pp.: HM 30535)

FISHER, Dorothy Frances (Canfield), *American novelist,* 1879–1958

Letters: 2 (1934)

FISHER, Mahlon Leonard, *American poet,* 1874–1947

Letters: 1 (1941)

FISKE, John, *American lecturer, philosopher,* 1842–1901

Prose:

American Political Ideas viewed from the standpoint of universal history: Three lectures delivered at Royal Institution of Great Britain in May 1880 (1 vol.: HM 18874)

American Revolution (2 vols.: HM 18875)

Appletons' Cyclopaedia of American Biography: [preface only] (3 pp.: HM 18873)

Are We Celts or Teutons? VII and VIII (final two of a series of articles, 23 pp.: HM 7228)

Autobiographical Notes (11 pp.: HM 18876)

The Beginnings of New England, or the Puritan Theocracy in its Relations to Civil and Religious Liberty (343 leaves: HM 18877)

The Boston Tea Party: [a lecture] (45 leaves: HM 18878)

A Candid Theologian: To the Editor of the *Christian Union* (13 leaves: HM 18867)

Civil Government in the United States, considered with some Reference to its Origins (1 vol.: HM 18879)

Cosmic Philosophy (a quotation, one paragraph only, 1 p.: HM 18872)

The Dutch and Quaker Colonies in America (2 vols.: HM 18880)

Essays on a Liberal Education (reviewed by John Fiske for the *North American Review,* 36 pp.: HM 18884)

Europe before the Arrival of Man (66 pp.: HM 18881)

Franklin, Benjamin: [a short biography, written for Appletons' Cyclopaedia of American Biography] (24 pp.: HM 18882)

The Genesis of Language (110 pp. [also another, incomplete, with 26 leaves]: FK 1288)

Herbert Spencer's Service to Religion: [an address at a farewell banquet to Spencer] (typewritten, 9 pp.: HM 13759)

History of the United States (306 pp.: HM 18883)

John Tyndall: a memoir (9 pp.: HM 18885)

Mass in B Minor: [score and vocal parts] (36 leaves [also another copy of the same, having 33 leaves]: HM 18893 [A and B])

Il Metauro, a Sonata for the Organ or Piano Forte (2 leaves: HM 18894)

The Mississippi Valley in the Civil War (219 numb. leaves followed by 7 plates maps: HM 18886)

New England: [an article drawn from Fiske's *The Beginnings of New England*] (26 leaves: HM 7230)

New France and New England (partly typewritten, 1 vol.: HM 18889)

Old Virginia and Her Neighbors (2 vols.: HM 18890)

The Peasant Girl and the Fairy (3 pp.: HM 18870)

Precisely the doctrine held and taught by Mr. Spencer (3 pp.: HM 13760)

Scenes and Characters in American History: [a series of lectures] (2 vols.: HM 18891)

Schubert (a biographical sketch, 51 pp.: HM 18887)

Shront: an Opera (18 leaves: HM 18895)

Spain and France in the New World: [a lecture delivered in Boston, October 21, 1892, on the 400th anniversary of the discovery of America] (incomplete, 7 leaves: HM 18871)

Thomas Hutchinson, Last Royal Governor of Massachusetts: [a lecture] (47 leaves: HM 18888)

The War for Independence (146 pp.: HM 18892)

Letters: 1,446 (1850–1901)

Documents: 11 (1858–1900)

Other:

[Annotation on letter of executors of S. J. Tilden estate] (HM 1247)

[A critical comment on the essay, "The Genesis of Language"] (1 p.: FK 1279)

[Mass in B minor: a memorandum giving the numbers and names of parts, with key of each, and number of pages of each] (1 p.: FK 1289)

[Notes for the first draft of "The Idea of God," written in the Little Kitchen at Petersham] (4 pp.: FK 1284)

Panorama of Pilgrim's Progress: [pencil sketch] (HM 43262)

[Sketch showing six lots on Berkeley Place, Cambridge] (1 p.: HM 18869)

FISKE, Minnie Maddern (Davey), *American actress,* 1865–1932

Letters: 15 (1890–1921)

FITCH, George Hamlin, *American editor, author,* 1852–1915

Letters: 2 (1887–1911)

FITZGERALD, Edward, *English poet, translator,* 1809–83

Letters: 4 (1869–70)

Other:

Corrections in translation of Aeschylus' *Agamemnon* (RB 32161)

Notes in *Charles Lamb* (RB 32137)

Corrections and additions in *The Downfall and Death of King Oedipus* (RB 46593)

Notes in *Virgil's Garden* (RB 46599)

Corrections in *The Mighty Magician* (RB 8567)

Corrections in *The Mighty Magician* (RB 8656)
Corrections in *The Downfall of King Oedipus* (RB 46594)

FITZGERALD, Francis Scott Key, *American novelist,* 1896–1940

Letters: 9 (1920–35)

FITZGERALD, William Thomas, *English versifier,* 1759?–1829

Letters: 2 (1795–1800)

FITZGIBBON, Robert Louis Constantine, *American author,* 1919–

Letters: 2 (1967)

FLANNER, Hildegarde, *American poet,* 1899–

Letters: 16 (1925–69)

FLANNER, Janet, *American journalist, author,* 1892–1978

Prose:

The Cubicle City (incomplete; 1 p. only: HM 8954)

FLAUBERT, Gustave, *French novelist,* 1821–80

Letters: 1 (n.d.)

FLECKER, Herman James Elroy, *English poet, dramatist,* 1884–1915

Letters: 1 (1914)

FLETCHER, John, *English dramatist,* 1579–1625

Verse:

[Poems ascribed to him in commonplace book] (HM 198)

Letters: 1 (n.d.)

FLETCHER, John Gould, *American poet*, 1886–1950

Verse:

Orange Blossom: [first draft] (OC 5)

Letters: 49 (1931–50), including 42 to Norreys J. O'Conor

FLOWER, Benjamin Orange, *American editor, social reformer, author*, 1858–1918

Letters: 5 (1900–09)

FOERSTER, Norman, *American educator, critic*, 1887–

Letters: 3 (1917–26)

FOLEY, James William, *American newspaperman*, 1874–1939

Letters: 57 (1905–ca. 1933), including 48 to Clara (Bradley) Burdette.

FOLEY, John Henry, *English sculptor*, 1818–74

Letters: 1 (1863)

FOLEY, Patrick Kevin, *American bookseller, bibliophile*, 1856–1937

Letters: 14 (1902–35)

FOOTE, Mary (Hallock), *American novelist, illustrator*, 1847–1938

Prose:

How the Pump Stopped at the Morning Watch (25 pp.: HM 43264)

The Story of the Alcazar (18 pp.: HM 45639)

The Rapture of Hetty (25 pp.: HM 43266)

Letters: 93 (1883–1933)

Other:

[Notes on Miner's War in Idaho, 1892] (HM 43265)

FORBES, Esther, *American author,* 1891–1967

Letters: 2 (1942–43)

FORBES, James, *American playwright,* 1871–1938

Letters: 1 (1913)

FORCE, Peter, *American archivist, historian,* 1790–1868

Letters: 12 (1835–56)

Documents: 4 (1840–42)

FORD, Ford Madox, *English author,* 1873–1939

Letters: 307 (1901–33), including 303 to his literary agent, James Brand Pinker

FORD, Paul Leicester, *American historian, novelist,* 1865–1902

Letters: 3 (1888–95)

FORD, Worthington Chauncey, *American editor, bibliophile, author,* 1858–1941

Letters: 41 (1889–1932)

FORMAN, Harry Buxton, *English scholar,* 1842–1917

Letters: 4 (1877–96)

Other:

[Note referring to a letter written by Mary Shelley] (1 p.: HM 15561)

FORMAN, Henry James, *American editor, author,* 1879–1966

Letters: 21 (1914–16)

FORREST, Earle Robert, *American author,* b. 1883

Letters: 24 (1936–49)

FORRESTER, Alfred Henry (Alfred Crowquill, pseud.), *English author, artist,* 1804–72

Verse:

The Stile (FR 105)

To Mary Ayris on her first Birthday (FR 106)

Prose:

The Crusader: a Very Romantic Opera (10 leaves: FR 94)

Doubt: a Vaudeville in two acts (18 leaves: FR 95)

False and True: play (21 leaves: FR 96)

Friar Rush or Harlequin and King Gold: a Comic Pantomime (17 leaves: FR 97)

The Little Pilgrim (8 leaves: FR 99)

My First Burglary (13 leaves: FR 100)

The Mysterious Chamber (20 leaves: FR 101)

Once Lost Twice Won (26 leaves: FR 102)

The Patchwork Quilt: Part 1st: The Duel (13 leaves: FR 103)

The Patchwork Quilt: Patch No. 2: The Roue (17 leaves: FR 104)

The Two Shoes (19 leaves: FR 107)

The Velvet Chair (17 leaves: FR 108)

Young Love and Old Constancy (18 leaves: FR 109)

Drawings:

The German Philosopher (FR 262)

Illustrations and proofs for The St. James's Hall Christy Minstrels' Christmas Annual (8 leaves: FR 98)

My first drawing made for Punch (pencil sketch of unicorn and lion seated at table: FR 93)

Pen and ink drawing of four persons aboard a wagon (FR 92)

Ringing Wet: pen and ink drawing (FR 263)

Sketchbook containing preliminary sketches and pen-and-ink drawings (FR 264)

Letters: 10 (1849–72)

FORSTER, Edward Morgan, *English novelist,* b. 1879

Prose:

Nassenheide (typewritten, 13 pp.: Russell Collection)

Letters: 4 (1951–60)

FORSTER, John, *English historian, biographer,* 1812–76

Letters: 56 (1828–75), and 142 addressed to Forster.

Other:

[4 miscellaneous notes] (Forster Collection)

[3 extracts from diary] (Forster Collection)

[Miscellaneous mss. about Forster] (Forster Collection)

FOSCOLO, Nicolo Ugo, *Italian poet, novelist,* 1778–1827

Letters: 2 (1820–21)

FOSS, Sam Walter, *American librarian, journalist, humorist, poet,* 1858–1911

Letters: 2 (1892 and n.d.)

FOSTER, Myles Birket, *English painter, illustrator,* 1825–99

Letters: 2 (1863–70)

FOSTER, Stephen Collins, *American author of songs and ballads,* 1826–64

Verse:

Oh! Boys, Carry Me 'Long: [Words and music] (HM 16511)

Letters: 2 (1851)

FOX, John William, Jr., *American novelist,* 1863–1919

Letters: 6 (1889–94)

FRAMPTON, Meredith, *English artist,* 1894–

Letters: 18 (1921–42)

FRANCKLIN, Thomas, *English miscellaneous writer,* 1721–84

Letters: 1 (1774)

FRANKLIN, Benjamin, *American inventor, printer, statesman,* 1706–90

Verse:

Copy of Verses on a Philadelphia Gent (HM 900)

To Madame B— (not autograph: MO 6836)

Prose:

Autobiography (1 vol.: HM 9999)

Letters: 25 (1753–86)

Documents: 8 (1756–90)

FRASER, James, *English publisher,* d. 1841

Letters: 2 (1840–41)

FREEMAN, Mary Eleanor (Wilkins), *American novelist,* 1862–1930

Verse:

The Giver (HM 1244)

Letters: 10 (1891–1902)

FRÉMONT, Jessie (Benton), *American author,* 1824–1902

Letters: 82 (1842–1902)

Other:

[To Horatio Nelson Rust: copy of Tennyson's "Crossing the Bar," followed by another poem and a note about the poems] (RU 1011)

FRÉMONT, John Charles, *American explorer, author,* 1813–90

Letters: 58 (1845–90)

Documents: 1 (1851)

FRENCH, Alice, *American novelist,* 1850–1934

Letters: 8 (1890–1910)

FRENCH, Anne (Warner), *American author,* 1869–1913

Prose:

The Minister's Vacation (38 pp.: HM 43321)

FRENCH, Benjamin Brown, *American poet,* 1800–70

Verse:

Consecration Hymn (HM 7236)

Letters: 9 (1843–70)

FRENCH, Nora May, *American poet,* 1881–1907

Verse:

After-Knowledge (Lafler Collection)

Change (Lafler Collection)

Growth (Lafler Collection)

Rewritten (Lafler Collection)

Spanish Girl IV: The Garden (Lafler Collection)

"To rosy buds in orchards of the spring" (Lafler Collection)

The Vine (Lafler Collection)

Wisteria (Lafler Collection)

Letters: 10 (1906) to Henry Anderson Lafler

FRERE, John Hookham, *English diplomat, author,* 1769–1846

Verse:

Poems and translations in printed copy of Frere's Works, including the following (RB 24370):

Catullus Carmen III, IV, X, XC

The Dirge in the Alcestis

Ed. Nucelia Esqr. 1833 Act 75. Dances—goes long journies and walks 6 miles an hour for two hours daily

Empedocles: Ed. Dominica Pavia Vol. II, p. 75.

Epitaph on Lord Lavington

Epitaph on Lord Nelson

[Extracts translated from the Cid]

Fable, followed by An appeal to the Professor of art and literature in the United Kingdom on behalf of Walter Savage Landor Esqre—

[Fragment, beginning], "The ideal ruling Law, like words to Deeds"

[Fragment, beginning], "The revelation of an element"

From the Diana of Montemayor

From Empedocles

From Euripides: Hercules furians

From Prosper Aquitanus

From the Spanish of Sanchez

Journey to Hurdingham to visit the Revd. W. Whites of Clare Hall

Lines describing the altered feeling and character of the Apostles after the effusion of the Holy Spirit

"Our fancies figure a Divinity"

Quid tibi visa

Suffolk Scenery: Lines

To a Lady with a present of a Walking Stick

Translation from Faust: Act III, scene vii

Written in the flyleaf of Mr. Pollock's Poem

FRITH, William Powell, *English artist,* 1819–1909

Letters: 6 (1841–89)

FROST, Frances Mary, *American poet, novelist,* 1905–59

[Signed quotation] (Kane Literary Collection)

FROST, Robert Lee, *American poet,* 1874–1963

Verse:

The Black Cottage (HM 7657)

The Blue Bird to Lesley (HM 7638)

Choice of Society (HM 7656)

Clear and Colder—Boston Common (HM 7639)

Collection of poems presented to Susan Hayes Ward at Christmas, 1911—(HM 7237)

Contents:

Death

Determent

The Little Things of War

My Giving

New Grief
On the Sale of My Farm
Pan Desponds
Pursuit of the Word
Pussy-Willow Time
The Rain Bath
Reluctance
To a Moth Seen in Winter
To the Loud Southwester
Tutelary Elves
Unchastened
Wind and Window-Flower
Winter Winds

Despair (HM 7640)

A Dream Pang (HM 7656)

The Flower Boat (HM 7641)

Genealogical (HM 7642)

In a Vale (HM 7654)

In White (HM 25361)

Love Being All One (HM 7643)

Midsummer Birds (HM 7644)

The Mill City (HM 7645)

My Butterfly (HM 7652)

Nature's Neglect (HM 7646)

Poem beginning, I had a love once . . . (Authorship of this poem has been repudiated by Frost: HM 1201)

A Riddle—Who Is Intended (HM 7642)

Sea Dream (Authorship of this poem has been repudiated by Frost: HM 7647)

A Summer's Garden (HM 7653)

The Trial by Existence (HM 7655)

What Thing a Bird Would Love (HM 7648)

When the Speed Comes (HM 7649)

A Winter's Night (HM 7650)

A Wish (HM 7651)

Letters: 37 (1894–1935)

FROTHINGHAM, Octavius Brooks, *American clergyman, biographer, hymn-writer,* 1822–95

Letters: 9 (1869–93)

FROTHINGHAM, Paul Revere, *American clergyman, biographer, essayist,* 1864–1926

Letters: 3 (1907–13), including 2 to Annie (Adams) Fields and 1 to Sarah Orne Jewett

FROUDE, James Anthony, *English historian, man of letters,* 1818–94

Letters: 85 (1861–92)

FULLER, Henry Blake, *American poet, essayist, novelist,* 1857–1929

Verse:

Song Without Words (HM 41908)

Prose:

His Little Life (18 pp.: HM 43312)

Letters: 64 (1873–ca. 1922)

FULLER, Margaret, see OSSOLI, Sarah Margaret (Fuller), Marchioness

FURMAN, Lucy, *American author,* 1869–1958

Letters: 8 (1895–97)

FURNESS, Horace Howard, *American Shakespearean scholar,* 1833–1912

Letters: 35 (1871–1912)

FURNESS, William Henry, *American Unitarian clergyman, author,* 1802–96

Letters: 19 (1852–81), including 18 to James Thomas Fields and Annie (Adams) Fields

Documents: 1 (1861)

FURNISS, Harry, *English artist, caricaturist,* 1854–1925

Letters: 16 (1880–1905)

Other:

[Two drawings] (Furniss Papers)

FURNIVALL, Frederick James, *English scholar,* 1825–1910

Prose:

[Copy for Working Men's College Program] (4 pp.: FU 298)

[Notes on Ludlow's lecture on] History of Parliamentary Legislation with reference to India (4 pp.: FU 299)

[Notes on English history] (4 pp.: FU 300)

[Report of inaugural meeting of the Browning Society] (incomplete, 3 leaves: FU 303)

Letters: 16 (1854–1908), and approximately 980 addressed to him

Documents: 1 (1852)

FUSELI, Johann Heinrich, *English painter, author,* 1741–1825

Letters: 1 (1803)

FYLES, Franklin, *American drama critic, playwright, author,* 1874–1911

[Signed quotation] (Kane Literary Collection)

G

GAINSBOROUGH, Thomas, *English painter,* 1727–88

Letters: 2 (1772)

GALBRAITH, Vivian Hunter, *English historian,* fl. 1950–1976

Prose:

An Autograph Manuscript of Higden's *Polychronicon* (corrected typescript, 20 pp.: HM 30666)

GALE, Norman Rowland, *English author,* 1862–1942

Verse:

Alice Ellaby (RB 129905)

Letters: 3 (n.d.)

GALE, Zona, *American novelist, playwright,* 1874–1938

Letters: 21 (1913–29)

GALLAGHER, William Davis, *American editor, poet,* 1808–94

Letters: 3 (1851–65)

GALSWORTHY, John, *English novelist,* 1867–1933

Prose:

The Freelands (2 vols.: HM 43320)

Letters: 3 (1907–22)

GALT, John, *English novelist*, 1779–1839

Letters: 8 (1813–38)

GALTON, Sir Francis, *English poet*, 1822–1911

Verse:

The Aged Philosopher: [rhymed couplet] (FI 1702)

Letters: 6 (1870–1904)

GANNETT, Lewis Stiles, *American journalist, author*, 1891–

Letters: 9 (1927–39)

GARD, Wayne Sanford, *American author*, 1899–

Letters: 1 (1936) to Eugene Lafayette Cunningham

GARDINER, Marguerite (Power) Farmer, Countess of Blessington, *English author*, 1789–1849

Prose:

Night Book (2 vols., 320 pp.: HM 12077)

Letters: 19 (1825–47)

GARDINER, Samuel Rawson, *English historian*, 1829–1902

Letters: 3 (1890–94)

GARLAND, Hamlin, *American novelist, playwright, author*, 1860–1940

Verse:

Camping Through (typewritten: California Poetry File)
The Fog-Horn (typewritten: California Poetry File)
The Force of the Wind (California Poetry File)
The Gold Seekers (Garland Collection)
Growing Old (Garland Collection)

In the Cold Green Mountains (typewritten, carbon copy: California Poetry File)

In Praise of the Plain (Garland Collection)

In Tippotee Land (Garland Collection)

"The mountains they are lonely folk" (California Poetry File)

Noon on the Plain (typewritten: California Poetry File)

The Red Man (Garland Collection)

The Stricken Mountaineer (California Poetry File)

The Tail of the Trail (California Poetry File)

Then It's Spring (HM 35075)

To a Captive Crane (Garland Collection)

The Ute Lover (Garland Collection)

"Van Amberg is the man, who goes into all the shows" (Garland Collection)

Prose:

Blinki (11 pp.: Garland Collection)

[Diaries, 1898–1940] (31 vols.: Garland Collection)

[Fragments of five manuscripts] (Garland Collection)

The Future of American Art (6 pp.: Garland Collection)

In the Interests of American Drama (4 pp.: Garland Collection)

Lorado Taft—Sculptor and Evangelist (typewritten, with corrections, 18 pp.: Garland Collection)

Must We Call It a Hoax (typewritten, 25 pp.: Garland Collection)

The New Daughter (typewritten, 3 pp., also 1 p. fragment: Garland Collection)

Osceola's Defiance (typewritten, with corrections, 5 pp., also: second typewritten copy: Garland Collection)

The Palace in the Mesquite (typewritten, with corrections: Garland Collection)

Paternity (15 pp.: Garland Collection)

Prairie Folks (18 pp. of printed pages with pencil corrections: Garland Collection)

Suggestions for a display ad for *Forty Years of Psychic Research* (typewritten, 1 p.: Garland Collection)

To the Women of Iowa (typewritten, 8 pp.: Garland Collection)

Letters: 97 (1893–1939)

Documents: 18 (1929–37)

GARNETT, David, *English novelist,* 1892–

Letters: 1 (1933)

GARNETT, Richard, *English author,* 1835–1906

Prose:

Life of Shelley (44 pp.: HM 43316)

Mandell Creighton, Bishop of London (20 pp.: HM 43315)

The Philosopher and the Butterflies (14 pp.: HM 44521)

Letters: 7 (1887–1900)

GARRICK, David, *English actor,* 1717–79

Verse:

Epilogue to the Andria of Terence (UP 217)

Prose:

Bon Ton; or, High Life Above the Stairs (copy, with autograph corrections, 88 pp.: HM 185)

The Jubilee (copy, with autograph corrections and notes, 43 leaves: HM 13)

The Meeting of the Company; or Baye's Art of Acting (copy, with request for permission to perform signed by Garrick, 32 pp.: HM 12)

Letters: 8 (1770–77)

GARRISON, Wendell Phillips, *American editor, author,* 1840–1907

Letters: 17 (1868–1901)

GARRISON, William Lloyd, *American editor, abolitionist, author,* 1805–79

Letters: 10 (1843–78)

Other:

[Two signed sentiments] (J. A. Ford Album and HM 8297)

GASKELL, Elizabeth Cleghorn (Stevenson), *English novelist,* 1810–65

Letters: 17 (1851–60)

GAY, John, *English poet, dramatist,* 1685–1732

Documents: 1 (1721/22)

GENLIS, Felicité Ducrest de St. Aubin, Mme. de, *French author,* 1746–1830

Letters: 1 (1783)

GEROME, Jean Léon, *French painter,* 1824–1904

Letters: 2 (1879–80)

GERSHWIN, George, *American pianist, composer,* 1898–1937

Letters: 1 (1931) to Sonya Levien

GERSWIN, Ira, *American lyricist,* 1896–

Letters: 1 (1932) to Carl Hovey and Sonya Levien

GHENT, William James, *American author,* 1866–1942

Letters: 3 (1909–14)

GIBBON, Edward, *English historian,* 1737–94

Letters: 2 (1781–93)

Documents: 1 (1787)

GIBBS, Arthur Hamilton, *American novelist,* 1888–

Letters: 1 (1937)

GIBBS, George, *American illustrator, fiction writer,* 1870–1942

Letters: 3 (1921–39)

GIBRAN, Kahlil, *American artist, author,* 1883–1931

Letters: 1 (n.d.)

GIBSON, John, *English sculptor,* 1790–1866

Letters: 1 (1818)

Documents: 1 (1863)

GIFFORD, Robert Swain, *American artist,* 1840–1905

Letters: 5 (1903–04)

GIFFORD, William, *English editor,* 1756–1826

Letters: 2 (1802–14)

GILBERT, Sir John, *English historical painter,* 1817–97

Letters: 4 (1873 and n.d.)

GILBERT, Sir William Schwenck, *English playwright*, 1836–1911

Prose:

Dr. Trusler's Maxims (10 pp.: HM 43319)

Letters: 11 (1869–1909)

GILCHRIST, Alexander, *English biographer*, 1828–61

Verse:

A Song Innonsense (RB 54039)
"Sure, my happy Pipe said it" (RB 54039)

Letters: 1 (1861)

GILDER, Jeannette Leonard, *American editor, critic, playwright*, 1849–1916

Letters: 12 (1879–1910)

Other:

[Signed quotation] (Kane Literary Collection)

GILDER, Joseph Benson, *American editor, author*, 1858–1936

Letters: 6 (1887–1911)

GILDER, Richard Watson, *American editor, poet*, 1844–1909

Verse:

Emma Lazarus (HM 1234)
On the Life-Mask of Abraham Lincoln (typewritten: HM 23840)
Sunset and Book (typewritten: CM 445)

Letters: 381 (1882–1909) and several hundred addressed to him.

Documents: 2 (1892–1904)

GILDER, Rosamond (deKay), *American author,* fl. 1916–34

Letters: 2 (1916–34)

GILES, Henry, *American clergyman, lecturer, essayist,* 1809–82

Letters: 39 (1849–65), including 35 to James Thomas Fields

GILFILLAN, George, *Scottish author,* 1813–78

Letters: 1 (1850)

GILLETTE, William Hooker, *American actor, playwright,* 1855–1937

Letters: 5 (1893–1911)

GILMAN, Charlotte (Perkins) Stetson, *American lecturer, author,* 1860–1935

Letters: 10 (1890–1925)

GILMORE, James Roberts, *American novelist, abolitionist,* 1822–1903

Letters: 3 (1861–96)

GILPIN, William, *English author,* 1724–1804

Letters: 3 (1796–97)

GISBORNE, Thomas, *English divine, author,* 1758–1846

Letters: 3 (1808–23)

GISSING, George Robert, *English novelist,* 1857–1903

Prose:

Born in Exile (236 pp.: HM 42718)

The Crown of Life (147 pp.: HM 42719)

Denzel Quarrier (133 pp.: HM 42720)
Eve's Ransom (67 pp.: HM 42721)
In the Year of the Jubilee (207 pp.: HM 42722)
[Memorandum book] (1899–1902; 96 pp.: HM 26182)
The Nether World (271 pp.: HM 42723)
Thyrza (321 pp.: HM 42724)
The Whirlpool (180 pp.: HM 42725)

Letters: 8 (1891–95)

GLADSTONE, William Ewart, *English statesman, author,* 1809–98

Verse:

The Shield of Achilles, wrought by Hephaistos (Kane Literary Collection)

Letters: 33 (1841–93)

Other:

[Note in Jerrold's *Life of George Cruikshank*] (RB 137399, vol. 4)

GLANVILL, Joseph, *English divine,* 1636–80

Letters: 2 (1652–62)

GLEIG, George Robert, *English chaplain, writer,* 1796–1888

Letters: 8 (1847–87)

GODKIN, Edwin Lawrence, *American editor, author,* 1831–1902

Letters: 1 (1879)

GODWIN, Mary (Wollstonecraft), *English author,* 1759–97

Letters: 2 (1789–97)

GODWIN, Parke, *American editor, author,* 1816–1904

Letters: 38 (1853–1901)

GODWIN, William, *English philosopher, novelist,* 1756–1836

Prose:

Deloraine (900 pp.: HM 43326)

St. Leon (1159 pp.: HM 43325)

Thoughts Occasioned, etc. by a perusal of Dr. Parr's Spital Sermon (56 pp.: HM 43327)

Letters: 19 (1794–1835)

Other:

[Manuscript explanations of the text in margins of *History of the Life of William Pitt*] (RB 145237)

[Manuscript note on p. 9 of *The Enquirer*] (RB 50080)

[Inscription in *Fleetwood*] (RB 118692)

GOLDMAN, Emma, *Russian-born American lecturer, editor, author,* 1869–1940

Letters: 18 (1910–32)

GOLDSMITH, Oliver, *English author,* 1728–74

Verse:

Song from the Vicar of Wakefield (translated into French by Henry W. Longfellow, and in his handwriting: HM 10479)

Prose:

The Grumbler (not autograph, 31 pp.: HM 23)

Preface and Introduction to the History of the Seven Years' War (20 pp.: HM 176)

Letters: 1 (1753), and forgery of letter dated September 30, 1766.

Documents: 1 (1758)

GOODALE, Dora Read, *American poet,* b. 1866

Verse:

Beneath the Linden-tree (HM 23028)

The Peddler of Long Ago (Kane Literary Collection)

The Seal of Hope (Kane Literary Collection)

Letters: 4 (1884–1912)

GOODALL, Frederick Trevelyan, *English painter,* 1848–71

Letters: 3 (1867)

GOODRICH, Arthur Frederick, *American novelist, playwright,* 1878–1941

Letters: 7 (1902–03)

Other:

[Signed quotation] (Kane Literary Collection)

GOODRICH, Samuel Griswold, *American publisher, author,* 1793–1860

Letters: 5 (1818–50)

GORDON, Charles William, *Canadian author,* 1860–1937

Letters: 1 (1902)

GORDON, Sir John Watson, *English portrait-painter,* 1788–1864

Letters: 1 (1855)

GORE, Catherine Grace Frances (Moody), *English dramatist, novelist,* 1799–1861

Prose:

The Champion (27 pp.: HM 849)

Letters: 6 (1840–41)

GORGES, Sir Arthur, *English poet and translator,* d. 1625

Verse:

The Olympian Catastrophe, a poem on the death of Prince Henry (EL 1130)

GOSSE, Sir Edmund William, *English author,* 1849–1928

Verse:

The Butchers' Row (HM 404)

Prose:

Austin Dobson (12 pp.: HM 11222)

Christina Rossetti (48 pp.: HM 11228)

[Diary kept while on a lecture tour in the United States, 1884–85] (34 pp.: HM 12258)

Gossip in a Library—Love and Business (8 pp.: HM 11224)

Lord de Tabley, a portrait (45 pp.: HM 12554)

The Romance of a Dictionary (12 pp.: HM 11225)

Rudyard Kipling (60 pp.: HM 7658)

[Review of] Travel Diaries of William Beckford of Fonthill (15 pp.: HM 11221)

Wolcott Balestier (18 pp.: HM 11223)

Letters: 44 (1874–1925)

Other:

[Inscription to R. L. Stevenson in *The Silverado Squatters*] (RB 285158)

[Note re "The Throstle" in printed copy of that poem] (RB 129096)

GOUDY, Frederic William, *American printer, type-designer, author,* 1865–1947

Letters: 6 (1904–36)

GOULD, Hannah Flagg, *American poet*, 1789–1865

Verse:

Trees for the Pilgrim's Wreath (HM 1896)

GRAND, Sarah, see McFALL, Frances Elizabeth (Clark)

GRANT, Robert, *American novelist, essayist, poet*, 1852–1940

Letters: 28 (1884–1939)

GRAY, Asa, *American botanist, author*, 1810–88

Letters: 26 (1847–80)

GRAY, Thomas, *English poet*, 1716–71

Verse:

An Elegy Written in a Country Churchyard (manuscript illuminated by Alberto Sangorski: HM 12548)

"Charmante Gabrielle" (HM 1266)

"Il etoit une Dame" (HM 1266)

"Thyrsis when he left me swore" (not autograph: HM 12550)

"With beauty with pleasure surrounded to languish (not autograph: HM 12550)

Prose:

Churches &c Worth Visiting in the County of Norfolk (2 pp.: HM 12552)

[Historical notes] (1 p.: SL 252)

Journal for 1754 (17 pp.: HM 12549)

[Notes on the barbaric invasions and the fall of the Roman empire] (4 pp.: HM 12553)

[Notes on Norwich Cathedral] (2 pp.: HM 12551)

[Notes on Persian geography and Alexander's march] (2 pp.: HM 43331)

Letters: 11 (1739–62)

Documents: 2 (1757)

Other:

[Manuscript notes in Latin in E. R. Bulwer-Lytton's *Life of Lord Lytton*] (RB 131334, vol. 1)

GREELEY, Horace, *American editor, reformer, author,* 1811–72

Verse:

Abraham Lincoln (HM 2038)

Prose:

Recollections of a Busy Life (an autobiography, 8 pp.: HP 28)

Free Thought (RB 102018, vol. 2)

Letters: 67 (1845–72)

Documents: 1 (1845)

GREEN, Anna Katharine, see ROHLFS, Anna Katharine (Green)

GREEN, Bartholomew, *American printer,* 1666–1732

Verse:

Verses upon Judge Dudley's character of Colonel Tyng in Gazette no. 218. Another character of him in News Letter no. 1043 (HM 7437)

Prose:

To William Dummer . . . : Memorial (2 pp.: HM 825)

GREEN, Henry, *English author,* 1801–73

Approximately 150 pieces (letters and booklets of ms. notes, 1869–70) relating to Andrea Alciati

GREEN, Julia (Boynton), *American poet,* 1861–1957

Verse:

993 pieces (California Poetry File, and Green Collection)

Prose:

72 pieces, including fiction, essays, etc. (Green Collection)

Letters: 39 (1930–47)

Other:

[249 notes and drafts] (Green Collection)

GREEN, Paul Eliot, *American educator, playwright, novelist,* 1894–

Letters: 1 (1944) to Sonya Levien

GREENAWAY, Kate, *English artist, book illustrator,* 1846–1901

Letters: 2 (1889–1901)

Handwriting on ms. of Sir Walter Scott (HM 1937)

GREENSLET, Ferris, *American editor, author,* 1875–1959

Letters: 6 (1907–26)

GREENWOOD, Grace, see LIPPINCOTT, Sara Jane (Clarke)

GREENWOOD, Mae Snowdrop, *American author,* 1897–

Verse:

Poems (approximately 65 pieces: GS 95–103)

Letters: 3 (1917)

GREER, Hilton Ross, *American editor, poet,* 1879–1949

Letters: 6 (1929–35) to Eugene Lafayette Cunningham

GREGORY, Isabella Augusta (Persse), Lady, *Irish author,* 1852–1932

Letters: 6 (1914–31)

GREW, Nehemiah, *English vegetable physiologist, author,* 1641–1712

Prose:

The Means of a Most Ample Encrease of the Wealth and Strength of England in a Few Years (207 pp.: HM 1264)

GRIEG, Edvard Hagerup, *Norwegian composer,* 1843–1907

Letters: 1 (1896)

GRIERSON, Francis, *English-born American musician, essayist,* 1849–1927

Prose:

[Article on Mary Austin] (4 pp.: AU Box 10)

Letters: 32 (1912–27), including 31 to Mary (Hunter) Austin

GRIEVE, Christopher Murray (Hugh McDiarmid, pseud.), *Irish poet, author, politician,* 1892–

Verse:

Direadh III (HM 27515)

Prose:

116 texts

Letters: 5 (1927–64)

Other:

[Autograph corrections in printed copy of *Stony Limits*] (RB 343623)

GRIFFITH, Matthew, *English Master of the Temple,* 1599?–1665

Prose:

[Sermon] (EL 6868)

GRINNELL, George Bird, *American author,* 1849–1938

Letters: 2 (1892–1924)

GRISWOLD, Rufus Wilmot, *American journalist, anthropologist,* 1815–57

Letters: 44 (1840–55), including 39 to James Thomas Fields

GROSVENOR, Gilbert Hovey, *American editor, author,* 1875–1966

Letters: 2 (1921–43)

GROTE, George, *English historian,* 1794–1871

Letters: 2 (1829 and n.d).

GRUBER, Frank, *American book collector, novelist,* 1904–

Letters: 10 (1955–56) to Eugene Lafayette Cunningham

GRUND, Francis Joseph, *American author, journalist, politician,* 1805–63

Letters: 3 (1850–52)

GUEDALLA, Philip, *English historian, essayist,* 1889–1944

Letters: 5 (1929–37)

GUEST, Edgar Albert, *American journalist, poet,* 1881–1959

Letters: 4 (1924–27)

GUEST, Edwin, *English historian,* 1800–80

Letters: 3 (1857–61)

GUINEY, Louise Imogen, *American essayist, poet,* 1861–1920

Verse:

Abelard (HM 7721)

Ad Patrem (HM 7702)

Amends (FI 1544)

The Anemone Japonica (HM 7715)

Athassel Abbey (HM 7661)

Chaluz Castle (HM 7662)

The Color-Bearer (HM 7722)

In Time (HM 7714)

The Japanese Anemone (HM 7716)

The Kings (HM 7663)

Mater Gloriosa (HM 7664)

Moustache (HM 7665)

On a Young Saint Dying in June (HM 7718)

On Helen's Cheek (HM 7712)

The Optimists (HM 7666)

The Recruit (HM 7717)

Letters: 182 (1884–1914), including 121 to Annie (Adams) Fields

GUITERMAN, Arthur, *American poet,* 1871–1943

Letters: 3 (1925–36)

GUIZOT, François Pierre Guillaume, *French historian, statesman,* 1787–1874

Letters: 6 (1840–76)

GUNTER, Archibald Clavering, *American novelist, playwright,* 1847–1907

Prose:

[Extract from] Mr. Barns of New York (HM 35075)

Letters: 3 (1891–1901)

GUTHRIE, Kenneth Sylvan, *American author,* 1871–1940

Verse:

"Fulfilled of years of glad activity" (HM 43332)

Letters: 3 (1910–11) to Daniel Berkeley Updike

GUTHRIE, Thomas Anstey, *English humorist, fantasist, playwright,* 1856–1934

Letters: 3 (1885–98)

H

HABBERTON, John, *American editor, author,* 1842–1921

Letters: 10 (1895–1901)

HABINGTON, William, *English poet,* 1605–54

Verse:

[Poems ascribed to him in commonplace book] (HM 904)

HACKETT, Francis, *American critic,* 1883–1962

Letters: 2 (1921)

HAGEDORN, Hermann, *American novelist, poet, biographer,* 1882–1964

Letters: 21 (1917–58)

HAGGARD, Sir Henry Rider, *English author,* 1856–1925

Prose:

Speech before The Imperial South African Association, seconding the motion for the appointment of the General Committee (typewritten, 6 pp.: HM 43500)

Notes for Discussion on Imagination. Its Advantages and its Evils (5 pp.: HM 43501)

Letters: 94 (1878–1925)

Documents: 1 (1900)

HAGHE, Louis, *English lithographer, water-color painter,* 1806–85

Letters: 2 (1866)

HAKE, Thomas Gordon, *English physician, poet,* 1809–95

Letters: 1 (1874) to Ford Madox Brown.

HALE, Edward Everett, *American clergyman, author,* 1822–1909

Verse:

New England's Chevy Chase (HM 12383)

"Short is the day and night is long" (FI 2428)

Letters: 109 (1845–1907), including 26 to James Thomas Fields

HALE, Sarah Josepha (Buell), *American editor, author,* 1788–1879

Letters: 6 (1841–76)

HALL, Anna Maria (Fielding), *English author,* 1800–81

Prose:

Waking Dreams (13 pp.: HM 12430)

Letters: 6 (1832–39)

HALL, Basil, *English author,* 1788–1844

Letters: 30 (1826–41)

HALL, David, *American printer, bookseller,* 1714–72

Letters: Six letters addressed to Hall from William Strahan

Documents: 1 (1770)

HALL, Samuel Carter, *English author, editor,* 1800–89

Letters: 20 (1832–82)

Other:

[Signed printed copy of his poem "Anniversary—56!"] (HM 13816)

HALLAM, Arthur Henry, *English poet,* 1811–33

Verse:

Lines Spoken in the Character of Pygmalion in an Acted Charade (SY 68)

Letters: 4 (1832)

HALLAM, Henry, *English historian,* 1777–1859

Letters: 8 (1828–40)

HALLECK, Fitz-Greene, *American poet,* 1790–1867

Verse:

[Billingsgate McSwell: verses beginning] "Ye gentlemen and ladies all" (HM 426)

Connecticut (HM 1226)

[Notebook of poems] (HM 10849)

The Fortunate Family

The History of New England

"Stern winters gone no more the flaking snow"

"Stern winter's gone no more it snows"

A View of the United States

[Poems ascribed to Halleck, and corrections and annotations in Joseph Rodman Drake's "Trifles in Rhyme: A Notebook of Verse"] (HM 35316)

Prose:

Notes on Biblical Reading (28 pp.: HM 425)

Letters: 12 (1831–67)

Other:

[Corrections and annotations on Joseph Rodman Drake's "Trifles in Rhyme: a Notebook of Verse"] (HM 35316)

HALLETT, Richard Matthews, *American author,* 1887–

Letters: 3 (1922–40)

HALPINE, Charles Graham, *American journalist, poet,* 1829–68

Verse:

"As Men Beneath Some Load of Grief" (HP 194)

Minnie my Doll-Wife (HP 41)

Sambo's Right to be Kilt (HP 44)

Prose:

The Marching Soldier. His Joys and Sorrows—A Lecture (45 pp.: HP 40)

[A novel] (incomplete; 106 leaves: HP 43)

Odds and Ends (2 vols.: HP 190)

Pocket Diary [for 1864] (1 vol.: HP 191)

Letters: 187 (1848–68), including 100 to Margaret Grace (Milligan) Halpine

Documents: 5 (1862–68)

Other:

[Miscellaneous prose and poetry] (12 leaves: HP 42)

HALSTEAD, Murat, *American editor, author,* 1829–1908

Letters: 5 (1873–90)

HAMERTON, Philip Gilbert, *English artist, essayist,* 1834–94

Prose:

The Mount (in hand of Eugenie (Gindriez) Hamerton, 166 leaves: HM 17251)

Letters: 3 (1877–90), and 2 (1896) by his wife, Eugenie (Gindriez) Hamerton

HAMILTON, Clayton Meeker, *American drama critic, playwright,* 1881–1946. HAMILTON, Diana, *American playwright,* fl. 1946

Prose:

Fear No More: [unrevised typescript] (1 vol., carbon copy: AIK 3775)

Fear No More: [revised version, with revisions by Diana Hamilton] (typewritten carbon copy, 159 pp.: AIK 3776)

Fear No More: [revised version, with revisions in ink and pencil by Diana Hamilton] (typewritten, carbon copy, 123 pp.: AIK 3777)

Fear No More: [first rewriting of the play, with numerous notes and corrections by Conrad Aiken] (typewritten, 199 pp.: AIK 3778).

Mr. Arcularis: [original version of the play] (typewritten, carbon copy, 1 vol.: AIK 3774)

Letters: 4 (1946)

HAMILTON, Gail, see DODGE, Mary Abigail

HAPGOOD, Norman, *American editor, author,* 1868–1937

Letters: 6 (1900–10)

HARBEN, William Nathaniel, *American novelist,* 1858–1919

Verse:

By the Light of Her Soul (Kane Literary Collection)

Letters: 3 (1907–12)

HARDING, James Duffield, *English landscape-painter, lithographer,* 1798–1863

Letters: 1 (1863)

HARDY, Arthur Sherburne, *American educator, engineer, editor, diplomat, novelist, poet,* 1847–1930

Letters: 1 (1888)

HARDY, Thomas, *English author,* 1840–1928

Prose:

A Committee-Man of the Terror (proof sheets with ms. corrections, 13 leaves: HM 6)

The Melancholy Hussar of the German Legion (27 pp.: HM 7)

A Sunday Morning Tragedy (7 pp.: HM 5)

Letters: 1 (1915)

Other:

[Volume of correspondence from various people concerning Hardy's 79th birthday tribute] (HM 39033–39087)

HARE, Augustus John Cuthbert, *English author,* 1834–1903

Letters: 3 (1887–1901)

Other:

[Signed quotation] (Kane Literary Collection)

HARLAND, Henry, *English novelist,* 1861–1905

Letters: 1 (1894)

HARNESS, William, *English divine, author,* 1790–1869

Letters: 5 (1835–67)

HARRIMAN, Karl Edwin, *American editor, author,* 1875–1935

Letters: 22 (1908–11)

HARRIS, Frank, *American author,* 1856–1931

Prose:

My Life: vol. 3 (extract; 2 pp.; in the hand of Elmer Gertz: HM 42085)

Letters: 14 (1901–21)

HARRIS, James, *English author, politician,* 1709–80

Verse:

To [John] Hoadly: [epistle in verse] (HM 6580)

Letters: 7 (1770–80)

HARRIS, Joel Chandler, *American editor, author,* 1848–1908

Verse:

A Song of the Mole (HM 12223)

Prose:

Free Joe and the Rest of the World (21 pp.: HM 12222)
Little Compton (60 pp.: HM 12419)
Mark Twain's 50th Birthday (2 pp.: HM 12420)
[The Old Bascom Place: fragment of a short story] (53 pp.: HM 43335)
A Rainy Day with Uncle Remus (revised as chapters vi–x of *Nights with Uncle Remus,* 60 pp.: HM 12422)

Letters: 2 (1883–84)

HARRISON, Constance (Cary), *American novelist, essayist,* 1843–1920

Prose:

The Three Misses Benedict (65 pp.: HM 12425)

The Fairfaxes of America (76 pp.: FAC 789)

Letters: 7 (1888–99)

HARRISON, Frederic, *English author, positivist,* 1831–1923

Letters: 24 (1889–1903), including 19 to Richard Watson Gilder

HARRISON, Henry Sydnor, *American journalist, novelist,* 1880–1930

Letters: 2 (1911–13)

HART, Jerome Alfred, *American editor, author,* 1854–1937

Verse:

"Charley the hurrying, fleeting years" (HM 35075)

HART, William Surrey, *American actor,* 1872–1946

Letters: 27 (1929–38)

HARTE, Francis Bret, *American short-story writer, poet, novelist,* 1839–1902

Verse:

At the Hacienda (HM 25925)

Mary's Album (HM 35075)

Prose:

83 texts

Letters: 45 (1868–1901)

HASLEWOOD, Joseph, *English antiquary,* 1769–1833

Verse:

Lyrical Gleanings, Comprising Madrigals, Odes, Songs, and Sonnets (material for a new edition; partly in manuscript and partly in print: HM 43338)

Letters: 5 (1808–31)

Other:

[Title page and notes in commonplace book, "Records of the Muse"] (HM 198)

HASSAM, Frederick Childe, *American artist,* 1859–1935

Letters: 22 (1891–1929)

HAWKES, Clarence, *American poet,* 1869–1954

Letters: 1 (1904) to Howes Norris

HAWKESWORTH, John, *English author,* 1715?–73

Letters: 7 (1759–67)

HAWKINS, Sir Anthony Hope, *English author,* 1863–1933

Prose:

La Mort a la Mode (4 pp.: HM 12255)

Letters: 6 (1898–1912)

HAWTHORNE, Julian, *American novelist, biographer,* 1846–1934

Verse:

Fathers of Freedom! (HM 12219)

Sunk Deep in a Sea (HM 12216)

Unshed Tears (HM 12218)

Prose:

The American of the Future (1 p.: HM 12217)

Hawthorne's Philosophy (20 pp.: HM 12215)

Millenial Reflections (3 pp.: HM 42678)

Millicent and Rosalind (100 pp.: HM 42679)

The Third of March (15 pp.: HM 42680)

Walking (10 pp.: HM 42681)

Letters: 19 (1901–32)

Other:

[Notes of authentication on a journal and verses by Nathaniel Hawthorne] (HM 561, HM 42560)

HAWTHORNE, Nathaniel, *American author,* 1804–64

Verse:

[Humorous verse on Amos Bronson Alcott] (HM 1220)

[Nonsense verses beginning] "Oh snow that comes" (written by Nathaniel and Una: HM 11042)

Prose:

[Fragment from The American Notebooks] (torn out by Mrs. Hawthorne, 2 pp.: HM 2854)

[Fragment from The American Notebooks] (torn out by Mrs. Hawthorne, 2 pp.: HM 2855)

[Diary kept during Hawthorne's residence in Florence] (68 leaves: HM 302)

[Doctor Grimshawe's Secret: preliminary draft] (31 leaves: HM 1699)

[The Dolliver Romance: experimental draft, incomplete] (2 leaves: HM 2863)

[Life of Franklin Pierce] (48 pp.: HM 10850)

[Notes used in writing Doctor Grimshawe's Secret, The Doliver Romance, Septimius Felton, and The Ancestral Footstep] 16 pp.: HM 2862)

[Septimius Felton: notes on the plan of the story] (1 leaf: HM 12131)

The Snow Image: a childish miracle (15 pp.: HM 12260)

[Subject index to the English Notebooks, with dates, and occasional page references] (2 pp.: HM 1401)

To a Friend: [inscription dedicating *Our Old Home* to Franklin Pierce] (2 leaves: HM 7173)

[Scribblings in Journal of a Passage to the East Indies and return by Nathaniel Hawthorne] (HM 561)

Letters: 233 (1822–64), including 165 to his wife; and 33 letters addressed to Hawthorne; also 2 letters (1864–67) by Sophia Amelia (Peabody) Hawthorne; and 39 (1870–76) from Elizabeth Manning Hawthorne to Una Hawthorne

Documents: 38 (1846–62), including 35 checks

HAY, John Milton, *American statesman, diplomat, journalist, historian, poet,* 1838–1905

Verse:

Two Fenians (HP 118)

Words (HM 35075)

Letters: 125 (1861–1904)

HAYDON, Benjamin Robert, *English historical painter,* 1786–1846

Verse:

"Benny has nothing more to say . . ." (BE 17)

Creditor (BE 42)

Debtor (BE 42)

Epitaph of a Great Man (HM 45445)

Letters: 275 (1819–46)

Documents: 2 (n.d.)

Other:

[Drawing] (BE 18)

HAYES, Helen, see MacARTHUR, Helen Hayes (Brown)

HAYES, Isaac Israel, *American physician, Arctic explorer, author,* 1832–81

Prose:

The Goblin of the Inn: [an outline for a drama in five acts] (7 pp.: HM 8958)

Letters: 33 (1858–72), including 27 to James Thomas Fields

HAYLEY, William, *English poet,* 1745–1820

Verse:

Epitaph on Mrs. Carlton of Woodside (RB 131334, vol. 2)

The Indian Viceroy, or The Slave of Passion (not autograph: HM 597)

The National Advocates (HM 43340)

[Three poems]: (HM 12587, vol. 2)

To Miss Catherine Thurlow

To William Wilberforce

Cowper! to you the Virgin's Bower belongs

To Miss Seward (in the handwriting of Anna Seward, followed by Seward's "To William Hayley" and by Hayley's reply: JE 475)

To Mrs. Mason (RB 220308, vol. 1)

Letters: 6 (1772–1803)

HAYNE, Paul Hamilton, *American editor, poet,* 1830–86

Verse:

Sonnets to Algernon Charles Swinburne (HM 9698)

Letters: 3 (1867–73)

HAYTER, Sir George, *English painter,* 1792–1871

Letters: 10 (1824–56)

HAYWARD, Abraham, *English essayist,* 1801–84

Letters: 2 (1861–75)

HAZARD, Caroline, *American educator, poet, essayist,* 1856–1945

Letters: 204 (1903–38), including 198 to the Merrymount Press

HAZELTON, Elizabeth Clara (Reynolds), *American writer,* fl. 1932–52

Prose:

Alaskan Forget-me-nots [compilation for book, and supplementary material] (46 pieces: Hazelton Collection)

Poppy of California [compilation for book, and supplementary material] (approximately 111 pieces: Hazelton Collection)

Letters: 10 (1932–52), and 64 letters addressed to her

HAZLITT, William, *English essayist,* 1778–1830

Prose:

On the Sun-dial (on verso of last leaf is part of an early version of On the Want of Money, 14 pp.: HM 12220)

Letters: 1 (1820)

Other:

[Manuscript note at the end of printed copy of *Conversations of James Northcote*] (RB 26244)

HEARN, Lafcadio, *American author, translator,* 1850–1904

Prose:

[Notes for] A Midsummer Trip to the West Indies (2 vols.: HM 12002)

The Scenes of Cable's Romances (31 pp.: HM 11963)
[Short autobiographical note] (1 p.: HM 38319)

Letters: 40 (1883–90)

HEARNSHAW, Fossey John Cobb, *English historian,* 1869–1946

Letters: 1 (1910)

HEBER, Reginald, *English bishop, author,* 1783–1826

Verse:

To Mary (HM 11587, p. 15)

Letters: 2 (1820–22)

HEBER, Richard, *English book-collector, editor,* 1773–1833

Letters: 3 (1817–24)

HECKER, Isaac Thomas, *American clergyman, author,* 1819–88

Letters: 2 (1844) to Henry David Thoreau

HECTOR, Annie (French), *English novelist,* 1825–1902

Letters: 1 (1885)

HEDGE, Frederic Henry, *American clergyman, poet,* 1805–90

Letters: 4 (1856–85)

HEINE, Heinrich, *German poet,* 1797–1856

Verse:

Florentinische Nachte [in zwei Teilen] (104 pp.: HM 12377)
"Als Republik ist Hamburg nicht" (HM 43341)

Du Bist wie Eine Blume: [translated by William Ford Aiken and in Aiken's hand] (AIK 3004)

Letters: 1 (1830)

HEINEMANN, William, *English publisher,* 1863–1920

Letters: 59 (1906–16)

HELLMAN, George Sidney, *American author,* 1878–1958

Prose:

Introduction [to an unpublished edition of the Poems of Henry David Thoreau; with design for the proposed title page] (6 leaves: HM 3143)

HELPER, Hinton Rowan, *American antislavery writer,* 1829–1909

Letters: 3 (1861–99)

HELPS, Sir Arthur, *English writer,* 1813–75

Letters: 6 (1858–73)

HEMANS, Felicia Dorothea (Browne), *English poet,* 1793–1835

Verse:

Angel Visits (HM 1829)

Bring Flowers (HM 12424)

Colonel Lovelace's Song to Lucasta (HM 42522)

Words for the Norwegian Air (HM 42524)

Prose:

Records of a Woman—No. 5, The Switzer's Wife (RB 131334, vol. 2)

Room in a Palace: [Act III, scene i only] (RB 6783)

Letters: 35 (1819–34)

HENDERSON, Archibald, *American educator, mathematician, author,* 1877–1963

Letters: 25 (1913–34)

HENDERSON, Charles Hanford, *American educator, author,* 1861–1941

Letters: 9 (1907–16)

HENLEY, William Ernest, *English editor, poet,* 1849–1903

Verse:

By the Seaside II (HM 30906)
A Contract; and Amantium Irae: [2 poems] (HM 30911)
Delirium (HM 30905)
A Love by the Sea XX (HM 30907)
My Last Song (HM 30908)
Poem, incomplete (HM 30904)
Romances IV: [4 poems] (HM 30910)
Tobacco I: Laus Tibi (HM 30909)

Prose:

London Types (36 pp.: HM 12378)

Letters: 53 (1872–1902)

Documents: 2 (1884)

HENN, Thomas Rice, *Irish educator, author,* 1901–

Letters: 3 (1964–65)

HENRY, Matthew, *English commentator, minister,* 1662–1714

Prose:

[Sermon] (16 pp.: HM 12418)

HENRY, O., see PORTER, William Sydney

HERBERT, Edward, 1st Baron Herbert of Cherbury, *English philosopher, historian, diplomat,* 1583–1648

Verse:

[Poems ascribed to him in commonplace book] (HM 198)

Documents: 1 (1646)

HERBERT, Henry William, *American novelist, sports writer,* 1807–58

Letters: 2 (1853)

HERFORD, Oliver, *American artist, humorist,* 1863–1935

Verse:

Night Thought (AP 726)

HERRICK, Robert, *English poet,* 1591–1674

Verse:

Poems included in commonplace book (HM 198) and in Dayly Observations (HM 93)

HERRICK, Robert, *American educator, novelist,* 1868–1938

Letters: 3 (1900–11)

HERSCHEL, Sir John Frederick William, *English astronomer,* 1792–1871

Letters: 8 (1821–61)

HESSE, Hermann, *German author,* 1877–1962

Verse:

Zwolf Gedichte: [12 autograph poems in German, presented to Wallace Stevens, each with a watercolor drawing] (WAS 223)

Letters: 2 (1951)

HEWITT, John Hill, *American editor, poet,* 1801–90

Verse:

Christmas Carol (BR 255)

Never Despair (BR 255)

HEWITT, Mary Elizabeth (Moore), *American poet,* b. 1818

Letters: 1 (1846)

HEWLETT, Maurice Henry, *English author,* 1861–1923

Verse:

The Letters Cross (a dialogue between "His" and "Hers": HM 41010)

Prose:

The Life and Death of Richard Yea-and-Nay (2 vols.: HM 12426

The Stooping Lady (353 pp.: HM 12003)

Letters: 5 (1915–29)

HEYWARD, DuBose, *American novelist, playwright, poet,* 1885–1940

Letters: 1 (1930)

HICKS, Granville, *American editor, author,* 1901–

Letters: 1 (1934)

HIGGINSON, Ella (Rhoades), *American novelist, poet,* 1862–1940

Verse:

Four-Leaf Clover (Kane Literary Collection)

Letters: 4 (1906–22)

HIGGINSON, Thomas Wentworth, *American clergyman, critic, poet,* 1823–1911

Verse:

Sub pondere crescit (HM 424)

To the Memory of H. H. (HM 423)

Prose:

The Health of Our Girls (30 pp.: FI 2563)

John Greenleaf Whittier (incomplete, 142 pp.: HM 12005)

Letter to a Young Contributor (30 pp.: FI 2564)

The Life of Birds (26 pp.: HM 12182)

Life of John Greenleaf Whittier (revised version, partly autograph, 257 pp.: HM 12004)

Letters: 99 (1851–1910)

Documents: 1 (1877)

Other:

[Quotation] (1 slip: HM 22632)

HILDRETH, Charles Lotin, *American novelist, poet,* 1858–96

Verse:

"Or slumbers she in palmy dells" (Kane Literary Collection)

HILL, Edwin Bliss, *American printer, author,* 1866–1949

Prose:

[Essay on the history of his private press] (typewritten, 5 pp. Also, list of works printed: Hill Collection)

Letters: 7 (1931–45), and several hundred letters addressed to him

HILL, Grace Livingston, *American novelist,* 1865–1947

Letters: 2 (1936–39)

HILL, John, *English author,* 1716?–75

Letters: 2 (1750–58)

HILL, Robert, *English learned tailor,* 1699–1777

Prose:

An Enquiry into the Nature of Apparitions (RB 131213, vol. 4)

Letters: 1 (1757)

HILLARD, George Stillman, *American lawyer, author,* 1808–79

Verse:

T. E. R. (Kane Literary Collection)

Letters: 173 (1835–78)

HILLYER, Robert Silliman, *American poet, novelist,* 1895–1961

Letters: 4 (1930–49)

HOARE, Prince, *English artist, author,* 1755–1834

Letters: 2 (1790–1808)

HOBART, Alice Tisdale (Nourse), *American author,* 1882–1967

Letters: 1 (1935)

HOBHOUSE, John Cam, Baron Broughton, *English statesman, author,* 1786–1869

Prose:

[Article inserted in "The Traveler," in *Letters and Journals of Lord Byron*] (3 pp.: RB 90327, vol. 4, p. 612)

Letters: 17 (1813–51)

HOCKING, William Ernest, *American educator, author,* 1873–1966

Letters: 13 (1929–41)

HODGE, Frederick Webb, *English-born American ethnologist, author of books on the American Indian,* 1864–1956

Letters: 50 (1893–1934)

HODGSON, John Evan, *English painter,* 1831–95

Letters: 1 (1882)

HOFFMAN, Arthur Sullivant, *American editor, author,* 1876–1966

Letters: 24 (1922–36), including 23 to Eugene Lafayette Cunningham

HOFFMAN, Daniel Gerard, *American author,* 1923–
Letters: 7 (1962–66)

HOFFMAN, Elwyn Irving, *American journalist, writer,* ca. 1870–ca. 1949

Prose:

Notebooks, 1939–48 (Hoffman Collection)

Letters: 27 (1900–45), and 250 addressed to him

Other:

[List of works published] (Hoffman Collection)

HOGAN, Robert Goode, *American educator,* author, 1930–

Prose:

An Introduction to Joseph Holloway by Robert Hogan and Michael J. O'Neill (typewritten, 17 pp.: Dublin Magazine Collection)

Letters: 8 (1962–67)

HOGARTH, William, *English engraver, painter,* 1697–1764
[Note on 2 pictures sold] (HM 7187)

HOGG, James, *Scottish poet-writer,* 1770–1835

Verse:

The Descent of Love (HM 12409)

Queen Hynde (HM 12412)

The Skylark (HM 12409)

Prose:

A Few Remarkable Adventures of Sir Simon Brodie (26 pp.: HM 12410)

Some Remarkable Passages in the Life of an Edinburgh Baillie (80 pp.: HM 12411)

Letters: 6 (1816–32)

HOLCROFT, Thomas, *English dramatist, author,* 1745–1809

Documents: 1 (1791)

HOLDER, Charles Frederick, *American naturalist, author,* 1851–1915

Letters: 6 (1911–14)

HOLL, Francis Montague, *English painter,* 1845–88

Letters: 1 (1882)

HOLLAND, James, *English water-color painter,* 1800–70

Letters: 2 (1863–65)

HOLLAND, Josiah Gilbert, *American editor, poet, novelist,* 1819–81

Verse:

False and True (HM 12188)

Jacob Hurd's Child (HM 12185)

A Threnody (HM 12186)

To My Dog "Blanco" (HM 12187)

Prose:

Art and Life (52 pp.: HM 12184)

Letters: 10 (1854–80)

Documents: 1 (1878)

HOLLEY, Marietta, *American humorist, writer,* 1836–1926

Prose:

On a Tower (incomplete, 12 pp.: HM 44985)

Letters: 1 (1895)

HOLLIDAY, Robert Cortes, *American editor, essayist, biographer,* 1880–1947

Letters: 1 (1919)

HOLLINGSHEAD, John, *English journalist, theater manager,* 1827–1904

Prose:

Report on the "Alhambra Music Hall and American Bar," Shoreditch (4 pp.: HD 98)

Letters: 13 (1872–89), and 309 letters addressed to him.

Documents: 15 (1860–86), including memoranda and notations concerning the Gaiety Theatre under his management

HOLME, Frank, *American illustrator,* 1868–1904

Prose:

Diaries: 1881–1904 (22 vols.: Hill Collection)

Letters: 134 (1899–1904), and 84 addressed to him

Other:

[Miscellaneous mss. and notes] in Hill Collection

HOLMES, Oliver Wendell, *American physician, essayist, poet,* 1809–94

Verse:

All Here (HM 1222)

"And if I should live to be" [The Last Leaf] (HM 44986)

The Army Hymn: [last stanza only] (HM 12839)

Astraea (HM 12436)

At the Unitarian Festival (HM 8961)

"Chained by the sable Stygian tide" (FI 2279)

The Chambered Nautilus (HM 12452)

[Extracts from a Medical Poem]: The Stability of Science [and] A Portrait (FI 2281)

"Had I the tongues of Greeks and Jews" (FI 2188)

"Lord of the universe, shield us and guide us" (HM 8282; and another copy in Kane Literary Collection)

The Last Leaf (copy, signed by Holmes: HM 12448)

The Last Leaf (incomplete: HM 12443)

"O sexton of the alcoved tomb" (HM 35075)

Old Ironsides (2 copies: HM 12442, HM 7730)

The Old Man of the Sea (fragment: HM 8962)

Reflections of a Proud Pedestrian (2 fragments: HM 12450, FI 2280)

A Rhymed Lesson (Urania): [extract] (FI 2272)

"The shadows of evening have fallen around us" (FI 2271)

A Song of Other Days (FI 2275)

The Star Spangled Banner: [an additional stanza] (HM 12449)

The Stethoscope Song (FI 2274)

An unpublished verse added to "The Dilemma" by O. W. Holmes at the request of Mrs. Greene of New Bedford (FI 2277)

Verses for After Dinner (FI 2276)

"Why linger round the sunken wrecks" (HM 44987)

Prose:

The Autocrat Gives a Breakfast to the Public (15 pp.: HM 12439)

From a letter of the author to the publisher: [preface to the 3rd edition of *Poems* by Oliver Wendell Holmes, Boston, Ticknor & Co., 1849] (2 pp.: FI 2273)

The Great Instrument (24 pp.: FI 2195)

Homeopathy and Its Kindred Delusions: [Lecture I] (39 pp.: HM 12441)

Homeopathy and Its Kindred Delusions: [beginning of Lecture II] (3 pp.: FI 2278)

The Human Wheel, its Spokes and Felloes (29 pp.: FI 2189)

Letter from the last man left by the deluge of the year 1964 to the last woman left by the same (3 pp.: FI 5080)

The Minister Plenipotentiary (16 pp.: HM 12438)

Oration Before the City Authorities of Boston on July 4, 1863 (HM 12440)

Our Progressive Independence (49 pp., part printed: FI 2269)

The Professor at the Breakfast Table (3 vols.: HM 12451)

A Visit to the Autocrat's Landlady (22 pp.: HM 12437)

The Wormwood Cordial of History (18 pp.: FI 2270)

Letters: 186 (1844–94)

Other:

[Marginal corrections in printed copy of the poem, "Each heart has its own secret"] (RB 71399)

[Manuscript correction in privately printed copy of *Poem for the opening of the Fifth Avenue Theatre,* December 3, 1873] (RB 89097)

HOLT, Francis Ludlow, *English legal writer,* 1780–1844

Letters: 2 (1809–36)

HOLT, Henry, *American publisher, author,* 1840–1926

Letters: 55 (1890–1923), including 40 to Mary (Hunter) Austin

HOLZAPFEL, Rudolph Patrick, *Irish author,* 1938–

Letters: 4 (1964–67)

HOME, Henry, Lord Kames, *Scottish judge and author,* 1696–1782

Prose:

The extracts Ld Kaimes made from my letter on ornament, with his alterations (2 leaves: MO 1163)

Letters: 11 (1766–73)

HOME, John, *English author,* 1722–1808

Letters: 12 (1799–1804)

HONE, William, *English author, bookseller,* 1780–1842

Verse:

[Sonnet beginning] "Dear to my soul . . ." (RB 137399, vol. 1)

Prose:

Manuscript Written for and Partly Used by Richard Carlile in His Trial (20 pp.: RC 544)

Letters: 11 (1821–31)

HOOD, Thomas, *English poet,* 1799–1845

Verse:

The Dream of Eugene Aram (forgery: HM 12385)

The Headlong Career and Woful Ending of Precocious Piggy (in the hand of his son, Thomas Hood, with the latter's drawings: HM 12406)

Letters: 24 (1826–44), plus one forgery (HM 12384)

Other:

[Two drawings] (FR 123, HM 13304)

HOOD, Thomas, *English humorist*, 1835–74

Prose:

Preface for an Edition of the Works of Thomas Hood, the Elder (HM 12386)

Letters: 9 (ca. 1865)

HOOK, James, *English organist, composer*, 1746–1827

Letters: 1 (n.d.)

HOOK, Theodore Edward, *English novelist*, 1788–1841

Verse:

Sacred to Genius be This Festive Day (RB 320006, vol. 2)

Chacun a Son Gout (HM 12382)

Letters: 17 (1830–40)

HOOKER, Forrestine (Cooper), *American novelist*, 1867–1932

Verse:

The Desert Sleeps (HM 34836)

The Prisoner (HM 34841)

The Star of Destiny (HM 34837)

Letters: 16 (1921–31)

HOOLE, John, *English translator, writer*, 1727–1803

Letters: 1 (1800)

HOPE, James Barron, *American poet*, 1829–87

Letters: 6 (1866–86)

HOPKINS, Samuel, *American clergyman, author*, 1721–1803

Prose:

Samuel Hopkins—his Book: [pocket-book containing memoranda on theological questions and related topics, accompanied by notes for 42 sermons] (42 pieces: HM 670)

Letters: 1 (1768)

HOPKINSON, Francis, *American jurist, musician, essayist, pamphleteer*, 1737–91

Verse:

Collection of Verse and Prose, in two volumes: (HM 1267)

Vol. I: Poems on several subjects

Vol. II: Miscellanies in Verse and Prose

Letters: 4 (1772–78)

Documents: 1 (1778)

HOPKINSON, Joseph, *American jurist, author of "Hail Columbia,"* 1770–1842

Letters: 5 (1801–38)

HORGAN, Paul, *American librarian, novelist*, 1903–

Letters: 3 (1953)

HORNE, Richard Hengist, *English author*, 1803–84

Verse:

[Ballad beginning] "There was a Lord of Scotland" (RB 132351)

Letters: 52 (1837–82)

Documents: 5 (1857–72)

HOSMER, Burr Griswold, *American poet,* fl. 1870–77

Letters: 11 (1870–77)

HOUDINI, Harry, *American magician, escape artist,* 1874–1926

Letters: 2 (1915–23)

HOUGH, Emerson, *American journalist, author,* 1857–1923

Letters: 3 (1906–21)

HOUGH, Henry Beetle, *American editor, publisher, author,* 1896–

[Signed quotation] (Kane Literary Collection)

HOUSMAN, Alfred Edward, *English classical scholar, poet,* 1859–1936

Letters: 1 (1919)

HOUSMAN, Laurence, *English writer, illustrator,* 1865–1959

Verse:

London in War Time: Amended Version (HM 30547)

Letters: 20 (1893–1902)

HOVEY, Richard, *American poet,* 1864–1900

Verse:

Last Songs from Vagabondia (written jointly with Bliss Carman): (HM 35548)

"Who's like us?" (RB 183571)

Prose:

The Plays of Maurice Maeterlinck (18 pp.: HM 12261)

Letters: 2 (1894)

HOW, Louis, *American novelist, poet,* 1873–1947

Letters: 23 (1921–46)

HOWARD, Sidney Coe, *American playwright,* 1891–1939

Letters: 5 (1916–31)

HOWE, Edgar Watson, *American editor, author,* 1853–1937

Letters: 1 (1893) to Albert Bigelow Paine

HOWE, Julia (Ward), *American reformer, author,* 1819–1910

Verse:

Craford's Statue at Richmond (HM 1241)
Battle Hymn of the Republic: [one stanza] (CW 204)
Lyrics of the Street: The Wedding (FI 2608)
The Manuscript (FI 2611)
A New Sculptor (FI 2609)

Letters: 86 (1840–1908)

HOWE, Mark Antony De Wolfe, *American author,* 1864–1960

Letters: 75 (1901–49)

HOWE, Will David, *American educator, editor,* 1873–1946

Letters: 1 (1937)

HOWELLS, William Dean, *American critic, novelist, poet, playwright,* 1837–1920

Verse:

In August (HM 1235)
In Earliest Spring: [last verse only] (HM 41386)
"What right have I to lift my head" (HM 35075)

Prose:

A Florentine Mosaic (157 pp.: HM 12427)

The Rise of Silas Needham: [synopsis of the plot published as *The Rise of Silas Lapham*] (5 pp.: HM 12428)

Letters: 288 (1860–1917), including 29 to James Thomas Fields and 70 to Annie (Adams) Fields

Other:

[List of] articles accepted [for the *Atlantic Monthly*] (1 p.: FI 2344)

HOWITT, Mary (Botham), *English miscellaneous writer,* 1799–1888

Verse:

The Ascent of the Spirit (HM 12373)

Letters: 13 (1847–59)

HOWITT, William, *English miscellaneous writer,* 1792–1879

Verse:

The Christ (HM 32123)

Letters: 5 (1845–69)

HUBBARD, Elbert, *American editor, publisher, author,* 1856–1915

Prose:

Robert Browning (17 pp.: HM 12257)

Letters: 8 (1896–1912)

HUDSON, William Henry, *English naturalist, author,* 1841–1922

Prose:

Fan, the Story of a Young Girl's Life: [corrected proof] (RB 108345)

Pelino Viera's Confessions: [pages from the *Cornhill Magazine,* with revisions for printing in *Tales of the Pampas*] (RB 136406)

HUGHES, John, *English author, artist,* 1790–1857

Verse:

"A is the Autograph, excellent Friend" (RB 109990, vol. 3, pt. 2)

HUGHES, Langston, *American poet, novelist, playwright,* 1902–67

Verse:

Declaration (6 drafts; typewritten, with autograph corrections: California Poetry File)

Let American be America Again (Charles Erskine Scott Wood Collection)

Uncle Tom (6 drafts; typewritten, with autograph corrections: California Poetry File)

Letters: 4 (1935–44)

HUGHES, Rupert, *American novelist, playwright,* 1872–1956

Letters: 10 (1920–52)

HUGHES, Thomas, *English author,* 1822–96

Letters: 13 (1857–70)

HUGO, Victor Marie, Comte, *French writer,* 1802–85

Letters: 6 (1842–74), also, one letter by Adèle Hugo

HUME, David, *English philosopher, historian,* 1711–76

Prose:

History of England: [memoranda and notes] (54 pp.: HM 12263)

Letters: 3 (1754–70)

HUMPHREYS, David, *American revolutionary soldier, statesman, poet,* 1752–1818

Letters: 6 (1780–1801)

HUMPHRIES, George Rolfe, *American educator, poet, translator,* 1894–1969

Verse:

For Good Greeks (GS 115)
"Go up, Thou Bald Head!" (GS 112)
One Flesh (GS 113)
Words to be Flung up a Stairway (GS 114)

Letters: 9 (1924–52)

HUNEKER, James Gibbons, *American musician, critic, author,* 1860–1921

Prose:

Franz Liszt, the Real and Legendary (17 pp.: HM 12417)

Letters: 2 (1905–12)

HUNT, Alfred William, *English landscape painter,* 1830–96

Letters: 2 (ca. 1863–74)

HUNT, James Henry Leigh, *English essayist, poet,* 1784–1859

Verse:

Argument in Brief Quotation (HM 12254)
"Charles, my boy, take heart, take heart" (HM 12250)
"Hear, all ye bold young men" (RB 132351)
Lines on the Birth of Her Majesty's Third Child (HM 12245)
The Love Letter (HM 12249)
Morgiana in England (HM 12243)

On Seeing a Pigeon Make Love (HM 12247)

The Palfry (HM 12252)

The Poets (HM 344)

"A sweet No, no,—with a sweet smile beneath" (HM 12250)

Talari Innamorati (HM 12253)

Three Visions Occasioned by the Birth and Christening of His Royal Highness the Prince of Wales (RB 150341)

Prose:

A line: [introduction only] (RB 131334, vol. 2)

Character of Will Hitter (1 p.: HM 12251)

Christianism (printed text with corrections, 8 pp.: HM 12262)

Commonplace Book (53 p.: HM 12242)

The Double (copy, with corrections in the hand of the author, 56 pp.: HM 12241)

Memorable Names, or a Critical Catalogue of Men Eminent in Literature, Philosophy, or the Arts (14 pp.: HM 12248)

The Religion of the Heart: Household Memorandum—of Religion (6 pp.: HM 12262)

Sayings of Confucius—The Oriental and Grecian Fabulists (8 leaves: HM 12781)

Letters: 24 (1818–55)

Other:

[Manuscript notes in Richard Polwhele's *Theocritus*] (RB 26263)

HUNT, William Henry, *English watercolor painter,* 1790–1864

Letters: 1 (n.d.)

HUNT, William Holman, *English painter,* 1827–1910

Verse:

Christ the Winnower (Hunt/Tupper Collection)

Letters: 227 (1849–1909)

Documents: 2 (1886)

HUNTER, Joseph, *English antiquary, author,* 1783–1861

Letters: 8 (1828–31)

HURLBERT, William Henry, *American editor, author,* 1827–95

Letters: 84 (1857–95)

HURST, Fannie, *American novelist,* 1889–1968

Letters: 35 (1917–57)

HUTTON, Laurence, *American bibliophile, editor, author,* 1843–1904

Letters: 4 (1889–1901)

HUTTON, Richard Holt, *English theologian, journalist,* 1826–97

Letters: 12 (1858–95)

HUXLEY, Aldous Leonard, *English author,* 1894–1963

Letters: 2 (1933–60)

HUXLEY, Thomas Henry, *English man of science,* 1825–95

Letters: 16 (1856–93)

HYNE, Charles John Cuteliffe Wright, *novelist, short-story writer,* 1866–1944

Letters: 13 (1893–1929)

Other:

[Signed quotation] (Kane Literary Collection)

I

INCHBALD, Elizabeth (Simpson), *English novelist, actress, dramatist,* 1753–1821

Letters: 2 (1817 and n.d.)

INGELOW, Jean, *English poet,* 1820–97

Verse:

Echo and the Ferry (in the hand of Mary E. Griswold: MC 545)

Prose:

John Jerome (315 pp.: HM 17250)

Letters: 10 (1865–89)

INGERSOLL, Charles Jared, *American lawyer, author,* 1782–1862

Letters: 5 (1808–61)

INGERSOLL, Robert Green, *American orator, agnostic, author,* 1833–99

Letters: 8 (1876–88)

INGRAHAM, Joseph Holt, *American clergyman, novelist,* 1809–60

Letters: 1 (1859)

IRELAND, Alexander, *English journalist, man of letters,* 1810–94

Letters: 10 (1868–86) to James Thomas Fields and Annie (Adams) Fields

IRELAND, Samuel, *English author, engraver,* d. 1800

Prose:

Annotations on the Shakespeare Manuscripts in Answer to Malone (240 pp.: HM 725)

Journal of Tours in England and France (109 pp.: HM 31435)

Catalogue of Hogarth's Works (12 leaves: HM 31426)

Journal of a Tour in North Wales (fragment, 1 p.: RB 287197)

IRELAND, William Henry, *English forger, writer,* 1777–1835

Verse:

"T' other morning the little God Love" (HM 7136)

Prose:

Frogmore Fete (not autograph, 35 pp.: HM 31427)

Letters: 13 (1805–30)

Other:

[Verses:] "To celebrate His Fame ye Virgin Choir" [ascribed by Ireland to his mother] (RB 287197)

[Many examples of his forgeries, including those in his *An Authentic Account of the Shaksperian Manuscripts etc.* (RB 143037)

[Typescript copied by G. Hilder Libbis from the 1799 edition of *Henry the Second*] (76 pp.: HM 31433)

IRVING, Sir Henry, *English actor,* 1838–1905

Letters: 120 (1875–1904), including 109 to Clement Scott

IRVING, Joseph, *English author, journalist,* 1830–91

Letters: 1 (1871) to Thomas Carlyle.

IRVING, Washington, *American author,* 1783–1859

Prose:

The Conspiracy of Neamathla (24 pp.: HM 3172)

Conversations with Talma (18 pp.: HM 3147)

[The Early Experiences of Ralph Ringwood] (58 pp.: HM 3175)

A History of New York (the 1854 edition extra-illustrated with numerous corrected proof sheets and pages from previous editions, and about 250 pages of manuscript additions, 2 vols.: HM 3131)

[Life of Washington: chap. IX, vol. 4] (92 pp.: HM 3190)

[Life of Washington: chap. XXIX and XXX, vol. 5] (46 pp.: HM 3160)

[Life of Washington: chap. XXXIII, vol. 4] (16 pp.: HM 3170)

[Life of Washington: chap. XXXIII, vol. 5] (14 pp.: HM 3161)

[Notebook of memoranda for his "History of New York"] (47 pp.: HM 3171)

[Notebook—containing notes for The Conspiracy of Neamathla] (21 pp.: HM 3151)

[Notes copied by Irving from an article in The British Review and Critical Literary Magazine] (4 pp.: HM 580)

The Seminoles (13 pp.: HM 2265)

[Tales of a Traveler] (7 tales, 185 pp.: HM 3183)

The Tuileries and Windsor Castle (12 pp.: HM 3133)

[Wolfert's Roost: notes] (66 pp.: HM 3150)

Letters: 41 (1819–59)

Documents: 1 (1839)

Other:

[Comments on his *History of the Life and Voyages of Christopher Columbus*] (RB 131334, vol. 2)

[Corrections on proof sheets of Allibone's biographical sketch of Irving] (RB 151882)

IRWIN, Wallace, *American author,* 1876–1959

Letters: 3 (1909–29)

IRWIN, William Henry, *American editor, author,* 1873–1948

Letters: 7 (1923–42)

Other:

[Signed sentiment] (Kane Literary Collection)

ISHAM, Samuel, *American artist, author,* 1855–1914

Letters: 1 (n.d.)

J

JACKSON, Helen Maria (Fiske) Hunt, *American novelist, poet,* 1830–85

Verse:

Aunt Jane's Lesson (HM 7836)

Burnt Offering (HM 7832)

A Funeral March (HM 7835)

Growths (HM 7830)

A Happy Woman's Fancy (HM 7833)

The Heart of a Rose (HM 11905)

The Indian's Cross and Star (HM 7828)

King Redwald's Altars (HM 11906)

The King's Friends (HM 7825)

The Last Words (HM 11907)

March (HM 7823)

A Measure of Hours (HM 7834)

My Little Argonaut (HM 7826)

Not As I Will (James Collection)

On the Death of Miss Charlotte Cushman: [2nd stanza only] (HM 7829)

The Pilgrim Forefathers (HM 7822)

The Prairie Dolly (HM 7824)

Refrain (HM 7827)

The Song He Never Wrote (HM 11904)

To Oliver Wendell Holmes on His Seventieth Birthday (HM 7205)

Torcello (HM 7821)

An Unknown Man Respectably Dressed (HM 7831)

Prose:

Bits of Travel at Home—A Colorado Week (44 pp.: HM 7820)

One Woman and Sunshine (25 pp.: HM 11908)

The Story of Clotilde Danarosch (93 pp.: HM 7819)

Letters: 154 (1852–85)

JACKSON, Henry Rootes, *American lawyer, editor, poet,* 1820–98

Letters: 1 (1892)

Documents: 15 (1861)

JACKSON, Joseph Henry, *American editor, literary critic,* 1894–1955

Letters: 2 (1939–40)

JAMES, Edwin, *American explorer, naturalist, author,* 1797–1861

Letters: 1 (1827)

JAMES, George Payne Rainsford, *English novelist, historical writer,* 1799–1860

Prose:

Life of Louis XIV (incomplete, 19 pp.: HM 11902)

Letters: 48 (1826–56)

Drawings: 1 (1852)

JAMES, George Wharton, *American editor, author,* 1858–1923

Prose:

81 sermons and lectures (James Collection)

51 articles on the West, California missions, and literature, religion, and travel (Also: a notebook on India, and miscellaneous notes: James Collection)

Letters: 76 (1899–1923)

Documents: 2 (1906–08)

Other:

[Personal accountbooks, 1883–88] (James Collection)

[2 Scrapbooks of correspondence and clippings] (James Collection)

JAMES, Henry, *American lecturer, author,* 1811–82

Letters: 4 (1870–74), including 3 to Annie (Adams) Fields and 1 to James Thomas Fields

JAMES, Henry, *American novelist,* 1843–1916

Prose:

The Correspondence of Carlyle and Emerson (27 pp.: HM 11911)

Four Meetings (71 pp.: HM 11910)

Letters: 173 (ca. 1883–1915)

Documents: 1 (1902)

JAMES, Will, *American artist, author,* 1892–1942

Letters: 1 (1927) to Neeta Marquis

JAMES, William, *American educator, psychologist, author,* 1842–1910

Letters: 4 (1894–1909)

JAMESON, Anna Brownell (Murphy), *Irish author,* 1794–1860

Letters: 6 (1844–55)

JANVIER, Margaret Thomson, *American poet,* 1844–1913

Verse:

Veiled (HM 34954)

JANVIER, Thomas Allibone, *American journalist, author,* 1849–1913

Verse:

Charity Children Going to Mass (HM 35075)

Prose:

Chiquita (54 pp.: HM 7862)

Letters: 3 (1898–1902)

JEFFERIES, Richard, *English naturalist, novelist,* 1848–87

Prose:

An English Deer Park (78 pp.: HM 11899)

JEFFERS, Robinson, *American poet,* 1887–1962

Verse:

Rock and Hawk (HM 44999)

Letters: 27 (1924–38)

JEFFERSON, Joseph, *American actor, author,* 1829–1905

Letters: 5 (1870–1903)

JEFFREY, Francis, Lord Jeffrey, *Scottish judge, critic,* 1773–1850

Letters: 13 (1804–47)

JENKS, Tudor Storrs, *American editor, author,* 1857–1922

Letters: 5 (1902–11)

JENNINGS, Leslie Nelson, *American author,* 1890–1972

Verse:

Encounter (GS 173)
The Gray Rain (GS 173)
Half-Past Two (GS 171)
Judith (GS 169)
The Last Grecian (GS 174)
Moment Triste (GS 168)
Passage (GS 170)
Refutation (GS 172)

Letters: 38 (1917–22) to George Sterling

JERNINGHAM, Edward, *English poet, dramatist,* 1727–1812

Verse:

The Queen of Diamonds to Miss Jerningham (JE 523)

Prose:

[Miscellaneous notes and compositions—5 pieces] (JE 533)

Letters: 12 (1764–95), and 1,103 letters addressed to him

JERDAN, William, *English journalist,* 1782–1869

Letters: 24 (1820–60)

Other:

[List of headings] (FI 2840)

JEROME, Jerome Klapka, *English novelist, playwright,* 1859–1927

Letters: 7 (1888–1911)

JERROLD, Douglas William, *English author,* 1803–57

Letters: 13 (1835–60)

JESSE, Edward, *English writer on natural history,* 1780–1868

Letters: 22 (1854–67) to James Thomas Fields and Annie (Adams) Fields

JEWETT, Sarah Orne, *American author,* 1849–1909

Prose:

The Coon Dog (36 pp.: HM 11900)

Jack's Merry Christmas (55 pp.: HM 1268)

Miss Tempy's Watcher's (fragment, 1 p.: HM 1905)

Letters: 6 (1902–06)

JEWSBURY, Maria Jane, *English author,* 1800–33

Letters: 3 (1827 and n.d.)

JODRELL, Richard Paul, *English dramatist, classical scholar,* 1745–1831

Prose:

On the Quadriga of Helios or the Sun (RB 131334, vol. 1)

JOHN, Augustus Edwin, *English painter, etcher,* 1878–1961

Verse:

Lines Written to a Young Lady on the Author Being Confined to His Bed of a Stiff Neck (HM 28269)

"Sometimes of a Lovely Umria forsook" (HM 28257)

Letters: 106 (1906–56) to Alexandra Schepeler

Other:

His son asleep at the cafe table (HM 28248)

Drawing of himself (1906: HM 28278)

Drawing, self-portrait (1907: HM 28281)

Drawing, self-portrait, back view, in new suit (1906: HM 28259)

Drawing: "Heard from Alick lately?" (HM 28291)

Three sketches (HM 28287)

JOHNS, Cloudesley Tremenhere, *American journalist and friend of Jack London,* fl. 1899–1955

Verse:

It's Nice to Be Alive (carbon copy: Borchart Collection)

Prose:

Who the Hell is Cloudesley Johns: [an autobiography] (typewritten, with corrections, 580 pp.: HM 42387)

Letters: 114 (1903–55)

Documents: 1 (1899)

JOHNS, Orrick, *American poet,* 1887–1946

Letters: 82 (1911–34)

JOHNSON, Burges, *American educator, poet, humorist,* 1877–1963

Letters: 3 (1926–27) to Mary (Hunter) Austin

JOHNSON, Helen Louise (Kendrick), *American editor, author,* 1844–1917

Letters: 1 (1902)

JOHNSON, Henry, *American educator, poet, translator of Dante,* 1855–1918

Letters: 1 (1874)

JOHNSON, James Weldon, *American novelist, poet,* 1871–1938

Letters: 2 (1924–25)

JOHNSON, Merle DeVore, *American illustrator, bibliographer,* 1874–1935

Letters: 2 (1912–22)

JOHNSON, Oliver, *American editor, abolitionist, author,* 1809–89

Letters: 2 (1882–87)

JOHNSON, Owen McMahon, *American author,* 1878–1952

Letters: 1 (1928)

JOHNSON, Robert Underwood, *American editor, poet,* 1853–1937

Verse:

"Oh, could Earth and Time assemble" (RB 130193)

Letters: 54 (1882–1921)

JOHNSON, Rossiter, *American editor, author,* 1840–1931

Letters: 4 (1869–1918)

JOHNSON, Samuel, *English lexicographer, writer, critic,* 1709–84

Verse:

Ad T[homam] L[aurentiam] (HM 675)

[Ode de Skia Insula] (HM 17355)

"Long-expected one and twenty" [satirical poem on the coming of age of Sir John Lade] (HM 2583)

Prose:

Diary (3 pp.: HM 2599)

[Queries on the Latin Language] (1 p.: HM 673)

[Suggested Improvements or Alterations in the Latin of Dr. Thomas Lawrence's *De natura animali*] (4 pp.: HM 674)

Letters: 26 (1746–84)

Documents: 1 (1759)

JOHNSTON, Mary, *American novelist,* 1870–1936

Letters: 5 (1900–09)

JOHNSTON, Richard Malcolm, *American educator, novelist, essayist,* 1822–98

Prose:

The Hotel Experience of Mr. Pink Fluker (21 pp.: HM 7213)

The Wimpy Adoptions (55 pp.: HM 7214)

Letters: 7 (1885–95)

JONES, Charles Colcock, *American historian,* 1831–93

Letters: 86 (1867–93)

Other:

[Manuscript corrections in printed copy of *The Siege of Savannah*] (RB 96376)

JONES, Charles Melancthon, *American author,* fl. 1865–76

Letters: 83 (1865–76) to Bayard Taylor

JONES, Henry Arthur, *English playwright,* 1851–1929

Letters: 7 (1885–95)

JONES, Richard, *English actor, dramatist,* 1779–1851

Letters: 3 (1817–35)

JONES, Thomas Samuel, *American poet,* 1882–1932

Letters: 2 (1917 and n.d.)

JONSON, Ben, *English dramatist, poet,* 1573?–1637

Verse:

An Expostulacion with Inigo Jones (copy: EL 8729)

The Gypsies metamorphos'd [a masque] (Contemporary copy, 61 pp.: HM 741)

[Poems ascribed to him in commonplace books] HM 172; HM 198; HM 904; EL 8729)

Other:

Note on fly-leaf of his *Seianus* (RB 60659)

JORDAN, David Starr, *American educator, author,* 1851–1931

Verse:

Viverols (typewritten: GS 175)

Letters: 52 (1892–1915)

JORDAN, Dorothy (Bland), *English actress,* 1762–1816

Letters: 536 (1796–1811)

JORDAN, Elizabeth (Garver), *American critic, novelist, playwright,* 1867–1947

Letters: 7 (1900–12)

JORDAN-SMITH, Paul, see SMITH, Paul Jordan

JOWETT, Benjamin, *English religious and classical scholar,* 1817–93

Letters: 10 (1860–89)

JOYCE, James, *Irish writer,* 1882–1941

Verse:

[Chamber Music: poems numbered I, V, XXIV, XXVIII, XXXIV] (HM 41119)

"Come out to where the youth is met" (HM 41120)

Pomes Penyeach (manuscript of ten of thirteen poems and the title-page; also typescripts: HM 41121)

Prose:

Before Sunrise (an English translation of Gerhart Hauptmann's *Vor Sonnenaufgang,* 199 pp.: HM 41118)

Ulysses: a portion of Penelope (typewritten with ms. corrections, 20 pp.: HM 41122)

Letters: 10 (1907–29)

JUDSON, Edward Zane Carroll, *American writer, "first of the dime novelists,"* 1823–86

Letters: 5 (1878–82)

Other:

[Quotation]: "My Country and my countrymen . . ." (HM 3163)

JUDSON, Emily (Chubbuck), *American author,* 1817–54

Verse:

The Flower (HM 1907)

The Weaver (Kane Literary Collection)

Letters: 1 (1846)

K

KAIN, Richard Morgan, *American educator, author,* 1908–

Prose:

Joyce's World View (typewritten, 14 pp.: Dublin Magazine Collection)

Letters: 8 (1962–65)

KAUFFMAN, Maria Anna Angelica Catharina, *English painter,* 1741–1807

Letters: 1 (1772)

KAUFFMAN, Reginald Wright, *American journalist, novelist, war correspondent,* 1877–1959

Prose:

The House of Bondage (721 pp.: HM 781)

Letters: 4 (1909–16)

KAYE-SMITH, Sheila, *English novelist,* 1887–1956

Letters: 1 (1923)

KAVANAGH, Julia, *English novelist, biographical writer,* 1824–77

Letters: 1 (1864)

KEAN, Charles John, *English actor,* 1811?–68

Letters: 15 (1838–62)

KEAN, Edmund, *English actor,* 1787–1833

Letters: 3 (1819 and n.d.)

KEAN, Ellen (Tree), *English actress,* 1805–80

Letters: 10 (1858–74)

KEATS, John, *English poet,* 1795–1821

Verse:

[The Cap and Bells: stanzas 9–12 only] (HM 7149)

[Nebuchadnezzar's Dream] (HM 1985)

[Otho the Great: Acts IV and V, fragmentary] (HM 11912)

Poems (1817 edition, interleaved copy with notes and additions in the hand of Richard Woodhouse: RB 151852)

Selected sonnets of John Keats (HM 11909)

To Mr. C. C. Clarke (HM 11903)

KEBLE, John, *English divine, poet,* 1792–1866

Verse:

[Volume of Poetry, labeled] "The Christian Year" (HM 44957), contents:

- Forms of Prayer to be Used at Sea
- Gunpowder Treason
- King Charles the Martyr
- The Restoration of the Royal Family
- The Accession
- Ordination

Letters: 2 (n.d.)

KEELER, Charles Augustus, *American poet,* 1871–1937

Verse and Prose:

Approximately 200 poems, articles, and miscellaneous notes as well as several notebooks, included in the collection of Keeler's papers

Letters: 101 (1915–37), and 980 letters addressed to him

Other:

[Manuscript proof of "The Live Oak"] (LF)

KEELER, Harry Stephen, *American editor, author,* 1894–

Letters: 2 (1934) to Eugene Lafayette Cunningham

KEELER, Ralph Olmstead, *American journalist, author,* 1840–73

Letters: 16 (1867–72)

KEENE, Florence Rosina, *American author,* 1878–ca. 1953

Verse:

[Typewritten copies of 40 poems] (California Poetry File)

Prose:

[Article] written in answer to Rev. Driver's attack on Ladies Improvement Club benefit bazaar (typewritten, 2 pp.: Keene Collection)

An Outstanding Individual (typewritten, 5 pp.: Keene Collection)

Letters: 26 (1901–55), and 2,458 letters addressed to her

KEENE, Laura, *English actress,* 1826?–73

Letters: 2 (1859–70)

KELL, Richard Alexander, *Irish educator, author,* 1927–

Letters: 1 (1964)

KELLER, Helen Adams, *American author, lecturer,* 1880–1968

Letters: 8 (1898–1955)

KELLY, Frances Maria, *English actress, singer,* 1790–1882

Verse:

Address (in rhymed verse: Kelly Collection)

Prose:

Memoirs (2 vols.: Kelly Collection)

Letters: 30 (1816–75), and 129 letters addressed to her

Documents: 2 (1826–30)

KELLY, George Edward, *American playwright,* 1887–

Letters: 1 (1926)

KELLY, Michael, *English vocalist, actor, composer,* 1764–1826

Letters: 2 (1800–25)

KEMBLE, Adelaide, see SARTORIS, Adelaide (Kemble)

KEMBLE, Charles, *English actor,* 1775–1854

Letters: 8 (1808–35)

KEMBLE, Elizabeth (Satchel), *English actress,* 1763?–1841

Letters: 1 (1795)

KEMBLE, Frances Anne, *English actress, author,* 1809–93

Verse:

Autumn—written after a ride by the Schuylkill (HM 45058)
Lines Written by the Sea Side (HM 45060)
Morning by the Sea (HM 45060)

On a Hollow Friendship (SL 232)

[Poems, including:] (FI 724)

Lines After a Summer's Walk . . .

Lines on a Young Woman . . .

On Reading with Difficulty Some of Schiller's Early Love Poems

Ode Written on the 22d of August—the Berkshire Jubilee

Sonnet: "Thou art to me, like one in a dream"

Lines Written by the Sea Side

Morning by the Sea Side

Noon Day by the Sea Side

Parting

"Silence—instead of thy sweet song my Bird" (HM 45059)

Sonnet Written among the Ruins of the Castle at Heidelberg (SL 232)

To Shakespeare (HM 45060)

"The voice of childhood blesses me and methought" (SY 219)

Written at Trenton (last 10 lines only: HM 45061)

Letters: 85 (1831–92)

Documents: 1 (1849)

KEMBLE, John Philip, *English actor,* 1757–1823

Letters: 6 (1800–14)

Other:

[Catalog of books and tracts relating to the stage] (81 pp.: HM 12214)

[Note referring to the plays of Mrs. Mary Pix] (1 p.: HM 45000)

KEMBLE, Maria Theresa (De Camp), *English actress,* 1774–1838

Letters: 1 (n.d.)

Documents: 1 (1827)

KEMBLE, Priscilla (Hopkins), *English actress,* 1756–1845

Letters: 1 (1823)

KEMP, Harry Hibbard, *American author,* 1883–1960

Letters: 5 (1915–49)

KENDALL, George Wilkins, *American editor, author,* 1809–67

Letters: 1 (1856)

KENDALL, William A., *American writer,* fl. 1863–67

Verse:

Bear to the Right (HM 35075)

Letters: 5 (1863–67)

KENEALY, Edward Vaughan Hyde, *English barrister,* 1819–80

Verse:

Fragments of verse (HM 38927)

Prose:

[Account of visit and talk with Benjamin Disraeli, 1st Earl of Beaconsfield] (3 pp.: HM 38634)

Memoranda relative to Dr. Maginn not inserted in my Life of him (6 pp.: HM 38640)

[Sketch of Francis Sylvester Mahony: an altered portion of Brallaghan] (2 pp.: HM 38641)

[Obituary of William Maginn] (RB 320006, vol. 1)

Letters: 170 (1837–76)

Other:

[Drawings] (HM 38635–639)

KENNAN, George, *American explorer, journalist, author,* 1845–1924

Verse:

Glamour: A Song of the Caucasian Mountaineers (HM 35075)

Prose:

The Mines of Kara (168 pp.: HM 11714)

Letters: 6 (1891–1907)

KENNARD, James, *American author,* 1815–47

Letters: 9 (1841–46) to James Thomas Fields

KENNEDY, John Pendleton, *American educator, editor, author,* 1795–1870

Letters: 7 (1842–65)

KENNEDY, William Sloane, *American author,* 1850–1929

Letters: 2 (1903)

KENNERLEY, Mitchell, *English-born American publisher,* b. 1878

Letters: 6 (1910–22)

KENNEY, James, *English dramatist,* 1780–1849

Letters: 4 (1808–35)

KENT, Rockwell, *American artist, travel writer,* 1882–1971

Letters: 12 (1881–1930)

KENYON, John, *English poet, philanthropist,* 1784–1856

Letters: 4 (1844–52)

KENYON, Theda, *American author,* ca. 1900–

Letters: 1 (1942)

KERR, Orpheus C., see NEWELL, Robert Henry

KESTER, Paul, *American playwright, novelist,* 1870–1933

Letters: 4 (1906–08)

KEY, Francis Scott, *American lawyer, poet,* 1779–1843

Letters: 3 (1817–38)

KILLIGREW, Thomas, *English playwright, courtier,* 1612–83

Letters: 1 (1649)

Documents: 1 (1676)

KILLIGREW, Thomas, *English dramatist,* 1657–1719

Letters: 2 (1715)

KILLIGREW, Sir William, *English dramatist,* 1606–95

Documents: 1 (1678)

KING, Charles, *American president of Columbia College,* 1789–1867

Letters: 8 (1828–65)

Documents: 1 (1852)

KING, Charles, *American soldier, author,* 1844–1933

Letters: 8 (1895–1916)

KING, Clarence, *American geologist, author, mining engineer,* 1842–1901

Prose:

Memo on Boxing Exercises (HM 27827)

[43 scientific notebooks, and miscellaneous notes and manuscripts] (King Collection)

Letters: 110 (1859–92); also, nine letterbooks containing approximately 229 letters (1879–90) (King Collection)

KING, Grace Elizabeth, *American novelist, short-story writer, essayist,* 1851–1932

Prose:

Balcony stories:

La Grande Demoiselle (29 pp.: HM 22755 [1])

Mimi's Marriage (18 pp.: HM 22755 [2])

The Miracle Chapel (17 pp.: HM 22755 [3])

The Story of a Day (31 pp.: HM 22755 [4])

A Crippled Hope (32 pp.: HM 22755 [5])

One of Us (23 pp.: HM 22755 [6])

The Little Convent Girl (35 pp.: HM 22755 [7])

Grandmother's Grandmother (22 pp.: HM 22755 [8])

The Old Lady's Restoration (21 pp.: HM 22755 [9])

Letters: 1 (1895)

KING, Henry, *English poet, Bishop of Chichester,* 1592–1669

Verse:

[Poems ascribed to him in commonplace book] (HM 172)

KING, Thomas, *English actor, dramatist,* 1730–1805

Letters: 3 (1776–1800)

KING, Thomas Starr, *American clergyman, orator, author,* 1824–64

Prose:

Dedication [to Charles Warren Stoddard] (HM 35075)

Letters: 18 (1853–63), including 10 to James Thomas Fields

KINGSLEY, Charles, *English author,* 1819–75

Verse:

Chartist Song (in the hand of Frederick James Furnivall: FU 456)

The Three Fishers (HM 17247)

Letters: 74 (1849–70)

KINGSLEY, Florence (Morse), *American author,* 1859–1937

Letters: 3 (1908–22)

Other:

[Signed quotation] (Kane Literary Collection)

KINNAIRD, Douglas James William, *English author,* 1788–1830

Letters: 1 (n.d.)

KINNEY, Elizabeth Clementine (Dodge) Stedman, *American poet,* 1810–89

Prose:

A Sabbath Among the Mountains of Pennsylvania (8 pp.: HM 1908)

KINNEY, Troy, *American artist, author,* 1871–1938

Letters: 1 (1922)

KIPLING, Rudyard, *English writer*, 1865–1936

Verse:

Barrack Room Ballads—VI, Soldier, Soldier (2 drafts: HM 11887)

How the Day Broke (HM 11886)

Job's Wife (not autograph: HM 1698)

The Lost Legion (HM 35075)

"Mother Rugen's teahouse on the Baltic" (HM 41844)

My Hat (HM 11877)

Retrocession (HM 2585)

Three Sonnets:

Their Consolation

Discovery

Escaped (HM 11882)

To A. E. W.—A Song of St. Valentine (HM 11884)

Prose:

At the End of the Passage (corrected proof: RB 71139)

From Sea to Sea (3 vols., two manifold notebooks, consisting of the original carbon with a few sheets of the duplicate carbon not removed, and one volume of photographs with comments by Kipling—see J. M. Stewart, *Rudyard Kipling, a Bibliographical Catalogue,* 1959, p. 173, for detailed description: HM 12429

Puck of Pook's Hill (corrected proofs for *Ladies Home Journal* for Jan., Feb., Mar. and Apr. 1906):

Weland's Sword (RB 29632)

Young Men at the Manor (RB 29631)

The Knights of the Joyous Venture (RB 29634)

Old Men at Pevensey (RB 29633)

Letters: 19 (1882–1935)

KIRK, John Foster, *American editor, author,* 1824–1904

Letters: 13 (1860–94)

KIRKE, Ellen Warner Olney, *American novelist,* 1842–1928?

Letters: 1 (1899)

Other:

[Signed quotation] (Kane Literary Collection)

KIRKLAND, Caroline Matilda (Stansbury), *American educator, editor, author,* 1801–64

Letters: 4 (1862)

KLEIN, Charles, *American playwright,* 1867–1915

Letters: 1 (n.d.)

KNAPP, Samuel Lorenzo, *American editor, orator, author,* 1783–1838

Letters: 1 (1835)

KNELLER, Sir Godfrey, 1st Bart., *German-born English painter,* 1646–1723

Letters: 2 (1693–1711)

Documents: 1 (1713)

KNIBBS, Harry Herbert, *American poet, novelist,* 1874–1945

Letters: 7 (1916–24)

KNIGHT, Charles, *English author, publisher,* 1791–1873

Letters: 6 (1844–67)

KNOPF, Alfred A., *American publisher,* 1892–

Letters: 72 (1913–55)

KNOWLES, James Sheridan, *English dramatist,* 1784–1862

Letters: 10 (1832–55)

KREYMBORG, Alfred, *American author,* b. 1883

Letters: 5 (1917–22)

KUMMER, Frederic Arnold, *American novelist, playwright,* 1873–1943

Letters: 1 (1921)

KYNE, Peter Bernard, *American novelist,* 1880–1957

Letters: 2 (1908–09)

L

LACY, Walter, *English actor,* 1809–98

Documents: 1 (1866)

LA FARGE, John, *American painter, author,* 1835–1910

Letters: 73 (1864–1909)

Documents: 1 (1893)

LAFLER, Henry Anderson, *American poet,* fl. 1905–06

Verse:

Her Pity (Lafler Collection)

Sonnet: "False, strangely false, am I beyond thy guess" (typewritten: Lafler Collection)

"To tread the strange land . . ." (Lafler Collection)

Letters: 12 (1905–06), including 10 to Nora May French; and 20 letters addressed to Lafler

LA FONTAINE, Jean de, *French poet, fabulist,* 1621–95

Verse:

Le Mari Confesseur: Conte tiré des cent Nouvelles nouvelles (HM 44958)

LAMB, Caroline (Ponsonby), Viscountess Melbourne, *English novelist,* 1785–1828

Verse:

Air—Amidst the flowers fresh and gay (HM 6603)

Letters: 3 (1816–25)

LAMB, Charles, *English essayist, humorist,* 1775–1834

Verse:

Acrostic against Acrostics (HM 11690)

Acrostic to E. B. (HM 11586)

The Boy, the Mother, and the Butterfly (HM 12286)

Catherine Orkney (HM 13302)

Christian Names of Women: To Edith Southey (HM 13302)

Epitaphium Alterum et Valde Melius (HM 11572)

The Fly (HM 13302)

For the Table Book: Gone or Going (signed Elia: HM 13300)

Free Thoughts on Several Eminent Composers (HM 7525)

Lines Suggested by a Sight of Waltham Cross (HM 11515)

On Being Asked to Write in Miss Westwood's Album (HM 11587)

Then Mrs. Gilpin sweetly said . . . (HM 13298)

To the Book (HM 13303)

What is an Album? (HM 11530)

Many additional poems are in letters, including:

To My Sister (HM 7482)

Four sonnets (HM 7483)

To a Young Lady (HM 7485)

The Tomb of Douglass (HM 7485)

To Charles Lloyd (HM 7492)

Written a Twelvemonth after the Events (HM 11637)

To Charles Lloyd (HM 11637)

The Witch (draft: HM 7494)

A Concept of Diabolical Possession (HM 11697)

A Ballad from the German (HM 11697)

Edward, Edward (copy: HM 11697)

The Case Plainly Stated (HM 11695)

Lamb's epilogue to William Godwin's tragedy "Antonio" (HM 11659)

Draft of an epitaph (HM 11571)

Draft of an epitaph (HM 11673)

Hester Savory (HM 13294)

Who first invented work? (HM 7519)

Prose:

An appearance of the Season (draft, 2 pp.: HM 13297)

Commonplace book (mostly in the handwriting of Mary Ann Lamb, 51 pp.: HM 2274)

The Defeat of Time, or A Tale of the Fairies (7 pp.: HM 2275)

Diamond Cut Diamond, or Manners of London Merchants a Hundred Years Ago (1 p.: HM 13299)

Dog Days (3 pp.: HM 7972)

Maid Marion to the Editor—a letter for the Table Book (1 p.: HM 7521)

[A Popular Fallacy] That the Poor Copy the Vices of the Rich (4 pp.: HM 7973)

The Squirrel (1 p.: HM 13296)

To Louisa (Holcroft) Badams (with notes on rules of whist, 3 pp.: HM 13301)

To the Editor of the Every Day Book: the humble petition of an unfortunate day (2 pp.: HM 13295)

Letters: 208 (1796–1834)
Also: handwriting on HM 12270
handwriting on HM 13293
handwriting on HM 510

LAMB, Mary Ann, *English writer,* 1764–1847

Verse:

"Small beauty to your book my lines can lend" (HM 11587)

Letters: 11 (1806–33)

LAMONT, Corliss, *American author,* 1902–

Letters: 4 (1936) to Sara Bard (Field) Wood

LAMPSON, Robin, *American poet, novelist,* 1900–1978

Verse:

Jack London (typewritten: Jack London Collection)
Laughter Out of the Ground (LF)

Letters: 19 (1933–40)

LANDON, Letitia Elizabeth, see MACLEAN, Letitia Elizabeth (Landon)

LANDON, Melville De Lancey, *American humorist,* 1839–1910

Letters: 5 (1898–1904)

LANDOR, Walter Savage, *English author,* 1775–1864

Verse:

130 pieces containing some 247 verses

Prose:

Ms. of the preface of *The Last Fruit off an Old Tree,* with corrections (RB 7864)

Ms. on politics in Bulwer-Lytton's *Life of Lord Lytton* (RB 131334, vol. 1)

Letters: 254 (1813–60); also, 37 (1839–54) by his sister, Elizabeth Savage Landor

Documents: 2 (1857–59)

LANDSEER, Sir Edwin Henry, *English animal painter,* 1802–73

Letters: 11 (1844–67)

LANE, Rose (Wilder), *American author,* 1887–

Letters: 7 (1917–18)

LANG, Andrew, *English scholar, poet,* 1844–1912

Prose:

Aucassin and Nicolette (20 pp.: HM 11384)
The Bishop and the Bogey (16 pp.: HM 11375)
A Black Kipling (11 pp.: HM 11377)
Confessions (3 pp.: HM 11383)
Dogs (12 pp.: HM 44068)
The French Milton (10 pp.: HM 11381)
Introduction to Joseph Shaylor's Pleasures of Literature and Solace of Books (24 pp.: HM 11378)
Irish Fairies (13 pp.: HM 11379)
Novels National and Local (15 pp.: HM 11380)
Parson Kelly (chaps. 1–7 only, 210 pp.: HM 11374)
Scotch Religious Changes (13 pp.: HM 11376)
The Second Sight (16 pp.: HM 17242)

Letters: 65 (1888–1910), including 56 to H. Clifford-Smith

LANIER, Clifford Anderson, *American author*, 1844–1908

Verse:

At Peace (HM 44725)

To Sidney Lanier (FI 2871)

LANIER, Henry Wysham, *American editor, publisher, author*, 1873–1958?

Letters: 21 (1901–13)

LANIER, Sidney, *American critic, musician, poet, novelist*, 1842–81

Verse:

At First (copy, in the hand of Mary [Day] Lanier: HM 44726)

Clover (HM 44727)

The Crystal (HM 44728)

Nilsson (copy, in the hand of John Banister Tabb: HM 44729)

On a Palmetto (copy in hand of Mary [Day] Lanier: HM 44730)

A Song of Eternity in Time (HM 44731)

Street Cries—VII. A Song of Love (HM 44732)

To Bayard Taylor (HM 7977)

Prose:

King Arthur and his Knights of the Round Table (30 pp.: HM 7996)

San Antonio Letters (14 pp.: HM 7971)

The Story of a Proverb (24 pp.: HM 7997)

Letters: 7 (1872–80)

LANMAN, Charles, *American explorer, librarian, artist, author,* 1819–95

Letters: 13 (1849–80)

LARCOM, Lucy, *American poet, editor, author,* 1824–93

Verse:

Asleep or Awake (HM 7994)

"The battle of our life is won" (RB 5751)

Elizabeth (HM 7981)

Gipsy Children's Song (HM 7988)

Good Bye! (FI 2893)

"Good friends, your entertainment" (HM 44733)

Grace's Friends (HM 7980)

Hal's Birthday (HM 7986)

His Burial Day (HM 7980)

In Time's Swing (HM 7987)

Misread (HM 1246)

The Rivulet (HM 7984)

"Round the rocks of Marblehead" (HM 44734)

Snow Fancies (HM 7989)

Swinging on a Birch Tree (HM 7983)

"There is no chance, no destiny, no fate" (RB 5751)

To the Unknown and Absent Author of "How They Climbed Chocorua" (HM 858)

Under the Trees (HM 44735)

Valley and Peak (HM 1906)

The Volunteer's Thanksgiving (HM 7993)

Prose:

How Margery Wondered (4 pp.: HM 7990)

The Lights on the Bridge (2 pp.: HM 7992)

Patty Mudge's Pies (7 pp.: HM 7991)

Letters: 42 (1855–92)

LARPENT, John, *English inspector of plays,* 1741–1824)

John Larpent, after posts in the foreign service and a term as secretary to the Duke of Bedford in Paris and to the Marquis of Hertford in Ireland, was appointed to the position of Examiner of Plays in November, 1778. This office had been created according to the enactment of the licensing act of 1737, requiring that all plays be submitted for licensing before their presentation. Larpent continued as Examiner until his death in 1824.

Subject matter: the collection consists of 2,502 official copies of plays submitted for licensing between 1737 and 1824.

Significant persons: a complete list of persons represented (as well as the unidentified items in the collection) appears in the Appendix of this guide.

Physical description: the plays are bound individually; most are written by professional copyists, while some are completely or partially in the authors' handwriting.

Source: acquired as part of the Ellesmere Collection in 1917.

Bibliography: MacMillan, Dougald, *Catalogue of the Larpent Plays in the Huntington Library,* San Marino, Calif., 1939.

Letters: 2 (1819–20)

LA SHELLE, Kirke, *American author,* fl. 1902–46

Letters: 10 (1902–46)

LATHAM, Harold Strong, *American editor, author,* 1887–1969

Letters: 99 (1910–22)

LATHROP, George Parsons, *American editor, author,* 1851–98

Letters: 8 (1887–97)

LATIMER, Mary Elizabeth (Wormeley), *American author,* 1822–1904

Letters: 2 (1892–94)

LATROBE, Christian Ignatius, *Moravian musician,* 1758–1836

Prose:

Journal of Journeys to Lyme Regis, Dorset (74 pp.: HM 31023)

Letters: 2 (1820–33)

LAUD, William, *English Archbishop of Canterbury,* 1573–1645

Letters: 22 (1630–40)

LAUT, Agnes Christina, *American author,* 1871–1936

Letters: 4 (1915–20)

LAWRENCE, David Herbert, *English novelist,* 1885–1930

Verse:

Eagle in New Mexico (HM 44740)

Letters: 4 (1914–20); also, 2 letters (1946) by Frieda (von Richthofen) Lawrence (in Walker Winslow Collection)

LAWRENCE, George Alfred, *English novelist,* 1827–76

Letters: 1 (n.d.)

LAWRENCE, Sir Thomas, *English painter,* 1769–1830

Letters: 15 (1801–29)

LAWSON, John Howard, *American playwright,* 1895–

Prose:

Memorial Services for Theodore Dreiser: two eulogies (joint author with Allan Hunter: HM 36322)

LAZARUS, Emma, *American poet, essayist,* 1849–87

Verse:

Sunrise (HM 1233)

Letters: 1 (1883)

LEA, Tom, *American artist, author,* 1907–

Letters: 2 (1963)

LEACH, Henry Goddard, *American author, editor,* 1880–1970

Letters: 2 (1927–37), including 1 to Anna (Strunsky) Walling

LEAR, Edward, *English artist, author,* 1812–88

Verse:

Mr. and Mrs. Discobbolos (FI 5083)

Nonsense Rhyme and drawing (Art Gallery 64.1)

Letters: 85 (1852–86), including 77 to William Holman Hunt

Other:

[Caricature of himself in his letter to James Thomas Fields on October 15, 1879] (FI 5083)

LECKY, William Edward Hartpole, *Irish historian, essayist,* 1838–1903

Letters: 10 (1865–98)

LEE, Albert, *American editor, author,* 1868–1946

Letters: 14 (1903–08)

LEE, Eliza Buckminster, *American author,* ca. 1788–1864

Letters: 16 (1842–63)

LEE, Sir Sidney, *English editor, scholar,* 1859–1926

Letters: 8 (1893–1904)

LEE, Sophia, *English novelist, dramatist,* 1750–1824

Letters: 1 (n.d.)

LEE, Vernon, see PAGET, Violet

LEECH, John, *English humorous artist,* 1817–64

Letters: 8 (1847–52)

Other:

[Miscellaneous pencil and ink sketches] (8 pp.: HM 10489)

LEFANU, Alicia (Sheridan), *English playwright,* 1753–1817

Letters: 1 (1817)

LE GALLIENNE, Richard, *English man of letters,* 1866–1947

Verse:

"All the wide world is but the thought of you" (HM 11701)
"And now the merry way we took" (RB 12781)
"At last I got a letter from the dead" (HM 11704)
A Ballad of Bindings (HM 44744)
A Ballade of Old Laughter (HM 44745)
"The dotted cays" (RB 12786)
"I said I care not if I can" (HM 11700)

June (HM 11699)

Love in Spain (HM 44747)

"Through the many to the one" (RB 279947)

"Time, like a spider . . ." (RB 13441)

To a Wild Bird (HM 11703)

Women and War (HM 44749)

Prose:

Delicatessen Days (6 pp.: HM 11698)

The English Countryside (12 pp.: HM 11709)

The Fourth of July (7 pp.: HM 44746)

Frederic Chopin and George Sand (16 pp.: HM 11706)

The Life Romantic (162 pp.: HM 11712)

The Love Story of Dante Gabriel Rossetti and Elizabeth Siddal (15 pp.: HM 11708)

The Love Story of Robert Browning and Elizabeth Barrett (18 pp.: HM 11705)

Mary Stewart and Pierre Chastelard (11 pp.: HM 11707)

The Migration of the Gods (9 pp.: HM 44748)

Neighbors (8 pp.: HM 11710)

The Quest of the Golden Girl (269 pp.: HM 848)

Rudyard Kipling, a Critical Causerie (128 pp.: HM 11711)

The Syncopated Lovers (10 pp.: HM 17243)

Letters: 8 (1897–1908)

LEGARE, Hugh Swinton, *American statesman, editor,* 1797–1843

Letters: 8 (1832–43)

LEGGETT, William, *American editor, author,* 1802–39

Letters: 1 (1834)

LEIGHTON, Frederick, Baron Leighton of Stretton, *English painter,* 1830–96

Letters: 25 (1856–90)

LELAND, Charles Godfrey, *American editor, humorist, essayist,* 1824–1903

Prose:

Visiting Gypsies (24 pp.: HM 10492)

Letters: 11 (1860–91)

LE MAY, Alan, *American novelist,* 1899–

Letters: 1 (1932) to Neeta Marquis

LEMON, Mark, *English writer, editor,* 1809–70

Letters: 15 (1843–70)

LENNOX, Lord William Pitt, *English miscellaneous writer,* 1799–1881

Letters: 3 (1829–30)

LENTON, Francis, *English poet,* fl. 1630–40

Verse:

Queene Ester's Haliluiahs and Hamans Madrigalls Expressed in a Sacred Poem, with the Translation and Illustration of the 83 Psalme (EL 6872)

Queene Esters Haliluiahs and Hamans Madrigalls . . . , a sacred poeme (HM 120)

LEONARD, Sterling Andrus, *American author,* 1888–1931

Letters: 2 (1928)

LEONOWENS, Anna Harriette (Crawford), *English author, teacher at court of Siam,* 1834–1914

Letters: 49 (1873–1911) to Annie (Adams) Fields

LESLIE, Charles Robert, *English painter,* 1794–1859

Letters: 4 (1837–58)

LESLIE, Eliza, *American author,* 1787–1858

Letters: 5 (1841–52)

LESLIE, Frank, *American wood engraver, publisher, editor,* 1821–80

Letters: 5 (1858–78)

LESTER, Charles Edwards, *American author,* 1815–90

Letters: 2 (1850–84)

L'ESTRANGE, Sir Roger, *English Tory, journalist, pamphleteer,* 1616–1704

Letters: 1 (1674)

LEVER, Charles James, *English novelist,* 1806–72

Prose:

Notebook, 1849–1860 (70 pp.: HM 270)
Notebook, 1861–1864 (140 pp.: HM 240)
Notebook, 1867–1870 (180 pp.: HM 241)
Notebook, 1870–1871 (79 pp.: HM 271)
Notebook, 1871–1872 (60 pp.: HM 269)
Post book, 1864–1867 (76 pp.: HM 272)

Letters: 321 (1835–70)

LEVIEN, Sonya, *American author, screenwriter,* 1888?–1960

Prose:

[Diaries: 1916–17, 1921, 1924] (Levien Collection)

[Miscellaneous notes and articles on woman's suffrage] (Levien Collection)

[Movie scripts] (approximately 100 scripts: Levien Collection)

Letters: 53 (1911–58), and approximately 400 addressed to her

LEWES, George Henry, *English writer,* 1817–78

Prose:

Copy of Fragmentary Notes in Various Books (in the hand of George Eliot, 70 pp.: HM 12995)

[Problems of Life and Mind: notes preparatory to posthumous publication of vol. 4 by George Eliot] (172 pp.: HM 12994)

Letters: 10 (1848–78)

LEWIS, Alfred Henry, *American editor, author,* 1858–1914

Letters: 10 (1895–1902) to Albert Bigelow Paine

LEWIS, Estelle Anna Blanche (Robinson), *American poet,* 1824–50

Verse:

The Angel's Visit (HM 34243)

"The Forsaken" (stanza 2 only; in the hand of Edgar Allan Poe: HM 34244)

Lament of La Vega (HM 34241)

My Study (HM 34242)

Other:

Marginal notes in William Hazlitt's *Liber Amoris* (RB 25295)

LEWIS, Grace (Hegger), *American author,* fl. 1919–32

Verse:

A Spinster's Holiday (1 p., typewritten: MS 26)

Letters: 18 (1919–32)

LEWIS, Harry Sinclair, *American novelist,* 1885–1951

Prose:

Mr. Cincinnatus: [plot summary] (Jack London Collection)
[Plots for eleven stories] (typewritten: Jack London Collection)

Letters: 48 (1909–49)

Documents: 1 (1914)

LEWIS, Julius Warren (Leon Lewis, pseud.), *American author,* 1833–1920

Prose:

The Millionaire Crook (53 pp.: HM 44750)

LEWIS, Leon, see LEWIS, Julius Warren

LEWIS, Matthew Gregory, *English author,* 1775–1818

Letters: 3 (ca. 1796 and n.d.)

Other:

[Copy, in Lewis's hand, of William Robert Spencer's "Epitaph on a Dog of Lady E. Foster's"] (HM 6627)

LEWIS, Sinclair, see LEWIS, Harry Sinclair

LEWIS, Wyndham, *English novelist, essayist, artist,* 1886–

Letters: 20 (1910–29)

LEWISOHN, Ludwig, *American critic, novelist,* 1883–1955

Letters: 1 (1921) to Mary (Hunter) Austin

LINCOLN, Joseph Crosby, *American author,* 1870–1944

Letters: 2 (1920)

LINDSAY, Nicholas Vachel, *American poet,* 1879–1931

Prose:

The Continental Mood and The American Psychology: Being a discussion of "The Last Laugh" and "He Who Gets Slapped": [motion picture review] (19 pp.: HM 41109)

In "The Golden Book of Springfield" . . . (14 pp.: HM 41107)

Poems and Motion Pictures: Being a Discussion of the $10,000 Adolph Zukor Motion Picture Prize (308 pp.: HM 41110)

The Progress of the Moving Pictures (typewritten, 215 pp.: HM 45443)

A Year with Your Mind: Lesson Three (typewritten, 7 pp.: HM 41108)

Letters: 7 (1913–30)

LINNELL, John, *English painter,* 1792–1882

Letters: 1 (1880)

LINSCOTT, Robert Newton, *American editor,* 1886–1964

Letters: 40 (1919–61)

LINTON, Eliza (Lynn), *English novelist, miscellaneous writer,* 1822–98

Letters: 14 (1858–95)

Other:

[Signed quotation] (Kane Literary Collection)

LINTON, William James, *English engraver, poet, political reformer,* 1812–97

Letters: 1 (1890)

LIPPINCOTT, Sara Jane (Clarke) (Grace Greenwood, pseud.), *American editor, author,* 1823–1904

Verse:

The Little Pilgrim—loquitur (FI 1729)

A Valentine for S[usan] B. A[nthony] (AF 48)

"Amid the poets and the wits" (HM 35075)

Prose:

Haps and Mishaps: [preface only] (2 pp.: FI 1730)

Letters: 85 (1848–1904), including 65 to James Thomas Fields

LIPPMANN, Walter, *American journalist, author,* 1889–1974

Letters: 15 (1915–45)

LITCHFIELD, Grace Denio, *American poet, novelist,* 1849–1944

Letters: 3 (1906–08)

LITTELL, Philip, *American author,* 1868–1943

Letters: 2 (n.d.) to Mary (Hunter) Austin

LIVERMORE, Mary Ashton (Rice), *American editor, reformer,* 1820–1905

Letters: 31 (1869–1904)

LIVINGSTON, Luther Samuel, *American editor,* 1864–1914

Letters: 8 (1902–13)

LLOYD, Charles, *English poet,* 1775–1839

Verse:

To Mr. Jerningham (JE 555)

Prose:

[Author's corrections in *Poems on the Death of Priscilla Farmer, by her Grandson*] (RB 180692)

[Pencil annotations in Coleridge's "Osorio, the Sketch of a Tragedy"] (HM 361)

LLOYD, Everett, *American editor, author,* 1881–1947

Letters: 1 (1931) to Eugene Lafayette Cunningham

LLOYD, Robert, *English poet,* 1733–64

Documents: 1 (1761)

LOCKE, John, *English philosopher,* 1632–1704

Prose:

An Essay Concerning Toleration (42 pp.: HM 584)

Letters: 3 (1678–1704). Also: forgery (HM 7979)

LOCKE, William John, *English novelist,* 1863–1930

Prose:

Joyous Adventures of Aristide Pujol (128 pp.: HM 7995)

Letters: 2 (1908–14)

LOCKER-LAMPSON, Frederick, *English poet,* 1821–95

Prose:

[Diaries: 1861–94] (35 vols.: HM 45378)

[Table of] Contents [of volume in which Edward Hawke Locker's correspondence was formerly bound] (2 leaves: LR 237)

Letters: 14 (1850–90)

LOCKHART, John Gibson, *English biographer, writer,* 1794–1854

Letters: 27 (1825–50)

LOCKLEY, Frederic E., *American soldier, journalist,* 1824–1905

Prose:

[Article re the Smoot Investigation] (Lockley Collection)

Memoirs of an Unsuccessful Man (Lockley Collection)

Reply to John A. Cockerill's "Brigham Young in Utah" (Lockley Collection)

Romance of a Suspender Buckle (Lockley Collection)

Letters: 320 (1862–75) to Elizabeth Metcalf (Campbell) Lockley

LOCKLEY, Frederic E., *American author, bookseller,* 1871–1958

Prose:

[Autobiographical notes] (Lockley Collection)

[Manuscripts of articles, interviews, stories, etc.] (61 pieces: Lockley Collection)

[Notes on interview with Edwin Markham] (Lockley Collection)

[Report of interview with Fanny (Kay) Bishop re Thomas Kay and the development of the wool industry in Oregon] (Lockley Collection)

Letters: 53 (1909–46)

LOCKWOOD, Francis Cummings, *American educator, author,* 1864–1948

Prose:

Reaping the Whirlwind—chap. 12 (44 pp.: Cunningham Collection)

Letters: 15 (1934–45)

LOGAN, Olive, *American actress, journalist, playwright,* 1839–1909

Letters: 2 (1868–1901)

LONDON, Jack, *American novelist, short-story writer, newspaper correspondent,* 1876–1916

A tramp, oyster pirate, seaman, socialist, laundryman, and miner, Jack London is as famous for the life he lived and the myths he wove around it as he is for the short stories and novels he wrote. Born in San Francisco, London's early life was one of some hardship; through his many adventures he tried to exchange the daily toil and adversity of his home life for the excitement of the new and unexplored.

Jack London's rise to fame came as a result of the Klondike Gold Rush. Unsuccessful in his attempt to break into the magazine market, London joined the flood of men rushing toward instant riches in the Yukon. He found little gold, but returned after the winter of 1897 with a wealth of memories and notes of the northland, the gold rush, and the hardships of the trail.

Jack London married Elizabeth May Maddern in 1900. The couple settled in Oakland, and soon added two daughters to the family. But the marriage was not successful; London divorced "Bess" and married Charmian Kittredge in 1905.

Charmian was adventurous, and she and Jack shared many exciting times, including a three-year trip to the South Seas aboard a tiny yacht. In order to pay for these adventures and for an extravagant life style, Jack London wrote at a furious pace, publishing fifty books by his fortieth year. His body could not withstand the brutal treatment it received, however, and shortly before his forty-first birthday he was dead. Rumors of suicide were prevalent after London's death, and, as were many of the events of his life, his death was controversial.

Subject matter: the author's personal archive, spanning roughly 100 years (1850–1950), contains some version, autograph or typescript, of almost everything Jack London wrote, including correspondence, literary notes, documents, and contracts, memos and letters regarding the operation of the Beauty Ranch, personal and family papers and documents, financial records, clippings and articles, and photographs. The Collection also contains letters and manuscripts pertaining to the Kittredge family.

Significant persons: Authors represented include Mary (Hunter) AUSTIN, Joseph CONRAD, Nora May FRENCH, Cloudesley JOHNS, Joaquin MILLER, Herbert Heron PEET, and Herbert George WELLS

Physical Description: 30,000 pieces: letters, documents, manuscripts and manuscript notes, photographs, and printed ephemeral pieces

Source: acquired from Charmian Kittredge London, 1925 and 1951, and from Irving Shepard, 1959. Gift of Irving Shepard, 1974

Bibliography: most of the manuscripts have been published by the Macmillan Company. Many of London's letters were published in *Letters from Jack London* in 1966. A three-volume edition of London's letters will be published in the 1980s.

Verse and Prose: approximately 2000 texts and notes

Letters: approximately 3000 (1898–1916) written by Jack London, and over 14,000 letters, most of which are written to Jack and Charmian (Kittredge) London

Documents: approximately 700

Other: over 7000 photographs and 5000 ephemeral pieces

LONG, John Davis, *American politician, author,* 1838–1915

Verse:

"At nightfall by the firelight's cheer" (HR 503)

Eulogy in Memory of Ulysses S. Grant (HM 1003)

Prose:

Abraham Lincoln (120 pp.: HM 1002)

Letters: 7 (1881–1902)

LONG, John Luther, *American novelist, playwright,* 1861–1927

Letters: 66 (1899–1920)

LONGFELLOW, Henry Wadsworth, *American poet, editor, educator,* 1807–82

Verse:

The Arrow and the Song (HM 1221)

Autumnal Night-fall (in the handwriting of Theophilus Parsons: HM 11885)

The Bridge of Cloud (HM 10472)

King Trisanku (HM 10473)

The Last of the Household (HM 7754)

Maiden and Weathercock (HM 10471)

Noël (copy; in French: HP 136)

A Song of Savoy (enclosed in letter: HM 7103)

Two Sonnets from the Spanish of Francisco de Aldana (HM 13017)

"Why waste the hours in idle talk" (HM 13019)

Woods in Winter (HM 7102)

Prose:

Literature of the Middle Ages (fragment, 1 p.: HM 13018)

The Youth of Mary Stuart (26 pp.: HM 10486)

Letters: 213 (1825–81), including 124 to James Thomas Fields

LONGFELLOW, Samuel, *American Unitarian clergyman, poet,* 1819–92

Verse:

Rock-burn (FI 3005)

Letters: 13 (1864–86)

LONGSTRETH, Thomas Morris, *American author,* 1886–

Letters: 1 (1921)

LOOMIS, Charles Battell, *American humorist, author,* 1861–1911

Letters: 1 (1905) to Albert Bigelow Paine

LOOS, Anita, *American author,* 1893–

Letters: 7 (1949)

LORD, William Wilberforce, *American clergyman, poet,* 1819–1907

Letters: 3 (1881–85)

LORIMER, George Horace, *American editor, publisher, author,* 1868–1937

Letters: 15 (1901–35)

LOSSING, Benson John, *American wood engraver, editor, author,* 1813–91

Verse:
To Helen (LS 1101)

Prose:
133 texts

Letters: 313 (1850–91)

Documents: 8 (1856–90)

Other:
30 drawings

LOTHROP, Harriet Mulford (Stone), *American author of children's books,* 1844–1924

Letters: 27 (1896–1922)

LOVEMAN, Samuel, *American author,* 1887–

Verse:
Ecce Homo (typescript signed: GS 217)
Ode to Apollo (typescript signed: GS 218)
Ode on the Passing of Youth (typewritten: GS 219)
The Triumph of Anarchy (typescript signed: GS 220)

Letters: 17 (1915–40)

LOVER, Samuel, *English song writer, novelist, painter,* 1797–1868

Verse:

The Reverie (HM 10755)

The War-ship of Peace (HM 10753)

Letters: 8 (ca. 1847–66)

Other:

[Fragment of music] HM 10756)

LOVETT, Robert Morss, *American educator, author,* 1870–1956

Letters: 3 (1913–19)

LOW, Will Hicock, *American painter, illustrator, author,* 1853–1932

[Note regarding Robert Louis Stevenson's departure for the South Sea voyages in 1888] (1 p.: HM 8951)

[Notes written by Low to accompany the letters of R. L. Stevenson addressed to him and to his wife, 1912] (HM 8908–8949)

LOWELL, Amy, *American poet, critic,* 1874–1925

Letters: 36 (1908–23)

LOWELL, James Russell, *American poet, critic, diplomat, educator,* 1819–91

Verse:

At the Exhibition (HM 10746)

A Fable for Critics (HM 10741)

His Ship (HM 10742)

"I know a girl (they say she's eighty)" (in the hand of Anne B. Procter: HM 42683)

In Far Japan (HM 10745)

"In woods . . ." (RB 7135)

The Present Crisis: [two stanzas only] (HM 1219)

"They are slaves who dare not be/ In the right with two or three:" [quotation] (HM 16636)

Prose:

Essay on Lessing (53 pp.: HM 10743)

Essay on Spencer (fragment, 2 pp.: HM 10744)

On Some Recent Sermons (1 p.: FI 5084)

[Review of Matthew Arnold's *On Translating Homer*] (5 pp.: FI 3058)

[Review of Max Müller's *Lectures on the Science of Language*] (4 pp.: FI 3057)

Review of W. H. Russell's *My Diary North and South* (10 pp.: HM 10738)

Satire on the Lowell family (4 pp.: SL 275)

Uncle Cobus's Story (12 pp.: HM 10739)

Letters: 154 (1849–91), including 50 to James Thomas Fields

Other:

[Manuscript corrections in George Chapman's *The Warres of Pompey and Caesar*] (RB 98552)

[Notes in Edward Herbert's *De Religione Centilium*] (RB 76966)

LOWELL, Robert Traill Spence, *American clergyman, novelist, poet,* 1816–91

Verse:

This Day, Countrymen!; and Call for True Men (2 poems: SL 42)

The Massachusetts Line (SL 248)

Letters: 12 (1861–89), including 11 to James Thomas Fields

LOWELL, Robert Traill Spence, *American poet,* 1917–1977

Letters: 5 (1947–56)

LOWENBERG, Bettie (Lilienfield), *American author,* 1845–1924

Letters: 1 (1920) to George Wharton James

LOWRY, Clarence Malcolm, *English novelist,* 1909–

Verse:

Byzantium; or, Where the Great Life Begins (AIK 2521)

Deserter (AIK 2521)

"The doom of each, said Doctor Usquebaugh" (AIK 2488)

[Four poems]: Spiderweb, Alcoholic, Dark Path, and Sonnet (AIK 2489)

"This wrestling, as of seamen with a storm" (AIK 2517)

Tom, by airmale: [notes for a poem?] (AIK 2490)

Work for Conrad: [four "prelude" poems written for Conrad Aiken] (AIK 3418)

Prose:

Ultramarine: [fragment of an early draft of novel, with revisions in ink and pencil by Conrad Aiken] (1 vol.: AIK 3381)

Ultramarine: [notes for chap. 1] (3 pp.: AIK 2491)

Ultramarine: [one page of an early draft] (typewritten, carbon copy: AIK 2492)

Ultramarine: [typewritten drafts on versos of letters] (AIK 2502–2503)

Letters: 49 (1929–54), including 44 to Conrad Potter Aiken

Other:

And then there came a wize man from over the hills . . . : [humorous pen and ink drawing] (AIK 2487)

LOWTH, Robert, *English bishop, scholar,* 1710–87

Prose:

Epitaph for Joseph Spence (1 p.: RB 131213, vol. 1)

Letters: 2 (1749–50)

LUBBOCK, Percy Samuel, *English essayist, historian, novelist,* b. 1879

Letters: 2 (1915–18)

LUCAS, Daniel Bedinger, *American jurist, poet,* 1836–1909

Letters: 4 (1871–78)

LUCAS, Edward Verrall, *English essayist, critic,* 1868–1938

Prose:

The Embossed Card (Hill Collection)

Letters: 2 (1928–34)

LUDLOW, Fitz Hugh, *American editor, author,* 1836–70

Verse:

"I will not wish thy life a tinted bubble" (HM 35075)

Letters: 2 (1865–67)

LUHAN, Mabel (Ganson) Dodge, *American author,* 1879–1962

Letters: 152 (1917–39)

LUMMIS, Charles Fletcher, *American editor, librarian, author,* 1859–1928

Prose:

[Review of Father Engelhardt's history of the missions] 1 p.: (HM 17216)

Letters: 252 (1895–1928)

LUNT, George, *American poet, journalist,* 1803–85

Letters: 2 (1838–77)

LUTYENS, Sir Edwin Landseer, *English architect,* 1869–1944

Letters: 1 (1914) to Charles Fletcher Lummis

LYNDE, Francis, *American novelist,* 1856–1930

Letters: 2 (1896–1903)

LYTTLETON, George, 1st Baron, *English public official, man of letters,* 1709–73

Verse:

The Squirrels of Hagley Park to Miss Warburton's Squirrel (MO 1264)

"T'other night, as they lay together in bed" (MO 1265)

Letters: 116 (1755–73)

LYTTON, Baron, see BULWER-LYTTON

M

MAAS, Willard, *American poet, critic,* 1911–70

Verse:

Landward Seabirds (typewritten: Charles Erskine Scott Wood Collection)

Letters: 8 (1937–54)

MABIE, Hamilton Wright, *American editor, critic,* 1846–1916

Prose:

America in Whitman's Poetry (87 pp.: HM 6264)

Letters: 8 (1877–1911)

MacARTHUR, Helen Hayes (Brown), *American actress,* 1900–

Letters: 27 (1942–46)

MACAULAY, Rose, *English novelist,* 1887–1958

Letters: 4 (1934–38)

MACAULAY, Thomas Babington, *English historian,* 1800–59

Verse:

[Two poems]: Moncontour; and Ivry (HM 32043)

Prose:

Translation of *Horace:* lib. ii, Ode XX (2 pp.: HM 44755)

Letters: 53 (1813–59)

MACAULAY, Zachary, *English philanthropist,* 1768–1838

Prose:

Diary (92 pp.: MY 2)

Journal (1328 pp.: MY 418 [1–28])

Letters: 227 (1794–1834)

McAULEY, James J., *Irish critic, educator, author,* 1936–

Letters: 1 (1963)

McCARTHY, Justin, *Irish novelist, statesman,* 1830–1912

Letters: 9 (1870–95)

McCARTHY, Justin Huntly, *English novelist, historian,* 1860–1936

Letters: 3 (n.d.)

McCLURE, Samuel Sidney, *American editor, author,* 1857–1949

Letters: 47 (1887–1908)

McCORD, David Thompson Watson, *American poet,* 1897–

Letters: 43 (1943–57)

McCRACKEN, Harold, *American explorer, lecturer, author,* 1894–

Letters: 9 (1912–16)

McCUTCHEON, George Barr, *American novelist,* 1866–1928

Letters: 4 (1910–27)

McCUTCHEON, John Tinney, *American cartoonist, author,* 1870–1949

Letters: 8 (1902–36)

McDIARMID, Hugh, see GRIEVE, Christopher Murray

MACDONALD, George, *Scottish novelist, poet,* 1824–1905

Verse:

A Fair Bargain (HM 44520)

Letters: 42 (1851–94)

McDONALD, James Robert, *American educator, author,* 1934–

Letters: 15 (1965–66)

McELHENNEY, Jane (Ada Clare, pseud.), *American actress, author,* 1836–74

Verse:

How Poets Sing (HM 35075)

McFALL, Frances Elizabeth (Clark), (Sarah Grand, pseud.), *English author,* b. 1862

Letters: 2 (1900–07)

MacGRATH, Harold, *American novelist,* 1871–1932

Letters: 1 (1908)

McGROARTY, John Steven, *American lawyer, writer,* 1862–1944

Letters: 41 (1908–44), including 10 to Louise (Ward) Watkins

McILWRAITH, Jean Newton, *Canadian writer*, 1859–1938

Letters: 2 (1920)

McINTOSH, Burr William, *American author*, 1862–1942

Letters: 5 (1901–38)

MACKARNESS, Matilda Anne (Planché), *English author*, 1826–81

Letters: 3 (1881)

MACKAY, Charles, *English journalist, poet*, 1814–89

Letters: 16 (1855–79)

MACKAY, Eric, *English poet*, 1851–98

Verse:

The Procession (HM 44756)

MACKAYE, Arthur Loring, *American author*, b. 1863

Verse:

Aloha! (Borchart Collection)

Prose:

Journal, 1872–1885 (14 pp.: Borchart Collection)

Letters: 4 (1904–38)

MacKAYE, Percy Wallace, *American poet, playwright*, 1875–1956

Letters: 21 (1909–52)

MacKAYE, Steele, *American playwright*, 1842–94

Letters: 1 (1886)

McKENNEY, Thomas Loraine, *American author, administrator of Indian affairs,* 1785–1859

Letters: 11 (1816–43)

Documents: 1 (1820)

MACKENZIE, Compton, *English novelist,* 1883–

Letters: 1 (1946) to Graham Greene

MACKENZIE, Henry, *English novelist, miscellaneous writer,* 1745–1831

Letters: 1 (1813)

MACKENZIE, Robert Shelton, *English miscellaneous writer,* 1809–81

Letters: 16 (1831–79)

Documents: 1 (1853)

MACKINTOSH, Sir James, *English philosopher,* 1765–1832

Prose:

Life of Sir Thomas More (96 pp.: HM 689)

Letters: 16 (1797–1818)

MACKLIN, Charles, *English actor, stage manager,* 1697?–1797

Letters: 1 (1785)

MACLEAN, Letitia Elizabeth (Landon), *English poet,* 1802–38

Verse:

Collection of Poems (not autograph: HM 7970)
"Beautiful slave go school thy brow" (RB 131334, vol. 2)
The Bridal Morning (RB 131334, vol. 2)

Daybreak (HM 1833)
The Fancy Struck Me Looking on the Boy (HM 7976)
Marius in the Ruins of Carthage (RB 131334, vol. 2)
Shuhur-Pegpore (RB 320006, vol. 2)
Letters: 31 (1825–38)

MacLEISH, Archibald, *American educator, poet, playwright,* 1892–

Letters: 6 (1925–56)

MACLISE, Daniel, *English historical painter,* 1806–70

Letters: 24 (1831–67), including 12 to Charles Dickens

Drawings: 1 (1852)

MacMANUS, Seumas, *American lecturer, author,* 1869–1960

Letters: 2 (1933–35)

McMASTER, John Bach, *American historian, author,* 1852–1932

Prose:
The Struggle for the West: [historical essay] (38 pp.: HM 44771)
Letters: 1 (1897)

MACNISH, Robert, *English author, physician,* 1802–37

Letters: 1 (1833)

MACPHERSON, James, *Scottish poet,* 1736–96

Letters: 1 (1773)

MACREADY, William, *English actor, manager,* d. 1829

Letters: 4 (1800–17)

MACREADY, William Charles, *English actor,* 1793–1873

Letters: 99 (1823–67)

Documents: 2 (1823–41)

MACY, John Albert, *American literary critic, poet,* 1877–1932

Letters: 11 (1912–31)

MADDEN, Sir Frederic, *English antiquary, paleographer,* 1801–73

Letters: 13 (1837–69)

MAGINN, William, *English poet, journalist, writer,* 1793–1842

Verse:

On a Couch of Sweet Roses (RB 320006, vol. 1)

"This is the ending of all noble blending" (RB 320006, vol. 1)

Prose:

Chap. 4: How He Sent for Dr. Wiggins (includes some lines in verse to the tune of "Yankee Doodle," 5 pp.: HM 44773)

Letters: 6 (1823–42), and 38 (1842–43) by members of his family

See also KENEALY, Edward Vaughan Hyde

MAGRUDER, Julia, *American novelist,* 1854–1907

Letters: 3 (1894–1900)

MAHONY, Francis Sylvester, *English humorist,* 1804–66

Prose:

[Fragment of a manuscript entitled] "End of Chapter XXXI where the Lady's manuscript breaks off" (2 pp.: HM 723)

Letters: 11 (1842–45)

MAJOR, Charles, *American novelist, lawyer,* 1856–1913

Letters: 6 (1910–21)

MAKIN, Bathsua, *English educator, writer,* fl. 1673

Verse:

In Mortem Clarissimi Domini Domini Henrici Hastings (Hastings Collection)

Upon the Much Lamented Death of the Right Honourable the Lady Elizabeth Langham (Hastings Collection)

Letters: 3 (1664–68)

MALLET, David, *English poet, miscellaneous writer,* 1705?–65

Letters: 1 (1762)

MALONE, Edmond, *English critic, author,* 1741–1812

Letters: 2 (1787–88)

MALONE, Walter, *American jurist, poet,* 1866–1915

Verse:

The Death of Poetry (RB 27597)

The One Thing Needful (Kane Literary Collection)

MANN, Edward Beverly, *American author,* 1902–

Letters: 1 (1953) to Eugene Lafayette Cunningham

MANN, Mary Tyler (Peabody), *American educator, author,* 1806–87

Letters: 4 (1835–61)

MANN, Thomas, *German author,* 1875–1955

Letters: 4 (1938–51)

MANSFIELD, Edward Deering, *American editor, author,* 1801–80

Letters: 1 (1864)

MANSFIELD, Katherine, *English short-story writer, critic,* 1888–1923

Letters: 28 (1921–22), including 27 to Mary Annette (Beauchamp) Russell, Countess Russell

MANUCHE or MANUCCI, Cosmo, *Italian-born dramatist,* fl. 1650–60

Prose:

The Banish'd Shepheardesse (78 pp.: EL 8395)

MARAT, Jean-Paul, *Swiss-born French revolutionary politician,* 1743–93

Prose:

Lettres Polonaises (231 leaves: HM 6263)

MARBLE, Manton Malone, *American editor, publisher,* 1835–1917

Letters: 90 (1862–88)

MARBURY, Elizabeth, *American author and author's representative,* 1856–1933

Letters: 30 (1906–14)

MARCH, Charles Wainwright, *American lawyer, journalist, author,* 1815–64

Letters: 21 (1854–58)

MARKHAM, Edwin, *American poet,* 1852–1940

Verse:

The Consecration of the Common Way (typewritten: HM 31197)

Five Quatrains for My Friend, Henry Meade Bland (IC 527)

Outwilled (MS 49)

[Savings deposit book containing first drafts of poems] (HM 44778)

Two at a Fireside (HM 34676)

Prose:

An Appeal of the Jewelled City to the Spirit (typescript with corrections and additions in author's hand, 15 pp.: HM 17379)

Lincoln, Man of the People (corrected proof sheets: RB 66584)

Letters: 41 (1894–1935)

Other:

2 printed poems, signed (Burdette Collection)

MARKHAM, Gervase, *English author,* 1568–1637

Prose:

The Muster-Master (attributed to him, 38 leaves: HM 27514)

MARKS, Jeannette Augustus, *American educator, author,* 1875–1964

Verse:

Rood—In Memory of the Trees at Wellesley College, November 29, 1921 (HM 20835)

Letters: 1 (1929)

MARQUIS, Donald Robert Perry, *American journalist, essayist, poet, playwright, humorist,* 1878–1937

Letters: 9 (1907–32)

MARQUIS, Neeta, *American author,* fl. 1922–56

Verse:

Apollonio: [narrative verse] (typewritten: California Poetry File)

Armistice (typewritten: Yeatman Collection)

Bafflement (Marquis Collection)

Bafflement (typewritten: California Poetry File)

By the Sea (typewritten, with corrections: Marquis Collection)

From the Desert's Edge (Marquis Collection)

Hardy Climber (typewritten: Yeatman Collection)

Heaven (typewritten: California Poetry File)

Inexorable Pattern (typewritten: Yeatman Collection)

Lilacs (typewritten: Marquis Collection)

Mission Vesper Call (Marquis Collection)

Wild Buckwheat Honey (typewritten: Marquis Collection)

Wisdom (typewritten: Marquis Collection)

Prose:

Bear Valley Backgrounds: Secessionist Echoes in Southern California (corrected typescript, 13 pp.: Marquis Collection)

Before the Red Man Vanishes (typescript, 3 pp.: Marquis Collection)

An Echo of Robert Louis Stevenson (corrected typescript, 5 pp.: Marquis Collection)

Report of Writers' Department, MacDowell Club of Allied Arts (typewritten, 2 pp.: Marquis Collection)

Letters: 151 (1922–56), and several hundred addressed to her

Other:

[Appointment books] (10 items: Marquis Collection)

[List of inscribed books] (Marquis Collection)

[Ms. notes re "Festival of Fire"] (Marquis Collection)

[Miscellaneous notes] (14 items: Marquis Collection)

[Notes for public talks on poetry] (Marquis Collection)

[Notes from lectures by Dr. Paul Shorey] (Marquis Collection)

Projected material for the Lyric West: [notes] (Marquis Collection)

[Scrapbooks containing letters, etc.] (3 vols.: Marquis Collection)

MARRIOTT, Charles, *English novelist, art critic,* 1869–1957

Letters: 2 (1908)

MARRYAT, Frederick, *English naval captain, novelist,* 1792–1848

Letters: 4 (1830–45)

MARSTON, John, *English dramatist, divine,* 1575?–1634

Verse:

[Ashby entertainment] The Ho^ble Lord and Lady of Huntingdons Entertainment of their Right Noble Mother, Alice Countesse Dowager of Darby the first nighte of her Honors arrival att the House of Ashby (partly autograph, 15 leaves: EL 34B9

The First Antimasque of Mountebanks (not autograph, 16 leaves: HM 21)

MARSTON, John Westland, *English dramatic poet,* 1819–90

Letters: 6 (1845–81)

MARSTON, Philip Bourke, *English poet,* 1850–87

Letters: 2 (1874 and n.d.)

MARTIN, Edward Sandford, *American editor, author,* 1856–1939

Letters: 66 (1912–35), including 63 to Daniel Berkeley Updike

MARTINEAU, Harriet, *English writer,* 1802–76

Prose:

Health in the Hospital (51 pp.: FI 3289)

Lady Noel Byron, a Defense (43 pp.: HM 6259)

Letter to a Student of History (6 pp.: HM 6260)

The Young Repealer (34 pp.: FI 3290)

Letters: 19 (1839–73)

MARTINEAU, James, *English Unitarian divine,* 1805–1900

Letters: 33 (1847–97)

MARVELL, Andrew, *English poet, satirist,* 1621–78

Verse:

[Further Advice to a Painter] (copy: EL 8870)

Letters: 1 (1676)

MASEFIELD, John, *English poet, playwright,* 1878–1967

Verse:

"O lovely lily clean" (HM 6509)

Letters: 11 (1902–57)

MASON, Charles, *English royalist divine,* 1616–77

Verse:

S.M.E.C.T.Y.M.N.U.U.S. vel Belua Multorum Capitum (attributed to Mason, or John Cleveland, or Robert Creswell: EL 8774)

MASON, Walt, *American humorist, writer,* 1862–1939

Letters: 6 (1895–1916)

MASON, William, *English poet, scholar,* 1724–97

Verse:

[Epistle, beginning] "Here pause fair Fancy!" (RB 108732)

Letters: 40 (1769–91)

MASSENET, Jules Émile Frédéric, *French composer,* 1842–1912

Letters: 2 (1911)

MASSEY, Gerald, *English poet,* 1828–1907

Letters: 10 (1857–80), including 6 to James Thomas Fields

MASSINGER, Philip, *English dramatist,* 1583–1640

Prose:

The Cure of Pride; or Every One in Their Way (generally conceded to be an adaptation of Massinger's "City Madam," 90 pp.: HM 95)

MASSON, David, *English writer, scholar,* 1822–1907

Letters: 8 (1860–69), including 7 to Frederick James Furnivall

MASTERS, Edgar Lee, *American poet,* 1869–1950

Verse:

37 of the poems published as *The Domesday Book* (LF)

Letters: 7 (1915–41)

MATHER, Cotton, *American clergyman, scholar, author,* 1663–1728

Prose:

Substance of Sermons Delivered by Several Ministers in Boston (302 pp.: HM 15212)

Notes for a Sermon (incomplete: HM 2154)

Sermon (2 pp.: HM 1347)

Sermon on a text from Ephesians 1:8 (4 pp.: HM 982)

To Ebenezer Bradshaw and George Hughes (presentation inscription, probably cut from the flyleaf of a volume, fragment: HM 1451)

Letters: 19 (1701–26)

Documents: 2 (1703–18)

MATHER, Increase, *American clergyman, educator, author,* 1639–1723

Prose:

An Essay for the Recording of Illustrious Providences: [preface and table of contents only] (7 pp.: HM 981)

Notebook—1656 (10 pp. in 2 vols.: HM 983)

Sermon (incomplete, 2 pp.: HM 2153)

Letters: 5 (1712–18)

Documents: 2 (1694–1718)

MATHEWS, Charles, *English comedian,* 1776–1835

Letters: 4 (1828 and n.d.)

MATHEWS, Charles James, *English actor, dramatist,* 1803–78

Prose:

Commonplace Book (324 pp.: HM 6513)

Letters: 27 (1840–77)

Documents: 2 (1846–52)

Drawings: 1 (1851: landscape: FR 167)

MATHEWS, Lucia Elizabeth (Bartolozzi) Vestris, *English actress,* 1797–1856

Letters: 4 (1836 and n.d.)

MATHEWS, Shailer, *American educator, editor, author,* 1863–1941

Letters: 1 (1906)

MATTHEWS, James Brander, *American educator, critic, playwright,* 1852–1929

Prose:

An Apology for Technic (typescript, 19 pp.: HM 23232)
Literature in the New Century (typescript, 19 pp.: HM 23403)
Review of *The Standard of Usage in English* (12 pp.: HM 23240)

Letters: 37 (1884–1921)

MAUGHAM, William Somerset, *English novelist, dramatist,* 1874–1965

Letters: 9 (1920–53)

MAUPASSANT, Guy de, *French short-story writer, novelist,* 1850–93

Letters: 1 (n.d.)

MAURICE, Arthur Bartlett, *American editor, author,* 1873–1946

Letters: 8 (1901–13) to Albert Bigelow Paine

MAURICE, Frederick Denison, *English theologian, founder of "Christian socialist" movement,* 1805–72

Letters: 36 (1854–62)

MAX MÜLLER, Friedrich, *German-born English orientalist, philologist, writer,* 1823–1900

Letters: 15 (1867–94)

MAXWELL, Perriton, *American editor, author,* 1868–1947

Letters: 7 (1905–16)

MAXWELL, William Hamilton, *Irish novelist,* 1792–1850

Letters: 2 (1838–41)

MAY, Thomas, *English author,* 1595–1650

Verse:

An Elegy on the Death of Lady Bridgewater (facsimile: EL 6843)

MAYER, Brantz, *American lawyer, historian, editor,* 1809–79

Prose:

[Notes on his trip to Yosemite Valley] (90 pieces: HM 4279)

Letters: 23 (1856–76)

MAYHEW, Henry, *English author,* 1812–87

Letters: 3 (1852–74)

MAYHEW, Horace, *English author,* 1816–72

Letters: 4 (1847 and n.d.)

MAYHEW, Jonathan, *American clergyman, author,* 1720–66

Verse:

Thoughts Occasioned by the Much Lamented Death of Miss Elizabeth Epes on Feb. 14, 1759 (not autograph, attributed to Mayhew: HM 44782)

Prose:

Sermons (8 pieces: HM 8046–8053)

MEANY, Edmond Stephen, *American educator, legislator, journalist,* 1862–1935

Verse:

[Collection of 28 poems] (HM 44783)
A Friendship Fire (TU Box 22)

Letters: 34 (1908–33)

MEARS, Mary Martha, *American author,* 1876–1939

Letters: 2 (1920)

MEGRUE, Roi Cooper, *American playwright,* 1883–1927

Letters: 1 (1909) to Albert Bigelow Paine

MELLEN, Grenville, *American poet,* 1799–1841

Letters: 2 (1837)

MELVILLE, Herman, *American author,* 1819–91

Letters: 1 (1890)

MENCKEN, Henry Louis, *American editor, essayist, critic,* 1880–1956

Letters: 167 (1912–55)

MENKEN, Adah Isaacs, *American actress, poet,* 1835–68

Verse:

"The poet's noblest duty is" (HM 35075)

Letters: 2 (1866)

MENUHIN, Yehudi, *American violinist,* 1916–

Prose:

Reactions and Ideas: the United States vs. India (typewritten, 20 pp.: Charles Erskine Scott Wood Collection)

Letters: 3 (1937–60)

MEREDITH, George, *English writer,* 1828–1909

Verse:

Alsace-Lorraine (typescript signed: HM 6753)
Archduchess Ann (HM 6763)
Bellerophon (HM 6768)
The Empty Purse (HM 7468)
The Empty Purse (an early draft: HM 7467)
Epitaph: The Emperor Frederick of Our Time (HM 7474)
Epitaph: Gordon of Khartoum (HM 7473)
Epitaph: J. C. M. (HM 7472)
Epitaph: The Year's Sheddings (HM 7475)
Foresight and Patience (HM 7463)
Foresight and Patience (an early draft: HM 7464)
The French Revolution (HM 6760)
Hard Weather (HM 6758)
Napoleon (also signed typewritten copy: HM 6756)

Nature and Life (HM 6755)

The Nuptials of Attila (corrected proof: RB 19162)

Penetration and Trust (also another copy: HM 7471)

Periander (HM 6766)

The Poet's Night (several versions; published as "Night of Frost in May": HM 6761)

The Riddle for Men (HM 6748)

Seed-Time (HM 6757)

Solon (HM 6767)

A Spanish Ballad (HM 6764)

The Teaching of the Nude (HM 6759)

To the Comic Spirit (HM 7469)

The Trance of Harold Hammerskull (HM 6765)

The Two Masks (HM 6762)

The Wind on the Lyre (also an early draft, entitled "Clear Singing": HM 7465)

With the Persuader (HM 7462)

Woodland Peace (HM 6754)

The Woodman (HM 6770)

Youth in Memory (HM 7470)

The Youthful Quest (also an early draft: HM 7466)

Prose:

Diana of the Crossways (93 pp.: HM 6769)

One of Our Conquerors (fragment, 1 p.: HM 6512)

[Reports as reader to Chapman and Hall] (5 leaves: HM 7476)

[Reports on manuscripts while acting as reader for Chapman and Hall] (235 leaves: HM 7477)

Letters: 9 (1849–1907)

MERIMÉE, Prosper, *French novelist,* 1803–70

Letters: 1 (1864)

MERIVALE, John Herman, *English scholar, poet,* 1779–1844

Letters: 1 (n.d.)

MERRICK, Leonard, *English novelist,* 1864–1939

Letters: 1 (1914)

MERWIN, Samuel, *American novelist,* 1874–1936

Letters: 3 (1911–17)

MEYNELL, Alice Christiana Gertrude (Thompson), *English poet, essayist, critic,* 1847–1922

Letters: 24 (1890–1914)

MIDDLETON, Thomas, *English dramatist,* 1570?–1627

Prose:

A Game at Chesse (partly autograph, 53 leaves: EL 34 B 17)
The Triumphs of Truth (30 pp.: HM 99)

MIGHELS, Ella Sterling (Clark), *American author,* 1853–1934

Letters: 21 (1928–31)

MILES, Nelson Appleton, *American army officer, author,* 1839–1925

Letters: 45 (1862–93)

Other:

Official Report of a Trip as Bearer of Despatches from General Miles' Command, Butler County, Texas, to Fort Leavenworth (Frank D. Baldwin Collection)

MILES, William Augustus, *English political writer,* 1753?–1817

Letters: 11 (1800–10)

MILL, John Stuart, *English philosopher,* 1806–73

Letters: 55 (1835–72)

MILLAIS, Sir John Everett, *English painter,* 1829–96

Letters: 205 (1850–96)

MILLARD, Bailey, *American editor, author,* 1859–1941

Verse:

Looking Landward (California Poetry File)

Letters: 20 (1905–37)

MILLER, Cincinnatus Hiner "Joaquin," *American poet, playwright,* 1839–1913

Verse:

153 texts

Letters: 287 (1863–1913)

MILLER, Henry, *American author,* 1891–

Prose:

[Review of] *If a Man Be Mad,* by Harold Maine (typewritten with autograph corrections, 4 pp.: Walker Winslow Collection)

Letters: 43 (1905–47), including 42 to Walker Winslow; also 57 letters from Winslow to Miller

MILLER, Joseph Dana, *American editor, publisher, poet,* 1864–1939

Letters: 3 (1937–38)

MILLER, Max, *American author,* 1899–1967

Letters: 2 (1934) to Eugene Lafayette Cunningham

MILLER, Samuel, *American clergyman, educator, author,* 1769–1850

Prose:

Compend of Church Government (42 pp.: HM 6717)

Letters: 3 (1800–47)

MILMAN, Henry Hart, *English author, scholar,* 1791–1868

Verse:

The Belvidere Apollo (MO 1553)

Letters: 5 (1835–61)

MILNES, Richard Monckton, Baron Houghton, *English poet, politician,* 1809–85

Letters: 22 (1842–80)

MINNIGERODE, Meade, *American author,* 1887–1967

Letters: 1 (1927)

MINOR, Robert Crannell, *American landscape painter,* 1839–1904

Letters: 1 (1891)

MITCHELL, Donald Grant, *American agriculturalist, author,* 1822–1908

Letters: 26 (1862–68) to James Thomas Fields

MITCHELL, John Ames, *American artist, editor, author,* 1845–1918

Letters: 2 (1911–12)

MITCHELL, Langdon Elwyn, *American poet, playwright,* 1862–1935

Letters: 1 (1894)

MITCHELL, Ruth Comfort, *American author,* 1882–1953

Verse:

My Grief That I Married a Gypsy Man (typewritten: California Poetry File)

Letters: 3 (1940 and n.d.)

MITCHELL, Silas Weir, *American poet, novelist,* 1829–1914

Letters: 21 (1866–1913)

MITFORD, Mary Russell, *English novelist, dramatist,* 1787–1855

Verse:

Alice (HM 44787)
"Fair spring beneath thy feet the grass is sweet" (FR 175)

Prose:

[An Autobiographical Sketch] (4 pp.: BE 101)

To Francis Bennoch Esqre: [a dedication and part of an introduction] (2 pp.: BE 102)

Letters: 252 (1821–55)

MODJESKA, Helena (Opid), *Polish-born actress,* 1840–1909

Letters: 33 (1870–1906)

MOIR, David Macbeth, *English physician, author,* 1798–1851

Prose:

Memoranda concerning the relationship between William Maginn and William Blackwood (10 pp.: HM 38897)

Letters: 5 (1828–43)

MONAHAN, Michael, *American editor, poet,* 1865–1933

Letters: 23 (1898–1933)

MONCRIEFF, William Thomas, *English dramatist,* 1794–1857

Letters: 3 (1819–52)

MONKHOUSE, William Cosmo, *English author,* 1840–1901

Verse:

With a Drawing by Boucher (HM 12081)

MONROE, Harriet, *American editor, poet,* 1860–1936

Letters: 34 (1914–36)

MONSEY, Messenger, *English physician,* 1693–1788

Verse:

[Verses addressed to Lord Lyttleton] (MO 1568 A and B)

Letters: 70 (1757–68)

MONTAGU, Elizabeth (Robinson), *English author,* 1720–1800

Verse:

[Seven lines of verse in French following letter from Joseph Warton] (MO 6620)

Prose:

[Critical review of "The Judgement of Paris" by James Beattie] (2 leaves: MO 2996)

[A dialogue between] Berenice and Cleopatra (3 leaves: MO 2998)

[A dialogue between] Simon or Simeon Stylites and Mr. Secretary (3 leaves: MO 2997)

Essay on the writing and genius of Shakespeare (fragment, 3 leaves: MO 2999)

To the Chronicle: [a letter on public parks] (5 pp.: MO 3000)

Letters: 3,526 (1732–99), and approximately 3,400 letters addressed to Mrs. Montagu

Other:

2 endorsements on letters (MO 991 and 1163)

Ms. in Italian of 5 leaves, ca. 1756 in the handwriting of Elizabeth (Robinson) Montagu (MO 6921)

MONTAGU, Matthew, Baron Rokeby, *English member of parliament, nephew of Elizabeth (Robinson) Montagu,* b. 1762

Verse:

"Think not, dear Greg, that I so long" (MO 3786)

Prose:

The Letters of Mrs. Elizabeth Montagu (three fragments of the ms., 3 pieces: MO 3785)

[Translations from classical texts, notes, etc.] (44 pieces: MO 3784)

Letters: 82 (1777–1810)

MONTAGUE, Charles, 1st Earl of Halifax, *English politician,* 1661–1715

Verse:

An Epistle to My Lord Chamberlain (EL 8788)

Letters: 1 (1710)

MONTAGUE, John Patrick, *American author,* 1929–

Letters: 5 (1963–67)

MONTGOMERY, James, *English poet, editor, hymn writer,* 1771–1854

Verse:

A Pilgrim's Retrospect (HM 7061)

Letters: 2 (1831–44)

MONTGOMERY, Robert, *English poet,* 1807–55

Letters: 4 (1829–38)

MOODY, William Vaughn, *American educator, poet, playwright,* 1869–1910

Verse:

Thammuz (Moody Collection)

Letters: 268 (1901–09) to Harriet Converse (Tilden) Brainard Moody

MOORE, Clement Clarke, *American educator, poet, Hebraist,* 1779–1863

Verse:

A Visit from St. Nicholas: [ballad beginning, 'Twas the night before Christmas] (HM 752)

Letters: 3 (1831–56)

MOORE, George, *English author,* 1852–1933

Prose:

The Brook Kerith (typescript, with author's corrections, 602 pp.: HM 41114)

Esther Waters: [acts IV and V only] (39 leaves: HM 6488)

Lovers of Orelay (corrected typescript and proof, 14 pp.: HM 26091)

A Mummer's Wife (incomplete, 109 pp.: HM 6489)

[A new paragraph added to the preface of the 1921 edition of *The Lake*] (RB 28663)

Letters: 63 (1889–1930)

MOORE, John Trotwood, *American editor, author,* 1858–1929

Letters: 1 (1912)

MOORE, Louise Kirby (Paine) Benjamin, *American author,* fl. 1900–18

Verse:

A Journey to Fairyland (AP 1186)

Letters: 13 (1900–18)

MOORE, Thomas, *English poet,* 1779–1852

Verse:

Account of an Extraordinary Dream in a Letter from—— to —— (HM 44792)

[Collection of Songs] (Many with music: HM 6279)

"Flow on thou shining river" (with music: HM 1886)

"Like one, who doom'd o'er distant sea" (with music: HM 1059)

More Church: a parody on Sir Charles Hanbury Williams's "Come, Cloe, and give me sweet kisses" (HM 6482)

My harp has an unchanging theme (musical score: HM 30635)

[Poem on Love] (with music: HM 6487)

Poems (HM 6258)

[Song beginning]: "Has sorrow thy young days shaded" (HM 27920)

Song from the Greek Anthology (Julian), beginning "Last night love I found" [musical score, with 2 copies] (HM 44793)

The Song of the Box (HM 19722)

The Song of the Box (corrected proofs: RB 152030)

Songs from Legendary Ballads (set to music by Bishop: HM 6481)

A Threnody on the Approaching Demise of Old Mother Cornlaw (HM 44794)

Prose:

Ali's Bride: [draft and notes] (11 pp.: HM 6278)

The Epicurean (incomplete, 128 pp.: HM 6275)

The Epicurean: [draft and notes] (63 leaves: HM 6274)

Letters: 72 (1802–46)

Documents: 1 (1813)

Other:

[Manuscript corrections, additions, notes and poems in *Epistles, Odes, and Other Poems*] (RB 28840)

MORAN, Thomas, *American landscape painter, etcher,* 1837–1926

Letters: 1 (1891)

MORE, Hannah, *English religious writer,* 1745–1833

Verse:

Bible Rhymes: an attempt to bring in the names of all the books of Scripture in their order (MY 724)

Bishop Bonner's Ghost (MO 3982)

A Midnight Hymn (RB 131334, vol. 2)

[Two poems]: "Yes! should ills beset me" and "To the Lady Elizabeth Monk" in letter of 1818, Dec. 1 (HM 25784)

Letters: 148 (1776–1830)

MORE, Henry, *English theologian,* 1614–87

Letters: 4 (1672–83)

MORE, Paul Elmer, *American editor, author,* 1864–1937

Letters: 2 (1904–18)

MORGAN, Angela, *American poet,* d. 1957

Verse:

Resurrection (AP 1197)

Letters: 9 (1909–20)

MORGAN, Charles, *English novelist,* 1894–1958

Letters: 1 (1946)

MORGAN, George, *American author, editor,* 1854–1936

Letters: 1 (1921)

MORGAN, Sydney (Owenson), Lady, *English novelist,* 1783?–1859

Verse:

To the Reviewer of the "odd volume" in the Athenaeum: [a poem beginning]: "My life is not dated by years" (HM 36051)

Letters: 12 (1805–59)

MORLEY, Christopher Darlington, *American novelist, journalist,* 1890–1957

Prose:

Gentles Attend (10 pp.: HM 11232)

Lecture Written for Cedric Crowell to Deliver at the A. B. A. Convention (7 pp.: HM 11231)

Thunder on the Left (206 pp.: HM 6262)

Letters: 3 (1920–42)

MORLEY, Henry, *English author,* 1822–94

Letters: 12 (1856–77)

MORRIS, Charles, *American compiler, dime-novelist,* 1833–1922

Letters: 1 (1921)

MORRIS, George Pope, *American editor, poet, playwright,* 1802–64

Verse:

Barcarolle (HM 44550)

"A woman with a beaming face" (HM 44549)

Letters: 12 (1832–61)

MORRIS, Gouverneur, *American author,* 1876–1953

Letters: 24 (1902–47)

Other:

[Commentary on picture of his house] (1 p.: MS 78)

[Drawings] (5 pieces: MS 74–77, 79)

MORRIS, Sir Lewis, *Welsh poet, educator,* 1833–1907

Letters: 7 (1864–1902)

MORRIS, Lloyd R., *American author,* 1893–1954

Letters: 2 (1917)

MORRIS, William, *English poet, artist, manufacturer, socialist,* 1834–96

Verse:

The Aeneid of Virgil (HM 6439)

[Child Christopher] (HM 36918)

The Deeds of Jason (incomplete: HM 6434)

The Defence of Guenevere (1907 illuminated ms. by Graily Hewitt: HM 25902)

The Doom of King Acrisius (HM 6462)

The Earthly Paradise (HM 6418)

Golden Wings (HM 6479)

The Hill of Venus (HM 6423)

Love is Enough (HM 6422)

[The Odyssey of Homer, done into English verse] (incomplete: HM 6448)

[The Odyssey of Homer, done into English Verse] (HM 6421)

The Ordination of Chivalry (from the French L'Ordené de Chevalerie: HM 6436)

Poems by the Way (49 poems: HM 6427)

The Story of Sigurd the Volsung (HM 6446)

"Think but one thought of me" (HM 6480)

[Two verses from Browning's Paracelsus, transcribed and illuminated by Morris for Browning] (HM 6478)

[Verses for pictures by Burne-Jones on Chaucer's "Romance of the Rose"] (HM 36919)

[Verses for pictures—stanza beginning]: "I am Winter that doth keep" (HM 36920)

Prose:

[Fragment: p. 96 of an unidentified novel] (HM 36917)

An Account of Three Socialist Lectures (4 pp.: HM 6444)

[Address Made in Behalf of the Work of the S.P.A.B.] (7 leaves: HM 6449)

Child Christopher and Goldilind the Fair (151 pp.: HM 6419)

The Glittering Plain: [original draft] (2 vols.: HM 6425)

The Glittering Plain (204 pp.: HM 6447)

The History of Over Sea (31 pp.: HM 6438)

Home Rule or Humbug (4 pp.: HM 6442)

Hopes and Fears for Art (incomplete, 9 pp.: HM 6432)

The House of the Wolfings (2 vols.: HM 6435)

[Magdalen Bridge: notes and memoranda relating to the efforts of the Society for the Protection of Ancient Buildings to save Magdalen Bridge] (2 leaves: HM 6451)

[Notes and sketches on verso of Socialist League leaflet] (1 p.: HM 36915)

Notes on Passing Events (2 pp.: HM 6443)

On the Artistic Qualities of the Woodcut Books of Ulm and Augsburg in the 15th Century (12 pp.: HM 6431)

Our Policy in This Crisis (7 leaves: HM 6465)

[Ravenna—Baptistry: petition re the raising and repair of the Baptistry at Ravenna] (1 leaf: HM 6455)

The Roots of the Mountains (455 pp.: HM 6424)

[St. Mark's at Venice: regarding the opinion of the S.P.A.B. on the restoration of St. Mark's] (1 p.: HM 6459)

[St. Mark's at Venice: re the S.P.A.B. and the restoration of St. Mark's] (15 leaves: HM 6461)

Some Thoughts on the Ornamented Manuscripts of the Middle Ages (7 pp.: HM 6440)

[The Story of Howard the Halt] (incomplete; from the Icelandic in collaboration with Erikr Magnusson, 33 leaves: HM 6426)

The Story of King Harold Greyfell (57 pp.: HM 6428)

The Story of King Magnus Son of Erling (from the Icelandic, in the hand of Magnusson, 126 pp.: HM 6437)

The Tables Turned, or Nupkins Awakened (68 pp.: HM 577)

The Tables Turned, or Nupkins Awakened: [draft] (24 pp.: HM 6433)

The Tale of King Coustans the Emperor (14 pp.: HM 6438)

To the Working People of Great Britain and of Ireland (3 pp.: HM 6464)

True and False Society (27 pp.: HM 6420)

Letters: 59 (1860–96), and 15 by May Morris

Documents: 5 (1881–96)

See also COCKERELL, Sir Sydney

MORROW, Honoré (McCue) Willsie, *American novelist, biographer,* 1880–1940

Letters: 1 (1938)

MORROW, William Chambers, *American author,* 1853–1923

Letters: 4 (1907–22)

MORTON, John Maddison, *English dramatist,* 1811–91

Prose:

After a Storm Comes a Calm (in one act, 32 pp.: HM 6715)

Letters: 1 (n.d.)

MORTON, Sarah Wentworth (Apthorp), *American poet, novelist,* 1759–1846

Verse:

[Poems] (251 pp.: HM 6272)
Stanzas to Memory (HM 6273)

MORTON, Thomas, *English dramatist,* 1764?–1838

Letters: 3 (1813–35)

MOSHER, Thomas Bird, *American publisher, printer, editor, author,* 1852–1923

Letters: 152 (1894–1923)

MOTLEY, John Lothrop, *American historian, diplomat,* 1814–77

Letters: 18 (1837–77)

Documents: 1 (1870)

MOTTRAM, Ralph Hale, *English novelist, miscellaneous author,* b. 1883

Letters: 1 (1926)

MOULTON, Ellen Louise (Chandler), *American editor, Author,* 1835–1908

Verse:

February (HM 1245)

Her Majesty (HM 23688)

How Long (HM 23474)

Life's Seasons (Kane Literary Collection)

The Lure (HM 44553)

Oh Latest Rose (HM 833)

Out in the Snow (HM 830)

A Poet's Second Love (HM 831)

Roses (HM 23920)

Throughout the Darkness (from Heine: HM 832)

Prose:

[Review notice of Mrs. Graham R. Thomson's poems] (1 p.: CM 187)

Letters: 57 (1854–1907)

MOWATT, Anna Cora (Ogden), see RITCHIE, Anna Cora (Ogden) Mowatt

MOXON, Edward, *English publisher, verse writer,* 1801–58

Letters: 3 (1831–39)

MUIR, John, *American naturalist, explorer,* 1838–1914

Prose:

[Fragmentary description beginning]: "joyful outburst of plant life, keenly emphasized by the chill baldness of the onlooking cliffs . . ." (1 p.; HM 15562)

Part of a journal relating to a visit in the Yosemite Valley (6 leaves: CA 145)

Steep Trails: a fragment (1 p.: HM 31315)

A Thousand Mile Journey (4 selected pages with drawings: FAC 624)

Letters: 174 (1860–1913)

MULOCK, Dinah Maria, see CRAIK, Dinah Maria (Mulock)

MUMFORD, Lewis, *American educator, editor, author,* 1895–

Letters: 6 (1952–72)

MUNBY, Arthur Joseph, *English poet,* 1828–1910

Letters: 1 (1891)

MUNDY, Talbot, *English-American novelist,* 1879–1940

Letters: 1 (1925)

MUNFORD, William, *American legislator, poet, classicist, court reporter,* 1775–1825

Verse:

The Iliad (translated into English, Books XXI–XXIV: BR 71)

Letters: 1 (1813)

Documents: 1 account book, (1795–1808) (BR 121)

MUNROE, Kirk, *American author,* 1850–1930

Letters: 1 (1897)

MURFREE, Mary Noailles (Charles Egbert Craddock, pseud.), *American novelist, short-story writer,* 1850–1922

Prose:

The Casting Vote: [final draft of a novelette] (138 pp.: HM 33799)

Letters: 5 (1885–87), including 2 to Sarah Orne Jewett and 3 to Annie (Adams) Fields

MURPHY, Arthur, *English author, actor,* 1727–1805

Prose:

The Way to Keep Him (Mr. Lovemore's part, in the handwriting of David Garrick, 34 pp.: HM 1263)

MURPHY, Henry Cruse, *American lawyer, book collector, editor, author,* 1810–82

Letters: 2 (1867–71)

MURPHY, Richard, *Irish poet,* 1927–

Letters: 2 (1964 and n.d.)

MURRAY, Alexander Stuart, *Scottish classical archaelogist,* 1841–1904

Verse:

A Greek Gem (HM 44070)

MURRAY, Charles, *English actor, dramatist,* 1754–1821

Letters: 2 (1818)

MURRAY, David Christie, *English novelist,* 1847–1907

Prose:

This Little World (191 pp.: HM 6716)

MURRAY, Gilbert, *English classicist, translator, publicist,* 1866–1957

Letters: 4 (1900–19)

MURRAY, John, *English publisher,* 1778–1843

Letters: 11 (1806–38)

MURRAY, Sir John, *English publisher,* 1851–1928

Letters: 3 (1899–1912)

MURRAY, John Fisher, *Irish poet, humorist,* 1811–65

Letters: 5 (1839–41)

MUZZEY, David Saville, *American educator and author,* 1870–1965

Letters: 2 (1936)

MYERS, Frederic William Henry, *English poet, essayist,* 1843–1901

Letters: 4 (1882–93)

N

NAPIER, Sir William Francis Patrick, *English general, historian,* 1785–1860

Letters: 5 (1844–57)

NASON, Leonard Hastings, *American author,* 1895–

Letters: 11 (1923–31) to Eugene Lafayette Cunningham.

NAST, Thomas, *American cartoonist,* 1840–1902

Prose:

[Satiric piece re Andrew Johnson] (in the hand of Sarah Edwards West, 1 p.: HM 27757)

Letters: 32 (1860–1902)

Other:

[Drawing]

NATHAN, George Jean, *American drama critic, editor, author,* 1882–1958

Letters: 5 (1920–31)

NATHAN, Isaac, *English composer, author,* 1791?–1864

Letters: 1 (1833)

NEAL, John, *American editor, novelist,* 1793–1876

Letters: 2 (1824)

NEIHARDT, John Gneisenau, *American poet, novelist,* b. 1881

Verse:

"Let me live out my years" (Jack London Collection)

Letters: 56 (1912–27)

NEMEROV, Howard, *American educator, author,* 1920–

Verse:

The Pond (OC 10)

Letters: 17 (1963–73)

NESBIT, Wilbur Dick, *American poet,* 1871–1927

Letters: 1 (1904)

NEWBOLT, Sir Henry John, *English poet, essayist, critic,* 1862–1938

Letters: 3 (1898–1927)

Other:

[Notes on Robert Seymour Bridges' "A Peace Ode"] (HM 36062)

NEWELL, Robert Henry (Orpheus C. Kerr, pseud.), *American editor, humorist,* 1836–1901

Verse:

"Who hath his birthright in immortal song" (HM 35075)

NEWMAN, Francis William, *English scholar, man of letters,* 1805–97

Verse:

What Is Germany? (HM 7138)

Letters: 10 (1849–76)

NEWMAN, John Henry, *English cardinal, author,* 1801–90

Verse:

Lead, Kindly Light: [2 lines copied from hymn by Newman] (HM 45674)

NEWTON, Alfred Edward, *American essayist, bibliophile, author,* 1863–1940

Letters: 22 (1918–40)

NICHOLS, John Gough, *English printer, antiquary, writer,* 1806–73

Letters: 4 (1832–49)

NICHOLS, Mary Sargeant (Neal) Gove, *American reformer, author,* 1810–84

Verse:

The Poet (HM 7147)

Letters: 8 (1879–80)

NICHOLS, Robert Malise Bowyer, *English poet, dramatist,* 1893–1944

Verse:

November (OC 1129)

Seventeen (OC 1128)

Letters: 8 (1934–42)

NICHOLSON, Meredith, *American novelist, diplomat,* 1866–1947

Letters: 1 (1920)

NICOLAS, Sir Nicholas Harris, *English antiquary, barrister,* 1799–1848

Letters: 19 (1826–44)

NIN, Anais, *American author,* 1903–77

Letters: 1 (1942) to Wallace Stevens

NIVEN, Frederick John, *Scottish-Canadian novelist,* 1878–1944

Letters: 1 (1921)

NOAH, Mordecai Manuel, *American lawyer, editor, playwright,* 1785–1851

Letters: 1 (1842)

NOEL, Thomas, *English poet,* 1799–1861

Verse:

The Poet (RB 109990, vol. 1, p. 1)

NOGUCHI, Yone, *Japanese-American poet,* 1875–1947

Verse:

Death of Lafcadio Hearn (HM 37864)
Epilogue: The Song of Songs, Which is Noguchi's (HM 37865)
Hymn of Spring (HM 37866)
Hymn of Summer (HM 37867)
In the Valley (HM 37868)
The Night Reverie in the Forest (HM 37869)
Prologue: The Song of Songs, Which is Noguchi's (HM 37870)
Song of Day [in] Yosemite Valley (HM 37871)
Song of Night in Yosemite Valley (HM 37872)
Upon the Heights (HM 37873)

Letters: 90 (1897–1919)

NORDHOFF, Charles, *American journalist, editor, author,* 1830–1901

Letters: 9 (1857–96)

NORDHOFF, Charles Bernard, *American author,* 1887–1947

Letters: 2 (1925–26)

NORMAN, Charles, *American artist, author,* 1904–

Letters: 3 (1945–61)

NORRIS, Kathleen (Thompson), *American novelist,* 1880–1966

Letters: 5 (1915–55)

NORTH, Francis, 4th Earl of Guilford, *English soldier, writer,* 1761–1817

Letters: 1 (1810)

NORTON, Andrews, *American biblical scholar, author,* 1786–1853

Verse:

"Thou best of friends, to whom I owe" (RB 150448)

Letters: 3 (1831–49)

NORTON, Caroline, see STIRLING-MAXWELL, Caroline Elizabeth Sarah (Sheridan) Norton

NORTON, Charles Eliot, *American educator, editor, author,* 1827–1908

Letters: 63 (1850–1907), including 21 to Annie (Adams) Fields and 17 to Richard Watson Gilder

NOYES, Alfred, *English poet,* 1880–1958

Verse:

[Two poems enclosed in letter] (HM 35925)

Letters: 46 (1919–57)

NOYES, John Humphrey, *American Perfectionist, reformer, author,* 1811–86

Prose:

How the *Essay on Scientific Propagation* Came to be Written and Published (2 pp.: RB 43854)

NYE, Edgar Wilson ("Bill"), *American journalist, humorist, lecturer, author,* 1850–96

Letters: 4 (1884–95)

O

O'BRIEN, Edward Joseph Harrington, *American poet, editor,* 1890–1941

Letters: 3 (1917–18) to Sarah (Hughes) Cornell

O'BRIEN, Fitz-James, *American journalist, playwright,* ca. 1828–62

Letters: 1 (1855) to James Thomas Fields

O'CALLAGHAN, John Cornelius, *Irish historical writer,* 1805–83

Letters: 1 (1866)

O'CONNOR, Ulick, *Irish author,* 1928–

Verse:

One Up (typewritten: Dublin Magazine Collection)

Prose:

The Dream Box: [play] (mimeograph copy, 16 pp.: Dublin Magazine Collection)

[Review of] *Apollinaire* by Margaret Davies (typewritten, 2 pp.: Dublin Magazine Collection)

Swift and Stella: [play] (typewritten, 37 pp.: Dublin Magazine Collection)

Theatre in Ireland: [review of Michael MacLiammoir] (typewritten with author's autograph corrections, 2 pp.: Dublin Magazine Collection)

O'CONOR, Norreys Jephson, *American author,* 1885–1958

Verse:

73 texts

Prose:

Amy Lowell: a Reminiscence (typewritten, 15 pp.: OC 11)

Bring Back the Years (typewritten: OC 21)

A British Hunter in Frontier Days (typewritten, 9 pp.: OC 22)

The Difference to Me (typewritten: OC 31)

Ear, Ear (typewritten, 5 pp.: OC 33)

E. H. Young (typewritten, 1 p.: OC 35)

Federal Union Talk: [notes for a speech] (partly typewritten, 8 pp.: OC 37)

Forgotten Country (typewritten, 3 pp.: OC 39)

Intrepid Lady (typewritten, 10 pp.: OC 49)

An Irish Sportsman in the Far West (typewritten, 11 pp.: OC 50)

It Happened in London (typewritten: OC 51)

John Gould Fletcher: An Impression (typewritten, 11 pp.: OC 52)

Magnificent Adventurer (typewritten, 12 pp.: OC 62)

Oh, to Glow in England (typewritten, 12 pp.: OC 74)

Portrait of Stephen (typewritten, 377 pp.: OC 79)

Thus the Story Might Begin (typewritten, 467 pp.: OC 94)

Letters: 261 (1891–1957)

Other:

[Autobiographical note] (OC 16)

Biographical note on H. S. Darlington (OC 4)

Biographical note on Norreys Jephson O'Conor (OC 18)

London Authors and London Scenes: [notes] (OC 59)

[Notes on U.S. Frigate *Constitution* and Commodore Jesse G. Eliot] (OC 9)

ODELL, Jonathan, *American Loyalist, satirist,* 1737–1818

Prose:

[The American Times: three-part satire, printed in 1870 under the pseudonym Camillo Querno] (in handwriting of John Howard Payne; incorrectly attributed to Jonathan Boucher, 49 pp.: HM 6249)

OGG, Frederic Austin, *American educator, author,* 1878–1951

Letters: 2 (1943–48)

O'HARA, John Henry, *American novelist,* 1905–

Letters: 6 (1950–56) to Sonya Levien

O'HARA, John Myers, *American author,* 1870–1944

Verse:

Epigrams of Nossis: [a translation] (HM 44945)

Fleurs D'Amour (HM 44946)

For Allah's Answer, by Ali Abu El-Imba: [a translation of poems] (HM 44947)

A Grecian Garland: [3 selections on Greece translated by O'Hara, followed by his poem, "Delos"] (HM 44949)

Greek Epitaphs by Charidas of Cyrene: [translation] (HM 44950)

Pagan Sonnets: [fifth edition of poems] (HM 44951)

Poems of Ming Wu: [translation] (HM 44952)

Te Fare Ute—Songs of Tahiti (HM 44953)

Xochicuicatl, by Xicontecatl—Flower Songs of Anahuac: [translation] (HM 44954)

Prose:

Christ and the Faun: [a play] (14 pp.: HM 44944)

Graffiti—Inscriptions on the Walls and Tombs of Pompeii: [translation] (97 pp.: HM 44948)

Letters: 17 (1907–42)

OLDER, Fremont, *American journalist, author,* 1856–1935

Prose:

Apricots as an Anaemia Remedy (6 pp.: HM 44559)

Communists in China (6 pp.: HM 44560)

Harvey, "the Circulator" (6 pp.: HM 44561)

Left Crime for Love of Mother (7 pp.: HM 44562)

Old Customs Survive (6 pp.: HM 44563)

The Problem of Fiat (6 pp.: HM 44564)

Reflections of an Editor (6 pp.: HM 44565)

Stop Torturing Rabbits (5 pp.: HM 44566)

A Street Girl Mother of a Duke (7 pp.: HM 44567)

Trying to "Save" the Eskimos (6 pp.: HM 44568)

Walking as Exercise for Policemen (7 pp.: HM 44569)

Letters: 13 (1912–34)

OLIPHANT, Margaret Oliphant (Wilson), *English novelist,* 1828–97

Prose:

An Anxious Moment (11 pp.: HM 44073)

Queen Victoria (6 pp.: HM 6255)

Letters: 12 (ca. 1880–90)

OLIVER, George, see ONIONS, Oliver

OLMSTEAD, Frederick Law, *American landscape architect, traveler, author,* 1822–1903

Letters: 10 (1860–77)

ONIONS, Oliver (George Oliver, pseud.), *English novelist* 1873–1961

Letters: 2 (1908–19)

OPIE, Amelia (Alderson), *English novelist, poet,* 1769–1853

Verse:

"He bade me remember him" (OP 37)

"Man's love is of man's life a thing apart" (OP 38)

"Oh bright was the pageant when England's throng" (OP 39)

To a Prism (OP 37)

To—With Cowper's Poems (OP 40)

To Thomas John Alderson on His Birthday (OP 41)

Letters: 331 (1794–1850)

OPPENHEIM, James, *American poet, novelist,* 1882–1932

Letters: 5 (1917–32)

OPPER, Frederick Burr, *American cartoonist, author,* 1857–1937

Letters: 123 (1898–1934)

ORCZY, Emmusca, Baroness, *Hungarian playwright, novelist,* 1865–1947

Letters: 1 (1914)

O'REILLY, John Boyle, *Irish revolutionist, author,* 1844–90

Verse:

Epigram (HM 1237)

Letters: 6 (1888–89) to Annie (Adams) Fields

ORME, Robert, *English military man, author,* 1728–1801

Letters: 6 (1776–94)

Documents: 2 (1765–74)

ORRERY, Earl of, see BOYLE, Roger, 1st Earl of Orrery

ORSAY, Alfred Guillaume Gabriel, Count d', *French artist,* 1801–52

Letters: 8 (1841–52)

OSBOURNE, Lloyd, *American author,* 1868–1947

Letters: 23 (1895–1928)

OSGOOD, Charles Grosvenor, *American educator, author,* 1871–1964

Letters: 6 (1916–36)

OSGOOD, Frances Sargent (Locke), *American poet,* 1811–50

Verse:

Discontent (HM 6254)

For Thee (HM 44570)

The Talisman (HM 6253)

O'SHAUGNESSY, Arthur William Edgar, *English poet, herpetologist,* 1844–81

Verse:

An Epic of Women and Other Poems (partly in the handwriting of Helen Snee: HM 6250)

An Epic of Women and Other Poems (proof sheets, final revision: RB 114301)

Music and Moonlight (HM 6251)

Notebook (HM 6252)

Prose:

An Account of an Occurrence in the South Sea Islands (15 pp.: HM 235)

On Russian Painting (incomplete, 7 pp.: HM 7072)

Portraits Charmants:

I—Alice (4 pp.: HM 7073)

II—Angora (6 pp. [and copy, 5 pp.]: HM 7074)

III—Zorahaida (4 pp. [and copy, 4 pp.]: HM 7075)

IV—Lady Greensleeves (6 pp. [and copy, 2 pp., incomplete]: HM 7076)

V—Cleopatra (16 pp. [and copy, 12 pp.]: HM 7077)

VI—Venus of Milo (5 pp. [and copy, 4 pp.]: HM 7078)

Letters: 1 (1877)

O'SHEEL, Shaemas, *American author,* 1886–1954

Letters: 1 (1938)

OSSOLI, Sarah Margaret (Fuller), Marchioness, *American journalist, social reformer, critic,* 1810–50

Verse:

"Church bells heard at evening" (HM 29617)

OUIDA, see DE LA RAMÉE, Marie Louise

OWEN, George, *English author of description and travel books,* 1552–1613

Prose:

The Description of Milford Haven (EL 1145)

OWEN, Robert Dale, *Scottish social reformer, author,* 1801–77

Prose:

Abraham Lincoln: a Eulogy (HM 2200)

in the Huntington Library

Letters: 8 (1853–74), including 4 to James Thomas Fields

Documents: 1 (1847)

OXBERRY, William Henry, *English actor,* 1808–52

Letters: 2 (ca. 1838–41)

P

PAGE, Curtis Hidden, *American educator, editor,* 1870–1946

Letters: 5 (1905–43)

PAGE, Thomas Nelson, *American diplomat, author,* 1853–1922

Prose:

Bred in the Bone (typescript with corrections and signature of author, 43 pp.: HM 6169)

A Soldier of the Empire (38 pp.: HM 7861)

[Ms. introduction in Pamela Colman Smith's *Annancy Stories*] (RB 109501)

Letters: 8 (1883–1903)

PAGE, Walter Hines, *American journalist, diplomat, publisher, author,* 1855–1918

Letters: 12 (1894–1914)

PAGET, Violet (Vernon Lee, pseud.), *English novelist, author,* 1857–1935

Letters: 8 (1884–1934)

PAINE, Albert Bigelow, *American editor, author,* 1861–1937

Verse:

To Edmund Clarence Stedman: On receiving from him a rare paste jar (AP 1430)

Letters: 15 (1902–31)

PAINE, John Knowles, *American educator, composer, author,* 1839–1906

Prose:

On John Fiske (3 pp.: HM 7860)

Letters: 2 (1905 and n.d.)

PAINE, Thomas, *American political philosopher, author,* 1737–1809

Verse:

The New Covenant (HM 170)

Letters: 4 (1782–95)

PALFREY, John Gorham, *American clergyman, editor, author,* 1796–1881

Letters: 6 (1848–50)

PALFREY, Sara Hammond, *American author,* 1823–1914

Letters: 11 (1861–1905), including 5 each to James Thomas and Annie (Adams) Fields

PALMER, Alice Elvira (Freeman), *American educator, poet,* 1855–1902

Letters: 3 (1886–91)

PALMER, John Williamson, *American author,* 1825–1906

Verse:

Stonewall Jackson Way (HM 7558)

Letters: 2 (1885–95)

PALMER, Samuel, *English painter,* 1805–81

Letters: 1 (1846)

PALMER, William Pitt, *American poet,* 1805–84

Letters: 2 (1843–57)

PANIZZI, Sir Anthony, *Italian-born librarian of British Museum,* 1797–1879

Letters: 6 (1842–69)

PARKE, John, *American poet,* 1754–89

Letters: 1 (1785)

PARKER, Sir Horatio Gilbert George, Bart., *English author, politician,* 1862–1932

Letters: 2 (1895–1915)

PARKER, Theodore, *American clergyman, abolitionist author,* 1810–60

Prose:

[Book Review for the Boston Courier of William Allen's *Psalms and Hymns for Public Worship*] (7 pp.: HM 25221)

[Book Review of a history of the Mexican War] (3 pp.: HM 25222)

Book Review of *The Old Testament Arranged in Historical and Chronological Order* (2 pp.: HM 25145)

Book Review of "Report of the Seventeenth Meeting of the British Association in Advancement of Science . . ." (8 pp.: HM 25220)

Journal (1831, May 16, 4 pp.: HM 25223)

Letters: 58 (1839–59), including 29 to Thomas Wentworth Higginson

Documents: 1 (1855)

Other:

[Memoranda] (6 leaves: HM 25382)

[Notes on] Duration of Life (3 pp.: HM 25238)

[Outline notes on intemperance, the Bible, slavery, etc.] (8 leaves: HM 25261)

Sketches: [reading notes] (15 pp.: HM 21638)

[Statement on slavery] (1 p.: HM 21637)

PARKMAN, Francis, *American historian, author,* 1823–93

Letters: 32 (1849–92)

PARR, Samuel, *English pedagogue,* 1747–1825

Letters: 8 (1790–1824)

PARRISH, Maxfield, *American artist, illustrator,* 1870–1966

Letters: 1 (1953)

PARRY, John, *English musician, composer,* 1776–1851
Pen-and-ink drawing (FR 187)

PARSONS, Thomas William, *American dentist, poet, translator,* 1819–92

Letters: 16 (1850–82)

Other:

[List of possible titles for translation of the first 10 cantos of the *Inferno*] (FI 3499)

PARTON, James, *American biographer,* 1822–91

Letters: 45 (1866–82)

Documents: 1 (1870)

Other:

[Four responses to requests for autographs] (Kane Literary Collection)

PARTON, Sara Payson (Willis) Eldredge Farrington, *American author,* 1811–72

Letters: 2 (1856 and n.d.)

PARTRIDGE, William Ordway, *American sculptor, author,* 1861–1930

Letters: 1 (1895)

PATER, Walter Horatio, *English critic, humanist,* 1839–94

Letters: 4 (1875–92)

PATON, Sir Joseph Noel, *English artist,* 1821–1901

Verse:

A Christmas Carol (HM 44069)

PAULDING, James Kirke, *American editor, author,* 1778–1860

Prose:

The millionaire (27 pp.: HM 6172)

Too Late and Too Early (25 pp.: HM 6168)

Letters: 5 (1817–55)

Other:

[Ink sketch of contemporary costumes with a satirical commentary] (2 pp.: HM 36828)

PAYN, James, *English novelist,* 1830–98

Letters: 5 (1882–ca. 1896)

PAYNE, John Howard, *American actor, playwright, editor, poet,* 1791–1852

Verse:

Eclogue the Fifth. Autumn. Interlocutory (HM 45664)

God Save Great George Our King (HM 1231)

Home, Sweet Home (HM 6046)

La Buccolica (HM 7839)

Letters: 51 (1811–50); also, letterbook (1813–18) containing copies of Payne's correspondence with the Von Hartens (HM 6048); and letterbook (1848–50) containing transcripts, in Payne's hand, of 57 letters to him from Anna Mary (Freeman) Goldbeck (HM 6049)

Other:

Account Book—1843 (89 pp.: HM 6045)

[Miscellaneous notes] (5 pieces: HM 7838)

PEABODY, Elizabeth Palmer, *American educator, author,* 1804–94

Letters: 2 (1846–90)

PEACOCK, Thomas Love, *English novelist, poet,* 1785–1866

Verse:

[The New Year]: Lines on George Cruikshank's Illustration of January, in the Comick Almanack for 1838 (HM 42738)

PEAKE, Richard Brinsley, *English dramatist,* 1792–1847

Letters: 1 (n.d.)

PEALE, Norman Vincent, *American clergyman, author,* 1898–

Letters: 2 (1941)

PEARSON, Norman Holmes, *American educator, editor,* 1909–

Letters: 21 (1937–71)

PEATTIE, Donald Culross, *American botanist, novelist,* 1898–1964

Letters: 1 (1943)

PECK, Samuel Minturn, *American poet,* 1854–1938

Verse:

The Dimple on Her Cheek (Kane Literary Collection)

A Knot of Blue (Kane Literary Collection)

The Old Songs (Kane Literary Collection)

Letters: 24 (1886–1912)

PEIXOTTO, Ernest Clifford, *American artist, author,* 1869–1940

Letters: 2 (1921 and n.d.)

PELLEGRINI, Carlo, *English caricaturist,* 1839–89

Letters: 2 (1876)

PENN, John, *English miscellaneous writer,* 1760–1834

Letters: 10 (1798–1824)

PENNELL, Joseph, *American artist, author,* 1857–1926

Letters: 22 letters (1894–1911) by his wife, Elizabeth (Robins) Pennell

Documents: 1 (ca. 1780)

PEPYS, Samuel, *English diarist,* 1633–1703

Letters: 3 (1684–90)

PERCIVAL, James Gates, *American editor, geologist, poet,* 1795–1856

Verse:

Ode (HM 8382)

Letters: 1 (1825)

PERCIVAL, Olive, *American writer*, 1869–1945

Prose:

Aunt Abby and Others (typewritten, 1 vol.: Percival Papers)

[Autobiographical sketch] (2 copies, typewritten: Percival Papers)

The Children's Garden Book (typewritten with ms. drawings, 1 vol.: Percival Papers)

Diaries: 1889–1939 (23 vols.: Percival Papers)

Los Angeles in part, 1847: [plan of parts of the city, with explanatory notes] (Percival Papers)

My First Visit to San Diego and La Jolla (typewritten, 9 pp.: Percival Papers)

Once, in Old Chinatown (typewritten: Percival Papers)

[Short stories, collected in a volume] (typewritten: Percival Papers)

Travel diaries: 1903 and 1910 (2 vols.: Percival Papers)

Letters: 2 (1914 and n.d.), and 14 letters addressed to her

PERCY, Thomas, Bishop of Dromore, *English editor*, 1729–1811

Verse:

Poetical Extracts: [miscellaneous 18th-century verse, gathered together by Thomas Percy, with several pieces written by Percy] (HM 216)

Prose:

Remarks on the History of China: [critical comments on volume 8 of the modern part of *An Universal History, from the Earliest Account of Time to the Present*] (8 pp.: HM 6511)

Remarks on the Hist[ory] of China: [abbreviated version of HM 6511] (9 pp.: HM 6173)

Letters: 11 (1776–1804)

PERCY, William, *English poet,* 1575–1648

Verse:

Comoedyes and Pastoralls with their songs (217 leaves: HM 4)

PERKINS, James Handasyd, *American author,* 1810–49

Letters: 1 (1838)

PERKINS, Maxwell Evarts, *American editor,* 1884–1947

Letters: 1 (1929)

PERRY, Bliss, *American educator, editor, author,* 1860–1954

Letters: 24 (1899–1913)

PERRY, James, *English journalist,* 1756–1821

Letters: 4 (1813–21)

PERRY, Nora, *American poet, journalist,* 1831–96

Letters: 3 (1885–92)

PERRY, Thomas Sergeant, *American lecturer, educator, author,* 1845–1928

Letters: 12 (1880–1920)

PETERKIN, Julia (Mood), *American author,* 1880–1961

Letters: 8 (1928–30)

PHELPS, Samuel, *English actor,* 1804–78

Letters: 7 (1837–78)

PHELPS, William Lyon, *American essayist, educator, author,* 1865–1943

Letters: 17 (1910–42)

PHILLEO, Calvin Wheeler, *American author,* fl. 1855

Prose:

Preface [to *Twice Married, A Story of Connecticut Life*] (LF)

Letters: 31 (1855) to Dix & Edwards Co.

PHILLIPS, Watts, *English dramatist, designer,* 1825–74

Letters: 4 (1867–73)

PHILLIPS, Wendell, *American orator, abolitionist author,* 1811–84

Prose:

The Louisiana Question (20 pp.: RU 110)

Letters: 33 (1841–83)

Other:

[Expression of patriotism] (1 p.: HM 8296)

Lines of poetry taught by John Brown to his children (typewritten, 1 p.: RU 164)

PHILLPOTTS, Eden, *English novelist, poet,* 1862–1960

Verse:

Remember (in the hand of Maurice Buxton Forman: HM 41824)

The Stars (in the hand of Maurice Buxton Forman: HM 41825)

A Vision of Spring (in the hand of Maurice Buxton Forman: HM 41826)

Letters: 41 (1893–1912), including 32 to William Morris Colles

Other:

[Quotation from "Jane's Legacy"] (1 p.: HM 44577)

PHOENIX, John, see DERBY, George Horatio

PIATT, John James, *American poet, journalist, editor,* 1835–1917

Verse:

Impromptu (HM 17266)

Letters: 2 (1862–63)

PICKARD, Samuel Thomas, *American printer, editor, author,* 1828–1915

Prose:

The Life and Letters of John Greenleaf Whittier (fragment, 4 pp.: HM 12998)

[Note regarding Whittier's *The Sycamores*] (1 p.: RB 55303 PF)

[Statement concerning anecdote about Whittier which appears in Annie (Adams) Fields's *Authors and Friends*] (typewritten, with 2 lines autograph, 1 p.: FI 2523)

Whittier-land: [rough notes] (6 pp.: HM 12999)

Whittier-land: [typescript of a portion of chapter 3] (7 pp.: HM 13000)

Letters: 2 (1904)

PICKERING, Henry, *American poet,* 1781–1831

Letters: 1 (1831)

PICKERING, William, *English publisher,* 1796–1854

Letters: 1 (1842)

PICKFORD, Mary, *Canadian-born American actress,* 1893–

Letters: 1 (1936)

PIDGIN, Charles Felton, *American inventor, novelist,* 1844–1923

Letters: 2 (1920)

PIERCE, Edward Lillie, *American lawyer, editor,* 1829–97

Letters: 6 (1859–86)

PIERCE, Frank Richardson, *American author,* 1887–

Letters: 1 (1934) to Eugene Lafayette Cunningham

PIERPONT, John, *American clergyman, poet, reformer,* 1785–1866

Letters: 1 (1852)

PIGOTT, Edward Smyth, *English Examiner of Plays,* 1826–95

Letters: approximately 400 letters addressed to Pigott, including 68 from Wilkie Collins

PIKE, Albert, *American lawyer, soldier, author,* 1809–91

Verse:

"We sit and watch the current of our life" (HM 6164)

Letters: 12 (1835–90)

Documents: 2 (1835–80)

PINERO, Sir Arthur Wing, *English dramatist,* 1855–1934

Letters: 7 (1886–1929)

PINKER, James Brand, *English literary agent,* 1863–1922

Letters: 149 (1903–13), and 306 letters addressed to him from Ford Madox Ford; also a collection (61 pieces) of letters to Pinker or one of his sons from a number of literary figures

PINKERTON, John, *Scottish antiquary, historian,* 1758–1826

Letters: 2 (1786–1801)

PIOZZI, Hester Lynch (Salusbury) Thrale, *English author, friend of Dr. Johnson,* 1741–1821

Verse:

Stanzas Written Among the Ruins of an Old Castle at Denbigh (HM 41047)

Prose:

Thraliana (6 vols.: HM 12183)

Letters: 39 (1780–1821)

Other:

[Notes in Edward Nares's *Eis Theos, Eis Mesites*] (RB 80677)

PITT, Christopher, *English poet, translator,* 1699–1748

Letters: 2 (n.d.)

PLACE, Francis, *English radical reformer,* 1771–1854

Letters: 9 (1813–41), including 7 to Richard Carlile

PLANCHÉ, James Robinson, *English dramatist, Somerset herald,* 1796–1880

Verse:

Farewell Address Spoken by the Countess Dowager of Essex (printed copy: JP 214)

A Literary Squabble (FI 4301)

Madame Vestris's Answer to the Alphabet (JP 211)

Prose:

King Christmas—a few words respecting the origin of this, last extravaganza (2 pp.: Planché Collection)

Mr. Buckstone's Voyage around the Globe (Planché Collection)

The Prince of Happy Land (Planché Collection)

Letters: 35 (1835–79)

Other:

[Drawings] (JP 206–210, 212–213)

[List of Planché's dramatic works] (Planché Collection)

PLANCHÉ, Matilda Anne, see MACKARNESS, Matilda Anne (Planché)

PLUMPTRE, James, *English dramatist, divine,* 1770–1832

Letters: 2 (1829)

PLUNKETT, Edward John Moreton Drax, 18th Baron Dunsany, *English writer,* 1878–1957

Verse:

The Waking Eye (HM 35483)

What garden since the close . . . (HM 35485)

Prose:

Clarity (11 pp.: HM 35484)

[Extract from The Book of Wonder] (1 p.: HM 7659)

Letters: 13 (1912–55)

Documents: 1 (1917)

POE, Edgar Allan, *American poet, critic, editor,* 1809–49

Verse:

Annabel Lee (HM 1186)

The Departed (in the hand of J. Hunt: HM 2510)

Dream-Land (possibly not autograph: HM 1725)

To Mrs. M. L. S. [Marie Louise Shew] (HM 2513)

To One Departed (possibly not autograph: HM 1182)

Prose:

About Critics and Criticisms (roll, 4 x 144 inches: HM 1188)

Criticism, and some stanzas from Hirst's "The Owl" (2 pp.: HM 1218)

Criticism of Simms's "The Wigwam and the Cabin" (11 pp.: HM 1185)

Literary America (15 pp.: HM 1184)

Marginalia: [excerpts] (1 p.: HM 2514)

[Marginalia—Reviews of Sarah Anne Lewis's "The Child of the Sea" and Eugene Sue's "The Wandering Jew"] (20 pp.: HM 1183)

Morella (2 pp.: HM 1726)

[Review of Sarah Anne Lewis's "Lament of La Vega"] (8 pp.: HM 2512)

Letters: 25 (1835–49), and one by Rosalie Poe (1873); also, forgery (HM 21873)

Documents: 1 (1843)

Other:

[Corrections in *The New Mirror,* edited by G. P. Morris] (RB 147099)

POLE, William, *English engineer, musician, authority on whist,* 1814–1900

Letters: 2 (1879–91)

POLLOCK, Channing, *American drama critic, playwright,* 1880–1946

Letters: 2 (1931 and n.d.)

POOLE, Ernest, *American novelist,* 1880–1950

Letters: 1 (1916) to Mary (Hunter) Austin

POOLE, John, *English dramatist, miscellaneous writer,* 1786?–1872

Prose:

Patrician and Parvenu (94 pp.: HM 6167)

Letters: 78 (1817–56)

POOLE, Paul Falconer, *English historical painter,* 1807–79

Letters: 3 (1867–76)

POOLE, Reginald Lane, *English historian,* 1857–1939

Letters: 4 (1897–1919)

POORE, Benjamin Perley, *American editor, author,* 1820–87

Letters: 6 (1852–86)

POPE, Alexander, *English poet,* 1688–1744

Verse:

Epistle to Arbuthnot (incomplete: HM 6006)

Epistle to Lord Bathurst (HM 6007)

Epistle to Lord Bathurst (HM 6008)

Epistle to Lord Bathurst: [leaves from 1735 quarto edition with variants in the hand of Jonathan Richardson] (HM 6009)

To Mr. Hughes on His Opera (RB 105725)

Letters: 10 (1716–41)

Other:

[Note in *Essay on Man*] (RB 106530)

See also SPENCE, Joseph

PORSON, Richard, *English Greek scholar,* 1759–1808

Verse:

Epitaph (HM 6170)

Letters: 1 (1784)

PORTER, Gene (Stratton), *American naturalist, author,* 1868–1924

Letters: 1 (1921)

PORTER, Jane, *English novelist,* 1776–1850

Letters: 18 (1803–32)

PORTER, Katherine Anne, *American author,* 1894–

Letters: 1 (1952)

PORTER, William Sydney (O. Henry, pseud.), *American short-story writer,* 1862–1910

Prose:

[Fragment of manuscript] (1 p.: HM 44582)

Letters: 7 (1895–97)

Documents: 4 (1894–95)

PORTEUS, Beilby, Bishop of London, *English bishop, author,* 1731–1808

Letters: 10 (1768–1808)

POTTER, Alfred Claghorn, *American librarian, author,* 1867–1940

Letters: 27 (1925–40)

POTTER, Paul Meredith, *English-born American playwright,* 1853–1921

Letters: 1 (n.d.)

POTTER, Robert, *English poet, politician,* 1721–1804

Verse:

The Oracle Concerning Babylon (MO 4153)

The Song of Exultation (MO 4153)

Prose:

Translations from the Persian Language (quotation, 2 leaves: MO 4154)

Letters: 54 (1778–1801)

POUND, Ezra Loomis, *American poet,* 1885–1972

Letters: 4 (1913–37)

Other:

[Annotation on letter from W. S. B. Braithwaite] (HM 30578)

POWELL, Edward Alexander, *American traveler, author,* 1879–1951

Letters: 1 (1938)

POWELL, Lawrence Clark, *American librarian, author,* 1906–

Letters: 3 (1944–65)

POWYS, Llewelyn, *English novelist, essayist,* 1884–1939

Letters: 17 (1920–39)

POYNTER, Sir Edward John, 1st Bart., *English painter,* 1836–1919

Letters: 35 (1866–1908)

Other:

Drawing for Howes Norris (1 p.: HM 30985)

PRAED, Winthrop Mackworth, *English poet,* 1802–39

Verse:

"Oh yes, her childhood hath been nurst" (HM 6165)
"They told me thou wilt pass again" (HM 6166)

Letters: 2 (1822–31)

PRATT, Samuel Jackson, *English miscellaneous writer,* 1749–1814

Letters: 9 (1775–1803)

PRENTICE, George Denison, *American poet, editor,* 1802–70

Verse:

The Bygone Year (HM 45334)
The Closing Year (HM 45335)
The Death of the Year (HM 45336)
The Departure of the Seasons (HM 45359)
A Dirge (HM 45337)
The Flight of Years (HM 45338)

in the Huntington Library

A Fragment [of a poem] (HM 45339)
Harvest Hymn (HM 45340)
I Think of Thee (HM 45341)
I Think of Thee: [variant] (HM 45342)
A Lady of Love (HM 45343)
Leaving Home (HM 45344)
Lines (HM 45345)
Lines for an Album (HM 45346)
Lines to a Lady (HM 45347)
Lines to a Lady: [variant] (HM 45348)
Lines [to a Lady: variant] (HM 45349)
Lines Written in a Beautiful Moonlight (HM 45350)
Lines Written in Cave Hill Cemetery (HM 45351)
The Lock of Hair (HM 45352)
A Moonlight Scene (HM 45353)
My Heart is with Thee (HM 45354)
New England (HM 45355)
Night in June (HM 45356)
Ode for an Agricultural Festival (HM 45357)
On a Distant View of the Ocean (HM 45358)
Progress of Liberty (HM 45359)
Recollections (HM 45360)
A Sabbath Night (HM 45361)
Scene on the Ohio (HM 45362)
To a Beautiful Girl (HM 45363)
To a Cousin Dying of Consumption (HM 45364)
To a Lady (HM 45365)
To a Poetess (HM 45366)
To Bell Smith (HM 45367)

To Julia [Bacon] (HM 45368)
To Laura (HM 45369)
To Miss B[enham]? (HM 45370)
To Miss H[enrietta] B[enham] (HM 45371)
To Miss Sue Spence (HM 45372)
To My Young Friend on Her Birthday (HM 45373)
To the Memory of Isabel (HM 45374)
To—(HM 45375)
To—(HM 45376)
Unhappy Love (HM 45377)

Letters: 1 (1862)

Documents: 1 (1861)

PRESCOTT, William Hickling, *American historian,* 1796–1859

Letters: 33 (1838–59)

PRESTON, Harriet Waters, *American editor, translator, author,* 1836–1911

Letters: 11 (1873–1910) to Annie (Adams) Fields

PRESTON, Margaret (Junkin), *American author,* 1820–97

Verse:

The Sphinx (BR Box 132 [1])
"There'll come a day" (HM 1914)

Prose:

William C[ampbell] Preston: [an obituary notice for "Willie" Preston, who fell at the 2nd Battle of Bull Run, Aug. 29, 1862] (9 leaves: BR Box 284)
Recent Literature (6 pp.: BR Box 183)
Book review (incomplete, 9 pp.: BR Box 183)

Publishers' Counters (incomplete, 5 pp.: BR Box 183)
[Literary Notes] (9 pp.: BR Box 183)

Letters: 7 (1872–87)

PRICE, Richard, *English nonconformist minister, writer,* 1723–91

Letters: 4 (1771–87)

PRIESTLEY, Herbert Ingram, *American historian, author,* 1875–1944

Letters: 1 (1928)

PRIME, Samuel Irenaeus, *American clergyman, editor, author,* 1812–85

Letters: 1 (1876)

PRINCE, John Critchley, *English poet,* 1808–66

Letters: 1 (1852)

PRIOR, Matthew, *English poet, diplomat,* 1664–1721

Verse:
Hans Carvel. De la Fountain Imitated (copy: EL 8907)

PROCTER, Adelaide Ann, *English poet,* 1825–64

Verse:
Grief (HM 3106)
King and Slave (HM 3105)
One by One (BC 1386)
Strive, Wait and Pray (BC 1386)

Letters: 1 (1861)

PROCTER, Anne Benson (Skepper), *English, wife of Bryan Waller Procter,* 1799–1888

Letters: 43 (1851–87)

PROCTER, Bryan Waller, *English poet,* 1787–1874

Verse:

Joy to Queen Victoria (HM 6940)

A Sleepy Song (FI 3552)

[A Song, beginning]: "Let us listen to the song" (HM 12323)

A Song, with a Moral [beginning]: "When the winter bloweth loud" (FI 3548)

To My Child (in hand of Mrs. Procter: HM 3103)

"Weave the words into a Song" (Kenyon Album)

Prose:

Charles Lamb (500 pp.: HM 656)

Letters: 35 (1819–73)

PROCTOR, Edna Dean, *American poet,* 1829–1923

Verse:

"This, too, will pass!" (HM 39114)

Letters: 3 (1890–1902)

PUTNAM, George Haven, *American soldier, publisher, author,* 1844–1930

Letters: 14 (1867–1914)

PUTNAM, George Palmer, *American publisher,* 1814–72

Letters: 6 (1839–63)

PUTNAM, George William, *American writer,* fl. 1881

Prose:

Charles Dickens and Washington Irving (7 pp.: FI 3593)

Incidents at New York (12 pp.: FI 3590)

Letters: 2 (1881) to James Thomas Fields

PUTNAM, Mary Traill Spence (Lowell), *American author,* 1810–98

Prose:

American Life in France (one paragraph only, in a letter to Fields: FI 3574)

Letters: 35 (1861–97), including 26 to Annie (Adams) Fields

PYE, Henry James, *English poet laureate,* 1745–1813

Letters: 2 (n.d.)

PYLE, Howard, *American artist, illustrator, author,* 1853–1911

Letters: 1 (1905)

Q

QUARLES, Francis, *English poet,* 1592–1644

Verse:

The Rejoyceing of ye Smects: or the Tryumph of the Roundheads (copy: EL 8884) [another copy] (EL 8890)

QUILLER-COUCH, Sir Arthur Thomas, *English author,* 1863–1944

Letters: 1 (1919)

QUILLINAN, Edward, *English poet,* 1791–1851

Letters: 1 (1836)

R

RACHMANINOFF, Sergei, *Russian pianist, composer,* 1873–1943

Letters: 1 (1942)

RACKHAM, Arthur, *English illustrator,* 1867–1939

Letters: 2 (1927)

RAEBURN, Sir Henry, *Scottish portrait painter,* 1756–1823

Letters: 3 (1814–30)

RAINE, William McLeod, *American novelist,* 1871–1954

Letters: 7 (1930–36) to Eugene Lafayette Cunningham

RALEIGH, Sir Walter Alexander, *English scholar,* 1861–1922

Letters: 4 (1895–1907)

RAMSAY, Allan, *Scottish wigmaker, poet, bookseller,* 1686–1758

Verse:

[Collection of his works] (65 pp.: HM 97)

[Collection of his works] (54 pp.: HM 211)

[Collection of his works] (43 pp.: HM 1490)

The Gentle Shepherd (4 pp.: HM 1489)

RANDALL, James Ryder, *American poet, journalist,* 1839–1908

Verse:

Magdalen (Arthur Bond Cecil Collection)

[Maryland, My Maryland: one stanza, beginning]: "Hark to an exiled son's appeal" (HM 45670)

My Maryland (HM 6043)

My Maryland (copy made for Edmund Clarence Stedman about 1888: HM 1996)

The Unconquered Banner (Arthur Bond Cecil Collection)

Letters: 3 (1888–1904)

RANDOLPH, Thomas, *English poet, dramatist,* 1605–35

Verse:

[Poems ascribed to him in commonplace books] (HM 116; HM 198; HM 172; HM 904)

Prose:

The Drinking Academy, or Cheaters Holy Day: [play] (20 leaves: HM 91)

RANKIN, McKee, *Canadian-born actor, theater manager,* 1844–1914

Prose:

Abraham Lincoln, a Historical Drama (contemporary typescript, 99 pp.: HM 6040)

Letters: 2 (1880–1909)

RANSOM, Will, *American book designer, printer, author,* 1878–1955

Letters: 27 (1925–48)

RASCOE, Arthur Burton, *American editor, author,* 1892–1957

Letters: 2 (1924–34) to Mary (Hunter) Austin

RATHBONE, Basil, *English-American actor,* 1892–1967

Letters: 1 (1934)

RAYMOND, Henry Jarvis, *American editor, author,* 1820–69

Letters: 5 (1855–66)

READ, Thomas Buchanan, *American painter, poet,* 1822–72

Letters: 7 (1846–69), including 4 to James Thomas Fields

READE, Charles, *English novelist, dramatist,* 1814–84

Prose:

The Cloister and the Hearth (4 vols.: HM 2299)
Dogs' Homes (10 pp.: HM 6000)
The Double Marriage (incomplete, 117 pp.: HM 2497)
The Picture (incomplete, 65 pp.: HM 2498)
Put Yourself in His Place (2 vols.: HM 2300)
The Wandering Heir (incomplete, 175 pp.: HM 2499)
What Has Become of Lord Camelford's Body: (19 pp.: HM 4252)

Letters: 103 (1855–83), including 42 to James Thomas Fields and 24 to Ticknor and Fields (firm)

Documents: 2 (1869–73)

Other:

Cuts to be made in the copy of [*It Is Never Too Late to Mend*] (6 pp.: FI 3651)

REALF, Richard, *American poet,* 1834–78

Verse:

The Children (EG Box 49)

Hymn of Pittsburg (EG Box 49)

Letters: 2 (1858–69)

REDGRAVE, Richard, *English painter,* 1804–88

Prose:

A Century of Painters of the English School with Critical Notices of their Works and an Account of the Progress of Art in England (797 pp.: HM 19801)

REDPATH, James, *American editor, lecture-promoter, author,* 1833–91

Letters: 9 (1860–86)

REEDY, William Marion, *American editor, essayist,* 1862–1920

Letters: 115 (1905–20)

REESE, Lizette Woodworth, *American educator, poet,* 1856–1935

Verse:

Immortality (HM 36068)

Letters: 1 (1896) to Annie (Adams) Fields

REID, Whitelaw, *American editor, diplomat, author,* 1837–1912

Letters: 41 (1864–1912)

REMINGTON, Frederic, *American painter, sculptor, author, illustrator,* 1861–1909

Letters: 5 (1891–99)

REPPLIER, Agnes, *American author*, 1855–1950

Letters: 4 (1891–93), including 3 to Annie (Adams) Fields

REPTON, Humphry, *English landscape gardener*, 1752–1818

Letters: 50 (1806–12)

REYNOLDS, Frederic, *English dramatist*, 1764–1841

Letters: 1 (n.d.)

REYNOLDS, John Hamilton, *English poet*, 1796–1852

Letters: 2 (1837)

REYNOLDS, Sir Joshua, *English portrait painter*, 1723–92

Letters: 4 (1773–90)

Other:
Samuel Johnson [pencil sketch] (HM 40961)

RHODES, Eugene Manlove, *American author*, 1869–1934

Verse:

At the Last Minute (typewritten, Rhodes Collection)

Recognition (Rhodes Collection)

Prose:

Aforesaid Bates (corrected proofs, 42 pp.: Rhodes Collection)

A Beggar on Horseback (corrected typescript, 12 pp.: Rhodes Collection)

Beyond the Desert (corrected typescript, 161 pp.: Rhodes Collection)

The Bird in the Bush (3 typewritten copies; 1 copy of proofs, 36 pp.: Rhodes Collection)

The Brave Adventure (typewritten, 50 pp.: Rhodes Collection)

The Brave Adventure (corrected typescript, 14 pp.: Rhodes Collection)

The Brave Adventure: [enlarged version] (corrected typescript, 47 pp.: Rhodes Collection)

A Change of Venue (corrected proofs, 7 pp.: Rhodes Collection)

Check (typewritten, 17 pp.: Rhodes Collection)

Check (corrected typescript, 22 pp.: Rhodes Collection)

His Father's Flag (typewritten, 12 pp.: Rhodes Collection)

The Hour and the Man (corrected typescript, 19 pp.: Rhodes Collection)

How the Dream Came True (corrected typescript, 6 pp.: Rhodes Collection)

An Interlude (typewritten, 17 pp.: Rhodes Collection)

The Little Eohippus: [ending only] (corrected typescript, 35 pp.: Rhodes Collection)

Loved I Not Honor More (corrected proofs, 9 pp.: Rhodes Collection)

Maid Most Dear (corrected proofs, 14 pp.: Rhodes Collection)

Neighbors (typewritten, 21 pp.: Rhodes Collection)

Old Times: chaps. 2 and 3, and Table of Contents (typewritten, 76 pp.: Rhodes Collection)

On Velvet (typewritten, 13 pp.: Rhodes Collection)

A Pink Trip Slip (corrected proofs, 6 pp.: Rhodes Collection)

The Prince of Tonight (corrected typescript, 39 pp.: Rhodes Collection)

The Prince of Tonight (printed copy with autograph corrections: Rhodes Collection)

The Punishment and the Crime (corrected printed copy, 7 pp.: Rhodes Collection)

The Ragged Twenty-Eighth (typewritten, 8 pp.: Rhodes Collection)

Rule-O'-Thumb (corrected proofs, 6 pp.: Rhodes Collection)

Shoot the Moon (corrected proofs, 30 pp.: Rhodes Collection)

The Simple Plan (corrected proofs, 11 pp.: Rhodes Collection)

Slaves of the Ring (corrected proofs, 9 pp.: Rhodes Collection)

Sticky Pierce, Diplomat (corrected proofs, 9 pp.: Rhodes Collection)

The Torch (corrected proofs, 12 pp.: Rhodes Collection)

Trail's End (corrected proofs, 28 pp.: Rhodes Collection)

Wildcat Represents (typewritten, 31 pp.: Rhodes Collection)

Letters: 644 (1899–1934), and several hundred addressed to Rhodes

RICE, Alice Hegan, *American novelist,* 1870–1942

Letters: 1 (1918)

RICE, Cale Young, *American poet, dramatist,* 1872–1943

Letters: 3 (1915–20)

RICE, Elmer L., *American playwright, novelist, stage director,* 1892–1967

Letters: 1 (1919)

RICE, James, see BESANT, Sir Walter

RICHARDS, Ivor Armstrong, *American educator, author,* 1893–

Letters: 9 (1966–73)

RICHARDS, Laura Elizabeth (Howe), *American author,* 1850–1943

Letters: 17 (1891–1911), including 6 to Sarah Orne Jewett and 11 to Annie (Adams) Fields

RICHARDSON, Charles Francis, *American educator, author,* 1851–1913

Verse:

Peace (Kane Literary Collection)

Letters: 2 (1879–96)

RICHARDSON, Samuel, *English novelist,* 1689–1761

Letters: 2 (1745–50)

Documents: 1 (1733)

Other:

[Manuscript notes in vol. 7 of *The History of Charles Grandison*] (RB 106535)

RICHMOND, George, *English portrait painter,* 1809–96

Letters: 3 (1874–79)

RICHTER, Conrad Michael, *American author,* 1890–

Letters: 4 (1910–53)

RICKETSON, Daniel, *American historian, poet,* 1813–98

Letters: 1 (1854)

RICKMAN, John, *English statistician, friend of Lamb and Southey,* 1771–1840

Letters: 500 (1798–1839), including 499 to Robert Southey

Other:

[Corrections on Southey's "Inscriptions for the Caledonian Canal"] (RS 1)

[Memorandum on letter from James Burney to Robert Southey] (RS 1247)

RIDDELL, Charlotte Eliza Lawson (Cowan), *English novelist,* 1832–1906

Letters: 1 (1866)

RIDDLE, Albert Gallatin, *American lawyer, biographer, novelist,* 1816–1902

Letters: 3 (1856–65)

RIDEOUT, Henry Milner, *American critic, editor, author,* 1877–1927

Letters: 1 (1922)

RIDGE, Lola, *American poet,* 1884–1941

Letters: 4 (1930) to Mary (Hunter) Austin

RIDLEY, Gloster, *English miscellaneous writer,* 1702–74

Letters: 3 (1746–47)

RIGGS, Lynn, *American playwright, poet,* 1899–1954

Letters: 1 (1930)

RIIS, Jacob August, *American journalist, reformer, author,* 1849–1914

Letters: 15 (1889–1911)

RILEY, James Whitcomb, *American poet,* 1849–1916

Verse:

"All hope of rest withdrawn me" (HM 6241)

The Assassin (Burdette Collection)

And Hushed Seraglios (HM 6174)

Dedication to Bliss Carman of his volume *Songs o' Cheer* (HM 44357)

Der Heimgang (HM 31086)

Dolores (HM 31083)

In the Muskingum Valley (HM 31084)

Last Christmas Was a Year Ago (HM 1232)

Mister Hop-Toad (HM 6176)

My Dancin' Days Is Over (HM 6175)

The Little Man in the Tin Shop (HM 31082)

Some "Breaks" in Poems Here at Home (HM 6181)

"There! little girl, don't cry (HM 35075)

To a Poet on His Marriage (HM 44358)

The Two Dreams (HM 6236)

When the Hearse Comes Back (HM 31085)

[Inscription from volume presented to Bliss Carman] (HM 44359)

[Inscription from volume presented to Bliss Carman] (HM 44360)

Letters: 155 (1879–1916)

Other:

[Signed portrait to Charles Warren Stoddard] (HM 6235)

RINEHART, Mary (Roberts), *American novelist, playwright,* 1876–1958

Letters: 3 (1920–29)

RIPLEY, George, *American reformer, editor, critic,* 1802–80

Letters: 1 (1876)

RITCHIE, Anna Cora (Ogden) Mowatt, *American actress, playwright, novelist, biographer,* 1819–70

Prose:

Armand (quotation from act I, scene i, 1 p.: HM 1911)

Letters: 11 (1848–58), including 7 to James Thomas Fields

RITTENHOUSE, Jessie Belle, *American poet, editor,* 1869–1948

Letters: 5 (1927–30) to Mary (Hunter) Austin

RIVES, Amelie, see TROUBETZKOY, Amelie (Rives) Chanler

ROBERTS, Sir Charles George Douglas, *Canadian novelist, poet,* 1860–1943

Letters: 30 (1888–1907)

ROBERTS, David, *English painter,* 1796–1864

Letters: 8 (1834–58)

ROBERTS, Kenneth Lewis, *American novelist, essayist,* 1885–1957

Letters: 2 (1942 and n.d.) to Norreys Jephson O'Conor

ROBERTSON, Walford Graham, *English painter, writer,* 1866–1948

Prose:

Notebook, I [includes dramatization of Thackeray's *Rose and the Ring*] (WR 3)

Notebook, II [includes Guildford Pageant] (WR 4)

Notebook, III [includes reminiscences for *Time Was*] (WR 5)

Notebook, IV: [notes on Ellen Terry, etc., in an old notebook of translation of Alcestis, from the Greek] (WR 6)

Letters: 840 (1908–48) to Kerrison Preston

Other:

[Lists of his works as artist] (WR 7–9)

Notebook-cum-sketchbook (WR 1)

Sketchbooks, 1–3 (WR 2)

ROBINSON, Edwin Arlington, *American poet,* 1869–1935

Letters: 13 (1912–27)

ROBINSON, Harriet Jane (Hanson), *American suffragist, author,* 1825–1911

Letters: 1 (1905)

ROBINSON, Solon, *American pioneer, agriculturalist, author,* 1803–80

Verse:

[Invitation to Edmund Clarence Stedman to visit him in Florida] (HM 6042)

ROBINSON, Tracy, *American author,* 1833–1915

Verse:

A Mia Nina (HM 6029)

Song of the Palm (HM 6030)

Letters: 1 (1908)

ROBINSON, William Henry, *American author*, 1867–1938

Prose:

The Bandar Log Press (typewritten, 4 pp.: Hill Collection)

Letters: 3 (1927–37)

ROCHE, James Jeffrey, *American poet, journalist, novelist*, 1847–1908

Verse:

"Half the race of life is over, and the wind is well abaft" (HM 35075)

Letters: 2 (1887–94)

RODWELL, George Herbert Buonaparte, *English author, musician*, 1800–52

Letters: 2 (1846)

ROE, Edward Payson, *American clergyman, novelist*, 1838–88

Prose:

An Original Belle (595 pp.: HM 17254)

Letters: 5 (1883–86); also, 2 letters by his wife, Anna P. (Sands) Roe, and 1 by his daughter, Martha Roe

ROGERS, Robert, *American colonial ranger, frontiersman, author*, 1731–95

Prose:

[Two extracts from his journal] (4 pp.: LO 1088, LO 1219)

Letters: 8 (1756–58)

Documents: 24 (1756–58)

ROGERS, Samuel, *English poet,* 1763–1855

Verse:

"Not now, his little lesson done" (RB 23973)

Prose:

Notes and Parts of Notes to be Added to "Italy" (10 leaves: HM 6041)

[Notes used in writing "Italy"] (25 pp.: HM 6028)

Letters: 24 (1785–1845)

ROHLFS, Anna Katharine (Green), *American novelist,* 1846–1935

Letters: 2 (1898)

ROLFE, William James, *American educator, editor, author,* 1827–1910

Prose:

The Flow of Sap in Early Spring: [one page of corrected proof with a note at the bottom by Rolfe] (Kane Literary Collection)

Letters: 2 (1886–1909)

ROLLE, Edward, *English writer,* fl. 1747–53

Prose:

[biographical sketch of Joseph Spence] (4 pp.: RB 131231, vol. 1)

Letters: 3 (1747–53)

ROLLINS, Alice (Wellington), *American poet, novelist,* 1847–97

Verse:

Remorse (Kane Literary Collection)

Letters: 1 (1887)

ROMNEY, George, *English painter,* 1734–1802

Letters: 2 (1762–95); also, 1 letter (1762) by Peter Romney

Other:

Account book, 1777–82 (HM 26343)

ROSCOE, Thomas, *English author, translator,* 1791–1871

Letters: 3 (1849 and n.d.)

ROSCOE, William, *English historian,* 1753–1831

Letters: 6 (1806–25)

Documents: 1 (1797)

ROSCOE, William Stanley, *English poet,* 1782–1843

Verse:

[Sonnet beginning], "I saw in Heaven before the throne of Jove" (enclosed in letter by William Roscoe: HM 6617)

Letters: 1 (n.d.)

ROSEBORO, Viola, *American novelist,* 1858–1945

Letters: 2 (1890–94)

ROSELIEP, Raymond, *American poet, author,* 1917–

Verse:

The Scissors Grinder (typewritten: Dublin Magazine Collection)

ROSSETTI, Christina Georgina, *English poet,* 1830–94

Verse:

[At Home] (incomplete: HM 6066)

Behold the Man (HM 6080)

Maude, a story in prose and verse (HM 6065)

[Sonnets: a collection of 28 sonnets] (HM 6076)

Uphill (HM 6066)

Prose:

A Safe Investment (13 leaves: HM 6079)

Letters: 9 (1867–87)

ROSSETTI, Dante Gabriel, *English poet,* 1828–82

Verse:

Bella's Bullfinch (published as "Beauty and the Bird": HM 6083)

Broken Music (HM 6081)

Concerning His Father (HM 6091)

He Would Slay All Who Hate Their Fathers (HM 6093)

Henry The Leper (translated from the German of Hartmann von Aue: HM 6077)

The King's Tragedy (HM 6095)

The King's Tragedy (incomplete: HM 6096)

The Landmark (HM 6082)

A Match with the Moon (HM 6084)

The Mission of Luke (HM 6085)

No More (published as "The Lady's Lament": HM 6088)

Of Love, in Honour of His Mistress, Becchina (HM 6089)

On the Death of His Father (sonnet in Italian: HM 6092)

The Orchard Pit (HM 6087)

Rails Against Dante Who Has Censured His Homage to Becchina (HM 6090)

Sonnet in Italian (HM 6094)

The Staff and the Script (incomplete draft: HM 6084)

To the Young Painters of England (published as "The Husbandmen": HM 6086)

Letters: 40 (1846–81)

ROSSETTI, William Michael, *English critic, poet,* 1829–1919

Prose:

[Preface to Frances C. Deverell's *The P. R. B. and Walter Howell Deverell: Letters from Dante Gabriel Rossetti and Others, with a Narrative and Illustrations*] (HM 12981) and typewritten copy (HM 12982)

Letters: 24 (1850–1903)

Documents: 1 (1895)

ROSSINI, Gioacchino Antonio, *Italian operatic composer,* 1792–1868

Letters: 3 (1835–53)

Other:

Zelmira, Dramma per Musica, Del Sigr. Gioachinno Rossini, Atto Secundo (orchestral score with words, 184 leaves: HM 1055)

ROTHENSTEIN, Sir William, *English artist, biographer,* 1872–1945

Letters: 5 (1921–39)

ROTHWELL, Richard, *English painter,* 1800–68

Letters: 2 (1855) to James Thomas Fields

ROUSSEAU, Jean-Baptiste, *French poet,* 1671–1741

Verse:

Ode VII. Le devoir et le sort des Grands Hommes (HM 17244)

ROWE, Nicholas, *English poet, dramatist,* 1674–1718

Verse:

Extempore on Lady Hewey (in the hand of Horace Walpole: JE 753)

On Mrs. Howe's Desiring Her Daughter to Go with Her (in the hand of John Montgomerie: LO 8707)

A Sad and True Account of a Dismal Accident (in the hand of John Montgomerie: LO 8708)

ROWLANDSON, Thomas, *English artist, caricaturist,* 1756–1827

Letters: 1 (1820)

ROWSE, Alfred Leslie, *English historian, writer,* 1903–

Prose:

Sir Walter Raleigh: the missing centerpiece to his life (16 pp.: HM 26295)

ROYALL, Anne Newport, *American author,* 1769–1854

Letters: 1 (1832)

ROYCE, Josiah, *American educator, philosopher, author,* 1855–1916

Letters: 18 (1884–1915)

RUSH, Benjamin, *American patriot, humanitarian, author, medical pioneer,* 1745–1813

Letters: 5 (1783–96)

RUSKIN, John, *English author, artist, social reformer,* 1819–1900

Verse:

"Be thou glad, oh my love" (JR 532)

Prose:

Arrows of the Chace (2 pp.: HM 21659)

The Elements of Drawing: [corrected proof with some corrections by W. H. Harrison] (RB 72948)

The Elements of Perspective (incomplete, 44 pp. and 11 pp. of corrected proofs: HM 7587)

Epitaphs on the Tombstones of John James Ruskin and Margaret Cox Ruskin in Shirley Church Yard (2 pp.: JR 534)

Expedition of Darius into Scythia (fragment, 1 p.: HM 21662)

Fors Clavigera (fragment, 1 p.: HM 7589)

Fors Clavigera, Letter the 94th: [corrected proof] (RB 129071)

[Fragment of notes relating to the competitive designs submitted for the new government buildings] (3 leaves: HM 21661)

Gold, a Dialogue (not autograph, 24 pp.: HM 6104)

Lectures on Architecture and Painting: "The Edinburgh Lectures" (201 pp.: HM 6099)

[Miscellaneous notes] (10 pp.: HM 7591)

[Notes for Essay on Baptism] (1 p.: HM 21660)

[Notes on the Royal Academy and other exhibitions] 53 pp. and 13 proof sheets: HM 6100)

[Notes on Prout and Hunt] (88 pp.: HM 6102)

Practical Geometry (an exercise book; inscription on flyleaf: Master Ruskin Jan. 21, 1833, 38 pp.: HM 6103)

Pre-Raphaelitism (17 pp.: HM 7586)

[Realistic Schools of Painting: D. G. Rossetti and W. Holman Hunt: fragment of an essay] (1 p.: HH 3)

The Seven Lamps of Architecture (2 vols.: HM 6097)

To Dear Dr. Acland, 2nd Letter on the Oxford Museum (incomplete, 12 pp., also: fragment of second draft: HM 7588 [1] and [2])

To Henry Swan (an article: Fra Filippo Lippi and Carpaccio, 9 pp.: HM 7590)

The Two Paths (170 pp., and 130 pp. of proof: (HM 6101)

Unto This Last (82 pp.: HM 6098)

Letters: 797 (1839–88); also, 1 letter (1848) by his mother, Margaret (Cox) Ruskin, and 4 letters (1857–63) by his father, John James Ruskin

Documents: 1 (1883–87)

Other:

[Revisions in *Hortus Inclusus* (1887) for a new edition] (RB 298058)

RUSSELL, George William, *Irish poet, artist,* 1867–1935

Prose:

New Songs, A Lyrical Selection made by A. E. from Poems by Padraic Colum (introduction in the hand of Russell, 56 pp.: HM 852)

Letters: 7 (1919–27)

RUSSELL, Irwin, *American poet,* 1853–79

Verse:

Rev. Henry's War Song (HM 6130)

Romaunt of Sir Kuss (HM 6132)

RUSSELL, John, 1st Earl Russell, *English statesman,* 1792–1878

Letters: 12 (1830–68)

Documents: 1 (1861)

RUSSELL, Mary Annette (Beauchamp), Countess Russell, *English author,* 1866–1941

in the Huntington Library

Prose:

[Account of days at the Chalet at the outbreak of World War I] (typewritten, 11 pp.: Russell Collection)

Account of Journey round Lake Geneva (typewritten, 3 pp.: Russell Collection)

Account of a visit to Nassenheide in 1920 (1 p.: Russell Collection)

The Anonymous in Poetry (typewritten, 20 pp.: Russell Collection)

Christmas in a Bavarian Village (7 pp.: Russell Collection)

Correspondence between a Lady and a Gentleman: Novel in Letters begun with L. G. (corrected typescript, 45 pp.: Russell Collection)

Das Abrudbrod: [a skit in German] (5 pp.: Russell Collection)

Der Pastor am Theetisch: [a skit in German] (typewritten, 4 pp.: Russell Collection)

Dramatisation of the Benefactress (corrected typescript, 79 pp.: Russell Collection)

Ellen in Germany (corrected typescript, 117 pp.: Russell Collection)

[Essay on women] (corrected typescript, 5 pp.: Russell Collection)

[Extracts of love letters received by Countess Russell] (10 pp.: Russell Collection)

[Fragment of lecture on Brontës] corrected typescript, 5 pp.: Russell Collection)

[Fragment of Thoughts on Virginia Woolf's *A Room of One's Own*] (corrected typescript, 4 pp.: Russell Collection)

I Travel with a Dog (4 pp.: Russell Collection)

Journals [from 1896 to 1920] (Russell Collection)

Journals [from 1921 to 1941] (Russell Collection)

Notes for dramatization of The Benefactress (Russell Collection)

One Thing in Common: Introduction (two typewritten copies, 3 pp. each: Russell Collection)

The Pastor's Wife: [two tentative beginnings] (corrected typescript, 13 pp.: Russell Collection)

Priscilla Runs Away (1 p.: Russell Collection)

Regurgitation: account of the pilgrimage to Nassenheide (corrected typescript, 21 pp.: Russell Collection)

Stray bits of a book not written (corrected typescript, 83 pp.: Russell Collection)

The Tea Rose (55 pp.: Russell Collection)

The Tea Rose: [later fragment] (typewritten, 4 pp.: Russell Collection)

[Typescript of journals of Elizabeth, with attached letters to her family] (Russell Collection)

Wieman sein Bernhard klein kriegt: [a play] (corrected typescript, 17 pp.: Russell Collection)

Letters: 594 (1898–1940)

RUSSELL, William Clark, *English writer,* 1844–1911

Prose:

My Shipment Louise (308 pp.: HM 6027)

Letters: 1 (1883)

RUSSELL, Sir William Howard, *English war correspondent,* 1820–1907

Letters: 27 (1854–91)

RYDER, Albert Pinkham, *American painter,* 1847–1917

Letters: 5 (1897)

S

SACKVILLE-WEST, Victoria Mary, *English poet and novelist,* 1892–1962

Verse:

The Garden (first draft: HM 43232)

The Garden (fair copy) [1945] (HM 46024)

The Land (HM 41088)

Letters: 8 (1939–55)

ST. JOHN, James Augustus, *English author, traveler,* 1801–75

Letters: 4 (1829–36)

SAINTSBURY, George Edward Bateman, *English critic, historian,* 1845–1933

Letters: 3 (1919–20)

SALA, George Augustus Henry, *English journalist,* 1828–96

Prose:

A Bad Time for Tommasi (6 pp.: HM 44460)

George Cruikshank in Mexico (incomplete, 6 pp.: FI 3776)

Gossip of the Month (5 pp.: HM 44461)

Letters: 19 (1855–84)

SALTUS, Edgar Evertson, *American author,* 1855–1921

Verse:

History (RB 13188)

Imeros (HM 44462)

Mara (HM 35075)

Prose:

[Article responding to his critics] (6 pp.: Hill Collection)

Transactions in Hearts (118 pp.: HM 2727)

The Waiting Room of the 400 (18 pp.; and 15 pp. typed copy, with contents differing: HM 44463)

Letters: 3 (ca. 1911 and n.d.)

SAMBOURNE, Edward Linley, *English artist,* 1844–1910

Letters: 3 (1890–91)

SAMS, William Raymond, *English publisher,* fl. 1847–70

Collection of 69 letters addressed to Sams from actors, playwrights, composers, and singers, covering the period from 1847–70.

SANBORN, Franklin Benjamin, *American editor, author,* 1831–1917

Prose:

First and Last Journeys of Thoreau: Addendum (corrected proof sheets, 22 pp.: HM 13189)

Letters: 27 (1859–1905)

SANBORN, Katherine Abbott, *American educator, lecturer, author,* 1839–1917

Letters: 11 (1891–93)

SAND, George, see DUPIN, Aurore Lucie

SANDBURG, Carl [Charles August], *American poet, biographer,* 1878–1967

Verse:

Hats (typewritten, with an autograph note to Wallace Stevens, in Sandburg's *Cornhuskers:* RB 296569)

Letters: 2 (1916–41), including 1 to George Sterling

SANDYS, Sir Edwin, *English statesman,* 1561–1629

Prose:

A View of Religion: [same as his "Europae Speculum," which was piratically published in 1605 as *A Relation of the State of Religion*] (EL 1147)

Letters: 1 (1620)

SANGSTER, Margaret Elizabeth (Munson), *American editor, author,* 1838–1912

Verse:

Out of the Dust and the Darkness (HM 44467)

Letters: 47 (1892–1912)

SANTAYANA, George, *American philosopher, poet, essayist,* 1863–1952

Verse:

"Cathedrals are not built along the sea": [sonnet in answer to one by Wallace Stevens] (WAS 2329)

A Dedication: [sonnet written for *Sonnets and Other Poems,* 1894, but not included] (WAS 2330)

Letters: 6 (1923–37)

SARDOU, Victorien, *French author,* 1831–1908

Letters: 2 (n.d.)

SARETT, Lew, *American educator, poet, lecturer, bibliophile,* 1888–1954

Letters: 2 (1928–29) to Mary (Hunter) Austin

SARGENT, Epes, *American editor, poet, playwright,* 1813–80

Verse:

The Light of the Lighthouse: [2 stanzas only] (HM 12870)

Letters: 6 (1858–66)

SARGENT, John Singer, *American portrait painter, muralist,* 1856–1925

Letters: 39 (1880–1914)

SARGENT, Lucius Manlius, *American antiquary, temperance reformer, author,* 1786–1867

Letters: 2 (1836–39)

SARGENT, Winthrop, *American author,* 1825–70

Letters: 8 (1863–69)

SARTAIN, John, *American engraver, editor, author,* 1808–97

Letters: 5 (1852–95)

SARTORIS, Adelaide (Kemble), *English vocalist, author,* 1814?–79

Letters: 3 (n.d.)

SASSOON, Siegfried Lorraine, *English poet, novelist,* 1886–1967

Letters: 9 (1919); also, numerous letters to him in the Thomas Hardy Tribute Collection

Documents: 1 (1919)

SAVAGE, John, *American journalist, author,* 1828–88

Letters: 2 (1876)

SAVAGE, Philip Henry, *American poet,* 1868–99

Letters: 1 (n.d.) to Annie (Adams) Fields

SAVAGE, Richard Henry, *American author,* 1846–1903

Verse:

Only (HM 35075)

Letters: 1 (1881)

SAVILE, Sir George, Marquis of Halifax, *English Royalist, governor,* 1633–95

Prose:

Character of a Trimmer (EL 8371)

Letters: 1 (1691)

SAXE, John Godfrey, *American poet,* 1816–87

Verse:

"Much have I mused if love and life were one" (HM 44501)

Rhyme of the Rail: [one stanza only, in a letter to Barry Alden] (HM 12871)

Which was King? (RB 50762)

Letters: 10 (1850–76)

Other:

[Six responses to requests for autographs] (Kane Literary Collection and J. A. Ford Album)

SCHEFFAUER, Herman George, *American poet, playwright,* 1878–1927

Verse:

An Amiable Child (GS 444)

Atlantis (GS 440)

The Bringer of the Dream (GS 449)

A Dedication (GS 442)

The Fire Funeral (GS 443)

Friedrich Nietzche (GS 441)

The Jewess in the Ghetto (GS 447)

The Pageant of the Sun (GS 446)

The Prayer of Beggarman Death (GS 445)

The Sleeping Galleon (GS 448)

Letters: 63 (1904–27)

SCHILLER, Ferdinand Canning Scott, *American educator, author,* 1864–1937

Prose:

201 books and essays

193 book reviews

Letters: 5 (1928–29)

SCHOOLCRAFT, Henry Rowe, *American explorer, ethnologist, author,* 1793–1864

Prose:

Ethnological Views and Inquiries Respecting the North American Indians (13 pp.: HM 13228)

Letters: 26 (1822–58)

Documents: 4 (1815–59)

SCHORER, Mark, *American novelist, literary critic, biographer,* 1908–77

Prose:

Sinclair Lewis: An American Life (typescript, 3 vols.: HM 26591)

Letters: 11 (1946–73)

SCHURZ, Carl, *American soldier, statesman, diplomat, editor, author,* 1829–1906

Prose:

Thoughts on American Imperialism (20 pp.: HM 2079)

Letters: 30 (1860–94)

SCHWARTZ, Delmore, *American poet, critic,* 1913–

Letters: 10 (1942–56)

SCOLLARD, Clinton, *American poet,* 1860–1932

Verse:

April Music (typewritten: Kane Literary Collection)

Skenandoa (HM 2600)

Sweet Clover (HM 44502)

'Tis ever the poet's part: [verse inscription] (RB 181850)

Letters: 2 (1900–15)

SCOTT, Sarah (Robinson), *English novelist,* d. 1795

Letters: 389 (1740–95), including 363 to Elizabeth (Robinson) Montagu

SCOTT, Sir Walter, *English novelist, poet,* 1771–1832

Verse:

Harold the Hardy (several pages of the original manuscript

are missing, for which Locker-Lampson substituted copies of the text in the handwriting of various literary figures among his friends—Browning, Swinburne, Emerson, Holmes, Longfellow, and many more: HM 1937)

[Poems ascribed to Scott in Lady Charlotte Bury's commonplace book] (HM 33691)

Prose:

The History of Scotland (3 vols.: vols. II and III were dictated to Laidlaw: HM 2726); also, a fragment (10 lines) of *History of Scotland* in Kane Literary Collection

Introduction to Chronicles of the Canongate (3 pp.: HM 1982)

Introduction to Chronicles of the Canongate (in the hand of Laidlaw corrected by Scott, 8 pp.: HM 979)

[Note in preface to his second edition of the *Works of Jonathan Swift*] (in the hand of James Smith); also, late 19th century copy (HM 14333 [A] and [B]), and pages from Nichols's 1808 edition, with revisions and additions in the hand of Scott and others (RB 141696)

The Pirate (corrected proof, 2 vols.: RB 110387)

A review of "Letters to and from Henrietta, Countess of Suffolk" (7 pp.: HM 6698)

Scroll of Warrant for Opening the Chest Deposited in the Crown Room of Edinburgh (4 pp.: HM 2011)

Letters: 132 (1795–1835)

Documents: 1 (1819)

SCOTT, William Bell, *English poet, painter,* 1811–90

Letters: 2 (1870–75)

SCOTT, Winfield Townley, *American author, editor,* 1910–68

Letters: 3 (1952–54)

SCUDDER, Horace Elisha, *American editor, author,* 1838–1902

Letters: 12 (1866–97)

SEARING, Laura Catherine (Redden), *American journalist, author,* 1840–1923

Letters: 9 (1871–95)

SEDGWICK, Anne Douglas, *American novelist,* 1873–1935

Letters: 28 (1900–08)

SEDGWICK, Catharine Maria, *American author,* 1789–1867

Prose:

Cousin Frank (11 pp.: HM 1956)

Letters: 9 (1843–65)

SEDGWICK, Ellery, *American editor, author,* 1872–1960

Letters: 5 (1902–34)

SEDGWICK, Henry Dwight, *American author,* 1861–1957

Letters: 2 (1916 and n.d.)

SEDGWICK, Theodore, *American lawyer, author,* 1811–59

Letters: 5 (1843–58)

SEDLEY, Sir Charles, *English wit, dramatic author,* 1639?–1701

Verse:

[Poems ascribed to him in commonplace book] (EL 8770)

SEELEY, Sir John Robert, *English historian, essayist,* 1834–95

Letters: 9 (1863–83)

SEITZ, Don Carlos, *American editor, author,* 1862–1935

Letters: 1 (1918) to Albert Bigelow Paine

SELDEN, John, *English jurist,* 1584–1654

Prose:

Judicature in Parliament (3 copies: EL 8392–94)

The Priviledges or Speciall Rights Belonging to the Baronage of England (not autograph: EL 2624)

Three Weeks Observation of the States Countrye and Especiallye Holland (not autograph, 43 pp.: HM 1420); also, another copy (11 leaves: EL 1181)

Letters: 1 (1638)

SELTZER, Charles Alden, *American novelist,* 1875–1942

Letters: 1 (1921)

SELWYN, Edgar, *American playwright,* 1875–1944

Letters: 1 (1925)

SETON, Ernest Thompson, *American naturalist, artist, author,* 1860–1946

Verse:

[Inscription on fly-leaf of *Monarch*] (RB 181748)

Prose:

The Drummer on Snowshoes (10 pp.: HM 153)

The Ovenbird (5 pp.: HM 1300)

The Pintail (5 pp.: HM 145)

Tracks in the Snow (12 pp.: HM 208)

Letters: 29 (1887–1932)

SEVERN, Joseph, *English painter*, 1793–1879

Verse:

The Art of Etching: a Parody (not autograph: HM 44503)

Letters: 7 (1842–79), including 6 to James Thomas Fields. There is also a signed authentication by him of the handwriting in the Keats manuscript of Otho the Great

SEWALL, Jonathan, *American lawyer, loyalist, author*, 1728–96

Letters: 1 (1776)

SEWARD, Anna, *English author*, 1747–1809

Verse:

"E'en as the Sun beneath the Line comes forth" (HM 38317)

"To deck lamented Simcoe's hallow'd tomb" (HM 38301)

Written after Reading Southey's *Joan of Arc* (JE 755)

Prose:

Memoirs: of the Beauties in Pope's Translation of the Odessy from Mr. Spence's Essay [in Thomas Addis Emmet's *Andreana*] (RB 8842, vol. 2)

Letters: 29 (1765–1807)

Documents: 1 (n.d.)

SEWARD, William Henry, *American statesman, author*, 1801–72

Letters: 92 (1840–68)

Documents: 4 (1850–67)

SHANNON, Charles Haselwood, *English lithographer, painter*, 1863–1937

Letters: 41 (1898–1904), including 33 to Harold Chaloner Dowdall

SHAPIRO, Karl Jay, *American poet, critic,* 1913–

Letters: 13 (1945–53)

SHARP, William, *English poet,* 1855–1905

Verse:

The Rune of the Passion of Women (London Collection)
Spring (HM 44505)

Prose:

The Last Voyage of Keir the Monk (7 pp.: HM 1952)

The Portraits of Keats (23 pp.: HM 1953)

Letters: 82 (1889–1905)

Documents: 2 (1895)

SHAW, Albert, *American editor, author,* 1857–1947

Letters: 5 (1896–1911)

SHAW, Anna Howard, *American minister, reformer, physician, author,* 1847–1919

Letters: 13 (1890–1913)

SHAW, George Bernard, *English playwright,* 1856–1950

Prose:

The Case of the Critic-Dramatist (typewritten with author's corrections, 11 pp.: HM 1946)

The Liberty Loan (3 pp.: HM 1954)

One of the Worst (typewritten with author's corrections, 1 p.: HM 1941)

The Two Latest Comedies (corrected proof, 6 pp.: HM 1948)

Woman Since 1860 (typewritten with author's corrections, 10 pp.: HM 30320)

Letters: 11 (1889–1949)

SHAW, John Byam Lister, *English architect,* 1831–1912

Letters: 1 (1913)

SHEA, John Dawson Gilmary, *American Roman Catholic historian, editor,* 1824–92

Letters: 14 (1865–85)

SHEIL, Richard Lalor, *English politician, dramatist,* 1791–1851

Letters: 4 (1824–40)

SHELDON, Charles Monroe, *American clergyman, author,* 1857–1946

Letters: 6 (1903–25)

SHELDON, Edward Brewster, *American playwright,* 1886–1946

Letters: 41 (1934)

SHELLEY, Mary Wollstonecraft (Godwin), *English author,* 1797–1851

Letters: 181 (1817–49)

SHELLEY, Percy Bysshe, *English poet,* 1792–1822

Verse:

Hellas (in the hand of Edward E. Williams, with corrections by Shelley: HM 329)

Letter to Maria Gisborne: a Poem (in the hand of Mary Shelley: HM 12338)

Lines Written Among the Euganean Hills (in the hand of Mary Shelley: HM 331)

Notebooks (3 vols.: HM 2111, 2176, 2177)

To a Skylark (illuminated ms. by Sangorski and Sutcliffe: HM 2790)

Written on Hearing the News of the Death of Napoleon (in the hand of Mary Shelley: HM 330)

Letters: 28 (1810–22); also, 21 letters of Harriet W. Shelley, 9 of Sir Timothy Shelley, and numerous genealogical papers

SHENSTONE, William, *English poet,* 1714–63

Letters: 2 (1758–62)

Other:

[Inscription of two lines, mounted with portrait of Shenstone] (HM 44507)

SHEPPARD, Elizabeth Sara, *English novelist,* 1830–62

Verse:

Louis Charles: A Relique (FI 3808)

Memorials of the Flight of Mendelssohn: No. II—The Last Improvisation (FI 3806) [followed by four other poems]:

To a Father on the Death of a Favorite Son

To Gerania, after a Long Moonlight Saunter in the Garden

"Oh! did the spell to me belong"

Choral Hymn of the Fireworshippers at Sunrise

[Miscellaneous verses and four sonnets]: (FI 3807)

"Summer brought sorrow in her smiling train"

"Bright is the future for thy smile is ours"

Sonnets: Poetry; Painting; Sculpture; Music

Letters: 1 (1859) to James Thomas Fields

SHERIDAN, Richard Brinsley Butler, *English dramatist, parliamentary orator,* 1751–1816

Verse:

Epilogue to the Tragedy of Semiramis (not autograph: MO 4974)

Monody (not autograph: HM 17433)

[Poems ascribed to him in Lady Charlotte Bury's commonplace book] (HM 33691)

Prose:

Geometry: The Elements of Euclid (176 pp.: HM 33618)

The School for Scandal (copy made for Fawcett when playing the part of Peter Teazle, 99 leaves: HM 2546)

Letters: 8 (1781–1813)

SHERIDAN, Thomas, *English actor, lecturer, author,* 1719–88

Verse:

The Five Ladies Answer to the Beau (not autograph: HM 14335)

Punch to the Ladies (not autograph: HM 14370)

To Jonathan Swift: [letter written in verse, followed by Swift's reply, also in verse] (HM 14336)

To the Dean of St. Patrick's (HM 14369)

Prose:

English Blunders (in the hand of Deane Swift, 2 pp.: HM 14371)

Documents: 1 (1784)

SHERMAN, Frank Dempster, *American author,* 1860–1916

Verse:

A Catch (HM 1959)

A Fairy Story (AP 1625)

Omar Khayyam (HM 1960)

A Real Santa Claus (AP 1624)

Letters: 42 (1878–1908)

SHERMAN, Stuart Pratt, *American educator, editor, critic,* 1881–1926

Letters: 4 (1917–26)

SHERWOOD, Mary Elizabeth (Wilson), *American poet, novelist, short-story writer,* 1826–1903

Prose:

Recollections of Brook Farm (incomplete, 16 pp.: HM 1978)

Letters: 6 (1864–73)

SHERWOOD, Robert Emmet, *American playwright,* 1896–1955

Letters: 4 (1933–38)

SHILLABER, Benjamin Penhallow, *American editor, humorist, poet,* 1814–90

Verse:

"This some call fun, but I with pain 'allow' " (RB 101693)

Letters: 35 (1852–86)

SHIPPEY, Henry Lee, *American journalist, author,* b. 1884

Letters: 5 (ca. 1930–38)

SHIRLEY, James, *English dramatic poet,* 1596–1666

Verse:

Cobblers and Coopers and the Rest (copy; attributed to Shirley: EL 8843)

Cupid and Death (not autograph: HM 601)

SIDDONS, Sarah (Kemble), *English actress,* 1755–1831

Verse:

Milton's Paradise Lost (in the hand of Mrs. Siddons: HM 2865)

Letters: 5 (1795–1823)

Other:

[Notes and corrections in Thomas Campbell's De Montfort: a Tragedy] (HM 32693)

SIGOURNEY, Lydia Howard (Huntley), *American editor, author,* 1791–1865

Verse:

The Benefactress (HM 24040)

The Departed Neighbor (HM 24039)

The Execution (HM 2952)

Gemini (HM 2953)

Honorable Thomas S. Williams, Late Chief Justice of Connecticut (HM 1980)

The Library of Dr. Bowditch (HM 44510)

My Country (HM 24732)

No Concealment (HM 1918)

Tribute to the Memory of Miss Charlotte Chester (HM 44511)

The Undaunted (HM 1979)

Prose:

Thoughts on Temperance: [essay included in letter] (4 pp.: HM 24042)

Letters: 20 (1827–56); also, one letter to Mrs. Sigourney from Joanna Baillie

SIMMS, Jeptha Root, *American author,* 1807–83

Prose:

[The Trappers of New York]:

Anecdote of Captain Dygert (2 pp.: HM 2006)

Anecdote of Captain Jacob Gardiner's Wife (1 p.: HM 1992)

Capture of the Sharer Children Near Fort Herkimer (4 pp.: HM 2009)

Fate of Capt. Woodworth and His Command (3 pp.: HM 1993)

Henderson's Town and Its Destruction (4 pp.: HM 1990)

Notes on the Captivity of the Olendorfs (2 pp.: HM 2010)

Novel Escape of Capt. Garret Putnam from the Enemy (1 p.: HM 1991)

Surprise of a Scout from Fort Dayton (2 pp.: HM 2008)

Surprise of a Scout from Fort Herkimer (1 p.: HM 2007)

SIMMS, William Gilmore, *American novelist, poet,* 1806–70

Letters: 12 (1847–69)

SINCLAIR, Andrew Annandale, *English author,* 1935–

Prose:

[Jack London Biography: first draft (9 chapters)] (typewritten with corrections, 246 pp.: HM 44532)

SINCLAIR, Catherine, *English novelist,* 1800–64

Letters: 2 (1862 and n.d.)

SINCLAIR, May, *English author,* 1865–1946

Letters: 13 (1905–12) to Annie (Adams) Fields

SINCLAIR, Upton Beall, *American author,* 1878–1968

Letters: 121 (1905–57)

Other:

[Inscription on George Sterling's *Sonnets to Craig*] (RB 285688)

See also DRYER, John

SINGMASTER, Elsie, *American author,* 1879–1958

Letters: 4 (1913–16)

SITWELL, Edith, *English poet,* 1887–1964

Verse:

"Ah, love on this strange autumn afternoon" (HM 32113)

Aspatia's Song (HM 32081)

At the Fair (HM 32073)

At the Fair (HM 32118)

Aubade (HM 32070)

Bacchanale (HM 32108)

Barcarolle (HM 32079)

Beyond Avalon (HM 32091)

Beyond Avalon (HM 32114)

The Burdened Wing (HM 32085)

Drowned Suns (HM 32090)

Drowned Suns (HM 32096)

Drowned Suns (HM 32116)
The Drunkard, Version I (HM 32071)
The Drunkard, Version II (HM 32072)
The Drunkard (HM 32118)
An Empty House (HM 32109)
Envoi (HM 32098)
The Fisherman (HM 32080)
From an Attic Window (HM 32074)
From an Attic Window (HM 32110)
"In an old cottage garden" (HM 32082)
"In an old cottage garden" (HM 32111)
Jester's Song (HM 32097)
Lament for Hyacinth (HM 32117)
Lament for Hyacinth (HM 32094)
Lost Love (HM 32092)
Lost Love (HM 32115)
Lullaby: "Gentle Slumber, lass his eyes" (HM 32078)
Lullaby: "Sweet shadow foot draw near . . ." (HM 32089)
Lullaby: "Sweet shadow foot draw near . . ." (HM 32086)
The Mother, Version I (HM 32068)
The Mother, Version II (HM 32069)
The Mother (HM 32095)
The Mother (rough draft: HM 32103)
The Mourner (HM 32087)
The Mourner (HM 32107)
Music (HM 32086)
Music at Eve (HM 32116)
Music at Eve (HM 32092)
Nocturne (HM 32093)

Nursery Rhyme (HM 32083)

Nursery Rhyme (HM 32104)

The Reapers (HM 32076)

Reverie (HM 32098)

Selene (HM 32088)

Serenade: "Now fall the trembling stars" (HM 32089)

Serenade: "The tremulous gold of stars within your hair" (HM 32115)

Serenade: "The tremulous gold of stars within your hair" (HM 32093)

Song (to Joan): "As sorrow lay a-sleeping" (HM 32077)

Song: "Tell me, where is sorrow laid" (HM 32101)

Song: "When daisies white and celandine" (HM 32100)

Song: "Your hair is like a jasmine bower" (HM 32099)

Sweet Music Dreaming Dwells (HM 32085)

Tom Tiddler (HM 32075)

Tom Tiddler (HM 32106)

The Two Archers (HM 32084)

The Two Archers (HM 32105)

The Web of Eros, or Gold Hair (HM 32112)

The Web of Eros, or Enchanted Gold (HM 32102)

Letters: 6 (1913–59)

SKELTON, Robin, *English educator, author,* 1925–

Prose:

Appendix A. The Case of Saint Augustine and the Novice: [portion of the typescript for *Poetic Pattern*] (9 pp.: HM 41038)

Letters: 7 (1954–65)

SKENE, William Forbes, *Scottish historian, author,* 1809–92

Letters: 1 (1885)

SKINNER, Knute Rumsey, *American educator, author,* 1929–

Letters: 1 (1967)

SMART, Sir George Thomas, *English musician, conductor,* 1776–1867

Letters: 2 (1816–26)

SMILES, Samuel, *English author, reformer,* 1812–1904

Letters: 1 (1888)

SMIRKE, Sir Edward, *English antiquary,* 1795–1875

Letters: 1 (1841)

SMIRKE, Richard, *English antiquarian draftsman,* 1778–1815

Letters: 1 (1809)

Documents: 1 (1803)

SMIRKE, Robert, *English painter,* 1752–1845

Letters: 21 (1789–1830)

Documents: 3 (1793–1818)

Other:

Prospectus of a new version of Don Quixote . . . (3 pp.: HM 18965)

SMIRKE, Sir Robert, *English architect, writer,* 1781–1867

Letters: 2 (1840–48)

Documents: 1 (1815)

SMIRKE, Sydney, *English architect,* 1798–1877

Letters: 1 (1842)

SMITH, Albert Richard, *English author, lecturer,* 1816–60

Prose:

Brown, a Travelling Portrait (15 pp.: HM 44512)

Letters: 8 (1842–56); and one letter to Smith from Charles Dickens

Documents: 1 (1855)

SMITH, Betty Wehner, *American author,* 1896–1972

Letters: 1 (1945)

SMITH, Charles Henry, *American journalist, humorist,* 1826–1903

Letters: 4 (1864–91)

SMITH, Charlotte (Turner), *English poet, novelist,* 1749–1806

Verse:

Passages from Mrs. C. Smith's Poems of the Emigrants (not autograph: HM 10810)

Letters: 47 (1784–1806)

SMITH, Elizabeth Oakes (Prince), *American lecturer, reformer, poet,* 1806–93

Verse:

Some Fell by the Wayside (HM 1920)

Letters: 3 (1854–66)

SMITH, Francis Hopkinson, *American artist, author,* 1838–1915

Prose:

A Night Out (typewritten, 27 pp.: HM 17222)

Letters: 2 (1915)

SMITH, Harrison, *American editor, critic,* 1888–1971

Letters: 38 (1937–46)

SMITH, Horatio, *English poet, author,* 1779–1849

Verse:

Brighton Bells (HM 2957)

Letters: 4 (1816–22); and 10 letters addressed to him from William Harrison Ainsworth

SMITH, James, *English author, humorist,* 1775–1839

Verse:

The Alphabet (JP 241)

Letters: 5 (1821–37)

SMITH, Paul Jordan, *American editor, bibliophile, author,* 1885–1971

Letters: 6 (1935–39)

SMITH, Samuel Francis, *American clergyman, poet, editor,* 1808–95

Verse:

America (two copies, signed, in author's hand: HM 44515)
America (another copy, made in 1894: HM 45668)

Prose:

Reminiscences re trip to India, 1877 (13 pp.: HM 29304)

Letters: 68 (1829–41)

SMITH, Sydney, *English canon, satirist, divine,* 1771–1845

Letters: 71 (1796–1844), including 40 to his father, Robert Smith

SMITH, Walter Chalmers, *Scottish poet,* 1824–1908

Verse:

Youth (HM 44524)

SMITH, William, *American clergyman, educator, author,* 1727–1803

Letters: 2 (1757)

SMITH, William, *American jurist, Loyalist, historian,* 1728–93

Letters: 1 (1771)

Documents: 1 (1758)

Other:

[Notes in 5 printed volumes] (RB 32441, 32488, 110798, 32474, 32432)

SMITH, William Henry, *English poet, essayist,* 1808–72

Letters: 1 (1867)

SMITH, Winchell, *American playwright,* 1871–1933

Letters: 1 (1913)

SMOLLETT, Tobias George, *English novelist,* 1721–71

Letters: 1 (1750)

SNOW, William Parker, *English mariner, explorer, writer,* 1817–95

Letters: 5 (1864–86)

SOMERVILLE, Mary (Fairfax) Grieg, *English scientific writer*, 1780–1872

Letters: 4 (1828–67)

SOTHEBY, William, *English author*, 1757–1833

Collection of 174 letters addressed to Sotheby, mostly from prominent literary friends acknowledging presentation copies of his writings

SOTHERN, Edward Askew, *English actor*, 1826–81

Letters: 7 (1860–80)

SOTHERN, Edward Hugh, *American actor, author*, 1859–1933

Letters: 1 (1913)

SOUSA, John Philip, *American bandmaster, composer*, 1854–1932

Letters: 3 (1883–90)

SOUTHEY, Robert, *English poet, man of letters*, 1774–1843

Verse:

A Ballad Shewing How an Old Woman Rode Double and Who Rode Before Her (HM 2728)

Epitaph (RB 320006, vol. 1)

Epitaph on Clement Francis, a nephew of Madame d'Arblay (HM 2876)

"Farewell to Westminster, my friend is gone" (HM 44800)

The First Book of Oliver Newman (HM 12264)

Funeral Song for the Princess Charlotte of Wales (LR 322)

Inscription Under an Oak (HM 4820)

Inscriptions for the Caledonian Canal: [three poems] (RS 1)

Inscriptions for the Caledonian Canal: [revised version of the verse for Fort Augustus only] (RS 2)

Inscriptions for the Caledonian Canal (HM 44795)

King Ramiro (HM 4845)

Miscellanea Poetica (HM 2733)

Ode on the Battle of Algiers (LR 321)

"Sovereign of the shivering hall" (HM 44796)

To Ignorance (HM 44797)

The Wedding: an Eclogue (HM 4817)

"Yes, now I may view the white sheep" (HM 44798)

The Young Dragon (HM 2634)

Prose:

Commonplace book: Orientaliana (partly autograph, 2 vols.: HM 2771)

[Extracts from the Order book of James Wolfe] (4 pp.: HM 9684)

[Notes on Indians and their corn in E. R. Bulwer-Lytton's *Life of Lord Lytton*] (RB 131334, vol. 2)

[Notebook—containing extracts from Davenant, Habington, Donne, Gascoigne, Ronsard, etc., as well as miscellaneous notes, sketches, and data] (1 vol.: HM 2099)

[Personal notebooks containing memoranda and notes used by him in the composition of various historical and literary works from 1808–11] (8 vols.: HM 2635)

A review of *Some Account of the Lives and Writings of Lope Felix de Vega,* by Henry R. Fox (48 pp.: HM 2589)

Letters: 897 (1796–1839), including 742 to John Rickman; also, 521 letters addressed to Southey. Several letters from Southey to Collins are written in verse form.

Documents: 2 (1810–12)

SPARKS, Jared, *American educator, historian, editor, biographer,* 1789–1866

Letters: 27 (1826–62)

SPEARMAN, Frank Hamilton, *American author,* 1859–1937

Prose:

62 addresses and essays (Spearman Collection)

19 novels (including 4 copies of *Whispering Smith:* 2 manuscript copies, a corrected typescript of the novel, and a typescript of the play: Spearman Collection)

12 plays (Spearman Collection)

174 short stories, of which 126 are bound in 12 volumes (Spearman Collection)

Letters: 910 (1874–1937), and more than 2,000 letters addressed to Spearman

Other:

Address book, account books, agreements, contracts, etc. (20 pieces: Spearman Collection)

Diary and miscellaneous family papers (110 pieces: Spearman Collection)

Royalty reports (192 pieces: Spearman Collection)

Statements and receipts (128 pieces: Spearman Collection)

SPEARS, Raymond Smiley, *American author,* 1876–1950

Letters: 6 (1946–47) to Eugene Lafayette Cunningham

SPENCE, Joseph, *English anecdotist,* 1699–1768

Prose:

Extracts Relating to English Poets, English Writers of Plays, English Prose Writers, Histories, Art, etc., from the Four Manuscript Volumes Written by Mr. Spence in the Possession of His Grace the Duke of Newcastle in 1782 (2 vols.: HM 2102)

Miscellaneous Thoughts, Anecdotes, and Characters of Books and Men Saved from the Conversation of Mr. Pope and Some Other Eminent Persons (incomplete, 230 pp.: HM 1271)

The Round of Mr. Shenstone's Paradise (with map of Leasowes, Worcs., in color and 2-page key by Robert Dodsley, 5 pp.: HM 30312)

Studies for a Clergyman (2 pp.: RB 131213, vol. 1)

The Suspicious Husband (52 pp.: HM 39463)

Letters: 4 (1735–40), and 33 addressed to Spence

Other:

[Translations of 2 lines of Albius Tibullus beginning], "Illam quicquid agit" (2 pp.: HM 41048)

See also LOWTH, Robert, and ROLLE, Edward

SPENCER, Herbert, *English philosopher,* 1820–1903

Letters: 51 (1864–94), including 42 to John Fiske

SPENCER, Theodore, *American educator, author,* 1902–49

Verse:

"Is this the truth we practised?" (AIK 817)

Letters: 9 (1930–48)

SPENCER, William Robert, *English poet, wit,* 1769–1834

Verse:

Enigma (in Latin: SY 152)

Epitaph on a Dog of Lady E. Foster's (in the hand of Matthew Gregory Lewis: HM 6627)

Letters: 2 (1795–1828)

SPOFFORD, Harriet Elizabeth (Prescott), *American poet, novelist,* 1835–1921

Verse:

"Come up, come up, soft spring airs" (HM 44517)

Letters: 13 (1867–1901 and n.d.)

SQUIRE, Sir John Collings, *English poet, critic, editor,* 1884–1958

Letters: 1 (1924)

STACPOOLE, Henry deVere, *English author,* 1863–1951

Letters: 3 (1915–23)

STALLWORTHY, John Howie, *English editor, author,* 1935–

Verse:

An Evening Walk (typewritten: Dublin Magazine Collection)

STANFIELD, Clarkson, *English marine and landscape painter,* 1793–1867

Letters: 10 (1836–51)

Other:

"Dick bets Stanny that Massaniello was produced, as an opera . . ." (1 p., coauthored with Charles Dickens, and in Dickens's hand: HM 18572)

STANHOPE, Philip Dormer, 4th Earl of Chesterfield, *English statesman, wit, letter writer,* 1694–1733

Verse:

Advice to Lady Nanny Shirley (MO 5071)

Letters: 53 (1747–69)

Documents: 1 (1731)

STANHOPE, Philip Henry, 5th Earl Stanhope, *English historian,* 1805–75

Letters: 7 (1836–74)

STANTON, Frank Lebby, *American poet, editor,* 1857–1927

Letters: 2 (1894–99)

STARRETT, Charles Vincent Emerson, *American critic, editor, bibliophile, novelist,* 1886–1974

Verse:

After Much Stirring for Fame (Hill Collection)

Dupin and Another (typewritten: Hill Collection)

Prose:

The Fellowship of Books (typewritten, 2 pp.: Hill Collection)

Sherlockian [several mss.] (Hill Collection)

Two Short Stories (typewritten, 4 pp.: Hill Collection)

Letters: 239 (1909–48)

Other:

[Miscellaneous mss. and proof sheets] (Hill Collection)

STEADMAN, John Marcellus, *American educator, author,* 1918–

Prose:

[Article on Richard Henry Wilde] (typewritten; 7 pp.: Steadman papers)

[Notes for article on Richard Henry Wilde] (27 pp.: Steadman papers)

Letters: 15 (1933–35), and 24 (1932–35) addressed to him; also, ca. 50 pieces of correspondence (1933) re Richard Henry White, for DAB article

STEDMAN, Edmund Clarence, *American poet, editor,* 1833–1908

Verse:

Ad Vatem (HM 2508)

Alice of Monmouth (HM 2266)

The Creole Lover's Song (HM 9)

Custer (HM 24733)

Gettysburg (HM 2272)

The Inland City (HM 2260)

Madrigal (HM 12853)

Meridian (HM 1968)

Ode to Pastoral Romance (HM 2500)

Pan in Wall Street (HM 2504)

Portrait d'une Dame Espagnole (HM 2507)

The Protest of Faith (HM 2502)

A Sea Change (includes corrected proofs: HM 2505)

Souvenir of Jeunesse (HM 12855)

Tribute to Walt Whitman (HM 12854)

The Undiscovered Country (HM 1228)

Youth and Age: [12 lines from 6th part of Dartmouth Ode] (HM 2501)

Prose:

Aerial Navigation (42 pp.: HM 2264)

Alfred Tennyson (40 pp.: HM 855)

Introduction to the Poems of Edgar Allan Poe (50 pp.: HM 2267)

Introduction to the Poems of Edgar Allan Poe (typescript, 35 pp.: HM 2503)

Introduction to the Tales of Edgar Allan Poe (58 pp.: HM 2268)

Keats (16 pp.: HM 2262)

Life "On the Floor" (72 pp.: HM 2269)

Memorial to James Russell Lowell (5 pp.: HM 2506)

[Review of Rudyard Kipling's *The Seven Seas*] (11 pp.: HM 12852)

The Twilight of the Poets (110 pp.: HM 2261)

Letters: 79 (1880–1905), and 94 letters addressed to Stedman

Other:

[Final page of a typewritten manuscript together with the author's signature and a pen-and-ink drawing of a monkey climbing a coconut tree] (HM 1973)

[Inscription in *Edgar Allan Poe*] (RB 14988)

[Inscription in verse, beginning], "Hast thou a golden Day, a starlit night" (RB 13143)

[Ms. copies of ninth verse of *The Star Bearer*] (RB 89192, RB 22905)

STEELE, Sir Richard, *English author, politician,* 1672–1729

Letters: 1 (n.d.)

Documents: 1 (1712)

STEEVENS, George, *English commentator on Shakespeare,* 1736–1800

Letters: 6 (1778–99)

Other:

[Notes on different editions of *The Paradice of Dainty Devises*] (HM 42755)

STEFFENS, Lincoln, *American editor, author,* 1866–1936

Letters: 49 (1901–36)

STEGNER, Wallace Earle, *American novelist,* 1909–

Letters: 1 (1945)

STEINBECK, John, *American novelist,* 1902–68

Letters: 1 (1937)

STELLMAN, Louis John, *American author,* b. 1877

Letters: 7 (1916–31)

STEPHEN, Sir James, *English colonial undersecretary, author,* 1789–1859

Letters: 18 (1815–52)

STEPHEN, Sir Leslie, *English biographer, essayist, editor, philosopher, man of letters,* 1832–1904

Letters: 7 (1865–90), and one letter to him from Mary Ann (Evans) Cross

STEPHENS, Ann Sophia (Winterbotham), *American editor, novelist,* 1813–86

Letters: 7 (1863–73)

STEPHENS, Charles Asbury, *American author,* 1844–1931

Letters: 5 (1903) to Albert Bigelow Paine

STEPHENS, James, *Irish poet, story writer,* 1880?–1950

Verse:

"I wish, my dear" (HM 35376)

"Let the skies" (HM 35376)

"Nothing do I withhold" (HM 35377)

"Wild am I" (HM 35377)

Letters: 7 (1908–36), including 5 to James Starkey

Other:

Drawing (HM 35378)

STEPHENSON, George Malcolm, *American author, historian,* b. 1883

Letters: 9 (1904–32)

STERLING, George, *American poet,* 1869–1926

Verse:

183 texts

Letters: 191 (1910–26), including 72 to Jack London; and 491 letters addressed to Sterling

Other:

The Meek Ranch: [a publicity write-up] (typewritten, with corrections: GS 453)

[Notebook containing vocabulary aid] (GS 569)

[Word list] (GS 570)

STERNE, Laurence, *English humorist,* 1713–68

Prose:

Temporal Advantages of Religion (30 pp.: HM 2100)

Letters: 5 (1758–68)

STETSON, Grace Ellery (Channing), *American author,* 1862–1937

Verse:

Pity, O God! (CA 160)

Letters: 3 (1911–27)

STEVENS, Louis Edwin, *Russian-born American novelist, writer,* 1897–1962

Prose:

A Long View Down the Road: [screenplay] (copy; typewritten, 236 pp.: Louis Edwin Stevens Collection)

The Straight Path: [play in 3 acts] (typescript; carbon copy, 110 pp.: Louis Edwin Stevens Collection)

Letters: 31 (1912–16) to Jack London

Documents: 3 (1916)

STEVENS, Thomas Wood, *American author,* 1880–1942

Letters: 3 (1927) to Mary (Hunter) Austin

STEVENS, Wallace, *American poet,* 1879–1955

Born in Reading, Pennsylvania, Wallace Stevens remained interested during his lifetime in his native Berks County, Pennsylvania. His wife, Elsie Viola (Moll) Stevens, came from Reading, and they both devoted considerable time and energy tracing their ancestries. Stevens began writing verse as a student at Harvard University, and had a number of his poems published in *The Harvard Advocate* and the *Harvard Monthly.* Between 1914 and 1923 he submitted poems to a number of journals, including *Poetry.* By 1923 his first book of poems had been published by Alfred A. Knopf, a firm which continued to publish his books for the rest of his life. Though Stevens refused to consider his life a dichotomy, his poetic activities were accomplished while he was holding a full-time position as a legal adviser for the Hartford Accident and Indemnity Company, the firm for which he acted as vice-president from 1934 until his death in 1955.

Subject matter: primarily letters written to Stevens, his carbon copy replies, and autograph manuscripts. Also included is an extensive collection of genealogical material, in form of letters, documents, and typescripts. Dates from 1856 to 1975.

Significant persons: authors represented include Edward Estlin CUMMINGS, Alfred A. KNOPF, Robert MC ALMON, Thomas MAC GREEVY, Archibald MAC LEISH, Marianne Craig MOORE, Jose RODRIGUEZ-FEO, and John Orley Allen TATE

Physical description: letters and manuscripts are the heart of the 6815-piece collection, which includes numerous photographs and genealogical documents.

Provenance: acquired from Holly Stevens, January, 1975. A few of the items were gifts from Wilson Taylor and Holly Stevens; some material was purchased later from Holly Stevens.

Bibliography: most of the manuscripts have been published in one of three places: a published work of Stevens; *Opus Posthumous* (1957) edited by Samuel French Morse, or *The Making of Harmonium* by Robert Buttel. Many of the letters from Stevens were published by his daughter in 1966 in *Letters of Wallace Stevens.*

Verse:

149 items containing 218 poems

Prose:

35 texts

Letters: 2381 (1895–1955)

Documents: 2 (1924–37)

Other:

[Lists of poems and published works] (4 pieces: WAS 1163, 4179–81)

[Notes on copyright] (2 pieces: WAS 1164–65)

Notes on Drawing and Engraving (WAS 2325)

[Recordings of Stevens reading his poetry]

Vassar Viewed Voraciously: [16 pencil sketches of Vassar College, with annotations by Stevens] (WAS 4052)

STEVENS, William Bagshaw, *English poet,* 1756–1800

Prose:

Journal, 1792–1800: [containing numerous letters and poems transcribed by Stevens] (6 vols.: HM 26405)

STEVENSON, Sir John Andrew, *English composer,* 1760?–1833

Letters: 1 (1823)

STEVENSON, Robert Louis, *English author, traveler,* 1850–94

Verse:

Auntie's Skirts (HM 2460)

Autumn Fires (HM 2460)

The Cow (HM 2460)

The Dumb Soldier (HM 2460)

Embro Hie Kirk (HM 2392)

The Fine Pacific Islands (HM 2416)

The Flowers (HM 2460)

The Garden Door (HM 2460)

Good and Bad Children (HM 2460)

A Good Boy (HM 2460)

Henry James (the version beginning, Who comes tonight?: HM 2389)

"Here for a Christmas card I send" (HM 498)

The Hunt Interrupted (HM 2460)

Keepsake Mill (HM 2460)

The Land of Counterpane (HM 2460)

The Land of Nod (HM 2460)

A Lowden Sabbath Morn (HM 2387)

The Maker to Posterity (HM 2463)

Marching Song (HM 2460)

My Shadow (HM 2460)

Nest Eggs (HM 2460)

Night and Day (HM 2460)

Phase Uulus Loquitur—the Canoe Speaks (HM 8914)

A Proper Pride (HM 2460)

R. L. Stevenson on W. H. Mallock (in the hand of William Ernest Henley: HM 2459)

Requiem (intermediate version, in three stanzas, written on paper watermarked 1883: HM 1998)

A Song of Days (HM 2460)

"Soon eyes are tired with sunshine": [first draft of the poem; these two stanzas were published in reverse order as "Death to the dead for evermore"] (HM 2399)

Summer Sun (HM 2460)

"Thought is driven out of doors tonight" (HM 2400)

A Visit from the Sea (HM 2460)

Where Go the Boats? (HM 2460)

Prose:

[Anecdotes of the South Sea Islands in the 1870s] (HM 20538)

The Beach of Falesá (59 pp.: HM 2391)

Catriona: [fragment of chap. XIII] (1 p.: HM 2461)

The Circumnavigation of Tutuila (incomplete draft, 11 pp.: HM 2413)

David Balfour: [draft of chapter headings only] (3 pp.: HM 2415)

[Essay on history] (incomplete, 2 pp.: HM 2393)

[For Grace: a prayer written at Vailimá] (8 p.: HM 36694)

The Hair Trunk (incomplete, 148 pp.: HM 2411)

Hawaii: [notes] (6 pp.: HM 20534)

Highlands: [notes] (34 pp.: HM 35317)

In the Lightroom (1 p.: HM 2394)

[Journal kept during the cruise of the "Janet Nicoll" in the South Seas, 1890] (fragment, 2 pp.: HM 20537)

[Journal kept during two visits to the South Seas during the period from July 15, 1888 to Dec., 1889] (242 pp.: HM 2412)

Kidnapped (last three chapters missing, 162 pp.: HM 2410)

The Master of Ballantrae: [fragment from the preface] (1 leaf: HM 20535)

The Master of Ballantrae: [fragment from chap. VI] (1 leaf: HM 2462)

[Memoir on Thomas Stevenson] (fragment, 1 p.: HM 20536)

A Mountain Town in France (with five pencil sketches, 12 pp.: HM 2396)

The New Lighthouse on the Dhu Heartach Rock, Argy Ushire (with corrections by Thomas Stevenson, 17 pp.: HM 2403)

[Notebook] (a fragment, 6 leaves: HM 2401)

[Notebook containing biographical notes on Thomas Stevenson and a draft of a story about John David Nicholson] (21 pp.: HM 2405)

[Notebook: fragments from two different books. Contains

"O Pilot tis a fearful night . . .", and lists and random notes] (7 leaves: HM 2458)

[Notebook kept as a student in Edinburgh] (68 leaves: HM 2406)

[Notebook kept during a severe illness, while not allowed to speak] (35 leaves: HM 2404)

[Notebook kept during a severe illness, while not allowed to speak] (43 leaves: HM 2407)

[Notebook kept during a walking tour in the Cevennes, 1878, Sept.–Oct.] (81 pp.: HM 2408)

Notes of Dr. Turner's Voyage in 1876 (2 pp.: HM 2398)

On the Choice of a Profession, in a Letter to a Young Gentleman (6 pp.: HM 401)

On the Lighthouse Roof (1 p.: HM 2395)

Plain John Wiltshire on the Situation (typescript, title in the hand of Lloyd Osbourne, 10 pp.: HM 2409)

Saint Ives (252 pp., including a few pages in the hand of Mrs. Strong: HM 2388)

The Silverado Squatters: [the original diary on which the book was based] (64 pp.: HM 650)

Some College Memories (12 pp.: HM 44527)

The South Seas—a Record of Two Years Travel (20 pp.: HM 2421)

Letters: 91 (1873–94), including 40 to Will Hicok Low; also, 13 by Fanny Osbourne Stevenson

Documents: 5 (1887)

Other:

[Drawings] (HM 2417–19)

[Manuscript corrections in *Father Damien: An Open Letter*] (RB 8654)

[Marginal notes and corrections in *The South Seas*] (RB 285157)

[Miscellaneous unidentified fragments of notes and a drawing] (HM 44078)

[Music scores] (7 leaves bound in two volumes: HM 2397)

Sketchbook kept during a visit to the Riviera (HM 2402)

STILES, Ezra, *American clergyman, educator, author,* 1727–95

Letters: 1 (1792) to Thomas Jefferson

STILLINGFLEET, Benjamin, *English botanist, author,* 1702–71

Letters: 11 (1757–71) to Elizabeth (Robinson) Montagu

STIRLING-MAXWELL, Cardine Elizabeth Sarah (Sheridan) Norton, *English poet,* 1808–77

Letters: 21 (1855–73), including 13 to James Hain Friswell

STIRLING-MAXWELL, Sir William, 9th Bart., *English historical writer,* 1818–78

Letters: 3 (1862–73)

STOCKTON, Francis Richard, *American author,* 1834–1902

Prose:

The Casting Away of Mrs. Lecks and Mrs. Aleshine (183 pp.: HM 2598)

The Clocks of Rondaine (47 pp.: HM 2592)

Derelict (110 pp.: HM 2594)

The King's Arena (published as "The Lady or the Tiger," 30 pp.: HM 1983)

The Later Years of Monticello (19 pp.: HM 2597)

The Poor Relations (34 pp.: HM 2596)

The Story of Viteau (445 pp.: HM 2595)

The Tricycle of the Future (40 pp.: HM 2593)

Letters: 8 (1876–1902)

STODDARD, Charles Augustus, *American clergyman, author,* 1833–1920

Letters: 1 (1892)

STODDARD, Charles Warren, *American author, poet,* 1843–1909

Verse:

The Cocoa Tree (HM 2541)

Madrigal (HM 45669)

Monterey (HM 38491)

Old Monterey (HM 38493)

"The parables of Nature run" (HM 2542)

The Poet as the Pervious; a Doleful Duty (HM 38494)

To Lizette Dennison (in the hand of Ina Donna Coolbrith: HM 38495)

To Lizette Dennison (Woodworth Collection)

To Theo. N. Vail (AP 1733)

Prose:

[Introduction to an unidentified article or book] (5 pp.: HM 38489)

[Notes on James] Boswell's [life of Samuel] Johnson (4 pp.: HM 38492)

Letters: 104 (1870–1908), including 52 to DeWitt Miller; also 419 letters addressed to Stoddard

Other:

List of poem titles (HM 38490)

STODDARD, Elizabeth Drew (Barstow), *American novelist, poet,* 1823–1902

Verse:

Mercedes (HM 2543)

Letters: 4 (1890–93)

STODDARD, John Lawson, *American lecturer, hymn writer,* 1850–1931

Verse:

[Inscription in verse in his *Poems:*] "Dear 'King of Books'—and hearts—thy gentle sway" (RB 69998)

Letters: 9 (1901–11)

STODDARD, Richard Henry, *American poet, critic, editor, author,* 1825–1903

Verse:

Ad Lycoris (HM 44079)

The Asphodel (RB 144848)

At Rest (incomplete, lacks 4th stanza: FI 3858)

At the Author's Club (HM 1962)

At the Author's Club (corrected typescript: HM 1963)

"The Christmas time drew slowly near" (HM 44080)

The Demon of Music (FI 3887)

A Gazelle (HM 2106)

"Go Slow, thou camel driver" (FI 3888)

Hymn to the Sea (HM 1964)

The Luteplayer's House (HM 1965)

My Way (HM 44079)

On the Sands: Full Fathom Five Thy Father Lies (published as "The Sea": FI 3886)

A Servian Song (HM 1966)

The Stork and the Ruby (FI 3857)

To George B. Butler (HM 1967)

To the Immortal Memory of Keats (HM 1961)

Prose:

Items, or Thoughts, That May Be of Use (2 pp.: HM 2545)

Letters: 53 (1851–91), including 45 to James Thomas Fields

Other:

Inscriptions (RB 75798, RB 21696, RB 75859)

STODDART, Isabella (Moncreiff-Wellwood), *English writer, wife of Sir John Stoddart,* d. 1846

Prose:

The Adventures of Pietro Bey the Albanian Chief and of Hellen Sinclair, by M. Blackford (212 pp.: HM 510)

Theodora or the Little Greek Slave (197 pp.: HM 510)

[Untitled text beginning] "Early in the month of August Mrs. Sullivan the wife of a respectable merchant who resided in Naples" (197 pp.: HM 510)

STODDART, Joseph Marshall, *American editor, publisher,* 1845–1921

Letters: 3 (1881–1900)

STONE, Irving, *American author,* 1903–

Letters: 8 (1938–53)

STONE, Melville Elijah, *American publisher, author,* 1848–1929

Letters: 15 (1894–1912)

STONE, William Leete, *American editor, author,* 1792–1844

Letters: 2 (1828–41)

STORK, Charles Wharton, *American poet, educator, editor, translator,* b. 1881

Verse:

To St. Francis (Kane Literary Collection)

Letters: 1 (n.d.)

STORY, William Wetmore, *American sculptor, essayist, poet,* 1819–95

Letters: 8 (1846–91)

STOTHARD, Thomas, *English painter, book illustrator,* 1755–1834

Letters: 1 (1826)

STOWE, Harriet Elizabeth (Beecher), *American author,* 1811–96

Verse:

"God's purposes will ripen fast" (HM 43372)

Knocking (FI 3957)

Prose:

Agnes of Sorrento (Chaps. 18–19, 27–32, 144 pp.: FI 3924)

"Behold the tabernacle of God": [religious statement] (2 pp.: HM 43371)

The Chimney Corner:

No. I (21 pp.: FI 3917)

No. III—Little Foxes, Part II (31 pp.: FI 3915)

No. IV—Little Foxes, Part III (25 pp.: FI 3916)

No. IX—Little Foxes, Part VII (37 pp.: FI 3919)

No. X—The Woman Question, or What Will You Do with Her? (27 pp.: FI 3920)

House and Home Papers:

No. II (10 pp.: FI 3913)

No. III (37 pp.: FI 3912)

No. III (brief portion, 3 pp.: FI 3910)

No. IV—The Economy of the Beautiful (31 pp.: FI 3911)

No. V—Raking Up the Fire (28 pp.: FI 3914)

No. VII (16 pp.: FI 3923)

No. VIII—Economy (27 pp.: FI 3922)

No. XI (59 pp.: FI 3918)

Lady Byron Vindicated (preface only, 4 pp.: HM 2547)

Little Pussy Willow:

Part I (15 pp.: HM 43373)

Part II (16 pp.: HM 43374)

Part III (18 pp.: HM 43375)

Part IV (10 pp.: HM 43376)

Part V (11 pp.: HM 43377)

Part VI (12 pp.: HM 43378)

Part VII—What Pussy Did with her Winters (18 pp.: HM 43379)

Part VIII—Pussy Willow Blossoms (8 pp.: HM 43380)

Part IX—What Pussy Willow Did (14 pp.: HM 43381)

Part X—Pussy and Emily at Sixteen (12 pp.: HM 43382)

Part XII—Emily's First Day with Pussy Willow (15 pp.: HM 43383)

Part XIII—Miss Emily Proudie Makes a Discovery (10 pp.: HM 43384)

Part XIV—Emily's New Resolution (16 pp.: HM 43385)

Part XV—Emily at Home Again (9 pp.: HM 43386)

Part XVI—Pussy and Emily Mature (12 pp.: HM 43387)

Queer Little People:

Aunt Esther's Rules (7 pp.: HM 43388)

The Daisy's First Winter (15 pp.: HM 43389)

The Hen that Hatched Ducks (14 pp.: HM 43390)

The History of Tip-Top (16 pp.: HM 43391)

Hum, the Son of Buz (20 pp.: HM 43392)

Miss Katy-did and Miss Cricket (10 pp.: HM 43393)

Mother Magpie's Mischief (11 pp.: HM 43394)

The Nutcrackers of Nutcracker Lodge (12 pp.: HM 43395)

Our Dogs (67 pp.: HM 43396)

The Squirrels that Live in a House (13 pp.: HM 43397)

[A Reply to the Address of the Women in England] (4 pp.: FI 3909)

Sojourner Truth, the Libyan Sybil (26 pp.: FI 3921)

Letters: 162 (1853–94), including 129 to James Thomas Fields and Annie (Adams) Fields

Other:

[Recipe, with drawing] (FI 3972)

[Signed sentiment] (J. A. Ford Album)

STRAHAN, William, *English printer and publisher,* 1715–85

Letters: 8 (1751–78), including 6 to David Hall

Documents: 1 (1745)

STREET, Alfred Billings, *American lawyer, poet, librarian,* 1811–81

Prose:

The Great Sun (170 pp.: HM 2103)

Pharsalius, the Avenger; a tragedy in five acts (93 pp.: HM 2544)

Letters: 2 (1857)

STREET, Julian Leonard, *American novelist,* 1879–1947

Letters: 27 (1912–38)

STREETER, Edward, *American humorist, author,* 1891–

Letters: 8 (1958–63) to Theodore Van Soelen

STRICKLAND, Agnes, *English historian,* 1796–1874

Verse:

The Advent of Peace (HM 44083)
Come Rally for Your Colors (HM 2107)
Fallen Leaves (HM 44084)
The Love Quarrel (HM 1951)
Prince Choo Kang (HM 2109)
Song for the Loyal and True (HM 2108)

Letters: 6 (1832–74)

STROBRIDGE, Idah (Meacham), *American author,* 1855–1932

Letters: 2 (1900)

STRODE, William, *English poet, dramatist,* 1602–45

Verse:

[Poems ascribed to him in commonplace book] (HM 16522)

STRONG, Leonard Alfred George, *English poet, novelist,* 1896–

Letters: 7 (1939–57)

STUART, Gilbert, *English historian, reviewer,* 1742–86

Letters: 1 (1770)

Documents: 1 (1770)

STUART, Jesse Hilton, *American poet, novelist,* 1907–

Letters: 1 (1934)

STUART, Ruth (McEnery), *American author,* 1849–1917

Prose:

Light (17 pp.: HM 44086)
Sonny's Schooling (44 pp.: HM 2601)
Uncle Mingo's Speculations (57 pp.: HM 44087)

Letters: 12 (1895–1905)

SUCKLING, Sir John, *English poet,* 1609–42

Verse:

[Poems ascribed to him in commonplace book] (HM 198)

Letters: 1 (1634)

SUCKOW, Ruth, *American novelist,* 1892–1960

Letters: 2 (1929–34)

SUE, Marie-Joseph (Eugéne, pseud.), *French novelist,* 1804–75

Letters: 1 (n.d.)

SULLIVAN, Sir Arthur Seymour, *English composer,* 1842–1900

Letters: 2 (1876 and n.d.)

SULLIVAN, Thomas Russell, *American novelist*, 1849–1916

Verse:

Inter Pocula (HM 35075)

Letters: 15 (1895–1912)

SUMNER, Charles, *American orator, statesman, abolitionist, author*, 1811–74

Prose:

[Draft of a speech in the Senate on a bill to regulate commerce among the several states] (56 pp.: HM 897)

Protest [and] Second Protest [upon being requested to appear before a committee appointed by the Senate to investigate the sale of arms to France] (32 pp.: HM 788)

Letters: 210 (1834–73)

Documents: 3 (1834–71)

Other:

[Signed sentiment] (J. A. Ford Album)

SWAIN, Charles, *English poet*, 1801–74

Verse:

Two Songs (HM 1950)

SWIFT, Jonathan, *English poet, satirist*, 1667–1745

The numbers in parentheses are page references to *The Poems of Jonathan Swift*, edited by Harold Williams, 1958.

Verse:

Advice to a Parson, An Epigram (807, not autograph: RB 143198–259)

An Answer to a Late Scandalous Poem (616: HM 14339)

An Answer to the Ballyspellin Ballad (440, not autograph: HM 14340)

The Beau's Reply to the Five Ladyes Answer (428: HM 14335)

Dr. Swift's Answer to Dr. Sheridan (1017: HM 14336)

An Epigram on Seeing a worthy Prelate go out of Church in the Time of Divine Service (809, not autograph: RB 143198–259)

An Epistle to a Lady (629, not autograph: RB 81494, vol. II)

The Grand Question debated, whether Hamilton's Bawn shall be turned into a Malt-House or a Barrack (866, not autograph: RB 143198–259)

On Bishop Rundle (819, in the hand of Deane Swift: HM 14345)

On Poetry (619, only the six so-called libelous passages—not autograph: RB 81494, vol. II)

On Wisdom's Defeat, In a Learned Debate (1118, not autograph: RB 352764–86)

On the Words Brother Protestant and Fellow Christian Which were Used by the Presbiterians (811, not autograph: RB 143198–259)

[Untitled verses on Swift's deafness beginning, Verticosus, inops, surdus] (672, draft: HM 14338, p. 23)

Verses wrote on the great Storm which happen'd about Xmas 1722 (302, not autograph: RB 143198–259)

"Your mouldring walls are mending still" (Swift is attributed author: HM 27942)

Prose:

Anglo Angli (some verse, including that on his deafness above, is to be found among the prose, 28 pp.: HM 14338)

A Consultation and other Lantin Angli: [part of Polite Conversation] (8 pp.: HM 14341)

A Dialogue in Hybernian Stile between A and B (2 pp.: HM 14342)

History of the Four Last Years of the Queen: [notes for vol. IV] (1 p.: HM 14380)

Irish Eloquence (2 pp.: HM 14343)

A Letter to a Young Lady upon Her Marriage, 1723 (18 pp.: HM 1599)

Men Famous for Their Learning, Wit, or Great Employments or Quality of My Acquaintance Who are Dead, and Men of Distinction and My Friends Who are yet Alive (3 pp.: HM 14344)

Preferments of Ireland (1 p.: HM 27943)

Proposal for Virtue: [the headings for a pamphlet which was apparently never written, with, on the verso, a draft of proposals for establishing a fellowship at Trinity College, Dublin, part of Swift's will] (3 pp.: HM 14346)

Recipe for Leaven Bread (2 pp.: RB 106660)

To Martha (Swift) Harrison Whiteway: directions to be followed in the event of his death (3 pp.: HM 14347)

Letters: 15 (1725–39); also, forgery (HM 24018); and early nineteenth-century copies of 10 letters in an 1808 edition of *The Works of Jonathan Swift* once belonging to Walter Scott (RB 141696)

There are also related papers and letters, salvaged from the effects of Theophilus Swift by James Smith, and other Swiftiana. See George P. Mayhew, *Rage or Raillery* (San Marino: Huntington Library, 1967), for detailed descriptions of the above material.

SWINBURNE, Algernon Charles, *English poet, critic,* 1837–1909

Verse:

After Death (HM 2782)

The Altar of Righteousness (HM 2777)

Astrophel and Other Poems [dedication only] (HM 2839)

At a Dog's Grave (HM 2775)

Atalanta in Calydon (HM 16286)

The Cliffside Path (HM 16295)

Cromwell's Statue (HM 2787)

Dedicatory poem for the 3rd series of Poems and Ballads (HM 2783)

Dickens (HM 2828)

Earl Robert (HM 16284)

The Emperor's Progress, study in three stages (HM 2850)

Ex Voto (HM 2842)

First and Last (HM 2837)

A Haven (HM 16293)

Hendecasyllables (HM 16287)

Hymn to Proserpine (a fragment: HM 27231)

In Memory of Barry Cornwall (HM 16288)

In the Water (HM 16294)

A Landscape by Courbet (HM 2772)

Loch Torridon (HM 2825)

March, an Ode (HM 2835)

Mary Stuart (fragment of act III, scene 1: HM 2779)

Memorial Verses on the Death of Richard Burton (HM 16296)

"'Mid the Mother . . . : [extract of poem] (HM 35075)

Ode on the Proclamation of the French Republic (HM 2773)

Ode to Athens (HM 2841)

On a Country Road (HM 16292)

On the Cliffs (HM 2840)

[On the Death of Colonel Benson] (HM 2788)
On the Verge (HM 16291)
Prologue to the Broken Heart (HM 2826)
Quia Multum Amavit (HM 2836)
Rosamund, Queen of the Lombards (HM 2830)
A Sea-mark (HM 16290)
Song (HD 267)
Song for the Centenary of Walter Savage Landor (HM 2846)
A Song in Time of Order, 1852 (HM 16285)
The Sunbows (HM 16289)
The Tragedy of the Duke of Gandia (HM 2831)
Tristram and Iseult (HM 2780)
The Two Dreams (HM 2813)
A Year's Carols (HM 2849)

Prose:

Ben Jonson (69 pp.: HM 2784, pt. 1)
Ben Jonson: Discoveries (34 pp.: HM 2784, pt. 3)
Ben Jonson: Miscellaneous Works (27 pp.: HM 2784, pt. 2)
Changes of Aspect (21 pp.: HM 2832)
Dickens (35 pp.: HM 2829)
Les Écoliers Britanniques (in French, 10 pp.: HM 2789)
The Fifth Chapter of Launcelot (3 pp.: HM 2848)
Lesbia Brandon (one chapter only, entitled Another Portrait, 3 pp.: HM 2847)
Mr. Arnold's New Poems (38 pp.: HM 2776)
Mr. Whistler's Lecture on Art (13 pp.: HM 16283)
Notes on Poems and Reviews (34 pp.: HM 2824)
The Poems of Dante Gabriel Rossetti (38 pp.: HM 2834)

Shelley (24 pp.: HM 2781)

Short Notes: Ibsen, Lewes, M[atthew] A[rnold] (2 pp.: HM 2786)

An Unknown Poet (31 pp.: HM 2833)

Victor Hugo: Choses Vues (11 pp.: HM 2844)

Victor Hugo: Dieu (9 pp.: HM 2827)

Victor Hugo: En Voyage (22 pp.: HM 2843)

Walter Savage Landor (11 pp.: HM 2845)

Wilkie Collins (22 pp.: HM 2838)

William Blake (fragment from part II, 3 leaves: HM 20609)

William Blake (fragment from part III, 1 leaf: HM 2778)

William Blake [a new introduction to a new edition] (4 pp.: HM 2785)

Letters: 46 (1866–1902), including 17 to Mary Charlotte Julia (Gordon) Leith

Other:

[Autograph presentation and ms. corrections in the text in his *The Queen-Mother, Rosamond, Two Plays*] (RB 26656)

[Autograph notes in Cyrano de Bergerac's *Les Oeuvres Diverses*] (RB 4067)

SWINNERTON, Frank Arthur, *English novelist,* b. 1884

Letters: 1 (1921)

SYMONDS, John Addington, *English poet, historian, biographer,* 1840–93

Verse:

Selection of Lyrical Verse Dedicated to George Rea (HM 2602)

Prose:

Life of Michelangelo Buonarrotti (3 vols.: HM 2725)

Letters: 3 (1887–89)

SYMONS, Arthur William, *English poet, critic,* 1865–1945

Verse:

Mary in Bethlehem (Hill Collection)

Letters: 6 (1904–23)

T

TABB, John Banister, *American clergyman, poet,* 1845–1909

Verse:

Good-night (RB 129849)

The Light of Bethlehem (HM 44094)

Remorse (HM 44095)

Stabat (HM 44096)

To a Rose (HM 44097)

Letters: 15 (1886–1907), including 8 to William Hayes Ward

TAGGARD, Genevieve, *American poet,* 1894–1948

Verse:

Man in the Wind (typewritten: Charles Erskine Scott Wood Collection)

Letters: 17 (1924–37)

TALFOURD, Sir Thomas Noon, *English judge, author,* 1795–1854

Verse:

Ion, a Tragedy (incomplete: TA 1)

To Mr. Macready (not autograph: RB 264486, vol. IV, p. 1)

To Mr. Macready on the Birth of His First Child (RB 264486, vol. I, p. 458)

Letters: 18 (1826–49), including 7 to Edward Vaughan Hyde Kenealy and 3 to Charles Dickens; also, 206 letters addressed to Talfourd

Other:

[Autograph quotation in Talfourd's *The Castilian*] (RB 69996)

TALMAGE, Thomas DeWitt, *American clergyman, lecturer, editor, author,* 1832–1902

Letters: 2 (1878–89)

TARBELL, Ida Minerva, *American author,* 1857–1944

Letters: 43 (1892–1928)

TARKINGTON, Booth, *American novelist, playwright, illustrator,* 1869–1946

Letters: 19 (1906–37); also: 3 letters (1919–29) by Susannah (Keifer) Robinson Tarkington

TATE, James, *English historian, author,* 1771–1843

Letters: 1 (1836)

Other:

To Geo[rge] Dyer: [transmitting a copy of Henry Francis Cary's] Epitaph on Charles Lamb in Edmonton Churchyard . . . (1 p.: HM 12288)

TATE, John Orley Allen, *American critic, poet,* 1899–1979

Letters: 155 (1941–73)

TAYLER, Frederick, *English landscape painter,* 1802–89

Letters: 2 (1863–80)

TAYLOR, Bayard, *American translator, author,* 1825–78

Verse:

Assyrian Night Song (HM 44277)

Bedouin Song: [first stanza only] (HM 14933)

Casa Guidi Windows (HM 14659)

The Dearest Image: [last stanza missing] (HM 14943)

Earth Life (HM 14947)

[Extracts from 2 poems] (HM 14884)

Faust: [2 stanzas from act III] (HM 14919)

The Fountain of Trevi (HM 14917)

Greeting to America, Written for Jenny Lind (HM 44278)

The Highland Chieftain (HM 14938)

Hymn to an American (not autograph, in German: HM 14862)

Hymn to the Beautiful (HM 14939)

Implora Pace (HM 14937)

Jane Reed (HM 14931)

Lars—a Pastoral of Norway: [extract—On the Fiord] (HM 14925)

March (HM 44279)

March (HM 14946)

May-Time: [last two lines only] (HM 14934)

The Mountains (HM 14916)

The Mountains (HM 14949)

My Farm: A Fable (HM 14936)

The Neva (HM 14942)

"Now part our paths awhile, my more than friend" (HM 14922)

"One shade, tonight, rests on our cheerful band" (HM 14923)

A Paean to the Dawn: [3rd stanza only] (HM 14941)

Poems of Home and Travel: [28 poems in the 1855 edition] (FI 4058)

Poems of the Orient: [all the poems in the 1855 edition except Bedouin Song and On the Sea] (FI 4057)

Song: [beginning, Daughter of Egypt, veil thine eyes] (HM 14948)

Song of the Camp: [last stanza only] (HM 14929)

Summer's Bacchanal (HM 14940)

Thanksgiving for Spring (HM 1227)

To the American People: [last stanza only] (HM 14935)

The Voice of Pennsylvania Volunteers through Balt[imore] (HM 14950)

"We've won! The sword in valiant hand" (HM 14924)

"When, through the gloom of years" (RB 82286)

Wind and Sea (HM 14945)

The Wisdom of Ali (HM 14944)

Prose:

At Home and Abroad: Day-Dreams-Departure (6 pp.: HM 14926)

At Home and Abroad: The First German Shooting Match (2 pp.: HM 14921)

Between Europe and Asia: [extract] (1 p.: HM 14932)

Dedicatory Address for the Monument to Fitz-Greene Halleck, Guilford, Conn., July 8, 1869 (16 pp.: HM 14930)

Farewell to the North—Second Interview with Humboldt (14 pp.: HM 14918)

Friend Eli's Daughter (15 pp.: FI 4059)

The German Burns (17 pp.: FI 4056)

Hannah Thurston: [extract from chap. IX] (1 p.: HM 14928)

Introductory Notice [to the American edition of Richard F.

Burton's *Personal Narrative of a Pilgrimage to El-Medinah and Mecca*] (8 pp.: HM 14920)

A Visit to India, China, and Japan: [chap. XLIII] (10 pp.: HM 14927)

Letters: 477 (1840–78), and 37 by Marie (Hansen) Taylor

Documents: 6 (1860–70) canceled checks

TAYLOR, Benjamin Franklin, *American editor, traveler, author*, 1819–87

Letters: 1 (1887)

TAYLOR, Sir Henry, *English author,* 1800–86

Verse:

To Ascario C. H. Tealdi (HM 26171)

Letters: 14 (1844–86)

TAYLOR, John, *English poet,* 1580–1653

Verse:

Sense upon Nonsense (fragment: EL 8753)

The Suddaine turne of Fortunes Wheele or A Conference holden in the Castle of St Angello betwixt the Pope the Emperor and the King of Spain (30 pp.: HM 122)

TAYLOR, John, *English miscellaneous writer,* 1757–1832

Verse:

Sonnet—To William Sotheby, Esqr. (SY 158)

Letters: 2 (1830)

TAYLOR, John, *English publisher,* 1781–1864

Letters: 11 (1821–58), including 2 in verse

TAYLOR, Meadows, *English Indian officer, novelist,* 1808–76

Letters: 1 (1874)

TAYLOR, Robert Lewis, *American author,* 1912–

Letters: 8 (1953–59) to Theodore Van Soelen

TAYLOR, Tom, *English dramatist, editor,* 1817–80

Letters: 29 (1853–80)

TEASDALE, Sara, *American poet,* 1884–1933

Letters: 7 (1914–24)

TENNANT, William, *English linguist, poet,* 1784–1848

Letters: 4 (1836–37) to Thomas Frognall Dibdin

Other:

[List of] Books bought, 1835 (2 pp.: DI 582)
[Transcript of George Gough's description of Oliver Cromwell's Great Seal, Jan. 21, 1798] (2 pp.: DI 581)

TENNYSON, Alfred, 1st Baron, *English poet,* 1809–92

Verse:

"Along this echoing gallery" (HM 19484)

"As thro' the corn at eve we went" (HM 19485)

"Ask me no more: the moon may draw the sea" (HM 19486)

"Be merry be merry: the woods begin to blow" (HM 19487)

"Black Bull of Aldgate may thy horns rot from the sockets" (HM 19488)

Boadicea (HM 19489)

"Break, break, break" (HM 19490)

The Bridesmaid (HM 19491)

The Captain (HM 19492)

Darwin's Gemmule (HM 19493)

The Day-Dream: [stanza IV from "L'envoi" section; varies slightly from printed version] (HM 19482)

Edward Gray (HM 1322)

Enoch Arden (HM 14951)

[Idylls of the King: first draft of a prelude] (not autograph: FI 4110)

Idylls of the King: [parts of "Balin and Balan," "The Holy Grail," and "The Last Tournament"] (HM 1323)

Idylls of the King: [parts of "Ninue"] (HM 1326)

Idylls of the King: [part of "Pelleas and Ettare" beginning] "The night was hot; he could not sleep: a lay" (HM 1324)

Idylls of the King: [part of "Pelleas and Ettare" beginning] "The night was hot: he cd not sleep: a sound" (HM 19494)

In Memoriam: [49 stanzas] (HM 1321)

Locksley Hall: [lines 31 to 34] (HM 19483)

Maud: [part I, section 22] (HM 19495)

Maud: [portions of part I] (HM 19496)

Milton (Alcaics: HM 19497)

Milton (Hendecasyllabics: HM 19498)

Minnie and Winnie (HM 18898)

Northern Farmer—Old Style (HM 19499)

"O sun that wakest all" (HM 19500)

Oenone (HM 19501)

On a Spiteful Letter (HM 1325)

[Poems and portions of poems published in the second volume of *Poems*, 1842] (HM 1320)

The Sailor Boy (HM 19502)

St. Agnes (HM 22255)

"Speak to the Lord: he is close at thy hand" (HM 19503)

"The tenth of April! is it not?" (HM 19504)

[Three epigrams] (HM 19505)

"While I live the owls" (HM 19506)

Letters: 43 (1835–88), including 19 to Frederick James Furnivall; also 24 by Emily, Baroness Tennyson, and 10 by Hallam, 2nd Baron

Other:

[Ms. corrections in printed copy of *Carmen Saeculare*] (RB 129214)

The Throstle (photostat of autograph ms. included with printed copy containing corrections by Hallam Tennyson: RB 129096)

TERHUNE, Albert Payson, *American author,* 1872–1942

Letters: 7 (1911–34), including 6 to Eugene Lafayette Cunningham

TERHUNE, Mary Virginia (Hawes), *American novelist,* 1830–1922

Prose:

The Sympathy Meeting (21 pp.: HM 44092)

Letters: 18 (1864–1901)

Other:

[Inscription in *Dr. Dale*] (RB 384396)

[Inscription in *Home of the Bible*] (RB 5604)

[Inscription in *Nemesis*] (RB 150652)

[Manuscript note in *Story of Mary Washington*] (RB 133884)

TERRY, Ellen, *English actress,* 1848–1928

Letters: 139 (1885–1931)

THACKERAY, William Makepeace, *English novelist,* 1811–63

Verse:

The Album and the Pen (HM 1621)

The Chronicle of the Drum (HM 1628)

A Mother's Greeting to Her First Born (forgery: HM 1623)

The Past—Looking Back (RB 110390)

A Quarter of an Hour (HM 15366)

Requiescant: [last verse of a poem from Proposals for a Continuation of Ivanhoe] (HM 15273)

Stranger (RB 110390)

Sweet Bird! (RB 110390)

"Sweet did she smile and graceful did she move" (RB 110390)

The White Squall: [chap. 9 of "Notes of a Journey from Cornhill to Grand Cairo"] (HM 15358, pp. 3–4)

Prose:

The Adventures of Philip (531 pp.: HM 239)

The Adventures of Philip: [fragment from vol. I, chap. III] (1 p.: HM 1630)

The Adventures of Philip: [fragment from vol. II, chap. XXI] (1 p.: HM 15364)

The English Humorists of the Eighteenth Century (the lecture on Swift, 30 pp.: HM 15362)

The Four Georges: [notes for a lecture] (23 pp.: HM 1622)

The Four Georges: [part of the lecture on George I, in the hand of George Hodder] (12 pp.: HM 15363)

The History of Pendennis: [fragment from chap. XXXIV] (1 p.: HM 1635)

The History of Pendennis: [fragment from chap. XLII] (1 p.: HM 1624)

Lovell the Widower: [corrected proof of chap. I] (11 pp.: HM 259)

Lovell the Widower: [part of chap. IV] (12 pp.: HM 1632)

The Newcomes: [fragment of chap. LXIX] (1 p.: HM 15365)

[Notes for a speech as Parliamentary candidate for Oxford] (5 pp.: HM 1625)

Our Street (The Bumpshers and part of Jolly Newboy Esq., 8 pp.: HM 1629)

Our Street (What Sometimes Happens in Our Street, Somebody Whom Nobody Knows, and part of The Man in Possession, 7 pp.: HM 1631)

[Part of an unpublished play] (13 pp.: HM 1633)

Roundabout Papers (part of De Juventute, 2 pp.: HM 1626)

Roundabout Papers: Round about the Christmas Tree (6 pp.: HM 1636)

Travels in Holland and Belgium (incomplete draft, 5 pp.: HM 15359)

Vanity Fair: [fragment of chap. XXXVIII] (RB 114203 PFX)

The Virginians: [fragment from chap. LXXXVII] (2 pp.: HM 1634)

Letters: 128 (1830–64); and 45 by Lady Anne (Thackeray) Ritchie

Drawings: 245, including 9 (RB 114203) for *Vanity Fair* and 78 (HM 15358; HM 40006) for *Notes of a Journey from Cornhill to Grand Cairo*

Other:

[Scrapbook containing pictures and clippings] (HM 40009)

THATCHER, Benjamin Bussey, *American lawyer, editor, author,* 1809–40

Letters: 3 (1835–38)

Documents: 1 (1835)

THAXTER, Celia (Laighton), *American author,* 1835–94

Verse:

"The barn was low and dim and old" (FI 4156)

Beethoven (second stanza only: FI 4148)

Content (published as "Discontent": FI 4142)

Farewell (FI 4141)

For Thoughts (FI 4192)

Guendolen (FI 4153)

Heartbreak Hill (FI 4145)

Imprisoned (FI 4146)

In Fredericksburg (FI 4151)

In Tuscany (contemporary typescript: FI 4172)

Leviathan (HM 1922)

May Morning (FI 4152)

The Minute-Guns (FI 4184)

A Morning Vision (FI 4149)

Mozart (FI 4143)

A Mussel Shell (HM 44098)

November Morning (FI 4147)

"O flying sails that scud before the gale" (FI 4155)

Off Shore (FI 4158)

The Pimpernel (FI 4159)

Poor Little Katy (FI 4140)

Renunciation (FI 4139)

The Sandpiper's Happy Call (FI 4137)

Schumann's Sonata in A Minor (FI 4154)

Song: "Above, in her bedchamber, her voice I hear" (FI 4138)

Song: "We sail toward evening's lonely star" (HM 44099)

Song: "We sail toward evening's lonely star" (FI 4150)

Submission (FI 4196)

A Summer Day (FI 4157)

Thora (FI 4144)

"Through the wide sky thy north wind's thunder roars" (FI 4193)

To J. Appleton Brown (HM 1242)

A Woman of Star Island (FI 4183)

Letters: 70 (1861–92), including 62 to James Thomas Fields and Annie (Adams) Fields

THOMAS, Augustus, *American playwright,* 1857–1934

Letters: 2 (1908–12), and 6 letters addressed to Thomas

THOMAS, Edith Matilda, *American poet,* 1854–1925

Verse:

Acer Saccharinum Loquitur (The Dryad Speaks: FI 4237)

Fighting the Wind (HM 26401)

Song: "Lonely art thou in thy sorrow—lonely art thou" (HM 1243)

To the Memory of Helen Hunt Jackson (HM 1923)

Letters: 15 (1885–1916)

THOMAS, Isaiah, *American printer, publisher, author,* 1749–1831

Letters: 4 (1791–1806)

THOMPSON, Dorothy, *American journalist, author,* 1894–1961

Letters: 1 (1933) to Walford Graham Robertson

THOMPSON, Sir Edward Maunde, *English paleographer, director of British Museum,* 1840–1929

Letters: 1 (1904)

THOMPSON, Henry Yates, *English book collector,* 1838–1928

Letters: 8 (1897–1904)

THOMPSON, John Reuben, *American editor, poet,* 1823–73

Letters: 10 (1868–72)

THOMPSON, Maurice, *American poet, novelist,* 1844–1901

Prose:

Nuts from Périgord (22 pp.: HM 44102)
An Autumn Shudder (3 pp.: HM 168)
A Race Romance (57 pp.: HM 214)
A Touch of Nature (20 pp.: HM 1305)

Letters: 2 (1887)

THOMPSON, Vance, *American author,* 1863–1925

Letters: 3 (1895) to Albert Bigelow Paine

THOMS, William John, *English antiquary, author, editor,* 1803–85

Letters: 5 (1853–72), and 9 letters addressed to Thoms

THOMSON, James, *English poet,* 1700–48

Verse:

Alfred, a Masque (not autograph, submitted for licensing by Garrick and Lacey, 50 pp.: HM 203)

THORBURN, Grant, *English author,* 1773–1863

Prose:

The Merchants of New York in the Last Century (5 pp.: RB 320006, vol. 2)

Letters: 7 (1847–59)

THORBURN, Robert, *English miniature painter,* 1818–85

Letters: 1 (1852)

THOREAU, Henry David, *American naturalist, poet, essayist,* 1817–62

Verse:

The Departure (HM 13184)
The Friend (HM 13188)
The Funeral Bell (HM 13185)
Godfrey of Boulogne (HM 13197)
Independence: [early draft] (HM 13186)
Morning (HM 13188)
[Poems, in the hand of Sophia E. Thoreau] (HM 13190)
Contents:

Haze
The Funeral Bell
Voyager's Song
Change Not
A Rural Scene
The Ark
Enoch
The Prayer
"Every little spring flows on"

"My feeble bark has reached the shore"

"Tell Shakespeare to attend some leisure hour" (HM 1225)

To the Mountains (HM 13183)

The Virgin (HM 13187)

Prose:

Calendar for March: [index to the Journal] (18 pp.: HM 13202)

[Cape Cod: draft, with later notes, corrections, and additions, bearing the title] A Course of Lectures on Cape Cod 322 pp.: HM 13206)

[College essays]: (30 pp.: HM 934)

Of Keeping a Private Journal

Whether the Cultivation of the Imagination Conduce to the Happiness of the Individual

[On the variety of energy in men]

[On the anxieties and delights of a discoverer]

Explain the Phrases—a Man of Business a Man of Pleasure, a Man of the World

[On becoming what others think us to be]

[On Henry N. Coleridge's book]

[On the advantages and disadvantages of foreign influence on American literature]

[Commonplace Book] (partly in the hand of Sophia E. Thoreau, 49 pp.: HM 957)

[An excursion to Canada; an early draft, in lecture form] (196 pp.: HM 949)

[An excursion to Canada: revised version of chaps. I and II, incomplete] (57 pp.: HM 950)

[An excursion to Canada: final revised version] (214 pp.: HM 953)

General Phenomena for April [and] Phenomena for Feb. 1860: [indexes to the Journal] (14 pp.: HM 13203)

Gratitude (with drafts and fragments of verse, 24 pp.: HM 13201)

Index Rerum (contains an index to the Journal, a library catalogue, and reviews of books, 76 pp.: HM 945)

Journal:

[fragment] (175 pp.: HM 13182)

[fragments: entries for] July 11–12, 1851, and Dec. 2, 8, and 15, 1853 (5 pp.: HM 933)

[fragment headed] Miscellaneous—At sundown on river (4 pp.: HM 931)

[fragment describing autumn foliage] (2 pp.: HM 13191)

Love and Friendship (27 pp.: HM 13196)

The Maine Woods: [early draft of Part III] (10 pp.: HM 13199)

[Miscellaneous observations on the phenomena of nature] (216 pp.: HM 954)

[Nature notes for the months of April and May] (1 p.: HM 13198)

[Notes on a journey from Concord, Massachusetts, to Minnesota, and return] (100 pp.: HM 13192)

Part of the Map in Loskiel's History (1 p.: HM 13200)

Pindar (fragments in translation, 24 pp.: HM 13204)

A Plea for John Brown (fragments; written on the backs of HM 13202 and 13203, 32 pp.)

Prometheus Bound, translated from Aeschylus: [draft] (44 pp.: HM 926)

Seven Against Thebes, translated from Aeschylus: [draft] (41 pp.: HM 13193)

Sir Walter Raleigh: [first draft] (103 pp.: HM 935)

Sir Walter Raleigh: [final draft] (83 pp.: HM 943)

Walden, or Life in the Woods: [includes parts of early versions] (1184 pp.: HM 924)

Walden, or Life in the Woods (corrected proof, 119 pp.: HM 925)

A Week on the Concord and Merrimack Rivers: [early, incomplete draft of Monday and Tuesday] (56 pp.: HM 956)

A Week on the Concord and Merrimack: [fragments of an early draft] (6 pp.: HM 13194)

A Week on the Concord and Merrimack Rivers: [early draft] (84 pp.: HM 13195)

Letters: 41 (1836–62), including 18 to Daniel Ricketson; also 11 letters addressed to Thoreau; and 13 by Sophia E. Thoreau, all addressed to Ricketson

Other:

[Ms. corrections in two printed copies of *A Week on the Concord and Merrimack Rivers*] (RB 11856, RB 110229)

Note on high-water mark in the river, June 30, 1860 (written on the back of a letter from Mary Mann, 1 p.: HM 13192)

THORPE, Rose (Hartwick), *American poet, novelist,* 1850–1939

Letters: 1 (1888), which includes one stanza from the poem, "Curfew Must Not Ring Tonight"

THRALE, Hester Lynch, see PIOZZI, Hester Lynch (Salusbury) Thrale

THURBER, James Grover, *American artist, author,* 1894–1961

Letters: 4 (1926) to Albert Bigelow Paine

THURSTON, Ernest Temple, *English novelist, dramatist,* 1879–1933

Letters: 1 (1924)

THYNNE, Francis, *English Lancaster Herald writer,* 1545?–1608

Prose:

Animadversions uppon the Annotacions and Corrections of Some Imperfections of Impressions of Chaucer's Works (116 pp.: EL 34/B/11)

Emblemes and Epigrames (140 pp.: EL 34/B/12)

The Names and Armes of the Chauncellors, Collected into one Catalogue by Francis Thynn . . . (101 pp.: EL 26/A/6)

Parte of the Fyrste Parte of the Commentaries of Britayne collected by Francis Thynne (360 pp.: EL 1137)

The Plea betwene the Advocate and the Ant'advocate concerning the Bathe and Bacheler Knightes . . . (85 pp.: EL 1138)

Letters: 1 (1607) to John Egerton

TICKNOR, George, *American educator, author,* 1791–1871

Letters: 35 (1822–64)

TICKNOR, William Davis, *American publisher,* 1810–64

Letters: 1 (1858), and 17 letters addressed to him

See also FIELDS, James Thomas

TIETJENS, Eunice (Hammond), *American poet, novelist,* 1884–1944

Verse:

Song (Kane Literary Collection)

Letters: 5 (1915–17)

TILTON, Theodore, *American poet, journalist, editor,* 1835–1907

Letters: 8 (1862–99)

TIMROD, Henry, *American poet*, 1828–67

Verse:

Charleston, 1862 (HM 1307)

Ode—Sung on the Occasion of Decorating the Graves of the Confederate Dead, at Magnolia Cemetery, Charleston, S. C. (BR Box 119 [2])

Written on passing at an early hour of the morning a dark swamp in Virginia, where a few Jessamines were blooming on the banks of a sluggish stream ("Gay flow'r of the forest! Thy bright sunny hues": Kane Literary Collection)

TINKER, Edward Larocque, *American author*, 1881–1968

Letters: 1 (1939)

TODD, Mabel (Loomis), *American lecturer, editor, author*, 1856–1932

Letters: 6 (1899–1928)

TOPHAM, Edward, *English journalist, play writer*, 1751–1820

Letters: 1 (1788)

TOPSELL, Edward, *English divine, author*, d. 1638?

Prose:

The Fowles of Heaven, or, History of Birds (487 pp.: EL 1142)

TORREY, Bradford, *American ornithologist, editor, essayist*, 1843–1912

Letters: 2 (1892–94)

TOURGEE, Albion Winegar, *American novelist*, 1838–1905

Letters: 4 (1871–93)

TOUT, Thomas Frederick, *English historian, teacher,* 1855–1929

Letters: 21 addressed to him; also: 2 letters (1920) by his daughter, Margaret (Tout) Sharp

Other:

[List of] subjects for theses (4 pp.: HM 44103)

Subjects for theses (4 pp.: HM 30546)

TOWNE, Charles Hanson, *American editor, author,* 1877–1949

Letters: 9 (1915–25)

TOWNLEY, James, *English author, dramatist,* 1714–78

Letters: 1 (1828)

TOWNSEND, Edward Waterman, *American congressman, author,* 1855–1942

Prose:

Chimmie Fadden, a Discussion of L'Aiglon and Women (15 pp.: HM 1301)

TOWNSEND, George Alfred, *American journalist, novelist,* 1841–1914

Verse:

Swede and Indian Cantico (HM 1319)

Letters: 5 (1865–90)

TOWNSEND, Virginia Frances, *American editor, author,* 1836–1920

Letters: 1 (1856)

TRAUBEL, Horace, *American editor, author,* 1858–1919

Letters: 32 (1906–19)

TRELAWNY, Edward John, *English author, adventurer*, 1792–1881

Letters: 3 (1833–73)

TRENT, William Peterfield, *American educator, editor, author*, 1862–1939

Letters: 15 (1889–1927)

TREVELYAN, George Macaulay, *English author, historian*, 1876–1962

Letters: 2 (1914–23)

TREVELYAN, Sir George Otto, *English historian, biographer*, 1838–1928

Letters: 19 (1863–1924), including 11 to James Beck

TRINE, Ralph Waldo, *American author*, 1866–1958

Letters: 3 (1897–1905); also, 201 letters addressed to Trine or his wife

TROLLOPE, Anthony, *English novelist*, 1815–82

Prose:

The Belton Estate (620 pp.: HM 1332)
The Lady of Launay (60 pp.: HM 1329)
Sketches of California (8 pp.: HM 1328)
The Small House at Allington (906 pp.: HM 1330)
South Africa (659 pp.: HM 1331)

Letters: 9 (1862–75)

TROLLOPE, Frances (Milton), *English novelist*, 1780–1863

Letters: 1 (1837)

TROLLOPE, Theodosia (Garrow), *English author,* 1825–65

Letters: 1 (n.d.)

TROLLOPE, Thomas Adolphus, *English author,* 1810–92

Letters: 4 (1863–73)

TROUBETZKOY, Amelie (Rives) Chanler, *American novelist,* 1863–1945

Prose:

The Quick or the Dead (206 pp.: HM 6044)

Letters: 8 (1888–1924)

TROWBRIDGE, John Townsend, *American poet, editor,* 1827–1916

Verse:

The Pewee (FI 4257)

Prose:

A Visit to Mt. Vernon (36 pp.: HM 44104)

Letters: 27 (1852–1912), including 18 to James Thomas Fields

Other:

[List of] Articles by Mr. Trowbridge in *Atlantic Monthly* (RB 91885)

TRUMAN, Benjamin Cummings, *American journalist, author,* 1835–1916

Letters: 20 (1869–1913)

TRUMBULL, James Hammond, *American philologist, historian, bibliographer,* 1821–97

Letters: 6 (1855–70)

TUCKER, George, *American political economist, author,* 1775–1861

Letters: 10 (1804–48)

Documents: 1 (1825)

TUCKER, Nathaniel Beverley, *American educator, novelist,* 1784–1851

Letters: 3 (1809–33)

TUCKER, St. George, *American poet,* 1752–1827

Letters: 6 (1793–1819)

Documents: 47 (1782–1823)

TUCKERMAN, Henry Theodore, *American essayist, poet, critic,* 1813–71

Verse:

"They who most bravely can endure" (HM 25700)

Letters: 31 (1846–69)

TULLY, Jim, *American author,* 1891–1947

Letters: 9 (1922–38)

TUPPER, Martin Farquhar, *English author,* 1810–89

Verse:

The Dioscuri (HM 10767)
"A Hundred thousand curses" (HM 35822)
The Queen's Return (HM 35821)

Prose:

[Autobiographical sketch] (16 pp.: HM 1306)

Letters: 86 (1845–86)

TURNER, Charles Tennyson, *English poet,* 1808–79

Letters: 2 (1873)

TURNER, Sharon, *English historian, attorney,* 1768–1847

Prose:

The History of the Anglo-Saxons: [resume of contents] (1 p.: CD 326)

Letters: 5 (1799–1818)

TURNER, Walter James Redfern, *English poet, novelist,* 1889–1946

Letters: 1 (1944)

TWAIN, Mark, see CLEMENS, Samuel Langhorne

TWISS, Horace, *English wit, politician,* 1787–1849

Letters: 6 (1824–30)

TYLER, Moses Coit, *American educator, author,* 1835–1900

Letters: 6 (1873–89)

TYLER, Royall, *American jurist, poet, novelist, playwright,* 1757–1826

Documents: 1 (1804)

TYNDALL, John, *English natural philosopher,* 1820–93

Letters: 36 (1865–89)

TYTLER, Alexander Fraser, *English historian,* 1747–1813

Letters: 7 (1797–1812)

U

UNDERWOOD, Francis Henry, *American lawyer, diplomat, author,* 1825–94

Letters: 4 (1882–93)

UNTERMEYER, Louis, *American poet,* 1885–

Prose:

A Note on Modern American Poetry (typewritten; with letter from editor of *American Minds in Miniature;* 2 pp.: AU Box 3)

Letters: 70 (1917–75)

UPCOTT, William, *English antiquary, autograph collector,* 1779–1845

Letters: 44 (1808–40)

UPHAM, Charles Wentworth, *American clergyman, author,* 1802–75

Letters: 6 (1854–56)

UPTON, George Bruce, *American merchant, capitalist,* 1804–74

Verse:

Age Hath Its Pleasures (HM 15575)

"Beneath a large and stately pile" (HM 15576)
"Good luck, by George here is a prize" (HM 15577)
Memory (HM 15578)
[Miscellaneous fragments of verse] (HM 15579)
"Raise your voices loud and free" (HM 15580)
"Shall we ever meet again" (HM 15581)
A Song for the Buck (HM 15583)
To the Lydian Society (HM 15582)
We're Here Once More (2 copies: HM 15584 A and B)
When the Puritans Came Over (HM 15583)
"The year, the year, o say what magic wand" (HM 15585)

Letters: 1 (1839)

Documents: 1 (1849)

USSHER, Percival Arland, *English author, critic,* 1899–

Prose:

Extracts from a Journal (typewritten, 13 pp.: Dublin Magazine Collection)

V

VACARESCO, Helene, *Rumanian author,* 1868–1947

Prose:

An Early Feminist, Tacitus (34 pp.: HM 34960)

King Alexander of Serbia and Queen Draga (51 pp.: HM 475)

The Last Emperor of Brazil (27 pp.: HM 44111)

Queen Alexandra (32 pp.; also corrected proofs: HM 44112)

VACHELL, Horace Annesley, *English novelist, playwright,* 1861–1955

Letters: 24 (1907–50), including 8 to Curtis Brown, literary agent

VALLENTINE, Benjamin Bennaton, *American journalist, playwright,* 1843–1926

Letters: 1 (1904)

VAN ALSTYNE, Frances Jane (Crosby), *American author,* 1820–1915

Letters: 1 (n.d.)

VANBRUGH, Sir John, *English dramatist, architect,* 1664–1726

Letters: 3 (1685–1725)

VAN DOREN, Carl Clinton, *American educator, editor, critic, author*, 1885–1950

Letters: 30 (1918–50), including 16 to Mary (Hunter) Austin

VAN DOREN, Dorothy (Graffe), *American author*, 1896–

Letters: 8 (1926–28)

VAN DOREN, Mark Albert, *American poet, editor, compiler*, 1894–1972

Letters: 69 (1915–66)

VAN DYKE, Henry, *American clergyman, poet, educator*, 1852–1933

Verse:

Angler's Wish in Town (HM 1273)

"A Book is like a beggar-child who stands before you pleading": [inscription in *The Story of the Other Wise Man*] (RB 14360)

God of the Open Air (HM 1275)

"I love thine inland seas": [2 verses to the tune of "America"] (HM 44144)

A Leaf of Spearmint (HM 1274)

"Life is an arrow,—therefore you must know": [inscription in *The Last Word*] (RB 11973)

National Monuments (HM 1272)

The Wild Bees (HM 44145)

Letters: 11 (1888–1927)

Other:

[Prose inscription in *The Poetry of the Psalms*] (RB 11394)

VAN LOON, Hendrik Willem, *American journalist, historian,* 1882–1944

Letters: 7 (1922–32)

VAN PATTEN, Nathan, *American librarian, bibliographer, author,* 1887–1956

Letters: 1 (1951)

VAN VECHTEN, Carl, *American critic, novelist,* 1880–1964

Letters: 1 (1931)

VAN ZILE, Edward Sims, *American author,* 1863–1931

Letters: 3 (1904–30)

VAUGHAN, Thomas, *English dramatist, solicitor,* fl. 1772–1820

Documents: 1 (1756)

VEILLER, Bayard, *American playwright,* 1869–1943

Letters: 1 (n.d.)

VERPLANCK, Gulian Grommelin, *American editor, author,* 1786–1870

Letters: 7 (1828–53)

VESEY, Elizabeth (Vesey) *English leader of literary society,* 1715?–91

Verse:

To Laura (MO 6911)

Letters: 96 (1761–85); and 260 letters addressed to Mrs. Vesey

VEZIN, Hermann, *American-born English actor,* 1829–1910

Letters: 6 (1872–91)

VICTOR, Orville James, *American author, publisher,* 1827–1910

Letters: 2 (1904)

VIERECK, George Sylvester, *American author,* 1884–1962

Letters: 6 (1912–37)

VIGNY, Alfred Victor, Comte de, *French poet, dramatist, novelist,* 1797–1863

Letters: 3 (1839–43) to William Charles Macready

VILLA-LOBOS, Heitor, *Brazilian composer,* 1887–

Letters: 1 (1944)

VILLARD, Henry, *American publisher, financier, author,* 1835–1900

Letters: 36 (1861–87)

VILLARD, Oswald Garrison, *American editor, author,* 1872–1949

Prose:

Free Speech and the Legion (typewritten, 2 pp.: Wood Collection)

The Truth about the American Legion:

A Super-Government (typewritten, 12 pp.: Wood Collection)

The Legion and Labor (typewritten, 10 pp.: Wood Collection)

Letters: 9 (1910–28)

VILLIERS, George, 2nd Duke of Buckingham, *English statesman, writer,* 1628–87

Verse:

A Familiar Epistle of Mr. Julian, Secretary to the Muses (copy: EL 8854)

VINAL, Harold, *American poet, editor, essayist, publisher,* 1891–

Letters: 16 (1925–50)

VINCENT, Frank, *American traveler, author,* 1848–1916

Letters: 2 (1884–87)

VOLTAIRE, François Marie Arouet de, *French philosopher, writer,* 1694–1778

Verse:

Epitaph on the King of Prussia (MO 6615)

Eulogy on Frederick the Great (HM 476)

Stanzas de L'Ode sur la Paix (HM 31180)

[Stanzas translated from Voltaire] (MO 6616)

Letters: 8 (1733–76)

VORSE, Mary Marvin (Heaton), *American author,* 1881–1966

Letters: 6 (1917–38)

WADE, John Stevens, *American poet,* 1927–

Verse:

The White Horse (typewritten: Dublin Magazine Collection)

WAGNER, Richard, *German composer,* 1813–83

[Copy of a Haydn symphony] (HM 746)

WAKEFIELD, Gilbert, *English scholar, writer,* 1756–1801

Letters: 4 (1795–1801), including 3 to Edward Jerningham

WALKER, Franklin Dickerson, *American educator, author,* 1900–78

Prose:

[Diary of trip to Yukon Territory] (1 vol.: HM 45281)

[Jack London Biography: 1st draft, 4 chapters] (typewritten with autograph corrections, 161 pp.: HM 45284)

Jack London's Apprentice Work: [Bibliography (partial) of London's early journalism uncollected in book form] (typewritten, carbon copy, 2 pp.: HM 45285)

[Notes re Jack London's death] (2 pp.: HM 45286)

Letters: 34 (1951–59)

Other:

[Index file: notecards for a biography of Jack London] (ca. 1300 pp.: HM 45282)

Index Translationem: [tabulation of translations of Jack London's works by title] (8 pp.: HM 45283)

WALKER, Frederick, *English painter*, 1840–75

Letters: 8 (1860–68)

WALKER, John Brisben, *American editor, publisher*, 1847–1931

Letters: 5 (1894–1914), including 3 to Albert Bigelow Paine

WALLACE, Charles William, *American educator, author*, 1865–1932

Prose:

[Transcripts of source material pertaining to the English drama and theater] (106 items: Wallace Collection)

[39 articles about English drama] (Wallace Collection)

Letters: 9 (1912–14)

WALLACE, Lewis (Lew), *American soldier, lawyer, diplomat, novelist*, 1827–1905

Prose:

Ben Hur (incomplete, lacks end of ms., 665 pp.: HM 485)

Letters: 27 (1860–96)

Documents: 1 (1879)

WALLACE, William Ross, *American poet*, 1819–81

Letters: 1 (1867)

WALLACK, James William, *English actor*, 1791?–1864

Letters: 5 (1828–54)

WALLER, Edmund, *English poet,* 1606–87

Verse:

On the Marriage of Mrs. Frances Cromwell with Mr. Rich (RB 58691)

[Poems ascribed to Waller in] commonplace book (HM 16522) and in Henry the Fifth by Roger Boyle, 1st Earl of Orrery (HM 11619)

Letters: 1 (ca. 1656) to Thomas Hobbes

Documents: 1 (ca. 1686)

Other:

[Sixteen lines in the hand of Waller added at end of *Instructions for a Painter, For the Drawing of the Posture and Progress of His Majesties Forces at Sea*] (RB 123687, p. 19)

WALLER, Lewis, *English actor, manager,* 1860–1915

Letters: 1 (1898)

WALLING, Anna (Strunsky), *American socialist author,* 1879–1964

Verse:

A Pleasure Trip (typewritten, with author's ms. corrections: Walling Collection)

Prose:

Diary (typewritten; incomplete, 42 pp.: Walling Collection)

[Dr. James Peter Warbasse] (a report on a dinner in his honor, printed copy, 1 p.; also 2 incomplete manuscripts, 2 pp.: Walling Collection)

Horace Traubel (typewritten, carbon copy, 4 pp.: Walling Collection)

Rosamond [reflections on her daughter] (typewritten, 1 p.: Walling Collection)

Letters: 179 (1902–58)

Other:

[Two pages of *Kempton Wace Letters* manuscript with brief note by Mrs. Walling] (Walling Collection)

WALN, Robert, *American businessman, writer, editor,* 1794–1825

Letters: 2 (1825)

WALPOLE, Horace, 4th Earl of Orford, *English author,* 1717–97

Verse:

[Verse]: "Inscription" [in Joseph Spence's *Spence's Anecdotes*] (RB 131213, vol. 4, p. 440)

Letters: 16 (1751–95)

Other:

Epitaph on George Vertue (with Vertue's Portrait of Milton: Art Gallery Acc. 60.6A)

[Marginal notes in Alexander Pope's *Additions to the Works of Alexander Pope*] (RB 55218)

[Note in *Life of Richard III*] (RB 106577)

[Translations of two lines of Albius Tibullus, beginning] "Illam quicquid agit" (HM 41048)

See also ROWE, Nicholas

WALPOLE, Sir Hugh Seymour, *English novelist,* 1884–1941

Letters: 8 (1932–40); and 112 letters addressed to Walpole

WALSH, Robert, *American editor, consul, author,* 1784–1859

Letters: 8 (1798–1826)

WALSH, Thomas, *American poet, critic, editor, compiler,* 1871–1928

Letters: 4 (1905–08) to Charles Warren Stoddard

WALTON, Izaak, *English author,* 1593–1683

Verse:

The Angler's Song (HM 44152)

WARBURTON, William, Bishop of Gloucester, *English writer,* 1698–1779

Letters: 1 (1750)

WARD, Christopher Longstreth, *American lawyer, author,* 1868–1943

Letters: 1 (1855)

WARD, Elizabeth Stuart (Phelps), *American author,* 1844–1911

Verse:

"If a New Year" (FI 5086)

Incompletion (HM 39098)

A Parable (FI 5086)

Unmasked (FI 5087)

Prose:

Sir Franklin (31 pp.: HM 17231)

Letters: 48 (1877–1909)

WARD, Lydia Arms Avery (Coonley), *American poet,* 1845–1924

Letters: 2 (1903)

WARD, Mary Augusta (Arnold), *English novelist,* 1851–1920

Letters: 60 (1888–1914), including 13 to Annie (Adams) Fields, 13 to Richard Watson Gilder, and 10 to Frances Power Cobbe

WARD, William Hayes, *American clergyman, editor, author,* 1835–1916

Prose:

Reminiscences of Sidney Lanier (typewritten with autograph corrections, incomplete, 16 pp.: HM 44154)

Letters: 9 (1874–1903); and 182 letters addressed to Ward

WARE, Eugene Fitch, *American author,* 1841–1911

Verse:

Ballad in G (AP 1968)

Prairie Children (AP 1967)

Superstition (AP 1966)

Letters: 64 (1890–1910), including 62 to Albert Bigelow Paine

WARE, William, *American clergyman, novelist, biographer,* 1797–1852

Letters: 2 (1834–42)

WARNER, Charles Dudley, *American editor, essayist, novelist,* 1829–1900

Prose:

Certain Diversities of American Life (53 pp.: HM 473)

The Gilded Age (joint author with Samuel Clemens: HM 453, 470, 1309–12, 1315, 1317)

In a Mexican Dugout (25 pp.: HM 471)

The National Pastime of Spain (52 pp.: HM 472)

Letters: 70 (1871–1900), including 28 to Annie (Adams) Fields, 14 to Robert Underwood Johnson, and 13 to Richard Watson Gilder

WARNER, Susan Bogert (Elizabeth Wetherell, pseud.), *American author,* 1819–85

Prose:

The Wide, Wide World (462 pp.: HM 87)

WARREN, Robert Penn, *American author,* 1905–

Letters: 7 (1937–70)

WARTON, Joseph, *English critic,* 1722–1800

Letters: 4 (1764–84)

WARTON, Thomas, *English historian of English poetry,* 1728–90

Letters: 1 (1785)

WASHBURN, Edward Abiel, *American clergyman, essayist, poet,* 1819–81

Verse:

Oxford Tracts (in the hand of John Greenleaf Whittier, in a letter to Annie [Adams] Fields: FI 4788)

Letters: 2 (1862–66)

WASHINGTON, Booker Taliaferro, *American educator, orator, author,* 1856–1915

Letters: 14 (1895–1912)

WASSON, David Atwood, *American transcendentalist, author,* 1823–87

Letters: 50 (1850–76), including 35 to James Thomas Fields

WATERSTON, Anne Cabot Lowell (Quincy), *American author,* b. 1812

Verse:

Alpha and Omega (FI 4407)

Letters: 19 (1860–80)

Other:

[Note re wedding anniversary] (1 p.: FI 4406)

WATKINS, John, *English miscellaneous author,* fl. 1792–1831

Letters: 1 (1821)

WATKINS, Vernon Phillips, *Welsh poet,* 1906–67

Letters: 10 (1966–67)

WATSON, John, *English divine, author,* 1850–1907

Letters: 3 (1889–97)

WATSON, Sir William, *English poet,* 1858–1935

Verse:

"Ah world, old world, unhappy, hapless world" (HM 1280)
A Dirge of Love (HM 1282)
The Father of the Forest (HM 67)
The Prince's Quest (HM 86)
The Raven's Shadow (HM 1284)
Sonnet: "O ye that seek but cannot, will not follow" (HM 1276)
Sonnet—Suggested whilst writing my name in the sands of the shore (HM 1279)
Sonnet—Written in a volume of Shelley (HM 1277)

Three Epigrams: To my dog Mephistopheles, In the Metropolitan Underground Railway, During a pedestrian excursion (HM 1281)

To E. D. (HM 1278)

To Edward Dowden (HM 1283)

The Triple Lordship (HM 1286)

Warm Weather in Winter (HM 1285)

Wordsworth's Grave (HM 494)

Letters: 11 (1879–1919)

Other:

[Ms. notes and corrections in *The Purple East*] (RB 85535)

WATTERSON, Henry, *American editor, author,* 1840–1921

Letters: 3 (1893)

WATTS, Alaric Alexander, *English poet, journalist, editor,* 1797–1864

Letters: 1 (1827)

WATTS, George Frederick, *English painter, sculptor,* 1817–1904

Letters: 58 (1848–1903)

WATTS, Isaac, *English hymn writer,* 1674–1748

Verse:

Faith and Diffidence (HM 483)

The Sluggard's Field (HM 483)

The Soul (HM 483)

"When I can call the blessed Jesus mine" (HM 483)

Documents: 1 (1715)

WATTS-DUNTON, Walter Theodore, *English novelist, poet,* 1832–1914

Letters: 6 (1884–1909)

WAUGH, Alec, *English novelist,* 1898–

Letters: 4 (1928–40)

WAYLAND, Francis, *American clergyman, educator, author,* 1796–1865

Letters: 4 (1848–62)

WEATHERLY, Frederick Edward, *English author,* 1848–1929

Verse:

A Bird in the Hand (typewritten: Kane Literary Collection)
Darby and Joan (typewritten: Kane Literary Collection)
Douglas Gordon (typewritten: Kane Literary Collection)
My Friend (typewritten: Kane Literary Collection)

Letters: 1 (1898)

WEAVER, John Van Alstyn, *American poet, novelist,* 1893–1938

Letters: 2 (1922–32)

WEAVER, Thomas, *English poet,* 1616–63

Verse:

Tom of Bedlam (copy: EL 8895)
[Poems ascribed to him in commonplace book] (HM 16522)

WEBB, Benjamin, *American poet,* 1695–1746

Verse:

On Heaven and Hell; and, Occasional Reflections Poetically Framed (HM 1302)

WEBB, Charles Henry, *American parodist, poet,* 1834–1905

Letters: 2 (1897)

WEBB, Walter Prescott, *American educator, author,* 1888–

Letters: 4 (1936–53) to Eugene Lafayette Cunningham

WEBSTER, Daniel, *American statesman, author,* 1782–1852

Verse:
"When you and I are dead and gone" (Kenyon Album)

Prose:
[An article referring to the "Reply to Hayne" address] (4 pp.: HM 777)

Letters: 48 (1806–52)

Documents: 2 (1838)

WEBSTER, Harold Tucker, *American cartoonist,* 1885–1952

Letters: 3 (1939–42)

WEBSTER, Henry Kitchell, *American novelist,* 1875–1932

Letters: 4 (1912–27)

WEBSTER, Noah, *American lexicographer,* 1758–1843

Prose:
[An American Dictionary of the English Language, 1828–a fragment: "Betake"—"Bilge"] (22 pp.: HM 19743)

Letters: 6 (1799–1839)

WEBSTER, Thomas, *English painter, etcher,* 1800–86

Letters: 2 (1866–67)

WEEMS, Mason Locke, *American clergyman, book agent, biographer,* 1759–1825

Letters: 3 (1805–16)

WEIK, Jesse William, *American author,* 1857–1930

Letters: 5 (1897–1916)

WEISS, John, *American clergyman, author,* 1818–79

Letters: 25 (1862–75), including 19 to James Thomas Fields

WELLES, Winifred, *American poet,* 1893–1939

Letters: 1 (1928)

WELLS, Carolyn, *American poet, parodist, novelist,* d. 1942

Letters: 10 (1902–25)

WELLS, Charles Jeremiah, *English poet,* 1799?–1879

Letters: 1 (1875)

WENDELL, Barrett, *American educator, author,* 1855–1921

Letters: 13 (1900–17)

WESLEY, Charles, *English divine, hymn writer,* 1707–88

Verse:

[Collection of anthems, songs, and other pieces, with music, 1775–1796] (HM 486)

Letters: 1 (1748)

WESLEY, John, *English evangelist, leader of Methodism,* 1703–91

Letters: 22 (1748–90)

Documents: 1 (1769)

WEST, Benjamin, *American-born English historical painter,* 1738–1820

Prose:

Address to the Royal Academy (3 pp.: HM 985)

Letters: 1 (n.d.); and 5 letters addressed to him

WEST, Gilbert, *English author,* 1703–56

Letters: 54 (1751–55), including 53 to Elizabeth (Robinson) Montagu

WEST, Rebecca, *English novelist, critic, essayist,* 1892–

Letters: 1 (n.d.)

WESTALL, Richard, *English historical painter,* 1765–1836

Letters: 2 (1795–1833)

WETHERELL, Elizabeth, see WARNER, Susan Bogert

WEYMAN, Stanley John, *English novelist,* 1855–1928

Prose:

Under the Red Robe (195 pp.: HM 921)

Letters: 5 (1894–1926); and 140 letters addressed to Weyman

WHARTON, Charles Henry, *American clergyman,* 1748–1833

Verse:

A Poetical Epistle to George Washington (HM 892)

WHARTON, Edith Newbold (Jones), *American novelist,* 1862–1937

Prose:

The Valley of Childish Things (16 pp.: HM 110)

Letters: 9 (1930–36)

WHEATLY, Charles, *English divine, author,* 1686–1742

Letters: 2 (1735)

WHEELOCK, John Hall, *American poet,* 1886–

Letters: 89 (1914–58)

WHEWELL, William, *English philosopher, writer,* 1794–1866

Letters: 4 (1850–54) to Alexander Dallas Bache; and a signature on a document

WHIPPLE, Edwin Percy, *American critic, lecturer, author,* 1819–86

Verse:

Anniversary Poem, delivered before the Mercantile Library Association (HM 44167)

The Progress of Humbug (LF)

Letters: 4 (1854–81)

WHISTLER, James Abbott McNeill, *American painter,* 1834–1903

Letters: 18 (1877–1900)

WHITE, Edward Lucas, *American novelist,* 1866–1934

Letters: 5 (1925) to George Sterling

WHITE, Gilbert, *English naturalist,* 1720–93

Prose:

[Sermon entitled] This do in remembrance of me (14 pp.: HM 481)

WHITE, Henry, *English clergyman,* 1761–1836

Prose:

Lichfield Monthly Gazette, or Newton Intelligencer:

1804, Dec. 1—1805, Jan. 1 (HM 38313)
1805, June 1—July 1 (HM 38314)
1805, Dec. 1—1806, Jan. 1 (HM 38315)
1806, July 1—1807, Jan. 1 (HM 38316)
1807, June 1—July 1 (HM 38317)
1807, Oct. 1—1808, Jan. 1 (HM 38318)

Letters: 34 (1803–08) to "Mrs. Parker"

WHITE, Richard Grant, *American editor, philologist, author,* 1821–85

Letters: 36 (1855–81)

WHITE, Stanford, *American architect,* 1853–1906

Letters: 7 (ca. 1885–1903)

WHITE, Stewart Edward, *American novelist,* 1873–1946

Prose:

Gold (819 pp.: HM 34992)
The Gray Dawn (first draft, 270 pp.: HM 34697)
The Gray Dawn (final draft, 949 pp.: HM 34698)
One Afternoon (typewritten, 35 pp.: HM 34908)
The Rose Dawn (705 pp.: HM 34907)

Letters: 26 (1902–45)

WHITE, Walter Francis, *American author,* 1893–1955

Letters: 2 (1924) to Mary (Hunter) Austin

WHITE, William Allen, *American editor, author,* 1868–1944

Prose:

[The Foreign Relations of Kansas: a speech to the Young Republicans Club] (3 pp.: AP 1997)

Letters: 58 (1891–1937)

WHITEFIELD, George, *American evangelist, author,* 1714–70

Letters: 4 (1740–68)

WHITEHEAD, William, *English poet laureate,* 1715–85

Verse:

"Clos'd are his toils, the fatal shaft has flown" (MO 6738)

"Dame Nature the Goddess, one very bright Day" (JE 1034)

Letters: 2 (1761–63)

WHITEING, Richard, *English journalist, novelist,* 1840–1928

Letters: 18 (1899–1921)

WHITING, Lilian, *American author,* 1859–1942

Letters: 5 (1850–1919)

WHITMAN, Sarah Helen (Power), *American poet,* 1803–78

Verse:

Summer's Invitation to the Little Orphan (HM 75)

Letters: 11 (1852–77)

WHITMAN, Walt, *American poet, editor, journalist,* 1819–92

Verse:

Beginners (title changed from Thought; published as one of the Inscriptions: HM 11202)

Come Said My Soul (HM 6713)

Fancies at Navesink—The Pilot in the Mist (HM 1190)

Inscription to Precede Leaves of Grass When Finished (HM 6714)

Leaves of Grass—extracts: (HM 1193)

You Lingering Sparse Leaves of Me (3 proof sheets, of which 2 are corrected)

Of That Blithe Throat of Thine (proofsheet)

With Husky-Haughty Lips, O Sea! (printed copy, with one pencil correction)

"Sometimes I see in ye, Disease and Death"

Longings for Home (published as O Magnet—South: HM 11200)

Queries to My Seventieth Year (HM 11207)

The Singer in the Prison (HM 11206)

Soon Shall the Winter's Foil Be Here (HM 1192)

Tests (HM 11203)

Thoughts (five poems: HM 11201)

Of the visages of things

Of persons arrived at wealth

Of waters, forests, hills

Of what I write from myself

Of obedience, faith, adhesiveness

To a Common Prostitute (HM 11205)

To Him That Was Crucified (HM 11208)

To Other Lands (published as one of the Inscriptions, To Foreign Lands: HM 11204)

A Twilight Song (HM 1224)

Prose:

[Autobiographical accounts] (2 pp.: HM 492)

[Autobiographical sketch] (2 pp.: HM 11199)

Authors at Home—No. VII. Walt Whitman, His Health and Condition Today (9 pp.: HM 1196)

Carlyle from American Points of View (30 pp.: HM 138)

The Dead in this War (2 pp.: HM 1194)

[Down at the Front, after First Fredericksburg] (4 pp.: HM 6708)

Facts in the Matter of Worthington Illegally Publishing Leaves of Grass (3 pp.: HM 6710)

Father Taylor (and Oratory, 11 pp.: HM 6711)

[Fragment of ms.] (2 sides of strip of paper 2″ × 8″: HM 39091)

Hospital Notebook (31 pp.: HM 1197)

Hospital Notes (10 pp.: HM 94)

Lafayette in Brooklyn (6 pp., with an introduction written by John Burroughs, 6 pp.: HM 1189)

Letter to the Santa Fe Anniversary Association [published also as *The Spanish Element in Our Nationality*] (printed broadside with ms. corrections: HM 6709)

[Memoranda during the war] (1 p.: HM 16537)

A Thought on Shakespeare (6 pp.: HM 6712)

A Visit to the Opera (8 pp.: HM 1191)

Letters: 13 (1857–91)

Other:

[Daily account of Whitman's last illness kept by his nurse, Mrs. Mary O. Davis] (HM 1198)

[A note regarding Emerson's remarks on greatness] (HM 490)

For more detailed descriptions of Whitman material, see the *Huntington Library Quarterly*, vol. 19, no. 1 (November 1955): 81–96.

WHITNEY, Adeline Dutton (Train), *American author,* 1824–1906

Verse:

My Daphne (FI 4499)

Under the Cloud, and Through the Sea (FI 4498)

Letters: 36 (1861–1902), including 28 to Annie (Adams) Fields

Other:

[Announcement of fund honoring George MacDonald, to appear in newspapers] (2 pp.: FI 4504)

WHITNEY, Anne, *American poet,* 1821–1915

Verse:

The Fugitive-Slave Bill (2 pp.: of corrected proofs: Merrymount Press Collection, 51)

Letters: 46 (1867–1911), including 20 to Annie (Adams) Fields

WHITNEY, Caspar, *American editor, journalist,* 1862–1929

Letters: 32 (1903–29), and 52 letters (1929–31) by Mrs. Whitney

WHITTIER, John Greenleaf, *American poet,* 1807–92

Verse:

[Acrostic for Lois Jones] (HM 13010)

Andrew Rykman's Prayer (incomplete, 1 p.: FI 4678)

"The aster-flower is falling" (John Anson Ford Autograph Album)

The Battle Autumn of 1862 (HM 76)

Between the Gates (with corrected proof sheets: HM 71)

Between the Gates (HM 6862)

Between the Gates (corrected proof sheet: HM 6863)

By Attitash (manuscript with printed copy; published, with changes, in *The Tent on the Beach* under the title "The Maids of Attitash": HM 493)

A Day's Journey (HM 24004)

The Dead Ship of Harpswell (FI 4679)

Divine Compassion (HM 13009)

The Dole of Jarl Thorkell: (23 stanzas only: FI 4680)

Esther Gyle's Ride (two drafts: HM 13015)

Garrison (HM 24006)

How They Climbed Chocorua (in the hand of Lucy Larcom: HM 856)

Hymn, Written for the Christmas Festival of the Oakland's School in St. Helena's Island, S.C. (HM 72)

"I, who have striven for freedom at the cost" (HM 1217)

"Lake of the Northland! keep thy dower" (HM 13003)

The Last Eve of Summer (HM 13005)

The Last Eve of Summer (HM 13006)

The Last Will and Testament of the Man in the Beartrap (in the hand of Lucy Larcom: HM 857)

Leggett's Monument (HM 191)

"Life's burdens fall, its discords cease" (HM 17370)

"Long has passed the summer": [extract from "The Garrison of Cape Ann"] (Kenyon Album)

"My dinner minds of autumn-time" (FI 4576)

My Meeting (HM 487)

"Not to the swift nor to the strong" (HM 13014)

"Over the grave . . ." (FI 4559)

The Quaker Meeting, from "The Germantown Pilgrim" (only the heading is autograph: HM 6855)

The Rejected (HM 12233)

Revelation (corrected proof: HM 188)

St. John De Matha's Mantle: A Legend of the Red, White and Blue (SL 317)

The Shadow and the Light: (17th stanza only: HM 189)

The Stars (HM 17376)

A Summer Pilgrimage (with corrected proof: HM 70)

Sweet Fern (HM 13013)

The Tent on the Beach: (includes Section I, last stanza of "The Wreck of Rivermouth," and one stanza of "The Grave by the Lake": FI 4681)

Thanksgiving (HM 13002)

To John C. Fremont (HM 98)

To John Pierpont (HM 13007)

The Two Elizabeths (with corrected proof sheet: HM 192)

The Vow of Washington (with corrected proof sheets: HM 69)

"We shut our eyes, the flowers bloom on" (HM 13004)

"What shall I wish him? Strength and health": [lines addressed to grandson of Theodore D. Wild] (HM 13001)

What the Birds Said (HM 13008)

What the Quaker Said to the Transcendentalist (not autograph: HM 74)

"Yet when the patriot cannon jars" (HM 24003)

Prose:

David Matson (12 pp.: HM 13012)

The Friends in New England (9 pp.: HM 488)

Life of John C. Brainard (Foreword, 3 pp.: HM 22225)

Life of Lydia Marie Child: (Introduction, 31 pp.: HM 489)

Margaret Smith's Journal: [extract] (1 p.: FI 4682)

Letters: 358 (1828–91), including 135 to James Thomas

Fields; and 155 to Annie (Adams) Fields; with 2 addressed to both

Other:

[Ms. corrections in *On the Big Horn*] (RB 54813)

[Ms. corrections and rewritten stanza in *The Two Elizabeths*] (RB 54815)

[Ms. correction on broadside of *The Captain's Well*] (RB 108164)

[Ms. corrections said to be in Whittier's hand in *Justice and Expediency*] (RB 7074)

[Letter at bottom and on back of printed copy of *R. S. S.: At Deer Island on the Merrimack*] (RB 85837)

[Ms. corrections in *A Summer Pilgrimage*] (RB 54816)

[Ms. and explanatory notation on *How the Women Went from Dover* (which begins "Through Dover Town in the chill, gray dawn")] (RB 54847)

[Corrected proof of *The Wind of March*] (RB 150335)

[Corrections of miscellaneous verses] (FI 4561 and FI 4602)

[Corrections for "Snowbound"] (FI 4594)

[Corrections for "The Panorama"] (FI 4615)

[Stanza to be added to the Dedication of *Songs of Labor*] (FI 4611)

WIDDEMER, Margaret, *American poet, novelist,* b. 1880

Verse:

A Holiday (AP 2047)

Letters: 12 (1900–32) to Albert Bigelow Paine

WIELAND, Christopher Martin, *German writer, translator,* 1733–1813

Letters: 1 (1782)

WIGGIN, Kate Douglas (Smith), *American editor, novelist,* 1856–1923

Prose:

Polly Oliver's Problem (450 pp.: HM 92)

Letters: 6 (1918–22)

WIGHT, Orlando Williams, *American author,* 1824–88

Letters: 1 (1858)

WILBERFORCE, William, *English philanthropist,* 1759–1833

Letters: 91 (1788–1832), including 24 to Matthew Montagu, 4th Baron Rokeby, and 39 to Zachary Macaulay

Documents: 1 (1790)

WILCOX, Ella (Wheeler), *American poet,* 1850–1919

Verse:

Consummation (GS 592)

Sonnets: Love letters of Abelard and Heloise (illuminated manuscript by a prisoner in the Charlestown Jail: HM 27965)

New Year '88 (HM 480)

Letters: 17 (1887–1916)

WILDE, Oscar Fingall O'Flahertie Wills, *Irish wit and dramatist, poet,* 1856–1900

Verse:

Griffiti [sic] d'Italia (HM 469)

Impressions de Paris (HM 467)

Impressions du Thèatre (HM 462)

"One sacrament one consecrate, the earth": [stanzas 21–23 of *Panthea*] (HM 44181)

Poems by Oscar Wilde: [title page, table of contents, and 16 stanzas from "Charmides"] (HM 464)

Santa Decca (HM 44182)

Prose:

[Lecture on the English renaissance of art] (incomplete, 89 pp.: HM 465)

[Notes for a lecture on America] (12 pp.: HM 466)

The Star Child (27 pp.: HM 463)

Letters: 9 (1887–93), including 5 to Walford Graham Robertson

WILDE, Richard Henry, *American poet, translator,* 1789–1847

Verse:

Lines for the Music to Weber's Last Waltz (HM 478)

Letters: 4 (1842–46)

WILDER, Thornton Niven, *American novelist, playwright,* 1897–1975

Letters: 4 (1929–50)

WILKIE, Sir David, *English painter,* 1785–1841

Letters: 63 (1815–40)

Other:

[Note concerning John Martin, in Blanchard Jerrold's *The Life of George Cruikshank*] (RB 149633, vol. 1)

WILLARD, Charles Dwight, *American editor, author,* 1860–1914

Prose:

[Diary for the years 1875 and 1878] (Willard Collection)

To "My dear Friend": [circular Christmas letter explaining

to his friends the simple philosophy of his life] (typewritten, 3 pp.: WI 458)

Letters: 553 (1879–1913), including 543 to family members; also, 355 letters (1907–14) from his daughter, Florence (Willard) Ryerson Clements

WILLCOX, Louise (Collier), *American critic, translator, editor, essayist,* 1865–1929

Letters: 14 (1906–07)

WILLIAMS, Ben Ames, *American short story writer,* 1889–1953

Letters: 3 (1930–33)

WILLIAMS, Helen Maria, *English author,* 1762–1827

Verse:

Lines on the Funeral of Mr. Brequet (HM 30856)

"Lines written . . . to the memory of Joel Barlow" (included in letter of Clara Baldwin Bomford: BN 134)

"Soothed, I receive the flowers you bring" (in the hand of Clara Baldwin Bomford: BN 449)

"What wounding thoughts this gift can make" (Kenyon Album)

Letters: 15 (1795–1822), including 7 to Edward Jerningham

WILLIAMS, Jesse Lynch, *American editor, playwright, short-story writer,* 1871–1929

Letters: 3 (1899–1916)

WILLIAMS, Oscar, *American poet, editor,* 1900–

Letters: 13 (1941–64)

WILLIAMS, William Carlos, *American physician, poet, novelist, essayist,* b. 1883

Letters: 16 (1916–53) including 13 to Wallace Stevens

WILLIAMSON, Henry, *English novelist, nature writer,* 1897–

Prose:

The Ackymals (corrected typescript, 15 pp.; also, corrected proofs, 5 pp.: HM 17232)

Letters: 2 (1929–31)

WILLIAMSON, Thames Ross, *American novelist,* 1894–

Letters: 2 (1921–32)

WILLIS, Henry Brittan, *English painter,* 1810–84

Letters: 1 (1867)

WILLIS, Nathaniel Parker, *American poet, editor, journalist, playwright,* 1806–67

Prose:

The Icy Veil, or The Keys to Three Hearts Thought Cold (20 pp.: HM 477)

[Portion of a manuscript about Job Smith] (4 pp.: HM 2084)

Letters: 21 (1829–65)

WILLMOTT, Robert Eldridge Aris, *English author,* 1809–63

Verse:

"Be mine thy winter evening's close" (RB 109990, vol. 1, pt. 1, p. 72)

WILLS, William Henry, *English miscellaneous writer, and assistant editor to Dickens of* Household Words *and* All the Year Round, 1810–80

Letters: 7 (1860–74), and 417 addressed to Wills by Dickens

Other:

[Memorandum:] Fame! [about insertion in *Morning Advertiser* of announcement of birth of one of Charles Dickens's sons] (1 p.: HM 18583)

WILMOT, John, 2nd Earl of Rochester, *English poet, libertine,* 1647–80

Verse:

A Letter from Artemiza in the Towne to Chloe in the Country (EL 8793)

My Lord Aupride (EL 8738)

On Poet Ninny (EL 8737)

A Very Heroicall Epistle in Answer to Ephelia (EL 8736B)

WILSON, Edmund, *American critic,* 1895–1972

Letters: 5 (1946), including 1 each to Graham Greene and Merle Armitage

WILSON, Francis, *American author,* 1854–1935

Letters: 7 (1888–1927)

WILSON, Harry Leon, *American novelist,* 1867–1939

Letters: 3 (1916)

WILSON, James Grant, *American soldier, editor, author,* 1832–1914

Prose:

[Speech for the] Proceedings of the 1st Annual Meeting of the Lincoln Fellowship (typewritten with autograph corrections: RB 40000)

Letters: 29 (1860–1912)

WILSON, John, *English essayist,* fl. 1852

Prose:

Notes on Living Writers—Robert Chambers (10 pp.: HM 156)

Letters: 1 (1852)

WILSON, Trevor Gordon, *New Zealand educator, author,* 1928–

Prose:

[Review of] *The Jerome Connexion,* by Seymour Leslie (typewritten with author's autograph corrections, 3 pp.: Dublin Magazine Collection)

[Review of] *Jonathan Swift* . . . , by Herbert Davis (typewritten with author's autograph corrections, 4 pp.: Dublin Magazine Collection)

The Swift Tercentenary: A Postscript (typewritten with author's autograph corrections, 7 pp.: Dublin Magazine Collection)

WINCHESTER, Caleb Thomas, *American editor, author,* 1847–1920

Letters: 1 (1882)

WINSOR, Justin, *American librarian, editor, author,* 1831–97

Letters: 43 (1853–94)

WINSTON, James, *English theater manager, actor,* 1773–1843

Prose:

Theatrical Records—1803–1830 (4 vols.: HM 19925)

Letters: 4 (1815–26), including 3 to William Upcott

WINTER, William, *American drama critic, historian, essayist, post,* 1836–1917

Verse:

Bethel (RB 306985)

Egeria (first stanza only: HM 3165)

"Life at the longest is not long" (RB 17345)

"No eyes can see man's destiny completed" (RB 30616)

The Yellow Rose (RB 306985 XPF)

Letters: 9 (1866–1910)

Other:

[Ms. correction on p. 169 of *The Poems of William Winter*] (RB 17345)

WINTERS, Yvor, *American educator, poet, critic,* 1900–68

Letters: 2 (1943 and n.d.)

WINTHROP, Robert Charles, *American senator, orator, author,* 1809–94

Letters: 56 (1846–94)

WIRT, William, *American statesman, author,* 1772–1834

Letters: 7 (1817–30)

WISE, Henry Augustus, *American naval officer, author,* 1819–69

Letters: 16 (1858–64)

WISE, John Sergeant, *American lawyer, author,* 1846–1913

Letters: 18 (1875–1903)

WISTER, Owen, *American novelist,* 1860–1938

Verse:

"I met a young horseman and to him I said" [inscription on fly leaf of Wister's *Lin McLean*] (RB 181875)

Letters: 14 (1895–1923)

WOLCOT, John, *English satirist, poet,* 1738–1819

Prose:

A Plaintive Epistle from John Ketch, Esq. of Newgate to William Pitt (8 pp.: HM 482)

WOLLSTONECRAFT, Mary, see GODWIN, Mary (Wollstonecraft)

WOOD, Charles Erskine Scott, *American poet, lawyer, army officer,* 1852–1944

Verse and Prose:

Approximately 5,600 pieces in the Wood Collection

Letters: ca. 2230 (1870–1943)

WOOD, Clement, *American poet, editor, compiler,* 1888–1950

Letters: 2 (1930–42)

WOOD, Ellen (Price), *English novelist,* 1814–87

Letters: 1 (1873)

WOOD, George, *American author,* 1799–1870

Letters: 2 (1861–66)

WOOD, Sara Bard (Field), *American poet,* 1882–1974

Verse and Prose:

Approximately 1200 pieces in the Wood Collection

Letters: ca. 2200 (1911–69)

WOODBERRY, George Edward, *American poet, critic, educator,* 1855–1930

Verse:

Divine Awe (HM 1236)

"When love in the faint heart trembles" (HM 35075)

Letters: 27 (1895–1927), including 15 to the Merrymount Press

WOODHOUSE, James, *English shoemaker, schoolmaster, poet,* 1735–1820

Verse:

Ode to [Elizabeth (Robinson) Montagu] on Her Birthday (MO 6781)

Letters: 15 (1764–71), including 13 to Elizabeth (Robinson) Montagu

WOODS, Margaret Louisa (Bradley), *American author,* 1856–1945

Prose:

The Princess of Hanover (180 pp.: HM 468)

Letters: 3 (1911) to Annie (Adams) Fields

WOODSON, Carter Godwin, *American author,* 1875–1950

Letters: 3 (1914–15)

WOODWORTH, Samuel, *American editor, poet, playwright,* 1785–1842

Verse:

"Each charm external, and each mental grace" (Woodworth Collection)

To Mrs. Mary Worthington Morris (HM 479)

Letters: 7 (1834–36)

Material about Woodworth is included among the papers of his son Selim E. Woodworth, 1600 pieces (1834–1947).

WOOLF, Leonard Sidney, *English historian, political essayist,* b. 1880

Verse:

2:30 A.M. (HM 42126)

To Ponamma (HM 42179)

Letters: 65 (1900–27), including 64 to Saxon Arnold Sydney-Turner

Other:

[Chronological List of Mystics for the Use of Contributors] (HM 42119)

WOOLLCOTT, Alexander Humphreys, *American critic, author,* 1887–1943

Letters: 14 (1933–42), including 8 to Walford Graham Robertson

WOOLLEY, Mary Emma, *American educator, author,* 1863–1947

Letters: 3 (1910–31)

WOOLNER, Thomas, *English sculptor, poet,* 1825–92

Letters: 2 (1855–57)

WOOLSEY, Sarah Chauncey (Susan Coolidge, pseud.), *American author,* 1835–1905

Verse:

Till the Day Dawn (signed "Susan Coolidge": FI 2966)

Letters: 9 (1883–1904), including 4 to Annie (Adams) Fields

WOOLSON, Constance Fenimore, *American novelist*, 1840–94

Letters: 1 (1886)

WORDSWORTH, William, *English poet*, 1770–1850

Verse:

The Country Girl [published as "The Gleaner"] (HM 2093)

Descriptive Sketches in Verse: [printed text with extensive annotations and corrections in the handwriting of Dorothy and William Wordsworth] (RB 25860)

The Excursion: [quotation of 2 lines from Book III] (HM 12310)

Grace Darling (corrected proof: HM 2092)

Selections from the Poems of William Wordsworth (corrected proof of title page, dedication, and preface; HM 2091)

Sonnet Suggested by Haydon's Picture of the Duke of Wellington (HM 12313)

The Wishing-gate Destroyed (HM 1270)

"Young England—What is Then Become of Old" (HM 2090)

Letters: 174 (1795–1848), including 120 to Edward Moxon; and 3 by Dorothy Wordsworth; also, forgery (HM 6881)

WOTTON, Sir Henry, *English diplomat, poet*, 1568–1639

Prose:

The State of Christendom (EL 8378)

WRANGHAM, Francis, *English classical scholar*, 1769–1842

Verse:

Cambridge (RB 109990, vol. 3, pt. 2, following p. 216)

Letters: 7 (1834–36)

WREN, Sir Christopher, *English architect,* 1632–1723

Letters: 1 (1706)

WRIGHT, Harold Bell, *American novelist,* 1872–1944

Letters: 1 (1924)

WRIGHT, Mabel (Osgood), *American author,* 1859–1934

Letters: 4 (1902–03)

Other:

[Signed sentiment] (Kane Literary Collection)

WRIGHT, Thomas, *English antiquary,* 1810–77

Letters: 5 (1851–72)

Y

YATES, Edmund, *English novelist,* 1831–94

Letters: 32 (1860–90)

YEARSLEY, Ann, *English verse writer,* 1756–1806

Verse:

Clifton Hill (MO 6805)

[Excerpts from several poems] (MO 3988)

[Verses at front of *Poems on Several Occasions*] (RB 87116)

Letters: 1 (1785)

YEATMAN, Jennette (Hayward), *American poet,* fl. 1925–56

Verse:

85 poems (some duplicates) in Yeatman Collection.

Letters: 307 (1925–56); and 1279 letters addressed to Mrs. Yeatman

YEATS, Elizabeth Corbet, *Irish publisher,* 1868–1940

Letters: 55 (1914–39)

YEATS, Jack Butler, *English artist,* 1871–1957

Verse:

Weary of Peace (HM 35383)

Letters: 6 (1910–45)

YEATS, William Butler, *Irish poet, dramatist,* 1865–1939

Verse:

Easter, 1916 (corrected typescript: HM 43250)

Prose:

The Bishop of Toronto on Emigration (17 pp.: HM 28173)

[A People's Theatre. A Letter to Lady Gregory] (27 pp.: Hill Collection)

Letters: 109 (1887–1929), including 72 to Katherine (Tynan) Hinkson

Other:

[Extensive corrections and additions in 1899 edition of *Poems* for a new edition] (RB 28902)

YONGE, Charlotte Mary, *English novelist, children's writer,* 1823–1901

Letters: 37 (1851–1901)

YOUNG, Charles Mayne, *English comedian,* 1777–1856

Letters: 3 (1824–30)

YOUNG, Edward, *English poet,* 1683–1765

Letters: 22 (1729–41), including 20 to Mrs. Judith Reynolds

YOUNG, Ella, *Irish poet, mythologist,* 1867–1956

Verse:

Bed-Time (RB 87651 PF)

A Face Remembered (Wood Collection)

Green Branches (RB 87651 PF)

in the Huntington Library

Heart's Desire (RB 87651 PF)

In a Wood (Wood Collection)

In Tir-na-Moe (Young Papers)

Inispail (Wood Collection)

Ode (Wood Collection)

Phantasy (Wood Collection)

Primavera (Wood Collection)

Recompense (Wood Collection)

The Rose (two different poems with the same title: Wood Collection)

Rose Leaves (RB 87651 PF)

Shasta (typewritten: Wood Collection)

Springtime (Wood Collection)

To the Little Princess: An Epistle (typewritten: Wood Collection)

The Vengeance of Fionn (Wood Collection)

"Was it our choice—the desert and the rod" (Wood Collection)

"When on the stone you write my name" (Wood Collection)

Prose:

Diary, 1917–18 (Young Papers)

Faerie Music (typewritten, 3 pp.: Young Papers)

Glencolumkille (4 pp.: Young Papers)

In an Oak Wood: [prose sketch] (typewritten, 1 p.: Young Papers)

Lilith: [draft] (6 pp.; also typewritten copy, 2 pp.: Young Papers)

Teigue Finds the Road to Fortune (15 pp.; also, typewritten copy, 7 pp.: Young Papers)

The Wonder-Smith and His Son [notes] (6 pp.: Young Papers)

[Miscellaneous notes and drafts] (14 pp.: Young Papers)

Letters: 102 (1927–56)

Other:

[Letters written on Ella Young's behalf and other material relating to the legal case regarding her citizenship] (Wood Collection)

YOUNG, Francis Brett, *English novelist,* 1884–1954

Letters: 2 (1919–27)

YOUNG, Gordon Ray, *American author,* 1886–1948

Letters: 1 (1921)

YOUNG, John Russell, *American journalist, diplomat, librarian, author,* 1840–99

Letters: 6 (1866–98)

YOUNG, William Wallace, *American playwright, poet,* 1847–1920

Verse:

The Maze (Kane Literary Collection)

Z

ZANGWILL, Israel, *English lecturer, novelist, playwright,* 1864–1926

Letters: 5 (1895–1917)

ZOLA, Émile Edouard Charles Antoine, *French novelist,* 1840–1902

[Presentation and signature on printed title page of *Nana*] (HM 44204)

APPENDIX

THE LARPENT PLAYS

Authors

Abbott, William
Addington, William
Ainslie, Whitelaw
Allen, ———
Allingham, John Till
Amherst, J. H.
Andrei, Antonio
Andrews, Miles Peter
Anelli, Angelo
Arne, Thomas Augustine
Arnold, Samuel James
Atkinson, Joseph
Auvigny, Jean du Castre d'
Ayscaugh, George Edward
Ayton, Richard

Baddeley, Robert
Badini, Charles Francis
Baillie, Joanna
Ball, Edward. *See* Fitzball, Edward
Banim, John
Bannister, John
Barker, James N.
Barlocci, Giovanni
Barlow, ———
Barrett, C. F.
Barrett, Eaton Stannard
Barry, Nathaniel
Barrymore, William
Bate, Henry [Bate Dudley]
Beaumarchais, de
Beaumont, Francis
Beazley, Samuel, Jr.
Behn, Aphra
Bell, Robert
Bellamy, Thomas
Bennett, George
Benson, ———
Bentley, Richard
Berio, ———
Berkeley, George Monck
Bernard, John
Berry, Mary
Bertati, Giovanni
Bickerstaffe, Isaac
Bidlake, John
Birch, Samuel
Bishop, Henry Rowley
Boaden, James
Boggio, G.
Bonnor, Charles
Bottarelli, Giovanni Gualberto
Brand, Hannah
Brandon, Isaac
Brewer, George
Bridges, Thomas
Bromley, George Percival
Brooke, Frances
Brooke, Henry
Brown, ———
Brown, Anthony
Brown, Charles Armitage
Brown, John
Bucke, Charles
Buckingham, J. S.
Bunn, Alfred
Buonaiuti, B. Serafino
Buonavoglia, ———
Burges, James Bland
Burgoyne, John
Burke, Miss
Burney, Charles
Burton, ———
Burton, Philippina
Butler, Richard, Earl of Glengall
Byron, George Gordon, Lord

Caigniez, L. C.
Calcraft, John William
Calsabigi, Ranieri dei
Caravita, Giuseppi
Carey, George Saville
Carey, Henry
Carr, George Charles
Carr, John
Celesia, Dorothea
Centlivre, Susannah
Challis, Henry W.
Chambers, Marianne
Chapman, George
Cheney, Miss. *See* Mrs. Gardner
Cherry, Andrew
Chiari, Pietro
Cibber, Colley
Cibber, Susannah Maria
Cibber, Theophilus
Cigna, V. A.
Clarke, C.
Clarke, Stephen
Clive, Catherine
Cobb, James
Code, H. B.
Coleridge, Samuel Taylor
Collier, George
Collins, John
Colman, Francis
Colman, George
Colman, George, the Younger
Coltellini, Marco
Congreve, William
Conway, Henry Seymour
Cooke, William
Cornwall, Barry
Cowdroy, W.
Cowley, Hannah
Craven, Elizabeth, Countess of (later Margravine of Anspach)
Crisp, Henry
Cromwell, Thomas
Cross, James C.
Cross, Richard
Cumberland, Richard
Cuthbertson, Miss

Dallas, Robert Charles
Dalton, John
Daniel, George
Da Ponte, Lorenzo
D'Arblay, Frances (Burney)
D'Aubigny
Dekker, Thomas
Delap, John
Dennis, John
Dent, John
Destouches, P. M.
De Vesle, de Pont
Dibdin, Charles
Dibdin, Charles Isaac Mungo
Dibdin, Thomas John
Dillon, John
Dimond, William
Diodati, G. M.
Dodd, James Solas
Dodsley, Robert
Dorman, ——— (of Hampstead)
Dossie, Robert
Dow, Alexander
Downing, George
Downs, W. A.
Dowton, William
Dryden, John
Dudley, Henry Bate. *See* Bate, Henry
Dunlap, William
Duval, Alexander
Dyer, Charles George

Earle, ———
Ebsworth, Joseph
Edmead, Miss
Edwin, John
Elliston, Robert William
Ewing, Peter
Eyre, Edmund John

Farley, Charles
Faucit, John Saville
Faucit, Mrs. John Saville
Favart, F. S.
Fawcett, John
Federico, Gennaro Antonio
Feist, Charles
Fennell, James
Fenwick, John
Ferretti, ———
Fielding, Henry
Finney, ———
Fitzball [or Ball], Edward
Fitzgerald, William Thomas
Fitzpatrick, Richard
Fletcher, John

Kean, Edmund
Keate, George
Keep, W. A.
Kelly, Hugh
Kemble, Charles
Kemble, Elizabeth (Satchell)
Kemble, Henry
Kemble, John Philip
Kemble, Marie Thérèse (De Camp)
Kemble, Stephen
Kemp, Joseph
Kenney, James
Kenrick, William
Kerr, John
King, Thomas
Kinnaird, Douglas James William
Kirby, ———
Knapp, Henry
Knight, ———
Knight, Edward P.
Knight, Thomas
Knowles, James Sheridan

Lake, John
Lamb, Charles
Lamb, William
Lambe, George
Lanfranchi-Rossi, C. G.
Langsdorff, Baron
Lathom, Francis
Lawler, Dennis
Lee, Harriet
Lee, Henry
Lee, Sophia
Lefanu, Alicia (Sheridan)
Leigh, Richard
Lennox, Charlotte
Lennox, W.
Lessing, Gotthold Ephraim
Levius, Barham
Lewis, Matthew Gregory
Lillo, George
Lindor, B.
Linley, William
Livigni, Filippo
Lloyd, Robert
Lockman, John
Logan, John
Lonsdale, M.
Lorenzi, Giambattista
Lunn, Joseph
Lynch, Thomas John

McDonald, Andrew
Macfarren, George
Mackenzie, Henry
Macklin, Charles
MacNally, Leonard
Macready, William
Male, G.
Mallet, David
Malone, Edmund
Man, Henry
Manners, George
Marlowe, Christopher
Marmontel, J. F.
Marsh, ———
Marston, John
Mason, William
Massinger, Philip
Maturin, Charles Robert
Maubray, ———
Mazzinghi, Giovanni
Mazzini, Cosimo
Meadows, Thomas
Mendez, Moses
Mercier, L. S.
Merivale, John Herman
Merry, Robert
Metastasio, Pietro
Metcalf, Catherine
Meyers, ———
Miles, William Augustus
Miller, James
Millingen, John Gideon
Milman, Henry Hart
Milner, Henry M.
Milton, John
Mitchell, Joseph
Mitford, Mary Russell
Molloy, Charles
Moncrieff, John
Moncrieff, William Thomas
Moore, Charles
Moore, Edward
Moore, Thomas
More, Hannah
Morell, Thomas
Moretti, F.
Morgan, McNamara
Morris, Edward
Morris, Thomas

Morton, Thomas
Moultru, The Rev. Mr.
Mozeen, Thomas
Murphy, Arthur
Murray, Charles

N., N.
Neville, Edward
Noble, Thomas
North, Francis

O'Beirne, Thomas
O'Brien, William
O'Bryen, Denis
O'Callaghan, P. P.
O'Hara, Kane
O'Keeffe, John
Oliphant, Robert
Opie, Mrs.
Oulton, Walley Chamberlaine
Oxberry, William Henry

Palmer, John
Palomba, A.
Palomba, Giuseppi
Panormo, F.
Parry, John
Parsons, Eliza
Paterson, William
Payne, John Howard
Paynter, David William
Peake, Richard Brinsley
Pearce, William
Peilde, Matthew
Penley, Samson
Penn, John
Pepoli, Alessandro Ercole
Petrosellini, G.
Phillips, Edward
Phillips, R.
Pilon, Frederick
Pinkerton, John
Pixérécourt, Guilbert
Planché, James Robinson
Plowden, Mrs. Frances
Plumptre, Anne
Plumptre, James
Pocock, Isaac
Ponte, Lorenzo da. *See* Da Ponte
Poole, John
Pope, Alexander
Portal, Abraham
Porter, Anna Maria
Porter, Walsh
Poujol
Povoleri, ———
Powell, William
Pratt, Samuel Jackson
Prior, Matthew
Proctor, Bryan Waller. *See* Cornwall, Barry
Pulham, ———
Pye, Henry James
Pye, J. Henrietta

Racine, Jean Baptiste
Ralph, James
Rannie, John
Raymond, Richard John
Reed, Joseph
Repton, Humphry
Reynolds, Frederic
Reynolds, G. N.
Rhodes, William Barnes
Rich, John
Richards, ———
Richardson, Elizabeth
Richardson, Joseph
Roberdeau, John Peter
Roberts, James
Roberts, William
Robinson, ———
Robinson, Horatio
Robinson, Mary
Rodwell, George Herbert
Rolli, Paolo Antonio
Rolt, Richard
Rose, John
Rossi, Gaetano
Rousseau, Jean Jacques
Ryder, Thomas
Ryley, Samuel William

S., F.
St. John, John
St. Just, de
Salvi, Antonio
Savage, Richard
Scawen, John
Schiller, Friedrich
Schmidt, ———
Schomberg, Ralph
Scott, Jane M.
Scott, Walter

Sedaine, M. J.
Sedley, Charles
Sernicola, Carlo
Shadwell, Thomas
Shakespeare, William
Sheil, Richard Lalor
Sheridan, Frances
Sheridan, Richard Brinsley
Sheridan, T.
Sheridan, Thomas
Shillito, Charles
Shirley, James
Shirley, William
Siddons, Henry
Simeon, Yve Felix St. Ange [T. Simeons?]
Simon, ———
Skeffington, Lumley St. George
Smart, Christopher
Smith, Charles
Smith, Charlotte
Smith, Horace
Smith, James
Smith, Lascelles
Smollett, Tobias
Snodgrass, Alfred
Soane, George
Sotheby, William
Southerne, Thomas
Spencer, William Robert
Stampiglia, Silvio
Starke, Mariana
Sterling, Edward
Stevens, George Alexander
Stewart, James
Stratford, Thomas
Street, J.
Stuart, Charles
Swift, Edmund L.
Swift, Jonathan

Taylor, J.
Taylor, John
Terry, Daniel
Theaulon
Theobald, Lewis
Thompson, Benjamin
Thompson, Edward
Thomson, James
Thomson, James
Tobin, John
Tomkis, Thomas
Tomlinson, ———
Toms, Edward
Tonioli, Girolamo
Topham, Edward
Tottola, Andrea Leone
Townley, James
Twiss, Horace

Upton, W.

Vanbrugh, John
Vanneschi, Francesco
Vaughan, Thomas
Verazzi, ———
Von Kotzebue, Augustus

Waldron, Francis Godolphin
Walker, C. E.
Wallace, Eglantine, Lady
Wallace, John
Wallis, George
Walpole, Horace
Walter, William Joseph
Walwyn, B.
Ward, C.
Ward, Charles
Wastell, William
Watson-Taylor, George
Whalley, Thomas Sedgwick
Whitehead, William
Wild, James
Willet, Thomas
Williams, H. C.
Williamson, ———
Wilmot, Mrs. Barberina (Ogle) (afterwards Brand, Baroness Dacre)
Wilson, Richard
Woodfall, William
Woods, William
Woodward, Henry
Wright, Waller
Wycherley, William

Yearsley, Anne
Young, Edward

Zeno, Apostolo
Zini, Saverio

Unidentified Items

Abel Drugger's Return from the Fete Champetre at Marylebone Gardens.

Address. "Call Hubert, Boy! 'Tis his task to begin."

Address for the English Prisoners in France.

Address. "From Isis Banks, just wing'd his daring flight."

Address. "Happy the Bard the Drama must confess."

Address. "Heavens! could these worthies once again arise."

Address Intended to Be Spoken on the Opening of the New Theatre Royal English Opera. "Well! here I am at last—& what's as true."

Address, Occasional, by Mr. Lacy.

Address, Occasional. "The long historic track of Time survey."

Address. "To carry Coal to Newcastle—Absurd!"

Address to the Volunteers of Great Britain.

Address. "When Rome's proud legions sought the Albion Throne."

Address. "When young Recruits by hard campaigns at length."

Address. "Whilst neighbouring nations fired with patriot rage."

ADDRESS. "Ye friends of Man whose generous hearts can feel."

ADDRESS. "Ye generous Friends, who so kindly appear."

ADDRESS. "Ye Liberal friends to the Arts & the Muses." By Thomas John Dibdin (?).

ADDRESS. "You who have shook the Trident of the Main."

THE DOCTOR AND HIS APPRENTICE. A comic tale. James Kenny.

EPILOGUE FOR MISS FALKNER. "As when a Bard, who long before in vain."

EPILOGUE. "Come on my hearts, Courage can ne'er be blam'd."

EPILOGUE. "Cramm'd to the Throat with wholesome moral Stuff."

AN EPILOGUE ("Critics—no frowns!—behold the authors pen") TO BE SPOKEN BY MRS. LEON IN THE CHARACTER OF MISS HARCOURT.

EPILOGUE. "Did ever author take so wide a field!"

EPILOGUE, [EDWARD III].

EPILOGUE FOR FATIMA. "Is the Stage clear?—bless me—I've such a Dread!"

EPILOGUE. "In all this bustle, rage, and Tragic roar."

EPILOGUE. "In former times—'tis long ago I own—"

EPILOGUE. "Ladies your servant—Servant Gentlemen all—"

EPILOGUE. "Long has the shameful License of the Age."

EPILOGUE. "Lord! what a stupid Race these Poets are!"

EPILOGUE. "Methinks I hear some youthful Critic say."

EPILOGUE TO MODERN TIMES.

EPILOGUE. "No longer now Camilla, I appear."

EPILOGUE. "Oh what will become of me? Oh what will I do? Nobody coming to marry me—nobody coming to woo."

EPILOGUE ON THE COMIC CHARACTERS OF WOMEN. "Some Poets say, if such we Poets call." [Joseph Addison's *The Drummer.*]

EPILOGUE. "Our Bard, midst doubts and fears—and strange dismay."

EPILOGUE. "Our Bards of late, so tragic in their calling."

EPILOGUE, SPOKEN BY THE LADY WHO PLAYED LADY ANNE IN THE TRAGEDY AND MARIA IN THE FARCE.

EPILOGUE, SPOKEN BY THE YOUNG LADY WHO PLAYED PRINCE EDWARD IN THE TRAGEDY & CORINNA IN THE FARCE.

[EPILOGUE.] "The transient Scene of Mimic Passions past."

EPILOGUE. "To night you've seen a faithful Bard reveal."

EPILOGUE, OCCASIONAL, TO BE SPOKEN BY MRS. POPE ON FRIDAY, 5TH MAY.

EPILOGUE. "Tho' the young Smarts I see begin to sneer."

EPILOGUE. "Trembling t'approach ye after what has past."

EPILOGUE. "Unhand me, Gentlemen, by Heaven, I say."

EPILOGUE. "We trust the Comedy perform'd tonight."

A FIG FOR THE FELLOWS. [EPILOGUE?] [1799?]

AN INTRODUCTORY DIALOGUE TO SOME IMITATIVE RECITALS.

UN JEU D'ESPRIT; OR, JERRY SNEAK'S INTENDED LAW-SUIT WITH THE MAJOR.

THE JEU D'ESPRIT, SONG ("The Waggoner") AND GLEE FOR.

LETTER FROM GEORGE COLMAN, THE YOUNGER(?) [TO LARPENT?].

[LINES,] "When Genius sinks to an untimely grave."

MOTHER SHIPTON'S REVIEW OF THE AUDIENCE. Application n.d., Thomas Harris, C.G.

PROLOGUE. "Ah, Sirs! it is an Axiom, and too true."

[PROLOGUE.] "Amidst the dread Commotions of the Age."

PROLOGUE. "Amidst the tumult of each bustling stage."

PROLOGUE. "Among the tawny Sons of Indian Lands."

PROLOGUE. "Aristophanes of the Modern Stage."

PROLOGUE, "As tender plants, which dread the boist'rous gale," AND EPILOGUE, "What part shall I assume? O tell me while I greet you."

PROLOGUE. "As wary Generals ere they risk a fight."

PROLOGUE. "Bold is the Man! who, in this nicer Age."

PROLOGUE. "Critics for once your dread decree Suspend."

PROLOGUE. "A Female Culprit at your Bar appears."

PROLOGUE. "Fond of your Praise—the Praise which most I love."

PROLOGUE [FOR THE OPENING OF COVENT GARDEN].

PROLOGUE FOR THE PRINCE'S BIRTHDAY. [By David Garrick?]

PROLOGUE FOR THE THEATRICAL FUND.

[PROLOGUE? TO SHE COULDN'T HELP IT(?)] "In these gay Days a little given to Riot."

PROLOGUE. "In vain would Satire with misguided rage."

PROLOGUE, "I've por'd on th'ancients till I'm almost blind," AND EPILOGUE, "Anon will be the Critic's busy Hour."

PROLOGUE. "Let Truths clear Eye, to Equity resign'd."

PROLOGUE. "May I take the Liberty—to intrude upon your Patience—for a minute?"

PROLOGUE, OCCASIONAL. "Of all the Victims which enamour'd Fame."

PROLOGUE, AN OCCASIONAL, TO THE MAN'S BEWITCH'D.

PROLOGUE, ON OCCASION OF A MONUMENT DESIGN'D TO BE ERECTED, BY CONTRIBUTION, TO SHAKESPEARE.

PROLOGUE TO OEDIPUS. John Lockman (?).

PROLOGUE ("Of all the Taxes, Custom's Power has made") TO THE NEW PIECE. Thomas John Dibdin.

PROLOGUE ("Oft has the trembling Poet sent me forth") BY MRS. POPE.

A PROLOGUE ON COMIC POETRY, [SPOKE BEFORE MR. ADDISON'S DRUMMER; OR, THE HAUNTED HOUSE, BY MR. RYAN].

PROLOGUE AND EPILOGUE TO OLIVER CROMWELL. [George Smith Green.]

PROLOGUE, "Our Comic bard, before whose roving Eye," AND EPILOGUE, "Truth has declar'd, and question it none can."

PROLOGUE. "Our modern Poets scarce know how to choose."

[PROLOGUE.] "Pray Sir come back—come back—the author swears."

PROLOGUE. "Prest by the load of life the weary mind."

PROLOGUE, AND ALTERATIONS [RICHARD III, BURLESQUE?].

PROLOGUE. "Since ev'ry rav'nous Critic's in his place."

PROLOGUE. "Studious the guilty passions to controul."

[PROLOGUE.] "Studious to please, but with a Conscious Fear."

[PROLOGUE.] "That Critics may [————?] nor malice grumble."

PROLOGUE, "Tho' I'm a Female, and the rule is ever," AND EPILOGUE, "I must, will, speak; I hope my Dress and Air."

PROLOGUE, TO BE SPOKEN AT THE OPENING OF THE NEW THEATRE IN GLASGOW.

PROLOGUE. "When e'er a new fledg'd Poet hither brings."

PROLOGUE. "When Fruits & Flowers Uncultivated lye."

PROLOGUE. "When the rude Masters of the early time."

PROLOGUE, "With modest Dread this Night I mount the Stage," AND EPILOGUE, "As it's the Form of Satire now in Vogue."

PROLOGUE. "Ye glitt'ring Train whom Lace & Velvet bless."

[RICHARD III (?)] Scene from (?).

A SNACK FOR THE TRAVELLERS. [A piece for recitation?]

SONG. "I was born beyond the Humber."

SONG. "Old Father Antic the Law."

SONG. "When I liv'd in Balenocrazy, dear."